SISTERHOOD DENIED

Race, Gender,
and Class
in a New South
Community

CLASS AND CULTURE
A series edited by
Bruce Laurie and Milton Cantor

Dolores E. Janiewski

SISTERHOOD DENIED

Race, Gender,
and Class
in a New South
Community

TEMPLE UNIVERSITY PRESS | PHILADELPHIA

Temple University Press, Philadelphia 19122
© 1985 by Temple University. All rights reserved
Published 1985
Printed in the United States of America

Library of Congress Cataloging in Publication Data

Janiewski, Dolores E., 1948–
Sisterhood denied.

(Class and culture)
Bibliography: p.
Includes index.
1. Women tobacco workers—North Carolina—Durham
Region—History. 2. Women textile workers—North Carolina
—Durham Region—History. 3. Durham Region (N.C.)—
Social conditions. I. Title. II. Series.
HD6073.T62U65   1985   305.4'2'09756563   84-2640
ISBN 0-87722-361-0

For all the sisters under their skins

The vast mass of human beings
have always been mainly invisible to themselves
while a tiny minority
have exhausted themselves in the isolation
of observing their own reflections.

Sheila Rowbotham
Woman's Consciousness, Man's World

Acknowledgments

The people who inspired this historical study include some who cannot be properly thanked. First, I owe a great debt to the many Durham workers who consented to be interviewed. Second, the woman who first taught me to think critically about the South never lived to see the completion of this book—or her daughter's metamorphosis into a historian. I hope she would have approved the results of her tutelage. Later, I was fortunate to study with Gerda Lerner, a historian who led many of her students to search women's past. Without her, this book would never have come to exist. Jack Maddex turned me into a historian of the South and forced me to change from the passive to the active voice. Anne Scott welcomed me to the South and the study of southern women. While at Duke, I also became a part of Durham through friendships and participation in the activist community. There I learned that scholars can not only analyze the world but also act on it. Although I cannot mention everyone, I must thank Lanier Rand, Bob Korstad, Peter Wood, Larry Goodwyn, Linda Guthrie, Sue Thrasher, Karen Sacks, Syd Nathans, Bill Chafe, Jackie Hall, and Esther Jenks, all of whom lived in the Durham–Chapel Hill area while I first grappled with the ideas presented here. Although my job at the Samuel Gompers Papers took me away from Durham, it also gave me the encouragement and the tangible help of Liz Fones-Wolf, Peter Albert, Stuart Kaufman, Dorotheé Schneider, and Celia Ramos Gray. On various stops along the way, I benefited from encounters with Patty Cooper, Joe Reidy, Mary Frederickson, Heidi Hartman, Julie Boddy, Alice Kessler-Harris, Elizabeth Higginbotham, Steven Hahn, Vicki Bynum, Marcia Douglass, and Bonnie Dill. Financial support came from the Rockefeller Foundation, the Woodrow Wilson Foundation, the Business and Professional Women's Foundation, the Center for Research on Women at Memphis State, and the National Endowment for the

ACKNOWLEDGMENTS

Humanities. Bruce Laurie, Milton Cantor, and the editorial staff of Temple University Press offered me breathing space in which to complete revisions in the midst of moving, teaching, and mothering. The staffs of the Southern Historical Collection and North Caroliniana Collection at the University of North Carolina, of Manuscripts and Archives in the William R. Perkins Library at Duke University, of the National Archives, and of Archives and Manuscripts in McKeldin Library of the University of Maryland all contributed by their patient attention to the needs of a researcher. Lastly, I must thank Maura Rigby, who taught me about motherhood as only a daughter can; Marie and Margaret, who first taught me about sisterhood; and Barry, Maura's father, who performed all the tedious tasks for which women are usually acknowledged. This work is very much the result of all who contributed to it and much of the credit must go to them.

Contents

Tables and Maps   xiii

Chronology   xv

I   INTENTIONS   3

II   MAKING FACTORIES WITHOUT WALLS   8

III   IN THE FIELDS   27

IV   THE HUMAN HARVEST   55

V   CAPITALISTS AND PATRIARCHS   67

VI   IN THE FACTORY   95

VII   THE OTHER WORKPLACE   127

VIII   BEYOND THE FRAGMENTS   152

Appendix   179

Notes   185

Index   237

Contents

Tables and Maps

TABLES

1	Age and Tenure Status for Heads of Rural Households in Durham, Person, and Granville Counties, 1880–1900	12
2	Tenure Status by Race of Household Head in Rural Durham, Person, and Granville Counties, 1880–1900	14
3	Tobacco Yields per Acre for Farmers by Race and Tenure Status, 1880–1900	15
4	Percentage of Farmers Owning Their Farms and Average Farm Size for Durham, Person, and Granville Counties, 1880–1930	25
5	Births per 1,000 Married Women, 15–44 Years of Age, by Race and Tenure Status for Five Rural Areas in North Carolina, 1915–1934	34
6	Tenure Status of Rural Households and Percentage of Employed Women in Such Households in Durham, Granville, and Person Counties, 1880–1900	37
7	Employed Women Aged 15 and Over by Race and Sex of Household Head and by Race of Women Employed, in Rural Durham, Person, Granville, and Wake Counties, 1880–1924	43
8	Percentage of Those Leaving Home Who Migrated to Urban Areas, by Race and Sex of Migrant	56
9	Sex Ratios for Durham by Race, 1890–1930	56
10	Percentages of Female-Headed Households in Rural, Urban, and Suburban Durham Areas, 1880–1900	59
11	Relationships of Women and Girls Aged 14 and Older to Household Heads in Durham, 1880–1900	60
12	Origins of Durham Tobacco Workers, 1935	62

TABLES AND FIGURES

13	Composition of Durham Tobacco Manufacturing Workforce, 1890–1917	71
14	Division of Labor between Black and White Female Tobacco Workers in Durham, 1900	101
15	Specific Occupations of Tobacco Workers by Race, Sex, and Skill, 1935	103
16	Gender and Age Division of Labor in North Carolina Textiles, 1907	104
17	Percentages of Females Employed in Durham, 1880–1930	109
18	Characteristics of Employed Females in Durham and Suburbs, 1900	110
19	Golden Belt Manufacturing Company Wages, 1904	111
20	Marital and Age Status of the Female Workforce in North Carolina Tobacco, Hosiery, and Textile Industries, 1920–1940	115
21	Status of Female Tobacco Workers in Durham Factories, 1935	116
22	Percentages of Women and Children in the Industrial Labor Force in Durham, 1880–1938	116
23	Percentage of Women Employed Having Children under Five Years of Age for Durham and Industrial Suburbs, 1880–1900	132
24	Number of Children under Five Years of Age per Woman of Childbearing Age in Durham, 1880–1940	132
25	Durham Households Keeping Boarders by Race of Household, 1880–1930	133
26	Distribution of Women's Employment in Durham and Industrial Suburbs, 1900	134
27	Background of Durham Industrial Workers Interviewed, 1900–1950	180

MAPS

1	North Carolina Counties Surrounding Durham	9
2	Migration to Durham from Counties in North Carolina, 1880–1900	58

Chronology

1854	North Carolina Railway comes to Durham's station.
1869	Blackwell Durham Tobacco Company is incorporated.
1870	Julian Shakespeare Carr, son of wealthy Chapel Hill merchant, buys into Blackwell firm producing Bull Durham smoking tobacco.
1874	James B., Washington, and Benjamin Duke move into Durham to establish a factory.
1881	County of Durham is formed. The Dukes decide to begin cigarette making in Durham; Blackwell Durham follows.
1884	W. Duke & Sons begins using the Bonsack cigarette-making machine. James B. Duke goes to New York to seek capital, markets, expertise, and cheaper labor; he establishes a factory in New York City. Durham Cotton Manufacturing Company is founded in East Durham.
1885	The Dukes begin full-scale mechanized production of cigarettes in Durham and begin hiring local workers.
1887	Cigarmakers Progressive Union and the Knights of Labor become active in Durham. Blackwell Durham Company abandons cigarette production.
1888	The last skilled hand-cigarette maker is displaced from the Duke factory.
1890s	Other textile mills are founded in Durham with profits from the tobacco industry.
1890	American Tobacco Company is founded by the merger of five leading cigarette companies; James B. Duke becomes president.
1892	Erwin Cotton Mills Company is founded.
1894	Golden Belt and Durham Hosiery Company are founded.

CHRONOLOGY

1894–98	The Populist-Republican fusion begins to win state offices.
1898	White supremacy campaign by the Democratic Party brings it back into office. The Carrs organize Durham Hosiery Mills. Blackwell Durham Tobacco Company is taken over by American Tobacco Company.
1900	Disfranchisement campaign succeeds in securing constitutional amendment to restrict suffrage. Textile workers strike Erwin Mills and other companies across the Piedmont.
1901	Major North Carolina textile companies, including Erwin Mills, meet and decide not to hire any worker dismissed from mills for union activity.
1903	Durham Hosiery Mills opens the first mill run with black labor.
1905	Washington Duke dies as the last Duke in active oversight of local industry.
1910	Erwin Mills builds No. 4 plant next to Erwin No. 1 in West Durham.
1911	U.S. Supreme Court breaks up American Tobacco Company into eight constituent companies. Liggett and Myers takes over the W. Duke Company factories; American Tobacco Company takes over the Blackwell Durham Tobacco Company; each receives one-fourth of the cigarette business formerly controlled by the trust. Cigarette production returns to importance in Durham tobacco industry.
1918–19	Following wartime inflation and labor scarcity, union activity begins in Durham among tobacco, textile, and hosiery workers.
1919	Durham Hosiery Mills begins experiment in industrial democracy for white employees.
1920–21	Panic and recession lead to a sharp drop in tobacco and cotton prices; wages are reduced 40 percent; industrial democracy experiment ends.
1924	Julian S. Carr dies.
1925–29	Workers renew efforts to organize; employers systematically use mutual cooperation, industrial espionage, welfare activities, dismissals, and other methods to prevent successful organization.
1933	Passage of the National Industrial Recovery Act gives workers the right to organize. TWIU sends an organizer into Durham; Local 176 at L and M and Local 183 at American are founded.
1934	United Textile Workers organize locals in Durham, stage General Textile Strike. Local 194 at L and M is founded; Local 193 at American is also founded but disappears. In September, all textile mills in Durham close down.
1935	L and M becomes the first employer to bargain with industrial employees in Durham.

CHRONOLOGY

1936   Local 183 wins its first contract from American Tobacco Company.

1937   Textile Workers Organizing Committee launches a drive to organize southern textile workers; TWOC organizer arrives in Durham to aid locals in West Durham and Golden Belt. Local 208 of the TWIU is founded, breaking away from Local 194 at L and M.

1938   Local 246 of TWOC wins a landslide victory at Erwin Mills, begins negotiations for a contract. Local 208 receives the first contract for a black industrial union in Durham from L and M. Passage of Fair Labor Standards Acts eliminates homework and imposes minimum wage. Tagging the bulls ends in Durham. Massive layoffs of black women employed as stemmers begins.

1939   Strike by Locals 176 and 208 wins preferential shop from L and M. Local 194 signs its first contract with L and M.

1940   Strike held at Erwin Mills over workloads and failure to negotiate contract.

1941   Under pressure from the federal government, Erwin Mills signs a contract with Local 246, Textile Workers Union of America (CIO).

SISTERHOOD DENIED

Race, Gender,
and Class
in a New South
Community

I
INTENTIONS

In September 1934 a series of events in Durham, North Carolina appeared to herald the birth of a new class. On Labor Day, a crowd gathered at the graveside of a Durham worker killed during a 1931 hosiery strike in Philadelphia, and its members dedicated themselves to achieving victory in a forthcoming confrontation with textile manufacturers. A speaker proclaimed, "More than half a million workers in the textile industry are halting work to achieve those aims for which Clem Norwood laid down his life." After that solemn moment, workers' gatherings took on the gaiety of a festival.

A local journalist, attending a Labor Day picnic in a Durham park, summed up the mood of the crowd: "Not only do they apparently believe they are battling for a righteous cause, but they boisterously display a keen spirit of unionism—a spirit which they feel sure will triumph." As he circulated among the people, he discovered that women sometimes spoke more forcibly in support of the labor action than men. Pearl Weaver told him, "We certainly are in favor of the strike and you can bet your life we will serve in the picket lines. I can't be there on Tuesday morning because I must take care of our ten children, but my husband will. And then I will shift with him." Mr. Weaver grunted his assent. The next day women joined with men as 5,200 textile workers, "grave in their intentions, remained in their homes or formed impregnable picket lines." They shared in the joking and the casual determination that "paralyzed seven local mills." Reporters detected only one unhappy note in the general excitement: tears came to the eyes of one mill official denied entrance to his office by "his employees, now pickets." Surely the birth of a class, an event predicted and feared by many observers, had taken place that September in Durham.

There were other signs that the vision of harmonious relations between capital and labor fashioned by New South propagandists had turned upside down. Local tobacco workers, black and white, voted financial support for the textile strikers. When the strike ended three weeks later, the workers were still unified. Shouts of "Victory is ours" and songs of rejoicing rang through Durham streets as workers celebrated in spontaneous dancing and parades.[1] Even after the manufacturers refused to negotiate with their returning employees, workers continued to agitate, protest, organize, and strike. In spring 1939, black and white workers at Liggett and Myers struck the company and won their demands for a preferential shop. A strike at Erwin Mills in March 1940 idled many workers for nearly a year but failed to weaken their resolve. Finally, in 1941, the largest textile mill in Durham, one of the leading mills in the South, grudgingly signed its first contract with its workers. A working class, divided into antagonistic racial communities, had somehow managed to articulate and defend its collective interests. Durham workers had forged a unity that apparently transcended racial and gender lines.

But the unity was flawed. One textile worker believed that God had sanctioned her participation in the 1940 strike; another dreamed that only those who repudiated the union would be saved from the lions' den. Many black women took no part in the L and M strike because their local was too weak to strike. A black woman who took part unwillingly summed up her impression: "Oneness," she called it, with a bitter twist. The bitterness is understandable. After marching on the picket line, workers returned to segregated communities; women went home to domestic chores; employers retained the right to assign jobs and pay wages based on a worker's race and sex. Nevertheless, the entrance of women into a common arena with men was as shattering to the cherished myths of the South as was cooperation across racial lines. The distance separating the races and the sexes had begun to shrink.

The story of the "New South" needs to be told through the experiences of the women who contributed to the region's wealth while remaining poor themselves. Both the women who picketed and the women who rejected the unions were the heirs to generations who worked in the Carolina Piedmont. Their attitudes grew out of the history of women's life and work. Black and white female hands provided labor for farms and mills and factories. They also performed the paid and unpaid tasks that fed, cleansed, clothed, and nursed other workers, and bore and nurtured the children who would become the next generation of workers. By the end of the 1930s, women had evolved collective forms of action rooted in their common position as industrial workers, although some women refused to participate. Yet these "sisters under their skins" never fully realized their kinship in a society where skin color was charged with fateful significance and employers possessed great power.² Their struggles against great odds to achieve common goals is an essential part of the history of the New South.³

Durham, North Carolina, is a particularly suitable area for study. The tobacco industry, which gave birth to Durham in the 1860s, and the textile industry, which followed in the 1880s and 1890s, employed large numbers of women throughout the sixty-year period between 1880 and 1940. The tobacco industry's policy of including black women in its labor force (in contrast to their exclusion from textile mills and their near exclusion from the hosiery industry) makes Durham one of the few cities where black and white women industrial workers can be compared. It becomes easier to reveal how different forms of labor control, race and gender discrimination, and manufacturing methods affected women workers. In addition, these events are close enough in time that we can recapture the women's experiences in their own words.

The process that brought women into the factories had roots both in the tobacco-growing areas surrounding Durham and in the industrializing process itself. The expanding cash-crop economy, with its rising levels of tenancy, sharecropping, and indebtedness, weakened traditional ties to the land. Women, the most expendable members of the agricultural population, were attracted to nearby Durham by the demand for their labor. There they evolved into industrial workers in a complex procedure that reconstructed racial, gender, and class relationships within the factory, the household, and the surrounding community. Unions faced not only the power of the males who dominated the political economy but also an internally divided work force. It was no easy task.

■ The research reported in this book was inspired by E. P. Thompson's study of English working-class culture and consciousness. As Thompson describes it, "Class happens when some men, as the result of common experiences (inherited or shared), feel and articulate the identity of their interests as between themselves, and as against other men whose interests are different from (and usually opposed to) theirs."⁴ Thompson's analysis, however, dealt with a racially homogeneous England. A historian of American southern workers must assess the impact of racial differences.⁵ Indeed, race usually replaced class in the collective consciousness of southern workers. Moreover, a student of women's lives cannot assume a congruence of interests between men and women in any society whose gender relationships were based on female subordination within the family and the denial of female power in the public realm.⁶

When gender and race are added to Thompson's description of class consciousness, the process of attaining group identification becomes a complex six-sided negotiation among unequal partners in each of three major relationships. In the New South, this process of group discovery took place within a community whose old patterns of social conduct were being eroded by emancipation, the expanding cash-crop economy, industrial production, and urbanization. Although blacks and whites were being forced into similar economic classes by the rapid changes, few individuals saw themselves as linked by such a novel and abstract notion as class. Distinctions of sex and color were much more obvious and time-honored. Threatened by forces of disorder beyond their control, whites were inclined to reassert control over former slaves, who might otherwise have competed with them for scarce resources. Men who had formerly been the heads of a patriarchal yeoman economy—or who had never attained authority over family members—were insistent on preserving female subordination. Further, white fears of racial intermingling tended to forestall any recognition of mutual interests with blacks as workers.[7] In the following analysis, I will explore the appeals for racial, gender, and class solidarity as competing forms of group and self discovery in a society where many felt victimized by forces outside their control.

■ This study draws on three major sources to illuminate the female experience in Durham: oral history, documents, and census data as interpreted by quantitative analysis. Large areas of women's lives, however, remain irretrievable by these tools. It is particularly difficult to recapture the texture of family life. Domestic routines were little recorded in the documents of the time, and women did not often discuss daily events in formal interviews. Perhaps encounters between two strangers separated by race, class, age, and sometimes gender were not likely settings for revelations about private lives.[8] For whatever reason, only a partial account of women's lives emerges in this study, one heavily slanted toward work in the factory and activities in public.

The study addresses concerns usually treated in several discrete areas of scholarship. In the field of labor history, it describes the making and unmaking of an industrial working class in a way that diverges in some particulars from other case studies.[9] It explores the effects on people who were uprooted from the land, but it discovers no harmonious peasant or yeoman culture disrupted by external forces; instead, it traces the tangled roots of racial, class, and gender domination in both country and city.[10] It reveals the inadequacies of a class-based strategy when social identities were powerfully shaped by gender and race, yet it recognizes the centrality of class conflicts in shaping the social order. This approach helps to explain the obstacles that hindered the agrarian and labor movements in the South.[11] In addition, in placing black and white women at the center of the analysis, the study departs from a historiographical tradition that too often took only the perspective of white or black males.[12] It thus contributes to the ongoing effort to make women's experience part of history.[13] Seeing women as active rather than passive brings scholarly attention to the issue of gender, and southern history can only benefit from this invigorating encounter.

Sisterhood Denied, as its title suggests, rebukes facile claims about the sisterhood of all women, yet the phrase also suggests the hope that infuses that feminist dream. The title, like the history that follows, should not avoid ambiguity. It affirms women's resistance but also describes their acceptance of subordination. A new society, a more inclusive view of community and sisterhood transcending racial boundaries, might have emerged in Durham. A "redemptive community" might have rendered the baggage of white supremacy obsolete.[14] Women might have created a life unbounded by inherited suspicion, pride, and fear. The title, however, states that this did not happen. Even so, women's involvement in the labor movement helped to breach some of the barriers that kept women apart. Their story is one of victory as well as defeat.

II
MAKING FACTORIES WITHOUT WALLS

Industrialization of the world leads to the single crop, and the single crop to the industrialization of the farm. Build a factory community, and it will gradually make a factory of the farm as well—a factory without walls, but suffering many of the evils of factory life.[1]

One root of the process that led women into the tobacco and textile factories of Durham lay in the rural Carolina Piedmont (see Map 1). Farmers were becoming increasingly dominated by the expanding market for tobacco and cotton in the post–Civil War era. The resulting transformation in agriculture provided the tobacco and textile industries with both the raw materials and the human labor needed to run factories. The human consequences were considerable: the entanglement of a majority of rural inhabitants in the constricting net of tenancy and the movement of many people off the land. Of course, some women remained on the land, but, because tobacco culture was considered man's work, women found fewer opportunities to stay. Durham, a city surrounded by tobacco fields, offered women a better chance to support themselves, especially if their country households lacked male labor. Although female members of tenant and farm laborers' households were the most likely candidates for migration, entire families fled a cash-crop economy that threatened to submerge them in hopeless poverty. Some perceived the move as an opportunity. Black women, more likely to be farm laborers or sharecroppers than white women, saw migration to urban areas as a means to escape racial, gender, and economic subordination.

Farming families did not give up easily, however. Rising rates of tenancy and indebtedness led to popular insurgencies in the 1880s and 1890s against the concentration of wealth and power in the control of landlords,

Map 1.
North Carolina Counties Surrounding Durham

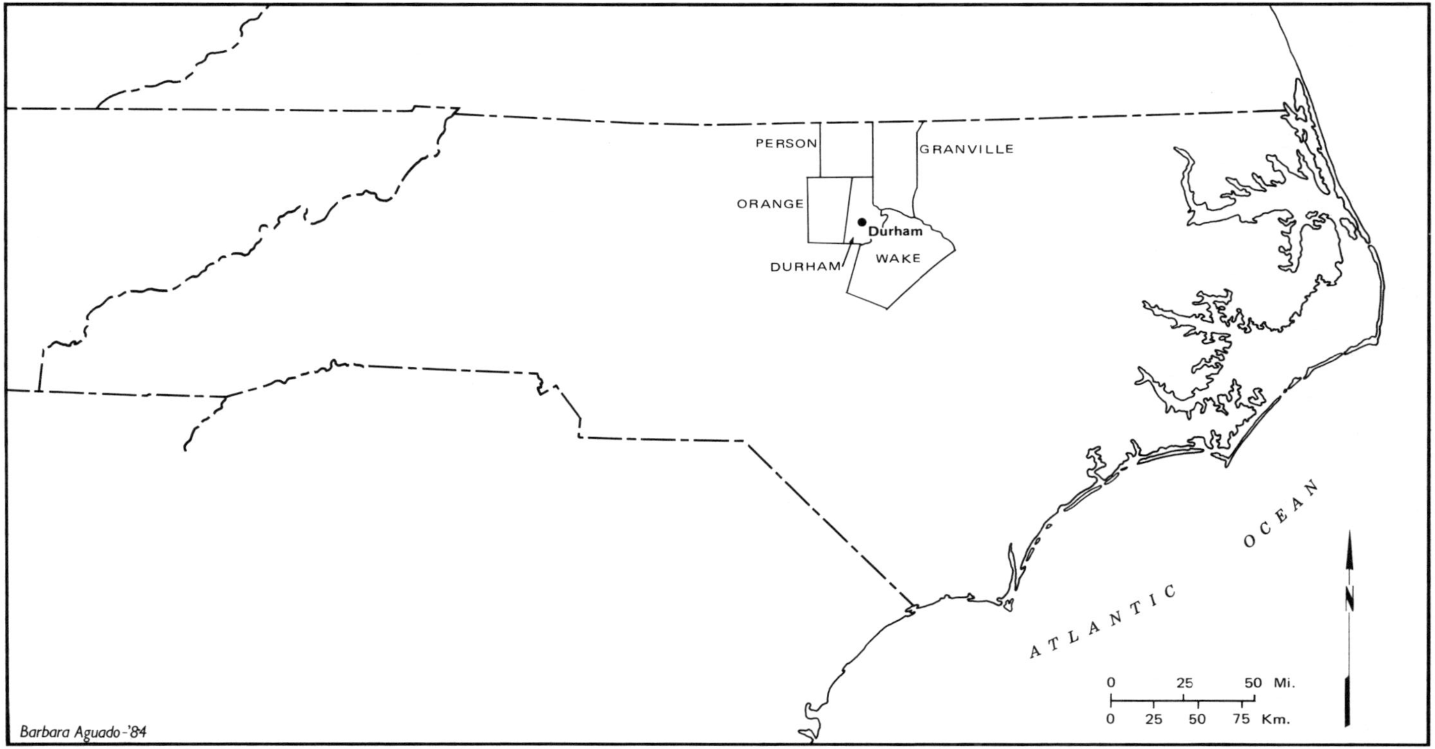

banks, and corporations. The industrial and landowning elites countered these protests with skillful appeals to white supremacist beliefs. After the failure of the movements to restore the security of the small farmer, forced migration from the land continued. As farm families became a landless rural proletariat, women became a part of the human flotsam flowing from field to factory.

Scholars have described this phenomenon, in its global form, as a process by which subsistence farming is "changed, by economic and political force, to plantation economies, mining areas, single-crop markets."[2] A new group of scholars has begun to examine the particular shape assumed by this transformation in the cotton economy. But similar developments occurred in the tobacco-growing areas of the Piedmont. There, too, the cash-crop economy expanded, and tenancy and sharecropping became the dominant forms of labor relations after the end of slavery. As in the cotton economy, this new biracial class of landless farmers heightened awareness of class divisions among white farmers, leading to the emergence of the populist movement as the voice of the yeoman class. But as white farmers faced declining expectations and as black farmers lost hope of owning land, competition for land, labor, and credit contributed to racial tensions. Ultimately, the appeals to racial solidarity in both the tobacco and cotton regions overwhelmed efforts to forge a class-based response to economic dislocation.

An analysis of developments in tobacco growing demonstrates how the agricultural crisis was linked to the expanding industrial economy. The effect on human lives is readily visible in the story of Durham, a New South city whose industrial growth depended on cheap cotton, cheap tobacco, and cheap labor—the products of an increasingly impoverished agricultural society. The examination of women's participation in commercial agricultural and industrial growth in Durham reveals the significance of gender in molding economic relationships. The men and women who became a rural proletariat in the Durham hinterland (in a process similar to that of the Cotton South) entered new workplaces—but bore with them the heritage of the old.

■ In the 1860s the northern counties of the Carolina Piedmont began to shift from a mixed economy of subsistence and market-oriented agriculture to an economy dominated by bright leaf tobacco, the variety best adapted to smoking. Farm tenancy became more common. The coming of the North Carolina Railroad (NCRR) in 1854 to a spot designated as Durham's Station, linking the area directly to tobacco markets in Virginia, gave impetus to this shift. Promoted by the largest local landowners, Duncan and Paul Carrington Cameron, the railroad eliminated the last major obstacle to the development of commercial agriculture.[3] The widespread adoption of the flue-curing process, the discovery that light and relatively infertile sandy gray soils were suitable for growing bright tobacco, the dissemination of intricate techniques essential to bright tobacco culture, and now the construction of crude tobacco factories along the NCRR, all stimulated local farmers to produce the new crop.[4] Other developments followed. In 1865–1866 the North Carolina legislature provided for a new system of farm credit; it passed a crop lien law that allowed a share of a future crop to be used as security for loans. Also, by marshalling their economic and political resources, the planters and landlords fashioned a legal framework for landlord-tenant relations that strengthened their control over a rural working class composed of former slaves and yeoman farmers.[5] The rise of tobacco auctions and warehouses in Durham, sponsored by local manufacturers, enhanced the crop's attraction to local farmers, who were eager to escape the area's chronic poverty. Moreover, high prices paid for the cured leaf seemed to offer a way to pay for the labor of newly freed blacks.[6] More and more farmers in the 1860s and 1870s believed that bright tobacco would become the agricultural equivalent of gold, a hope symbolized by the optimistic name coined for the region, the Golden Belt.

Less than two decades later, tobacco farmers, like cotton farmers in eastern North Carolina, discovered that their growing dependence on a market economy beyond their control had mortgaged their future. Surveys conducted by the North Carolina Bureau of Labor Statistics from the late 1880s to the early 1900s revealed widespread disillusionment in the Golden Belt. According to a Chatham County farmer in 1887,

> There is quite a depressed condition seen and felt on every hand among farmers on account of short crops and low prices. There is much unrest and dissatisfaction. I have been on a farm for more than fifty years and I have never seen so much desire for a change. Farmers are moving to towns, leaving very good farms to grow up untenanted.

A Granville farmer reported, "The notorious mortgage system so extensively practiced in other sections is beginning to infest this section. The farmers of this section (I am sorry to say) paid so much attention to the cultivation of bright tobacco for the past decades that education has been fearfully neglected." Another farmer from Harnett County stated, "Labor is down, so is the farmer. The merchant is the prosperous man now. Half the farms are mortgaged to the commission merchants who charge 50 percent above cash prices."[7] A Person County farmer wrote in 1891,

> Tobacco is our money crop, and since our products are priced before we plant, the future is quite gloomy. Before the American Tobacco Trust was organized [in 1890] we got much better prices, as we raise bright tobacco in this section; but now the price is just half. Farmers

are gloomy and making no money. We hope to see the time when trusts and futures are to be no more.⁸

Other farmers shared his desperation and hope.

The same conditions that plagued tobacco farmers in the 1880s and early 1890s—tobacco prices hovering below ten cents a pound, heavy expenses for fertilizer and curing bright tobacco, and rates of interest ranging between 25 and 50 percent for purchased supplies—troubled farmers in the early twentieth century. Once-confident farmers discovered that prices like the 7.5 cents a pound paid for bright tobacco in 1904 translated into a loss of $2.50 per hundred pounds despite the four hundred hours of labor invested in each acre of tobacco. The rural population discovered that the chances of becoming landowners had diminished for farmers in their middle years, although older farmers had experienced some marginal improvements (see Table 1). The changing shape of the tenure ladder suggests that the cash-crop economy had fostered an upward shift from laborers to tenant farmers—while limiting any further upward mobility. Half the rural households, however, would never attain the greater prestige and independence associated with landholding status.⁹

Even owning land no longer guaranteed real security. Some landowners shared the feelings expressed by one Chatham County farmer in 1891: "When a man mortgages his property, he can't help thinking about it, consequently, he can't work like a free man." Increasingly, tenants and owners

Table 1.
Age and Tenure Status for Heads of Rural Households in Durham,* Person, and Granville Counties, 1880–1900

AGE	1880				1900			
	OWNERS	TENANTS	LABORERS	N	OWNERS	TENANTS	LABORERS	N
0–25	19%	12%	69%	14	27.2%	36.4%	36.4%	11
26–34	17	32	51	23	25	50	25	32
35–44	48	26	26	18	32.1	55.4	12.5	56
45–54	36	34	30	30	41.2	51	13.8	51
55+	49	17	34	28	50	43.3	6.7	30
				113				180

*Durham County was formed in 1881 from parts of Orange and Wake County; sampled households for 1880 come from those parts of original counties later incorporated into Durham County.

SOURCES: 10th Census of the United States, 1880 (manuscript) Population and Agricultural Schedules; 12th Census of the United States, 1900 (manuscript) Population Schedules for the Counties Sampled, National Archives (see Appendix for description of sampling techniques).

alike feared that nearly all farmers were "mortgaged to a few merchants and capitalists," that there were "too many middle men" pocketing the proceeds of their labor, and that the Yankees in charge of "the present financial system" were using their power to bleed Piedmont farmers dry.[10] The rising levels of tenancy and indebtedness frustrated the expectations of white men who had hoped to assume an independent status as yeoman farmers. These farmers, who had optimistically begun planting bright leaf in the 1860s and 1870s, found themselves mired in an economy that mocked their hopes and snared their descendents.

For those who began the 1880s as farm laborers, incorporation into the tenant class was an improvement, offering relief from a life of unremitting toil and hopeless deprivation. Letters from North Carolina farm workers to the *Journal of United Labor,* the organ of the Knights of Labor, depicted the situation of most black farm laborers in the cotton-growing counties: "There are here common laborers who work steadily, yet the proceeds of their labor will not furnish bare necessities—luxuries are unknown." A Knight from Orange County, which was a mixed cotton-, tobacco-, and corn-growing area, reported the prevailing wage rates: "Farm hands, $10 per month and from 40 to 50 cents per day; railroad section hands, 50 cents per day, and $13 per month; train hands, $20 to $30 per month; firemen, $20 to $30 per month; section master, $40 per month; cooks, $3 to $5; nurses, $1.50 to $3; house maids, $3 to $5 per month; carpenters, $1 to $1.50 per day; brick masons, $2 to $3 per day."[11] Because living expenses totalled about $220 a year for a family of five, only railway employees and construction workers (from the wage list just quoted) could hope to keep their families above the poverty line. Black Congressman George White's testimony to the United States Industrial Commission in 1900 summed up the bleak conditions endured by his constituents in the cotton-growing counties of North Carolina's Second District, which bordered on the Golden Belt:

> A great many men are keeping families with a wife and four, five, six, or eight children, and they do not get over $10. But remember that the man is hired out, the wife is hired out, and every child is hired out, and the wife takes the babies along with her. A great many families live on less than $10 a month. The provision is very coarse but it is common food. It is usually corn, a little molasses and Western side meat. They live on the coarsest food, wear the coarsest-textured clothing. They can not do otherwise.[12]

The history of one generation in a white Wake County family illustrates the difficulties that faced even white farm laborers. Newly married in the 1870s, the young couple survived originally on the husband's wages of $8 per month for farm labor and the wife's occasional earnings of 25 cents per day for chopping or picking cotton. The wife took her young children into the fields so that she could continue to work. On Saturdays she took in washing to supplement the family income. Seven children reached working age, but the family never acquired tools, livestock, or land. After the children began to leave home, the ageing couple sank back into poverty.[13] Whether black or white, farm laborers in the areas near Durham could afford only a life of grim privation that appeared to doom their children and destine the aged to nearly hopeless poverty.

The expansion of market-oriented agriculture in the tobacco-growing region was paradoxical; it simultaneously undermined the security of many landowners and enhanced the position of those able to rise from laboring to tenant status (see Table 2). Tobacco tenants gained greater control over their labor and its product than wage earners could attain. As in the Cotton Belt, tenancy was linked to the cash-crop economy. The rise of the predominantly black farm-laborer class into the tenant class represented a compromise between the intentions of agricultural employers and the desires of former slaves. The destruction in the 1870s of the protections offered small farmers and laborers under the 1868 constitution enacted by the Republican government placed blacks at a disadvantage in pursuing landownership. Potential employers, on the other hand, had to contend with the difficulties of paying laborers an attractive wage, of supervising reluctant workers, and of keeping labor available at the critical periods in the agricultural cycle. Tenancy seemed a way to avoid these problems. It saved employers the eco-

Table 2.
Tenure Status by Race of Household Head in Rural Durham,*
Person, and Granville Counties, 1880–1900

TENURE	1880				1900			
	WHITES	N	BLACKS	N	WHITES	N	BLACKS	N
Landowners	57.1%	32	8.8%	5	48.7%	56	12.7%	8
Tenants	21.4	12	31.6	18	42.6	49	65.1	41
Laborers	21.4	12	59.6	34	8.7	10	22.2	14
		56		57		115		63

*Durham County was formed in 1881 from parts of Orange and Wake County; the sampled households come from those parts of the original counties later incorporated in Durham County.

SOURCES: 10th Census of the United States, 1880 (manuscript) Population and Agricultural Schedules; 12th Census of the United States, 1900 (manuscript) Population Schedules, for the Counties Sampled; National Archives (see Appendix for description of sampling techniques used).

nomic burden of paying wages, gave tenants a greater stake in production, and afforded the lucky tenant a chance to accumulate the capital needed to purchase land. An expanding group of black tenants joined a growing number of white tenants, and a few black households managed to acquire title to land.

Although some economic historians have argued the contrary, tenancy seems to have grown out of the imbalance of political, racial, and economic power between the poor and wealthy classes, not from a market-induced rationality. Indeed, by 1900, after the techniques of tobacco cultivation had been widely disseminated, farmowners and tenants seemed almost equal in productive efficiency (see Table 3). Certainly white tobacco farmers proved most efficient, even as their ranks were thinning and the number of tenants was rising. The comparisons among black farmers present a more ambiguous result, but the averages for output per acre do not suggest that economic efficiency was being rewarded. If black sharecroppers were more efficient farmers than black farmowners, why was the first group receiving the smallest share of its total product and the less efficient group the largest? While econometricians might insist that these comparisons disclose the superior ability of white managers and landowners in supervising black sharecroppers, a plausible explanation must also consider the quality of land available to white and black farmers; racial differentials in access to information, technology, and credit; and the grossly unequal distribution of wealth and human capital that contributed to the different levels of performance.[14]

While former laborers rejoiced at their rise to tenant status, residents of

Table 3.
Tobacco Yields per Acre for Farmers by Race and Tenure Status, 1880–1900

TENURE	POUNDS PER ACRE, 1880*		POUNDS PER ACRE, 1900†	
	WHITES	BLACKS	WHITES	BLACKS
Owners	537	411	822	595
Renters	388	500	805	596
Croppers	527	341	797	627

*1880: Person, Durham, Granville Counties.
†1900: United States.
SOURCES: 10th Census of the United States, 1880 (manuscript) Population and Agricultural Schedules for Granville, Person, and Durham Counties (parts of Orange and Wake which became Durham in 1881); 1900 figures from Meyer Jacobstein, *The Tobacco Industry in the United States* (New York: Columbia University Press, 1907), p. 67.

the tobacco regions who lost power complained. Agricultural employers resented losing an accustomed supply of cheap and dependent labor. As early as the 1870s, landowners began to grumble about the scarcity of farmhands and the weakening of controls that they had exercised over "the old slave negro." By the late 1880s, the complaints were filling the pages of the surveys collected by the North Carolina Bureau of Labor Statistics. Black women's confining their labor to the household or their own fields, a tendency discovered by other scholars of the post-emancipation South, appears to have contributed to the growing labor scarcity. This particular unwillingness of black women was noted by one Granville farmer in 1887: "Very few females engaged in farm work. They will not hire for regular work." Twenty years later, another Granville farmer declared, "The negro as a laborer on our farms or as a servant in our homes is almost a thing of the past. In many localities it is difficult to get the washing done by the colored race." Favoring immigration from Europe as a substitute for unavailable black labor, he explained, "We want a class of people we can control; then we are willing and want to pay them what is just and right for their service." Unfortunately for disgruntled North Carolina employers, they could find no immigrant group to replace the black laborers who became tenants or abandoned the land.[15]

There is no need to exaggerate the gains of the tenant class. The conditions actually faced by many tenants explains the anger expressed by those unable to become yeoman farmers. Forced to borrow "furnishing" money at the beginning of the planting season, tenants paid exorbitant interest rates, purchased needed items at steep prices from the landlord and often sold their crop to their landlord at rates below the market price. Depending on the terms of their contracts, they received one-fourth, one-third, one-half, or three-fourths of the actual returns of their labor. When prices fell, their indebtedness rose. A correspondent from Rich Square in Northampton County described the situation faced by black tenant farmers in a letter published in the *Journal of United Labor*:

> In spite of the good crops the tenant receives but a very small share of the results of his labor, frequently only $15 or $20, so that men with families, after working the entire year, are seldom free from debt. In other words, what the landlord does not get, the merchant under the mortgage system does, which leaves the man who toils from sunrise to sunset to raise the crops as poor as when he started.[16]

The story of the second generation in the Wake County family discussed above demonstrates the forces that controlled the tenant farmer, white or black. The children of the farm laborer began their adult lives in the 1890s, when the tenant system was displacing the wage-labor system in Wake County. One son, whose story was recorded, bargained for a one-horse crop—twenty acres of cotton and five acres of corn. Lacking draft animals and tools, he could do no better than farm "on thirds"; the landlord agreed to pay him one-third of the cotton and one-third of the corn. Because the entire farm was planted in cash crops, the family bought its food and clothing—meal, meat, flour, sugar, cloth, molasses, and shoes—on credit at the landlord's store. Together the young couple made eighteen bales of cotton that year and received $206 for the six bales that comprised their share, plus twenty-five bushels of corn. After paying their debts, they kept $6. The next year the wife's difficult first pregnancy kept her out of the fields, so their share amounted to less than their debts. When another landlord offered to assume the debt, they moved to a new farm. The family arranged to buy a mule on time so that it could take a bigger share of the crop, but the landlord insisted that all of the land be devoted to cotton. This required buying corn to feed the mule while paying off the debt, and in this fashion the family moved from farm to farm. The wife carried her babies into the fields so that she could work. When the oldest boy reached ten, old enough to plow, the father bought another mule on credit so that the family could cultivate thirty acres. After more children grew to working size, the father tried to buy land. When the crops failed one year, the family lost everything.[17] Years of hard labor had brought this family to a precarious perch on the second rung of a tenure ladder that, for the vast majority of landless farmers, no longer led upward. Because the price of tobacco stayed higher than the price paid for cotton, conditions were marginally better for tobacco tenants than for cotton tenants, but all lived within severe constraints.

As in both generations of the Wake County family, women's fates were tied to the well-being of the family economy. If their husbands enjoyed the opportunities bestowed by close kinship to landed families, patronage by merchants and bankers, a sufficient supply of sons to work in the fields, and favorable crop prices during their early years, women found their burdens eased. Women in landowning families could remove themselves from the fields because their children remained longer with their parents and thereby added to the family labor supply. When children were too young or the couple too old to farm, landowners could rent land to tenants, house other relatives to work in the fields, or hire laborers. Only a minority of families owned land, however. The painful ascent of the Wake County family from laboring to tenant status illustrates the unceasing labor of the women who carried their infants into the fields. Children in such families began their labors in early childhood, rapidly became full hands, and left their parents to establish their own tenant households. Early and frequent childbearing yielded the family's major resource—labor power—but beleaguered tenant households could not retain their children past early adolescence. Gradually the parents lost their ability to rent and cultivate land as the family labor force shrank. Some families fragmented under the strains of tenant or laboring conditions; when that occurred, female households encountered even greater obstacles. Male labor was generally crucial for renting land and raising a profitable crop. Unless women belonged to the ranks of the landowning minority, widowhood or desertion forced them into dependency in a relative's household, sent them into low-paying "public work," or uprooted them from the land altogether.[18]

■ Fearful and growing desperate in the 1880s, farmers responded to several organizations that offered hope for attaining more control over land and credit. Some farmers and farm laborers heeded the appeals of the Knights of Labor to join a biracial crusade pledged to end the exploitation of all members of the producing classes. The whites-only North Carolina Farmers' Alliance recruited planters, yeomen, and tenants across the state. Later the Colored Farmers' Alliance entered the state to help aspiring black landowners to advance their interests in association with their white counterparts. These organizations found the North Carolina Piedmont, where the expansion of the market was unsettling traditional social and economic relationships, a favorable environment for their recruiting efforts.[19]

While the organizations clearly attracted different (and sometimes antagonistic) class and racial constituencies, each offered its members rituals and goals that bound isolated rural folk to a common cause. A Tarboro Knight described a ceremonial march in which black members of the male Fidelity and female Rosebud Local Assemblies participated. Meeting at St. Stephan's Colored Missionary Baptist Church, the Tarboro Knights heard an appeal to "be diligent in their duties, to be brotherly in their dealings with each other, to remember each other in the hour of need, and to discard forever the ways of traitors." They were "encouraged to wait, watch, and work for the reward that is coming." Like the Knights, the Farmers' Alliances engaged the interest of their members through elaborate rituals called the "secret work," but later submerged the fraternal elements in a public "movement culture" that included mass gatherings, camp meetings, and co-operative institutions. Gatherings like a Vance County picnic in October 1890 attracted 1,500 people from the area just north of Durham.[20] The rhetoric in speeches and publications drew on the republican political heritage to criticize the millionaires, corporations, and trusts "in their insatiate greed" who had driven many laboring people and farmers into debt and wage slavery. Both movements argued that labor must evolve out of its "present condition in the wage-system into a co-operative system," into "one great solidarity." Each spoke for the "producing classes" who must strive collectively to create a "cooperative commonwealth."[21]

The two organizations also strove to deal with the issues of gender and race. Race, the most immediate source of division among their potential supporters, elicited the most attention. Committed to the "abolition of distinctions maintained by creed and color," Knights' organizers tried to persuade their white North Carolina constituency to cooperate with black members. Believers in the "domestic moral order," the Knights welcomed working women and the wives of members into the order, while endorsing the notion of a separate female sphere centered in the home. "Equal rights" in the Knights' political vocabulary extended to women while still preserving their distinct roles as wives and mothers. The Farmers' Alliance dealt less forthrightly with the racial issue. Like most whites, they wished to restrict blacks and whites "from anything but the most necessary and strictly controlled economic and social contact." When the racist fears of white men called up visions of sexual contact between white women and black men, the combination became even more explosive. White women, however, could be welcomed into the segregated Alliance, where they were promised "equal privileges to the men." The Alliance allowed women to join in discussion of the economic and political issues, taught them "all the secret words and signs," encouraged them to find "constant, honorable, and remunerative employment," and urged them to serve as the helpmates of their menfolk. Unlike the Knights, however, the Alliance evaded the more divisive issue of political rights for women. Perhaps its very commitment to the patriarchal family economy militated against woman suffrage. At one rally the Alliance lecturer refused to "invite" the women "to suffrage" although he acknowledged that some people were proposing that reform. At another gathering, the speaker warned women to "be contented in the sphere the Lord hath placed you in."[22] Yet the wholehearted endorsement of equal rights expressed by the Knights, and even the equivocal support offered by the Farmers' Alliance, seemed radical threats to the conservative ideologies embraced by many southerners.

The Knights of Labor entered North Carolina committed to engaging all members of the producing classes. Only the idle and the corrupt were to be excluded. Beginning its campaign in 1885 in Raleigh and nearby Durham County, the Knights initially succeeded in attracting whites and blacks in rural and urban North Carolina. The order elected a master workman from Raleigh to the U.S. Congress in 1886, but the interracial alliance soon unraveled. A Knight in Oxford, just north of Durham, listed the tactics used by enemies to create "ill-feeling" against the order. "The disregard of the 'color-line' by the Richmond General Assembly and the partial success of the Republican party in our State last November was also used against us. They pointed at us with scorn, and kept crying 'Nigger! Nigger!' until the two words 'Nigger' and 'Knights' became synonymous terms." Members reported to the *Journal of United Labor* that "the white people do not take to the Knighthood in these parts; but it is growing well among the colored folks."[23] As other correspondents made clear in the *Journal* and in letters to the Knights' leadership, the Knights began drawing their members almost exclusively from a black rural constituency.[24] Racist appeals, repeatedly invoked by white Democrats and other opponents of the Knights' radical programs, discouraged white members.[25] In the late 1880s, the Knights and the Alliance, ostensibly dedicated to a common defense of the producing classes, began to function as antagonists in the Piedmont despite efforts at cooperation on the national level.[26]

In May 1887 the National Farmers' Alliance and Industrial Union (the Southern Alliance) moved into Wake County. By August the Farmers' Alliance organizer was marveling, "The farmers seem like unto ripe fruit—you can gather them by a gentle shake of the bush."[27] In October the Alliance held its first state-wide meeting, electing Leonidias L. Polk secretary. The *Progressive Farmer,* the journal edited by Polk, became the official newspaper. The new organization declared that it would admit all white farmers, farm laborers, mechanics, country teachers, physicians, ministers of the gospel and the female members of their families, but its early leadership primarily came from the ranks of large landowners like Polk or Elias Carr, the first state president.[28]

The Knights and the Alliance soon clashed. The local suballiances were concerned about defeating "the combines" that paid their members low prices for their tobacco, but did not want to pay higher wages to farm workers.[29] The farm laborer, on the other hand, wanted "to better his condition." Referring to the "big farmers" who opposed laborers' demands, a Knight explained, "Our intention is to work gradually to at last conquer the great monster." A Caswell County Knight informed the order, "it has slipped out here that the so-called Farmers' Alliance proposes to see to it, and is instructing its members to pay no more money to wage-workers. They are to be paid in orders on stores . . . We fear that this so-called Farmers' Alliance in our State means nothing more nor less than oppression and death to the laborer." Other Knights insisted on the need to work secretly because of widespread opposition from Alliance members determined to maintain a cheap source of farm labor.[30] The imbalance in political and financial resources between landowners and laborers, coupled with white willingness to use violence against black advances, crippled the efforts made by black Knights to defend their rights. Gradually, reluctantly, black farmers and farm laborers lost faith in the ability of the order to deliver justice and a better life in cooperation with enlightened whites.[31]

When the Colored Farmer's National Alliance and Cooperative Union came to North Carolina in 1888 to organize farmers excluded from the whites-only Alliance, Elias Carr described the new body as "a separate and distinct group with which we have nothing to do."[32] Other Alliance members convinced Carr that, in the opinion of one farmer, it would be "adviceable to incourage their organization in our state" because cooperation would "stop the tide of emergration from the cotton countrys of our state."

In addition, the Alliance member argued, cooperation might prevent the radical Knights of Labor from enlisting black farmers and laborers, a coalition more threatening to white agricultural employers.[33] By the end of 1888, the two Alliances had begun a hesitant partnership within the constraints imposed by racism among the whites and the sympathies of black farmers toward black farm laborers. When the black organization collapsed in 1891, following an unsuccessful strike of farm laborers in the cotton-growing regions of the Deep South, the white North Carolina Alliance saw no need to continue its controversial partnership. The issue of a political alliance with blacks surfaced again after the People's Party was formed in the 1890s, but the recent destruction of a biracial movement weakened the already limited ability of class interests to transcend racial antagonisms.[34]

The populist movements' interests were not limited to politics. The Alliance, and for a brief period, the Knights, set up cooperatives to sell food, implements, seed, fertilizer, and other necessities to their members. By establishing warehouses, the suballiances in the tobacco-growing region hoped to reduce the power of "the combined tobacco interest of the United States," who were reaping "enormous profits, directly taken from the disorganized producers." An Oxford warehouse saved members an estimated 20 percent of the total crop value formerly paid in marketing and storage charges. Alliance stores and warehouses enabled farmers to reduce their dependence on credit; in Durham County mortgage indebtedness fell by half in 1888. The Alliance followed the lead of the Knights in setting up tobacco factories in Durham, Granville, Vance, and Person counties to provide additional insurance that growers would receive a fair price for their leaf.[35]

By the 1890s, having grown discouraged by the difficulties in operating cooperatives in the face of merchant and banker opposition, the Alliance directed its efforts toward securing state regulation of the economic forces that impinged on farmers' lives. Major targets included a bank-controlled credit system and a corporate-controlled transportation system that charged farmers high fees and rates of interest.[36] Frustrated by the lack of response to its lobbying efforts and by the reluctance of the two major political parties to support reforms, the North Carolina Alliance joined with the national Alliances to form the People's Party at St. Louis in 1892. In North Carolina the Populists rode to victory by fusion with the racially mixed Republican Party in 1894 and 1896. Arguing for state regulation of the railroads, the establishment of a legal maximum for interest rates, increased support for schools, and the return of home rule taken away from the predominantly black counties (to limit black officeholding), the fusionists elected state legislators, congressmen, and a U.S. senator, and captured the governorship in 1896. The Populists and the Republican Party had created a successful coalition of blacks and whites.

Even before its first victories, however, the coalition had begun to fray.

The Populists were trying to appeal to blacks while defending their party against the charge that it advocated "social equality." After the death of Leonidias Polk in 1892, the *Progressive Farmer* and the new leadership of the North Carolina People's Party abandoned attempts to include blacks directly in their movement. Gradually the issue of free silver replaced the more radical schemes for economic reforms. By July 1893, the *Progressive Farmer* declared that the "white men" of the South and West, in contrast to "the politicians and the negroes," would unite as populists to defeat "Wall Street slavery." By 1894, the state Populist platform denounced the use of strikes as a weapon: "We sympathize with the oppressed everywhere, but we are opposed to all lawless combinations of men, whether representing capital or labor. We believe in peace and strict obedience to law." Evidently reacting to the disorders associated with the 1894 Pullman strike, the platform recommended that workers vote rather than strike or riot. In 1895, Marion Butler, a U.S. senator and chairman of the North Carolina party, began organizing free silver clubs to attract Democrats to a racially and economically conservative Populist movement.[37]

After the 1896 victory, the fusion strategy collapsed. Daniel Russell, the new Republican governor, suspended the lease of the NCRR to the Southern Railway system controlled by the J. Pierpont Morgan interests. Probusiness Republicans broke away from the coalition. Populists, eager to strengthen their electoral chances, offered the Democrats another opportunity for an alliance in 1898, but party leaders refused because they feared that joining with economic radicals would split party ranks. Instead, the Democratic Party campaigned on a white supremacy ticket as the most potent method of uniting its members and attracting frustrated whites from the other parties. The election, marked by violence to intimidate Republicans and Populists, vigilante tactics, and a vicious propaganda campaign, succeeded in raising racial antagonisms to new heights. Shortly after the Democrats claimed victory in the legislature, a mob in Wilmington drove black officeholders from town and killed almost twenty black residents.

Once back in office, the Democrats dismantled the reforms, abolished the railroad commission, eliminated home rule, and, in direct violation of campaign pledges, moved to disfranchise black voters. In 1900 they cemented their victory over the populist coalition of poor whites and poor blacks by passing a constitutional amendment disfranchising all illiterate male citizens except those who could claim descent from voters eligible before 1867. After eight years had passed, the grandfather clause would no longer apply. Josephus Daniels, the editor of the Raleigh *News and Observer* and a leading propagandist for the white supremacy campaign, explained that the constitutional amendment would remove the curse of "negro rule," prevent "demagogues" from gaining power, and would keep "dissatisfied whites" from uniting with the "immense ignorant negro vote."[38] Political participation by poor whites and poor blacks plummeted, and North Carolina joined the ranks of the Solid South. Although Democrats generally defended the measure on racial grounds, it served the class interests openly backed by Daniels. The victorious new governor, Charles Aycock, the first of a long line of "progressive" Democrats, proclaimed his intention to broaden education so that all men could meet the literacy requirement for suffrage by 1908. The state, however, never provided enough funding to educate its population, white or black. Education, like political participation, was a privilege and not a right in the one-party South.[39]

■ Tobacco farmers had lost their ability to appeal to the state for protection. They appeared more defenseless than ever against the forces of the market. The prices paid for tobacco continued to hover below ten cents a pound, as did cotton.[40] Tobacco farmers met in futile efforts in Raleigh, Danville, and Rocky Mount to denounce the American Tobacco Company for "putting the prices of tobacco below the cost of production."[41] A slight improvement in tobacco prices during the early 1900s enabled some tenants to enter the ranks of farmowners in Caswell, Durham, Granville, Orange, and Vance counties (all in the Golden Belt), but tenancy rates in the mixed cotton- and tobacco-growing areas of Edgecombe, Greene, Johnston, Nash, Wilson, and Wake continued to climb.[42]

Finally, in 1909 and 1910, tobacco prices exceeded ten cents a pound and kept above that mark for several consecutive years. Consequently, farmers channeled their energies toward tobacco and adopted more productive methods such as "priming," or picking individual leaves. Tobacco culture expanded into cotton-growing areas. The rapid rise in tobacco and cotton prices during the war years spurred farmers' efforts generally, but the spread of the boll weevil favored the substitution of bright tobacco for insect-ravaged cotton in Georgia and South Carolina. Delighted by their profits, farmers began to make long-needed improvements in their households and farms. Some purchased their first cars. North Carolina tobacco production doubled between 1916 and 1919 and, in the latter year, prices went above fifty cents a pound as farmers reveled in the wealth now flowing from the golden weed.[43]

Despite some premonitions that good fortune would not last, most farmers hoped for still better prices in 1920. Cotton growers as well as tobacco growers planted large crops. Prices climbed until mid-1920 and then suddenly slumped to less than half the previous year's average. A few farmers resorted to burning warehouses and threatening bankers and buyers to prevent foreclosures. Tobacco growers tried to improve their market position under the leadership of the Tri-State Tobacco Growers Association. The attempt failed; the reluctance of many farmers to conform to voluntary production restrictions, the refusal by two of the big four cigarette companies to purchase from the association, and a scandal involving private profiteering by leaders of the group led to its demise in 1926.[44] Small tobacco growers were forced to market their crops in order to pay their debts or satisfy their landlords. They appeared unable to organize against the large manufacturers who dictated price levels that earned the tobacco farmer less than half the average income of other farmers in the United States.[45]

The coming of "Hoover" times in the early 1930s pushed thousands of struggling farmers into destitution. Forced sales claimed 150,000 farms in 1930; 93 banks closed their doors in the same year. Farmers who had earned almost $600 in 1928 for their share of the tobacco crop pocketed less than $150 for the 1932 equivalent. Landowners, pressured by a credit squeeze, responded by eliminating 25 percent of their tenants in 1932; this action deprived 15,000 to 20,000 farmers of their livelihood.[46] The combined impact of a sharp decline in foreign demand, manufacturers' reluctance to buy tobacco in a time of economic uncertainty, and the upheaval in the financial system forced many of those who had survived the bleak 1920s to abandon farming. Rates of migration from rural to urban areas in North Carolina reached their highest levels for white men in 1930, for white women in 1933, and for black women in 1931; the rates for black men almost equaled the previous highs set in the late 1920s.[47] "Hoover carts," rather than automobiles, brought crops to markets that offered prices matching the lows recorded in the 1890s.

The arrival of the "poor man's friend" in the White House and the surge of activity from the Roosevelt administration evoked hope among those still clinging to the land. The Agricultural Adjustment Act, passed in May 1933, promised to justify those hopes by including cotton and tobacco among the crops to be controlled by government action. Incomes rose after federal regulations limited tobacco acreage and placed a floor under prices. An allotment system set up in the late 1930s, after the original AAA had been declared unconstitutional, made the changes permanent. Yet the reforms, intended to restore rather than radically transform the agricultural economy, could not rebuild a way of life already shattered by the cash-crop economy. Small farms and family labor still produced much of the bright tobacco crop, but the social cleavage dividing the rural population remained fixed.[48] As one disgruntled farmer remarked, landlords continued to skim the cream while tenants got the sweat. This unequal division of labor and rewards operated under the new, regulated economy as it had under the old.[49]

The human consequences of the "industrialization of the farm" appeared in the decline in farm ownership (see Table 4). Although farmers made some gains in the first two decades of the twentieth century, the favorable trend reversed in the 1920s. Whatever the percentages of owners and tenants, however, the size of the average farm dropped steadily throughout the pe-

Table 4.
Percentage of Farmers Owning Their Farms and Average Farm Size for Durham, Person, and Granville Counties, 1880–1930

COUNTY	1880 AV. FARM SIZE	1880 ALL	1880 WF	1880 BF*	1900 AV. FARM SIZE	1900 ALL	1900 WF	1900 BF	1910 AV. FARM SIZE	1910 ALL	1910 WF	1910 BF	1920 AV. FARM SIZE	1920 ALL	1920 WF	1920 BF	1930 AV. FARM SIZE	1930 ALL	1930 WF	1930 BF
Durham†	115	61.4	NA	NA	95.8	36.5	49.7	9.3	85.0	42.6	53.6	20.5	75.9	44.7	53.3	25.5	70.6	41.2	53.0	20.0
Granville	136	51.3	NA	NA	98.6	32.5	49.3	15.0	96.4	42.1	53.8	25.0	85.2	44.7	55.7	30.8	75.0	33.7	49.4	23.0
Person	168	62.0	NA	NA	116.1	37.1	50.9	13.8	100.5	40.0	52.2	18.7	82.5	51.4	59.2	39.8	65.1	27.8	48.0	22.0

*Size in acres; All = all farmers, WF = white farmers, BF = black farmers.
†1880 figures for Durham County are those for Orange County, from which Durham was formed in 1881.
SOURCE: U.S. Bureau of the Census, 10th, 12th, 13th, 14th, 15th Censuses for Agriculture (see Appendix for publication information).

riod as land became subdivided into one- and two-horse tenant farms. A new system of class relations emerged in the tobacco-growing region paralleling the trends in the cotton economy. Landless farmers worked in "factories without walls," where they produced the raw materials demanded by an industrial economy that developed in conjunction with commercial agriculture. Although black farmers benefited by their climb into the ranks of tenancy and, for a minority, landownership, most whites and blacks found themselves confined to a permanently landless class that toiled "from sunrise to sunset to raise the crops." They were thwarted in their efforts to better themselves by bitter racial antagonisms and the ruthless tactics of those who exploited them. No longer so firmly attached to the land by ownership, or by expectations that they would one day become landowners, this rural proletariat felt "free" to move from one tenant farm to another or toward the center of the industrial economy. Women, whose labor was less valued, lost or abandoned their places on the land more readily. By the 1890s, Durham was attracting more women than men from the nearby countryside. To comprehend why this pattern of migration persisted into the 1930s, we must recreate the conditions of life and labor as women experienced them in the rural Piedmont.

III
IN
THE
FIELDS

Women experienced the transformation of the countryside in distinctly female ways. From infancy, they encountered patriarchal social relations rooted in a gender-based division of labor, authority, prestige, and reward.[1] In young girlhood, they learned the rules that regulated access to resources and power on the basis of race.[2] Yet the forces undermining the rural economy prevented many women from repeating the lives of their mothers and grandmothers. Torn from a past that could not be relived, some ventured onto new terrain. They traveled, however, still burdened with their upbringing in a hierarchical society.

A story told by a Piedmont farmer illustrates how the crop lien system endangered the rural population. The farmer was reacting to the low price paid for cotton in the late 1890s:

> At the winding up of the year, the crop lien began to draw and it kept on drawing. It drew all the cotton and the corn, and wheat and oats, the shucks, the hay and the fodder, the horses, and the mules, the cows, the hogs and the poultry, the farm utensils and the wagons . . . and not being satisfied with its drawing outside, it drew the household and the kitchen furniture; and . . . it didn't quit drawing until it got the table, the plates and dishes, the cups and the saucers, the knives and the forks, and when it had gotten everything else, it reached for the dish rag and wiped up the whole concern, not leaving even a grease spot.[3]

The male narrator emphasized his own concerns, but he acknowledged that hard times did not stop at the kitchen door. If we are to understand women's situation, the subject added by the farmer as an afterthought must become the focus of our discussion. It must be stressed, however that women's working lives were not confined within the walls of the farmhouse but extended into the fields; a sizeable minority of the female population even ventured into "public work." Indeed, given the intimate links between domestic concerns and agricultural prosperity, women who labored in both arenas were doubly affected by the forces undermining family economic self-sufficiency.

As agricultural production increasingly centered in the tenant family household, its women became a more important part of the family's labor supply. Childbearing and childrearing brought additional hands that allowed the family's income to grow, making it possible to buy mules, tools, and, for a very few, additional land. Nearly all rural women carried out the exhausting chores that transformed coarse provisions into food, clothed the family, battled the dirt, nursed the sick, instructed daughters in domestic tasks, gardened, and tended the domestic animals. Women also worked in the fields when necessary, which was especially frequent while children were young. In addition, women engaged in wage labor to help lift a household out of desperate poverty. The state census, however, consistently underestimated the importance of women's wage contributions to rural households. Taking in laundry, providing for boarders, and working as occasional farmhands were occupations that often went unrecorded. Active in all three arenas of work—domestic labor, field labor, and hired labor—women exhausted themselves in the unrelieved drudgery necessary to sustain a farm household in the emerging cash-crop economy.

Women carried out their duties in a society that was evolving from a simple to a more complex system of market-regulated economic transactions. A woman's labor in a prosperous property-holding household might take place entirely outside the market. That is, she did not help to produce the crop. In a tenant or sharecropping household, however, her labor was recompensed in the family's share of the crop produced by its combined efforts. Some tenant women and even more women in laboring households participated in wage labor; here the employers appropriated the product. Whether women's labor had become a commodity in a formal sense, it typically occurred within a family labor system that distributed tasks among the family members according to gender, age, and the requirements of the crop cycle.[4] Ideally, the father presided over the farm "autocracy" like an "overlord . . . in the ancient patriarchal fashion" that had prevailed among the yeomen of the pre-Civil War South. The mother fulfilled domestic responsibilities and directed her daughters' labor whenever they could be spared from the fields.[5] Tobacco culture, with its varied range of light and heavy, skilled and unskilled duties, was suited to the family labor system. As a cash crop produced by tenants, however, tobacco production undermined both the independence of the family economy and patriarchal authority. The farm household remained the site where production took place in the rural

Piedmont, but increasingly landlords assumed control over the family's labor resources.[6]

Bright-leaf tobacco was a labor-intensive crop, requiring more than 400 hours of labor per acre.[7] The father and older sons would prepare the seedbed in January and transplant the young seedlings in the spring after they had plowed the fields. Small children could drop the young plants in rows while the father and older hands planted them. Later the father would direct the labor of the older children (and perhaps the mother) as the family labor force chopped the weeds in repeated trips through the fields and picked off the tobacco worms before they damaged the leaves. A nursing mother would bring her infant to the fields, lay the baby on a quilt, and tend it between trips up and down the rows. Men performed the harder and more skilled tasks, such as topping (breaking off the just-formed flower buds), which prevented the tobacco going to seed before harvest. The women and children could then break off the suckers that grew after the loss of the flower bud.

The father and other male hands took charge of the most laborious work of the year—harvesting and curing the leaf—which took over 250 hours of labor per acre.[8] Originally, male strength was employed to split the stalk in two with a single stroke of the knife, while children held the sticks over which the bisected plants were draped. As the technique of priming (picking each leaf as it ripened up the stalk) supplanted cutting, women and children took a more active part in the harvest after the father had determined that a layer of leaves was ready to be cured. Where priming was the method of harvesting, women and girls would loop the individual leaves into "hands" and drape the hands over sticks to be inserted into racks in the curing barns.

Men then took charge of the five-day process that cured the leaf. Day and night they carefully regulated the fires that sent smoke through the flues of tobacco barns, slowly heating the leaf to fix the color and produce the most marketable shade and texture. Men, but sometimes women, then graded and sorted the cured leaf by color, size, thickness, texture, and original position on the stalk. Finally the head of the household or the landlord took the cured leaf to town and sold it. Proceeds were disbursed to creditors, landlords, and merchants.

As women in the tobacco-growing region around Durham affirmed into the late 1930s, men, not women, "toted the pocketbook."[9] Although age- and sex-divided tasks gave each participant a sense of purpose in the collective enterprise, tradition designated the male household head as "the farmer" and the rest merely as "family labor."[10] The patriarchal cast of the tobacco culture was reflected in the secular ritual of the tobacco auction, the climax of the thirteen-month crop cycle. Jonathan Daniels, who sympathetically depicted the plight of the grower, somewhat inadvertently recorded the racial and sexual subordination that permeated the public ceremonies surrounding tobacco production:

> Some of them [tobacco farmers] do only get a poor frolic for a driven year. There were . . . more Indian boys and purse snatchers and prostitutes and liquor stores and high pressure business men all waiting beyond the time merchant and the landlord for what is left. But there is thrift, too. You could see it in the eyes of some of the women waiting for their husbands to come back from the warehouses . . . The farmer is at the end of the line, waiting and working, working and hoping, but not getting rich out of the richest crop in the world. But once a year, while the auctioneer chants and sways and the buyers march to his chanting, the intoxication of riches spreads through the towns and overflows on the land. That exaltation is emphasized by the sadder years when the chant is a wail and merchants and bankers and farmers walk together in sorrow. Too often the whole region is nigger rich or nigger poor. And both, like the black man under all his laughter, can sometimes be sad.

Daniels was a compassionate observer, but he missed in one detail. It was the farm wives and farm families and not the farmer who were actually "at the end of the line, waiting and working, working and hoping." Women, moreover, despite the "driven year" they had endured in the service of the family economy, could enjoy the "poor frolic" offered their husbands only at the risk of their respectability.[11] Instead, the women waited at the farm or somewhere in town to learn how much would be left after the merchant, the landlord, and the family head had taken their shares.

Women rarely questioned the sexual division of labor that marked the patriarchal enterprise. They accepted their roles as helpmates fitted for work of lesser prestige. According to the daughter of a black landowner who lived in northern Durham County in the late nineteenth and early twentieth centuries,

> Men's work was for men. Women crossed over more doing whatever was needed. They worked in the fields when necessary, but that was man's work. Men chopped wood, shoveled snow, cut tobacco when it was ready to be primed. Women held the sticks and men draped the tobacco leaves over the sticks . . . Women didn't do much of the barn curing. Men did the sorting but women tied it up in bundles. Men just understood what grades the tobacco leaves should be put in. It was based upon the color of the leaf and there were four to eight grades. It seemed that men could detect the grades better. Men took the tobacco into town and sold it. Women didn't go into town much.[12]

IN THE FIELDS

Bertie Loman, a black woman who lived all her adult life on a Person County tobacco farm, took pride in a life of "crossing over" to do men's work:

> When my daddy died, I was older than my brother. Of course, I knowed how to plow before he died, because I'd had to rest him. I plowed up until he [her brother] got bigger. Still I loved to plow and I plowed after I got married. I cut wheat with a cradle. I did everything but drive a tractor. I cut wheat, grubbed, cleared the ground, primed tobacco. I done my part of hard work.[13]

When not occupied with fieldwork, caring for six children, and housework, Mrs. Loman strung Bull Durham tobacco bags "to pay for the fertilizer that went on the tobacco." A similar pride was expressed in the interviews conducted by Margaret Hagood among white tenant farm women in the Durham area during the 1930s. These women accepted the distinction between men's and women's work, but also testified to the frequency with which women crossed the boundaries. Displaying a detailed knowledge of tobacco culture, they delighted in their husbands' or fathers' praise of their skills as tobacco hands. Like their black counterparts, they recognized which work carried the greatest prestige.[14]

When discussions turned to "women's work," the evidence suggests that women's unpaid labor in the home was losing status in an agricultural economy increasingly oriented toward the market. As cash, not the usefulness of labor to the household, became the major measure of labor's value, the partnership between men and women rooted in a simple market society began to erode. Analyses of women's position in Farmers' Alliance publications and public forums reflect the decline. When the journal *Progressive Farmer* functioned as the organ of the Farmers' Alliance and the Populists under the editorship of Leonidias Polk, it simultaneously offered articles on housekeeping, encouraged women to defend the independent producer, and asked its male readership to provide "conveniences for the good and faithful wife." Polk urged farmers to rescue themselves from the perils of the cash-crop economy by diversifying their crops and becoming more self-sufficient in food production. He justified "progressive agriculture" in the name of the farm woman, who would be able to adorn her home and "attend to her milk and butter, eggs, bees, chickens, and other poultry," rather than wear out "her life in cooking for a lot of negroes to work the cotton." The female supporters of the *Progressive Farmer* and the Alliance enthusiastically responded to such appeals, and sometimes went beyond the rhetoric of wifely submission. In 1888, one correspondent wrote:

> Let us all put our shoulders to this great wheel, the Alliance, and push with one purpose in view—independence and freedom. As sisters of

this Alliance we may feel we are silent factors in this work . . . [but] let us so entwine ourselves around our brothers that should we be taken away they will feel they are tottering."[15]

When the *Progressive Farmer* under Polk's successor became a booster of commercial agriculture (having abandoned the political definition of "progressive"), its pages became a forum for women's frustrations with chronic overwork and isolation, economic dependence on their husbands, lack of adequate resources to ease household chores, and men's indifference to their concerns. Although women in more prosperous tenant and landowning families could eventually purchase labor-saving devices—such as fireless cookers, gas or oil stoves, gasoline-powered irons and mechanical washers in the 1920s and 1930s—mere access to appliances did not always produce satisfaction for even the most privileged women.[16]

Surveys of women's lives in the tenant and sharecropping classes in rural North Carolina revealed little enthusiasm for domestic labor. Investigators from the U.S. Children's Bureau in 1916 discovered that black women preferred work in cotton fields because it paid better, allowed greater sociability, and offered opportunity to display skills. White women were less adamant about their preferences. The investigators also documented the arduous nature of household chores in ill-equipped houses. Both black and white women (more than three-quarters of whom also worked in the fields) carried water from springs or distant wells, cooked over wood-burning stoves that made homes stifling hot in summer, and cleaned cramped and ramshackle cabins that lacked screens, indoor plumbing, or privies.[17] A study of white tenant families in Caswell County in the early 1920s recorded similar conditions.[18] In the late 1930s, Margaret Hagood's survey of white tenant farm women in the Durham area found that the typical house lacked electricity, running water, a radio, or a phonograph; it did possess, however, a sewing machine, "inadequate screens," a wood-burning stove, a safe for storing and keeping food, and drab interiors decorated with calendars. Having systematically inventoried these conditions, Hagood expressed no surprise at women's enthusiasm for outdoor work. She wondered only that those she interviewed were "able to keep up the level of energy output during almost every waking hour, day in and day out, year after year, which is demanded for getting big families fed, cleaned after, washed and sewed for, with such meager and inadequate equipment, and with such antiquated methods." She understood why one older woman felt it necessary to apologize for doing only housework: "I just can't hold out any more in the field, though I used to work like a man."[19] Working like a woman brought little recognition or reward.

Detailed study of white farm family budgets in North Carolina during the

1920s explains the lack of labor-saving equipment in farm households. Expenditures for "home and household" equaled 3 percent of the average landowning or tenant household budget, while "farm and investment" consumed 48.9 percent of the yeoman budget and 33.1 percent of the tenant budget. In 1929, with the average tenant farm income at $800 per year, household needs were far behind the farm; food, clothing, auto, and health concerns in priority.[20] Men's work took precedence because it produced cash and satisfied creditors. The "crop lien" story related above got things backward: the insatiable system devoured spoons and plates first. Horses and farm utensils had to be preserved to the last. Virtually all family income (after paying creditors) went into supplies for the next crop and for food during the winter and early spring.

The informal swap work exchanges between relatives and neighbors also distinguished between men's and women's work. Groups of men often shared the tasks of hog killing, corn shucking, wood chopping, wheat threshing, and barn or house building. Women often worked for days preparing food for the men involved in swap work, as they also did for church suppers, family reunions, and neighborhood picnics—while the men relaxed.[21] When black men and white men jointly participated, the women were required to cook and serve three separate meals: one for white men, one for white women, and one for black men. Black women, if present, ate after all others had finished.[22] When women gathered for shared work, they met in small groups, "just three or four," to piece together quilts, knit, and talk. Their work was more often restricted to a circle of kin and nearby neighbors than done in the wider community where men performed.

Whether they worked in the household or earned wages, women received less reward for their labors than did men. Nevertheless, they rarely protested. Even an ardent feminist like Margaret Hagood could detect little resentment against the pervasive assumption of female subordination. Men, of course, benefited from their privileged position. Even the least successful men believed in their rightful superiority over their wives.[23] Women's acceptance of this situation is harder for us to understand. The general absence of any public forum available to rural women may be partial explanation. If women had complaints, they vented them in privacy and left no trace for a curious historian.

In the pages of the *Progressive Farmer*, a few farm wives criticized domineering husbands, but most women kept their views out of the public media.[24] Women rarely expressed resentment of male authority even in interviews. They were more likely to complain when husbands failed their patriarchal responsibilities; women faulted the incompetent farmer and manager and not the successful household head. The few women able to confine themselves to women's work because of the success of their husbands took pride in their good fortune. Less favored women took pride in their ability to do men's work. Both attitudes equally reflected acceptance of the social status quo.[25]

Women's initiative in childbearing is harder to document than their role in the production of tobacco or cotton. Reproduction was considered inevitable and took place within one patriarchal family unit. Except for the occasional problem of determining paternity, motherhood rarely became an issue in the public world of men. Only later, following controversy over women's employment outside the home, did scholars take an interest in the subject. And just as white women's employment provoked more debate, so too did white women's reproductive activities. A few studies compared black and white women's fertility in the rural Piedmont, but most researchers concentrated on white women's experiences—despite black women's higher birth rates (see Table 5). The same cultural assumptions that valued white women for their reproductive capacities (while extolling their sexual purity) devalued black motherhood (while exploiting black women's sexuality). Researchers, apparently influenced by the same attitudes, wrote books such as *Mothers of the South*, which referred primarily to white women.

A few researchers went beyond simple comparisons of fertility by racial or tenure group. Margaret Hagood gathered detailed information from 117 tenant farm women concerning their involvement in the "producing and rearing of children." She noted that these women produced an average of 6.4 children during the average 18.9-year marriage. She also reported the

Table 5.
Births Per 1,000 Married Women, 15–44 Years of Age, by Race and Tenure Status for Five Rural Areas in North Carolina, 1915–1934

RACE/TENURE	1915–1919	1920–1924	1925–1929	1930–1934
All rural women	329	316	262	237
White women	313	299	248	223
Black women	342	337	291	250
Owners	302	271	214	223
Renters	343	322	273	230
Croppers	366	365	302	259
Laborers	278	288	249	209

SOURCE: C. Horace Hamilton, "Recent Changes in the Social and Economic Status of Farm Families in North Carolina," North Carolina Agricultural Experiment Station, *Bulletin* No. 309, May 1937, p. 157.

pride shown by her subjects as they related their experiences in "those most fundamental of realities." Although the "lines of class distinction" vanished in their conversations, Hagood was always conscious that economic pressures were one of the major factors perpetuating the high rates of fertility. The women whom she interviewed were adding "field workers of economic value" to their family economies. She also sensed ambivalence in the frequent remark, "I hope this is the last one." But if women wished "to keep from having them," they took no direct action to stop conception. Some relied on withdrawal: one woman explained, "If you don't want butter, pull out the dasher in time!" The majority complied with their womanly duties. The 1934 birth rate, however, was about a third less than the 1915–1919 average.

Hagood's study ventured beyond the concerns of demographers, census takers, and labor supply specialists and examined the process of socialization within the Piedmont household. She was particularly sensitive to the rearing of the next generation of tenant farm women. Girls learned early to perform household chores so that "by ten they can clean house, make beds, and straighten up and by twelve or thirteen can cook a meal if they have to." They also shared the farm work with their brothers when young, but encountered greater restrictions when they entered puberty. Fear that a girl would "get in trouble" led to parental anxiety but not to sex education. Daughters were warned against breaking a rigid code of sexual purity and punished for infractions, but the mysteries of the code were never fully explained. Such girls replicated their mother's lives because they lacked other opportunities—for education, for occupational mobility, or for relationships with men outside their own class. Although about a fifth of the tenant farm women had sought outside work by the late 1930s, the majority were "resigned to the fact that their economic goals cannot be achieved," accepted their deprived existence through "moralizations," tolerated mild discontent "without being bitter," and hoped that their daughters might realize their dreams.[26]

The actual balance of power within a household depended on resources and force of character, but males enjoyed unchallenged authority outside. A public patriarchy controlled by white men enforced the power of the male household head over all other household members. Public areas—the tobacco auction, the county courthouse, the jury box, the judge's bench, the lawyer's office, the legislature in Raleigh, the pulpit, the bank, and the state university in nearby Chapel Hill—were white male territory. Any white women present were self-effacing and silent. Black men and women, if present, were required to defer to whites. The two hierarchies of gender and race enhanced the status of the white men, who dominated both. Even white men who were poor and powerless enjoyed a privileged status; they ventured into town more frequently than women to do the family shopping, to sell the family crop, to arrange for loans, and to acquire information about economic, political, and social affairs.

Although women were more devout than men, the rural church was a male-controlled institution. Preaching a literal interpretation of the Bible, rural ministers insisted on female subordination as a fitting punishment for Eve's original sin. The Baptists and, to a lesser extent, the Methodists stressed women's position as "helpmates" to males. Feminism, implicitly and sometimes explicitly, was damned in fundamentalist teaching as unchristian, unwomanly, antifamily, and contrary to the sacred traditions of the South. Many rural churches reinforced gender consciousness by seating women on one side and men on the other. Some women, particularly in black churches, might assume positions of leadership, but their careers were less likely to reach the highest governing bodies. An implicit feminist critique (conveyed by women missionaries, teachers, and female organizations) countered the patriarchal version of Christianity in some churches, but rural ministers overwhelmingly opposed the notion that women had an equal right with men to interpret God's word.[27]

Exhorted to obey their fathers and their husbands, women rarely found encouragement to challenge a male authority endorsed by the church, the state, and popular opinion. Yet the forces undermining the family economy made it difficult for men to maintain control over their households. The tenant or the mortgaged farmowner could not operate like an independent producer. Landlords and creditors insisted that a tenant plant a large cash crop to ensure repayment of the family's obligations at the end of the year. The pressure of the debt could force the entire family into the fields in order to produce the maximum yield. Tenants could not always keep women out of the fields or send their children to school. Wives became an essential part of the family labor force, as comparisons between the amount of field labor performed by women in tenant and landowning families demonstrates. Families that lacked other resources utilized their potential labor power with less distinction between male and female, adult and child, than occurred in more economically advantaged households. Finally, the most impoverished families would surrender some labor power by sending women in pursuit of the meager wages paid to female labor in the rural countryside (see Table 6). Such a strategy may have declined in popularity as migration into cities became an attractive alternative to remaining on the land for families dependent on female wage-earning. In either case, fathers and husbands gradually lost their monopoly over the labor of their womenfolk and their ability to shield them from potential sexual encounters.

Studies that compared the rates at which rural households lost labor power as children moved away disclosed that tenant children were more likely to leave home at younger ages and more likely to live further away than were the children of landowners. In one study of late-1920s white farm

IN THE FIELDS

Table 6.
Tenure Status of Rural Households and Percentage of Employed Women in Such Households in Durham,* Granville, and Person Counties, 1880–1900

HOUSEHOLDS	OWNERS (%) 1880	1900	N	TENANTS (%) 1880	1900	N	LABORERS (%) 1880	1900	N
With white male heads	60.0	47.4	NA	22.0	44.3	NA	18.0	8.2	142
With black male heads	10.0	10.5	NA	35.0	68.4	NA	55.0	21.1	106
With white female heads	45.0	55.6	NA	18.0	33.3	NA	37.0	11.1	29
With black female heads	-0-	33.3	NA	12.5	33.3	NA	87.5	33.3	14
With employed women aged 14+	32.6	14.0	101	33.4	17.5	120	34.4	28.8	73

*1880 figures for parts of Orange/Wake County that became Durham County in 1881.
SOURCE: 10th and 12th Censuses of the United States (manuscript) Population Schedules for 1880 and 1900, sample from counties indicated, National Archives, Washington, D.C. (See Appendix for description of sampling techniques used).

households in Wake County, 39.2 percent of the owners' sons lived in the same township as their parents, compared with 21.3 percent of tenants' sons. The variations for daughters was less extreme but still significant: 34.9 percent of owners' daughters lived near their parents, compared with 25.3 percent of tenants' daughters. Another 30 to 40 percent from each category had moved to cities, primarily Raleigh and Durham. Since tenants' children left earlier and tended to live further away, the study made clear that a tenant family more quickly depleted its most important resource—the labor of its children—than did the household that could promise its offspring an inheritance.[28] A study conducted in 1935, however, found fewer differences in migration patterns between children of landowning and landless families. This later study also examined racial variations in the distance between migrant children and their parents. Black women were the least likely to live in the same township as their parents, followed by white women, then black men, and then white men; in fact, 44.2 percent of white men lived in the same township as their parents. Of all the tenure classes, sharecroppers' children moved the greatest distance from the parental home; less than 38 percent lived in the same township, and 33 percent lived in other parts of North Carolina or in an adjoining state. Taken together, the surveys indicated the tenuous hold that landless patriarchs had on their children. The landowner enjoyed a further advantage: he could replace family labor with tenant or hired labor. A comparison of income, acreage under cultivation, and expenditures makes clear the tenant household's greater dependence on family labor. Although average incomes peaked when children reached their teen years, the tenant income never exceeded slightly more than half of the average landowner income. As children left the household, the incomes of both groups dropped, but the tenant income fell to $750 while the landowner income dropped to $1,200, an amount equal to the highest tenant income.[29] More vulnerable to the vagaries of biology and less able to command the labor of their children, aging tenant couples often moved into the households of married children to end their days in dependency.

Although all households grew more vulnerable to a market increasingly beyond their control, households headed by women were less secure. Landlords preferred to rent the most desirable farms to families boasting a healthy male head and a full complement of sons. Many women abandoned the fight to remain on the land. Widows and ex-widows who remained on tenant farms always "stressed the economic value of a husband," according to Margaret Hagood, as well as their struggles to farm and raise children on "the little they had to eat." When they turned to paid work, women's choices were limited to domestic work and farm labor, and their wages rarely averaged more than half the average male wage. In the late nineteenth century, women earned about 25 cents a day for domestic labor and about $5 a month for farm labor. During the labor scarcity of the First World War, male farm laborers' wages climbed to $3.50 a day but females earned only half that.[30] When wages fell in the 1920s and 1930s, women's wages remained at a fourth to a half of those received by men.

Women who wanted to avoid working away from their families supplemented their incomes at home by making, stringing, and tagging sacks for Bull Durham smoking tobacco. Gradually, however, that supplementary income was lost to mechanization and governmental regulation against homework. In the late 1880s a machine began manufacturing the bags at the Bull Durham factory, but the bags were still sent out to be strung with drawstrings and tagged with the Bull Durham label. In the 1910s the sacks began to be strung mechanically. Finally, in the late 1930s, a machine took over "tagging the Bulls," ending the last part of a production process that enabled rural women to earn money without going into "public work."[31] As the security of the family economy dissolved along with the opportunity for landownership, rural women, especially in female-headed households, found it difficult to stay on the land in a market that paid them little for their labor or their crops.

■ Race, not class, represented the most visible social category that divided women from one another and determined the men with whom they could form acceptable relationships. Like class, race was a powerful determinant of female access to security and prestige. Yet race was something more than a biological equivalent or mask for class. Southern racial traditions and institutions incorporated caste-like practices that regulated access not only to the privileged race but to all desirable resources. Concern about property rights, the focus of the class system, became inseparable from concern about sexual property. Women, whose fertility and sexual availability were the medium of exchange in the reproductive system, became the objects for whom property rights were claimed or denied in conflicts between men. Sexual relations between white women and black men, originally prohibited because their issue would create an anomalous group of free blacks, were particularly dangerous. White women, the symbolic and actual agents whose choice of sexual partners protected or defiled "white" bloodlines, were both elevated and subordinated to the cause of racial purity. Black women, seen as the negative image of the white virgin-mothers, were assigned roles as sexual prey whose carnality made them willing accomplices to the desires of white men. Black men, the group most likely to compete for patriarchal status with white men, threatened the racial order to the extent that their aspirations most resembled white men's. In the set of emotional appeals developed by white racists to defend their supremacy, the image of the black beast contrasted with the white man's chosen role of the knight. White or black, women belonged to racial communities whose boundaries hemmed them in while men guarded the racial frontiers.[32]

Although men generally took a more aggressive role in defending or attacking white dominance, women participated in the brutal encounters that reconstructed race relations after the end of slavery. Opposed to the radical reforms of the Republican-dominated legislature in the late 1860s and to the new state constitution of 1868, North Carolina's traditional elite—the major controllers of wealth, land, and labor, "chose to draw the color line in politics." In the name of virtue, property, and intelligence, conservative leaders condemned the political reforms that had put power into the "hands of mere numbers." As part of their "total struggle" against Republicanism, the elite embarked on a campaign of terrorism through secret organizations such as the White Brotherhood, the Constitutional Union Guard, and the Invisible Empire. Both black people, particularly those active in Republican campaigns or the Union League, and white Republicans were the targets of terrorist assaults. The specter of the black rapist supplied one pretext for intimidating any advocate of political or "social equality." After a lynching in Hillsborough, a town twelve miles northwest of Durham, the killers left a note saying, "All Barn-burners, all women offenders, we Kuklux hang by the neck till they are dead, dead, dead." The widow of one of the victims, assured that she would be protected by "good men" if she identified the perpetrators, replied, "The Lord knows who the good men were, I didn't." A white woman suffered an assault at the hands of the nocturnal raiders, who whipped her crippled husband for teaching in an integrated school.[33] A black man who came South to teach the freedmen was advised by the county official in charge of education that he would "do better in the field" than in the classroom. Nightly visits from "masked Klansmen" convinced Robert Fitzgerald that the secret organization and public officials shared a common hostility to the cause of "educating the black race for their own future welfare."[34] While the Fitzgeralds refused to be intimidated, other white and black Republicans fled from rural Orange, Chatham, Wake, and other counties, seeking a place "where there was no Ku Klux."

The use of the Klan aided the Conservative Party in its goal of recapturing the state legislature in 1870. Once in power, the Conservatives consolidated the victory by pressing impeachment proceedings against the Republican governor who had commanded the state militia to do battle against the Klan. After Governor Holden had been driven from office in 1871, the Conservatives reorganized district boundaries, lengthened residential requirements, and disfranchised voters arrested for petty crimes in order to cleanse the voting rolls of blacks and poor whites. Finally, in 1875, the Conservatives, now reconstituted as the Democratic Party, seized control of a new constitutional convention that took away many of the reforms imposed under Radical Reconstruction. The next year they climaxed their drive to regain power by electing a Democrat as governor.[35] A mixture of terror against opponents and incitement to racist fears among white men had succeeded in restoring the former rulers to political control.

Although denied the right to participate actively in the electoral process, women could not be sheltered from the turmoil that was altering the political economy of the Piedmont. Black farm laborers of both sexes rose to tenant status by refusing to accept the lesser rewards of wage labor. Black women participated in the struggle for education, for land, and for the political rights that could advance those goals. White women, frightened by the threat of rape and perplexed by the unsettling economic changes that forced many of them to occupy the same class position as former slaves, generally applauded the actions conducted by white men to advance white supremacy. Some women, however, joined the Alliances and the Knights in attempts to create a class-based solidarity. A few black women sought to escape from outbreaks of racial violence by joining an exodus in the late 1870s and the late 1880s that brought black settlers to Kansas, Arkansas, Texas, Mississippi, and Indiana territories.[36] The majority remained in the state despite the indignities visited upon their people. They supported black men even when women's needs were not completely incorporated into the agenda established by black leaders. They shared the vision evoked by George White, the representative of North Carolina's Second District and the last black man to serve a district from the South until modern times. Speaking to Congress in 1898, White told his audience:

IN THE FIELDS

Despite all the oppression which has fallen upon our shoulders, we have been rising, steadily rising and in some instances we hope ere long to be able to measure our achievements with those of all other men and women in the land. This tendency on the part of some of us to rise and assert our manhood along all lines, is, I fear, what has brought about this changed condition.[37]

Although White did not call on black females to assert their womanhood, they lost a champion when the aggressive campaign for disfranchisement intimidated enough black voters in the Second District that White was forced out of office in 1901. White women, on the other side of the widening racial divide, enthusiastically endorsed the notion of white supremacy and the defense of white womanhood. In a tense atmosphere, the *Progressive Farmer,* initially sponsored by the Knights and the Farmers' Alliance, carried white farmers' recommendations that the "whipping-post" be reestablished and education for black children be eliminated because literate blacks would become "a disturbing element in politics." Women, coming to consciousness in this environment, could not escape the contagion of racial hatreds that classified blacks as enemies to be rendered powerless, ignorant, and abjectly dependent on their white overlords.

Not content with a political victory, some white leaders sought still stricter controls over black life. Clarence Poe, heir to the farmers' movement of the late nineteenth century, broke sharply with its tradition of racial cooperation. Writing as a defender of the "laboring white man who must compete industrially with a race with lower living standards," Poe, the editor of the post-Alliance *Progressive Farmer,* argued for segregation in rural areas to prevent economic competition between the races. He denounced black tenants for living in "shabbier houses," eating "meaner food," and wearing "dirtier clothes," and argued that competition with the cheaper labor of black tenants forced white farmers into tenancy or out of agriculture altogether.[38] Probably because white landlords benefited from the very conditions Poe sought to eliminate, rural segregation statutes were never passed. Rigid social boundaries, however, operated without explicit legal sanction. There were taboos against eating together, sitting together, or participating in any social event where the white was not clearly defined as superior. When taboos were violated or hard times intensified white anger, lynching and other terrorist acts deflected the attention of poor whites from powerful white landlords to the black victims of the same class.

Informal controls kept blacks economically subordinate through low wages and limited access to land. The *Christian Recorder* carried a letter from a Hillsborough, North Carolina, reader describing the situation that forced many blacks to leave the state:

> The cause of our people leaving the state was, first, for a living. The average wage in North Carolina for men is about $8 to $10 . . . They hope to be able to keep us from even being able to buy land . . . Should you ever become able to make them an offer they will charge you from $10 to $12 per acre for land that would not produce five bushels to the acre . . . The women get from $3 to $4, $5 or $6 and find their own room. Should they accidentally break an old plate, they charge them 50 to 75¢.[39]

Arthur Raper, who was born into a landowning family, argued that black farmers still faced the same constraints in 1929: "The definition of 'his place' hedges the Negro landowner about by restrictions similar to those which define and enforce the chronic dependency of the landless Negroes."[40] A black farmer, as reported by a black agricultural agent born in northern Durham County in the early twentieth century, needed a white patron before he could expect to acquire land. Even then, he would probably be sold the "backbone and spareribs" rather than the prime farm land. Late into this century, the workings of a white-controlled system of credit, patronage, and political power operated to prevent blacks from gaining control over land, to detach black farmers from the land, and to retain white control over black labor.[41]

Black women, more likely than their white counterparts to be attached to a propertyless household, bore the economic consequences of a mutually reinforcing system of racial, class, and gender subordination that drove them from the land when they were widowed or deserted. As a result, black women were less likely than white women to head rural households. In 1880, almost 20 percent of white households in the rural areas sampled were headed by women, compared with only 14 percent of black households; in 1900, almost 17 percent of white households had female heads, compared with less than 10 percent of black households. It was harder for black women to sustain viable households in an economy that severely restricted their access to resources. The destiny of black women who headed households and remained on the land was suggested by the high proportion of such women listed in the ranks of the laboring class in the 1880 census (see Table 6). Although the remaining female-headed households moved up the tenure ladder between 1880 and 1900, the decrease in their proportions in the total farm population reflects a propensity of the less advantaged to migrate rather than marked improvements for their standing in commercial agriculture. Those female heads able to rent or own land, a small number in any case, were more likely to remain as farmers; those forced to subsist on farm laborers' wages found it preferable to migrate to cities instead. Furthermore, as the higher rates of female labor from members of female-headed households testify, women clung to the land only by taking on paid employment or by acting as unpaid field labor and domestic labor within their households. Such households, especially those headed by black women, inevitably endured greater hardships than did those whose members could devote their energies entirely to farming (see Table 7).

The exhausting round of work pursued by Mrs. Callie Ruffin, whose family sharecropped on the Stagville portion of the old Cameron plantation, illustrated the plight of black women who lacked an adult male farmer to lead the family enterprises. Tilling a small farm on the estate where her elderly husband had been enslaved, Mrs. Ruffin struggled to support him and their eleven children in the 1920s. In addition to performing all the domestic chores, she nursed the family with her knowledge of herbs and roots. She worked in the fields beside her sons. She also washed clothes for the inhabitants of a small mill village five miles from her home in northern Durham County. Carrying "one bundle on her head and two up under her arms," Mrs. Ruffin walked to and from Orange Factory. Rubbing the clothes on a

Table 7.
Employed Women Aged 15 and Over by Race and Sex of Household Head and by Race of Women Employed, in Rural Durham,* Person, Granville, and Wake Counties, 1880–1924

PERCENTAGE OF WOMEN EMPLOYED	1880	N	1900	N	1924	N
In households headed by:						
White men	11.3%	45	9.4%	97	NA	142
Black men	17.0	49	10.9	57	NA	106
White women	14.7	11	45.6	18	NA	29
Black women	46.5	8	66.7	6	NA	14
Heads of households only:	21.0	19	58.3	24	NA	43
White women	9.0	11	50.0	18	NA	29
Black women	37.5	8	66.7	6	NA	14
All rural women:	16.5	468	15.5	482	25.2%	10,826
Black women	30.5	143	34.6	167	36.0	4,637
White women	17.4	81	24.0	116	17.0	6,189

*1880 figures for parts of Orange/Wake County that became Durham County in 1881; 1924 figures for rural Wake County.

SOURCES: 10th, 12th Censuses of the United States (manuscript) Population Schedules for 1880 and 1900, sample from the counties indicated, National Archives, Washington, D.C. (see Appendix for description of sampling techniques used); 1924 figures from U.S. Department of Commerce, Bureau of the Census, *Farm Population of Selected Counties* (Washington, D.C.: G.P.O., 1924).

washboard, cleaning them with homemade soap, and boiling the clothes in a large iron pot, she washed and rinsed them with water she transported from a nearby spring. After washing, boiling, rinsing, blueing, and starching the shirts, she ironed them with a heavy flatiron heated on a wood-burning stove. Upon returning the bundles to her mill village customers, she received fifty to seventy-five cents for each family's wash. This laborious process consumed two to three days a week. Rather than lamenting her hard lot, however, Callie Ruffin expressed gratitude to Bennehan Cameron for allowing her the privilege of sharecropping his land when her children were young. When she moved to Snow Hill in 1935, she took pleasure in the family's new-found access to a privy.[42] Mrs. Ruffin was aware that other women lacked her blessings. Her landlord was willing to rent to a female-headed family, and she commanded the loyalty of sons who remained unmarried to help support their mother and younger siblings. Many were less fortunate.

Black women's heavier responsibilities for labor outside the immediate household were compounded by frequent childbearing. Crude ratios, like the number of children under five years of age per women of reproductive age (roughly fifteen to forty-four), consistently revealed heavy reproductive activity among rural black women in the 1930s. By 1931, largely rural Granville and Person Counties were recording birth rates of 28.2 and 29.5 per thousand black women in those areas, with white birth rates of 21.8 and 26.5, while the city of Durham in the predominantly urban county of Durham posted birth rates of 19.9 for black women and 22.1 for white women. Black women were also bearing children under less favorable conditions: their infant mortality rates were more than double those faced by white mothers. In 1931 the rural death rate per thousand black infants in North Carolina approximated 92.8, compared to 58.7 for white infants; in the city of Durham the black infant death toll reached 126.9 compared to 58.8 for white babies.[43] Government researchers, attempting to reduce the infant mortality rates, attributed the greater susceptibility of black children to their mothers' heavy workloads. Observing childbearing among black and white households in 1916, they noted that white women rested at least nine days after childbirth before resuming their labors, where black women got up within five days. The researchers pointed out that 71 percent of white mothers and 95 percent of black mothers combined fieldwork with housework and childcare, and concluded that overwork deprived black mothers of sufficient strength and time to fulfill their maternal duties. They also noted that inferior housing, inadequate supplies of water, and lack of inside plumbing made it more difficult to provide a healthy environment for mother or child.[44]

Racial oppression went beyond the merely quantifiable. In addition to poisoning contacts between the races, it corroded relationships within the black family and community. A particularly cruel manifestation arose from the parental need to teach children survival skills. It was a black mother's duty to socialize her children to their subordinate place in the racial hierarchy. Nearly sixty years later, Zina Riddle remembered the whippings her mother had given her when she forgot to "put a handle" to white people's names.[45] Other parents imparted the same bitter lessons. Failure to instruct children might cost the life of a child; one young boy was lynched for throwing a rock at a white-owned car.[46] On the other hand, instructing daughters and sons in degrading behaviors commonly led to anger between parent and child. Often black children were never explicitly told to defer to whites; they learned by seeing their parents enact self-effacing rituals in the presence of whites. Children were instructed to ignore rather than resist hostile or sexually insulting attentions from white men.[47] When parents could not protect their children or explain why they should submit to injustice, respect between family members was damaged.

Memories of relationships with whites revealed a range of emotions from resignation to open rage. Callie Ruffin taught her children by her patient, long-enduring example to accept their situation as the will of God. Living through "hard times and tribulations," Mrs. Ruffin left her daughter with peaceful memories:

> She worked all her life as long as I knowed her and never had nothing, but was a very happy person . . . They had religion, they had faith . . . They didn't have nothing else to believe . . . I can remember about how my mother used to wash and she would be singing those hymns, "Amazing Grace" . . . But what could you do? You didn't have any other choice 'cause there wasn't anywhere else to go . . . They had to stay there. There wasn't anywhere else and this is why that I say that they made themselves happy.[48]

Zina Riddle, who was the daughter of a farm laborer, painted a bleaker picture of her early life: "Back then we had it rough. Sometimes it seemed like the white folks hated the black folk, but there wasn't nothing you could do about it. They were so mean."[49]

Mamie Gray, whose family bought land through the combined labors of herself, her husband, and their twelve children, reported a more satisfying life. She liked farming, she explained, because "you could be your own boss. When you got tired, you could sit down and rest. It wasn't like it is now . . . White and black would help each other sometimes, but not too often. It wasn't like it is now. It was much more separate."[50] As a member of a landowning family, Mamie Gray was able to avoid the most bruising encounters with white employers. Most black laborers were not so fortunate, and years of unrewarded labor had taught black women like Zina Riddle and Callie Ruffin to accept what they could not change as a sign of God's "amazing grace."[51]

Against odds, black women, along with black men, created a set of social institutions that helped maintain their personal integrity. Black families, churches, schools, and self-help organizations offered protection against the often brutal interactions with whites, as well as with more conventional life crises. Elastic networks of household and kinship provided care for the old and young; children were taught to become contributing members to the family economy and to respect the authority of their parents. Churches, which attracted a predominantly female membership, offered perhaps the fullest opportunity for blacks to assume positions of leadership. Boards of stewards or deacons might deliberate over the hiring of local teachers, the building of a school, or ways to gain needed services from a hostile, white-dominated local government. Churches and schools provided gathering places where a dispersed rural population met for worship, lectures, picnics, courtship, and funerals. There, news was exchanged about local affairs and family matters. Black women also gained a sense of power through church activities. They worked as Sunday School teachers, supported missionary societies, and served on church governing boards—although they faced opposition when they challenged male authority. Black school teachers also filled a position of respect. Battles over equal funds for black schools and equal pay for black teachers placed teachers on the front lines of one of the major black campaigns in the state in the 1930s. Finally, community organizations like the Masons, Eastern Star, and insurance societies advanced the collective interests of the black community while enhancing the lives of individual members.[52]

Unlike their black counterparts, white women benefited in obvious ways from racial domination. Black women assisted them in household chores and sometimes relieved them from work in the fields. White women could bully their servants if they chose. Although some white women lived in families as poor as many blacks, many others enjoyed the benefits of higher incomes and better living conditions. As a consequence, white women enjoyed longer life spans despite the hardships that they also endured.[53]

Black women's degraded social status also enhanced the white women's image of superior virtue. Indeed, the presumed superiority underlay white men's fierce determination to defend their women against the allegedly predatory black male. Yet, this same system simultaneously trapped white women, as a small group of female reformers recognized. Dependent on white males for protection, women were expected to obey those who guarded their virtue. Furthermore, the notion of defending white womanhood assumed that white women's sexuality was the private possession of their present or future husbands; while black women's bodies were the common property of white men. This sexual double standard punished white women for behavior that their men tolerated in themselves.⁵⁴

Most white farm women accepted the tenets of this deeply racist culture. The theology preached in rural churches declared that God had annointed whites to rule over the inferior races. The religious press endorsed white supremacy as morally correct and socially necessary. The editor of the *Biblical Recorder*, a Baptist newspaper published in Raleigh, advised his readers in 1873 on dealing with black farm laborers:

> Never so lose sight of your own self-respect so as to socialize with him; if you do, you at once subvert your influence and destroy your mutual interest . . . avoid the suicidal policy of making him believe he is as good as you are—he will drop you at once, and naturally and justly should.⁵⁵

The Methodists and Baptists, whose congregations worshiped in segregated churches, also urged racial separation unless blacks could be clearly defined as subordinate. Although southern churches usually insisted that religion should not mix with politics, the religious press actively supported the Democratic campaigns for white supremacy and black disfranchisement during the 1890s. One Baptist newspaper expressed the sweeping sentiment, "Old Baptists believe in white supremacy in church matters and so do all churches." Southern Methodists also conformed to the practice of white supremacy, although they criticized its more savage abuses.⁵⁶ The decision by black Protestants to form independent churches confirmed the justness of segregation in the eyes of southern whites.

The poorest white women, often scarcely connected to the churches of their more affluent neighbors, thoroughly embraced white supremacist attitudes. They used the threat of the "Big Black Nig" to keep their children obedient. Sometimes they ignored the very existence of black homes, churches, or schools when discussing the local community—even when giving directions. Unable to demonstrate their superiority by employing black maids, white tenant women might denounce the practice of having white children cared for by "niggers."⁵⁷ According to their testimony, these women cherished a system that ensured that someone, at least, would always remain fixed beneath them.

White women were deeply implicated in some of the most brutal racial incidents. Newspapers reports of lynchings noted the presence of white women in the crowds that watched and cheered.⁵⁸ While researching the causes of lynching, Arthur Raper investigated the circumstances surrounding the hanging of a black tobacco tenant in Edgecombe County, not far from Durham. According to the Raleigh *News and Observer*, families flocked to see the "show of the countryside." Parents brought young children to educate them in the workings of white justice, men traded jokes, and young girls giggled beside the dangling body of the black victim. The local paper justified the hanging, although some ministers in the large town churches criticized the use of mob violence. When Raper asked local residents about race relations in the county, he was told repeatedly, "We've got the best Negroes of any county in the State; they are good workers and 'they know their place.'" White men and women, Raper explained, saw lynching as a method of ensuring that blacks never strayed beyond the narrow limits of "their place."[59]

Black women, subject to the same constraints as black men, rarely challenged the system in overt ways that might invite retaliation. When asked how her mother or other croppers on the Cameron lands had survived under oppressive conditions, Anna Ruffin Whitted replied:

> They had to believe in God and have a lot of faith to do this. I never heard them say like people say, "I will not do this. Before I do this I'll kill." If anybody on that plantation where we used to be ever said that, I can't remember . . . They just went on ahead . . . They said one day we will overcome. I may not see it but my children will see it.[60]

Another woman, reared in a cotton-growing area of South Carolina, remembered a confrontation between a white stationmaster and her cousin, the son of a prominent local landowner, who "didn't know what it was to bow to white people." The black man won that battle, but the family, like many other rural blacks, eventually left South Carolina to escape racial and sexual exploitation.[61] Although Durham blacks were never free of both heavy-handed and subtle reminders of their subordinate position, their plight could have been worse. Urban life in the Upper South "lacked the savage racial prejudice" that was unleashed in rural areas of the lower states.[62]

Paralleling their secular estrangement, black and white women worshiped separately. Black women's membership in the church invited them into a sisterhood that extended beyond biological or marital kinship, but not across racial lines; their ties to the church set them more firmly apart from whites.[63] Becoming a sister marked a young black woman's rite of passage into full adulthood. Her allegiance to the church—where an essential part of her earthly identity was forged—often continued throughout her life.[64] A young white woman's conversion experience also marked her rite of passage to adulthood, but her identity was less linked to a specific congregation than to a Protestant affiliation. Her church membership was more easily transferred to a new church when she left her original home.[65]

The diverse experiences of the two races deeply influenced their interpretations of the Christian message. White Christians, who conceived of God in profoundly moral terms, placed their greatest emphasis on avoiding sin in order to achieve salvation. Black Christians, conscious of evil as an inescapable part of their condition as an oppressed people, more often defined salvation as the release from bondage and suffering rather than from sin. The Devil was an outside force that sought to entrap them rather than an evil force from within that had to be subdued.⁶⁶ And so, despite their common identity as Christians, black and white women found no meeting place in the church; the most important public institution in the rural Piedmont reinforced the racial segregation that shaped all areas of social life.

■ The major forms of human interaction that this study calls race, gender, and class have been relatively easy to demonstrate. How those relationships manifest themselves in human consciousness is harder to establish. Whether an individual or group wholeheartedly subscribed to the prevailing view of racial, gender, or class relationships cannot be determined by simple questioning. The majority of relevant witnesses are not accessible. What can be reliably examined, however, are the sets of analytical frameworks, the "languages" by which people explained their place in the world. Understanding the messages women both gave and received helps to illuminate the ongoing negotiations between the dominant and the dominated.⁶⁷

Although the post-Civil War period saw an ongoing conflict between the propertied and the propertyless, class allegiances were usually submerged beneath racial alliances and conflicts. In the 1880s and 1890s, however, following emancipation and the expansion of the cash-crop economy, class tensions erupted with an uncommon intensity. Frustrated white farmers, thwarted in their desires to become yeomen or planters, began to identify as enemies the bankers, industrialists, warehousemen, and landlords who profited from their impoverishment. This political warfare gave the majority of whites a brief "democratic moment" of choice: to align themselves with white elites on the basis of racial solidarity or to unite with black farmers on the basis of class lines. As members of the Farmers' Alliances and the Knights of Labor, women joined in the discussions that defined their problems as rooted in economic and political domination by small elites rather than in competition between the races. Yet the appeal to common class identities was blunted by the realities of economic conflicts and the deep-seated traditions of racial antagonism. When even the editor of the Tarboro *Farmers' Advocate* could ask "why the colored man should aim a blow at the white farmer who gives him employment and pays the best wages he can afford," it was clear that the Populist appeal to common class interests could not counteract the deep prejudices and economic differences that divided whites and blacks into separate racial blocs.⁶⁸

The publications of the Populists and Knights record only the words of white women, though acknowledging the activities of rural women, black and white. Letters to the *Progressive Farmer* demonstrate women's enthusiasm but also their skepticism about men's acceptance of their full participation in the activities of the movement. The editor, who received the letters pouring in from women, detected an "undercurrent of unrest." One woman advised male voters against swallowing "the whole Democratic Party." She added, "I could say a good deal more on this line, but will stop for fear some fool will ask: 'Are you a woman?'" As subordinated partners in patriarchal family economies, female Populists may well have sensed some inadequacies in the male-dominated movement representing the interests of those who only "located exploitation in the sphere of exchange" and not within the patriarchal household.[69]

Despite internal contradictions, the Populists presented southerners with an agrarian version of the social gospel that challenged the New South orthodoxy. Dr. Cyrus Thompson, a president of the North Carolina Farmers' Alliance in the mid-1890s, preached that the degradation of the farmer was contrary to the will of God. Thompson, an active Methodist, criticized more conservative church members for supporting the "corporate interest" and ignoring the "masses [who] are impoverished, degraded, and enslaved." The western editor of the North Carolina *Christian Advocate,* a Methodist journal, supported the Populist claim that economic exploitation was of "great moral significance." Ultimately defeated by a conservative Methodist leadership that chose to ally itself with tobacco manufacturers like James B. Duke, the Populist-inspired religious spokesmen instructed some women in a version of the gospel that included a critique of "money domination" as well as of personal morality.[70]

The destruction of the Populist movement deprived women of an opportunity to develop a complex vocabulary by which to analyse their plight. It obviously retarded the ability of white women to examine their racial and class assumptions; it also decreased the likelihood that black women would ever conceive of whites as allies. Black and white, good and evil, remained the basic reference points. By the 1920s and 1930s, black and white women spoke about "mean" or "kind" landlords and employers. Black women condemned the "meanness" of whites, but saw no way to escape except through the mercy of God. A tenant told one interviewer in the late 1930s that her family moved "around in cricles like the mule that pulls the syrup mill." Another woman told Margaret Hagood, "Things is unbalanced and the poor don't get their share." Yet, as Hagood concluded, their analysis was content with condemning particular landlords. After the Populists vanished, the area surrounding Durham never produced another movement that invited women to examine their social roles. Black and white, rural women understood their situation as being rooted in the personal depravity of individuals and, therefore, as unchangeable except by relocating under a better landlord.[71]

Profoundly aware of their class, yet unable to envisage an alternative to their subordination, the women of the expanding rural proletariat adapted

IN THE FIELDS

as best they could. For the most part, they learned to live within their meager means. The most restless and the least bound by kin or property ties saw migration into towns as the major escape from rural deprivation. For a brief interlude, the wistful Mollie Goodwin, the prototype of the tenant woman presented by Margaret Hagood, fulfilled her dreams by following her cousin into a Durham tobacco factory. Called back by her father to resume the unrewarding tasks of a dutiful daughter, she determined that her own daughter would one day work in town, where she would "never have to do field work or heavy housework."[72] Some "made themselves happy," in one black woman's words, by accepting overwork and chronic poverty without complaint.[73] A few were able to ascend the tenure ladder; many others avoided the pain that came from failure by never striving for a goal that appeared unattainable. Burdened as they were by childcare, housework, and agricultural labor, women's energies were largely absorbed by the laborious process of making next-to-nothing go a long way. Their menfolk handled most of the transactions in the larger world. As in the Populist movement itself, therefore, women's encounters with economic and political forces were often mediated through their relationships with men and expressed through a male-formulated vocabulary.[74] Under such conditions, women were too involved with dealing with the status quo to challenge it.

Like other groups with limited resources, rural women in the tenant and laboring classes depended on extended networks of kin and neighbors to provide services. Yet the conditions of tenant life lessened contact with kin and neighbors. Frequent moves could disrupt these networks. Lack of suitable clothing could keep some women and children from taking part in school, church, or social gatherings. In white communities, tenants were less likely to attend church than were their wealthier neighbors; in rural black communities class distinctions were less sharply developed. Among tenant and sharecropping families, mothers' activities outside the household were also restricted by repeated childbearing (see Table 5). Even trips to town or church were less frequent while children were young.[75]

It is difficult to determine the average woman's isolation without diaries or personal observation. Data from the census, because the census takers were oriented to the static household unit, tended to overlook the elastic quality of human relationships, even in the household itself.[76]

Since women's lives were inextricably bound up in these daily interactions, many of their activities escaped notice. Still, to the extent that such activities were measurable, women appeared to have lived in greater social isolation than men. The same fragmentary evidence also suggests that women from the propertyless classes were more likely to live enclosed within the narrow boundaries of the household and were less likely to be involved in schools, churches, or the marketplace.

The nearly universal practice of defining women as wives, mothers, sisters, or daughters in relationship to individual men, rather than as farmers, landlords, merchants, or ministers, symbolized their subordinate class identities.[77] The unattached woman found it almost impossible to survive on the land. The attached woman's position depended on the economic status of her menfolk. A black landowner like Oscar Suitt, who prohibited his daughters from "working out" in some "white man's kitchen," offered them protection while demonstrating his ability to control their labor and guard them from sexual exploitation. A black tenant farmer, unable to subsist without a wife's wage-earning, could afford more limited protection: his wife could wash clothes at home rather than do "menial labor in someone's kitchen or in the field."[78] More desperate male tenants or laborers surrendered their women to outside service because the household needed all the wages its members could earn.

Thus a man's economic status correlated with his ability to monopolize the services of his wife and daughters. Conversely, higher economic status for women resulted in their greater dependence on the male household head and in their sexuality being more tightly controlled.[79] Black men's protective instincts were activated by white men's refusal to respect their sexual claims over black women. Operating by the same measures of male prestige and economic status, white men restricted the types of labor performed by their women and zealously defended their sexual honor (while attempting to deny the same prerogatives to black men). Even a white tenant farmer, whose daughters' labor was essential to making the tobacco crop, could elevate his status by restricting "pulling or stripping fodder" to women in the families of his black subtenants. In the mind of Lacey Turrentine, tobacco was a fit crop for a white woman to tend, but transforming cornstalks into animal feed was "nigger's work."[80] More successful white tenants or farmers affirmed their claims to superiority by employing black women as domestic labor and fieldhands and regarding them as sexual prey. White male standing was enhanced by the ability to control white women's behavior while dishonoring black women and men in sexually-specific assaults. In an anachronistic demonstration of the current feminist slogan, "the personal is the political," sexual intercourse assumed the "character of a truly 'political' act" and became a "dominant idiom for political relations."[81] Just as crucially, the "politics of housework" in the rural Piedmont expressed the interconnections between the "private" household and "public" power.[82] Intertwined in a complex social hierarchy, the interaction among gender, race, and class prevented women from ever occupying the same social space as men, or from wielding the same power.

By the same token, class and racial differences rendered the feminist ideal of sisterhood inconceivable to rural women. The encounters between the wife of Paul Cameron, the wealthiest landowner in Durham County, and her domestic servants, the Camerons' former slaves, illustrated the gulf between privileged white women and impoverished black women. Paying her cooks and maids wages of twenty-five cents a day in the 1880s, Mrs. Cameron deducted a dollar for each plate or cup broken. The business practices of her husband, simultaneously a landlord, employer, and storekeeper, made wage-earning a necessity for the women whom his wife employed.[83] Rather than sympathizing with the women forced to work in the hot tobacco fields, a landowner's wife was more likely to take pride in her ignorance of agricultural methods and to forbid her daughters to go into the tobacco patch. Margaret Hagood observed a woman from a white farm family during a corn shucking. Having hired a black woman to assist her, she ordered the woman to wash the dishes in the three separate batches required to feed the white men, the black men, and the white women. When the black woman refused to do that much work, the white employer exclaimed that she hated that "independent type of nigger."[84] Possibly because of Hagood's presence, however, the white women present washed the dishes while the black woman savored a small victory in the one-sided conflict between white employers and black labor. Significantly, the white women never challenged the custom that men eat before the women; nor did the black men demand to be fed at the same table as the whites.

Still lower on the tenure ladder, the daughter of a white tenant was expected to keep silent in the tobacco fields rather than join in the singing of her black coworkers in order to maintain her superiority to black people. A half century later, one woman still refused to join the communal singing in an integrated senior citizens residence although she knew the words to every song.[85] Anna Ruffin Whitted affectionately remembered the mill workers who had given her biscuits, but such gestures also bore the stamp of charity toward the children of the woman (Anna's mother) who washed clothes for the residents of Orange Factory.[86] Without being explicitly instructed, the children of a black landowner learned to defer to whites as an inescapable fact of life in northern Durham County.[87] Whether black women responded to white condescension and brutality with anger, with subtle diplomacy, or by avoiding contact with whites whenever possible, they learned to distrust white motives, to shelter their opinions from inquiring whites, and to deceive them when necessary.[88] Under such conditions, the parallels between black and white women's situations were submerged by more powerful antagonisms.

Within each racial community, women from the more privileged classes strove to maintain distance between themselves and their social inferiors. The pressures of racial oppression forced black women to associate across class lines in church or school, but some prided themselves on their lighter skin color, on their reputation for sexual restraint, or on other badges of respectability. Daughters in such families were sometimes warned against consorting with men not their social equals. A young girl, born in a rural black community in Durham County in the early 1930s, found that dark skin was looked down on at her segregated country school—prizes always went to girls with the lightest skin and the straightest hair.[89] Rural whites, reared in a more economically stratified community, were even more likely to express awareness of class differences. Tenant children occasionally disliked school because they might be laughed at by better-off children. Tenant parents did not like their children to pick up "notions" at consolidated schools. One woman's children, for example, refused to eat corn bread after beng exposed to store-bought "loaf bread" at school in town. Another mother refused to let her children play with neighbors who were not the "right sort." Such attitudes, which more often inculcated a sense of shame among those looked down upon than outrage at "biggity" owners, indeed nurtured an "awareness of separation from the owning class," but in the absence of "farm union organizers," it did not lead to collective resistance.[90]

Hostage to low prices, indebtedness, weather, and biology, few families could maintain a secure footing on the land. Some families shattered after a household head died, a couple broke up, or debts mounted. Working in factories without walls, some members of this rapidly expanding rural proletariat began to consider a move to factory communities. Their decision, as reflected in variable rates of migration, depended in part on their own positions in the rural hierarchy. More likely to move if female or black or both, these victims of economic and social dislocation did not journey alone. In addition to family and friends, they brought with them the legacy of exploitation by landlords and merchants, embittered relations between the races, and a general acceptance of patriarchal authority. However few their possessions, rural women traveled into Durham encumbered with other baggage.

Nevertheless, their legacy included countervailing strengths. They were proud of their ability to work "like a man" and were grittily determined to improve their lives. They brought with them the faith that had sustained them through hard times. The contradictory ideas in which they believed included notions of human dignity and equality, the right to challenge unjust authority, and codes of morality and decency by which everyone should be judged. These ideas clashed with other notions, including conventional deference to male authorities, the inevitable separation of the races, and the impossibility of "social equality" or of the poor ever getting "their share." Whether individual women accepted these contradictions uncritically or sought ways to preserve some traditions and escape others, they embarked on a journey to a new society bringing with them expectations rooted in the past.

IV
THE
HUMAN
HARVEST

As the agricultural crisis deepened, increasing numbers of migrants poured out of the countryside. The intensity and the direction of the flow depended on the prices paid for tobacco and cotton, the cost of land, the level of indebtedness among farmers, and the economic opportunities available. At times, employers influenced the migrants: during labor shortages, they actively solicited particular types of workers. The attractiveness of rural life vis à vis town life and industrial employment also played a role in determining who would migrate and who would remain. Because agriculture rewarded female labor less than male, young women were more likely to move into town. Among men, migration was concentrated among those over twenty, whose parents could no longer command their labor, and under forty. More blacks migrated than whites, a reflection of blacks' more limited access to resources. Also, the destinations of black males and black females varied: women migrated to cities like Durham that welcomed their labor; men traveled longer distances in search of work (see Tables 8 and 9).[1] The earliest waves of migration included the most vulnerable members of rural society: blacks of both sexes and white women. The labor demands of the First World War and the restriction on foreign immigration intensified the pull off the land. Durham's population grew as a result of this differential migration; out in the countryside, males outnumbered females among those who remained.[2]

Tracing the intricate connections between individual journeys and urbanization requires a creative understanding of data, because migration, particularly short-range migration within a single state, has rarely been well-documented.[3] A few results are clear: between 1890 and 1930, Durham became a city where women, particularly black women, outnumbered men (see Table 9). When we turn to the issues that determined migration, the dif-

Table 8.
Percentage of Those Leaving Home Who Migrated to Urban Areas, by Race and Sex of Migrant*

DATE	WHITE		BLACK	
	MALES	FEMALES	MALES	FEMALES
Before 1920	19.0%	20.6%	30.0%	30.8%
1915–1919	28.8	23.0	37.5	37.2
1920–1924	28.2	24.2	40.3	48.5
1925–1929	22.7	24.5	43.4	42.5
1930–1934	23.1	25.8	31.4	47.5
Overall	24.6	24.0	37.5	42.6

*N = 1,999 from five rural areas in North Carolina.

SOURCE: C. Horace Hamilton, "Recent Changes in the Social and Economic Status of Farm Families in North Carolina," North Carolina Agricultural Extension Station *Bulletin* no. 309, May 1937, p. 128.

Table 9.
Sex Ratios* for Durham by Race, 1890–1930

CATEGORY	1890	1900	1910	1920	1930
White males	1,768	3,150	5,456	6,512	15,797
White females	1,829	3,421	5,196	7,368	17,155
White sex ratio	.96	.92	1.05	.88	.92
Black males	860	1,024	3,106	3,637	8,616
Black females	999	1,217	3,763	4,017	10,101
Black sex ratio	.86	.84	.825	.905	.85
Durham sex ratio	.93	.90	.956	.89	.896

*A sex ratio is derived by dividing the total number of males in a population by the total number of females. When females outnumber males, the sex ratio is less than one.

SOURCE: 11th, 12th, 13th, 14th, 15th Censuses of the United States, Population, 1890, 1900, 1910, 1920, 1930, published volumes of the U.S. Bureau of the Census (see Appendix for publication information).

ficulties are compounded by the failure of most demographers and census takers to deal adequately with class, family structure, women's marital status, and other influential factors. Except for a few relatively systematic surveys, we must depend on the laments of planters for departed farm laborers, the biographies of migrants, and the histories of successful migrants who became leading businessmen. Entrepreneurs like Washington Duke, Julian S. Carr, John Merrick, and C. C. Spaulding came to Durham equipped with capital, connections, and business expertise. In contrast to less celebrated migrants, they did not come from the fields to the factory. They had already acquired the experience that prepared them to set up enterprises in the city where "the wheels begin to turn, the smoke rolls in massive clouds from every stack and the sweet assuring music of busy machinery is heard."[4] Their success pulled other migrants into Durham. The Duke and Carr companies attracted a continuing stream of black labor. Mechanization in the 1880s induced the migration of white men and women to operate the machines. New industries like textiles and hosiery intensified the demand, shifting from a predominantly female and child labor force to a family labor system by the early twentieth century. Until the end of the 1930s, when the mechanization of the stemmeries lessened the demand for labor, Durham's factories drew a steady stream of recruits from the rural Piedmont.

Leaving agricultural for industrial occupations was the major economic motivation for the move to Durham. Forty-five out of forty-eight stable Durham households had migrated between 1880 and 1900 (see Map 2). Almost all had come from tobacco or cotton-growing areas relatively near to Durham. In 1880, forty of these households had engaged in farming; by 1900, only five included a member designated as a farmer. By the last year of the nineteenth century, 41 percent of the household members then living in Durham were employed in textiles, 16 percent worked in the tobacco industry, and another 9 percent, who were listed as laborers, may have worked in the same industry. The other 31 percent of the employed household members filled occupations in the building trades, assorted industries, and retail. These new Durham residents symbolized the transformation of a rural population into an urban workforce.

Although it is clear that the city offered single women greater opportunities than were available in the rural Piedmont, the available data demonstrate that most women migrated as part of a family. A comparison of female-headed households suggests that black female-headed households were disproportionately likely to migrate, while white female-headed households could more readily stay on the land (see Tables 6 and 10). The differences in available resources probably accounted for the contrasting strategies of these households. Such racially-distinct migratory strategies helped to engender a markedly unbalanced sex ratio for black Durhamites.

Map 2.
Migration to Durham from Counties in North Carolina, 1880–1900

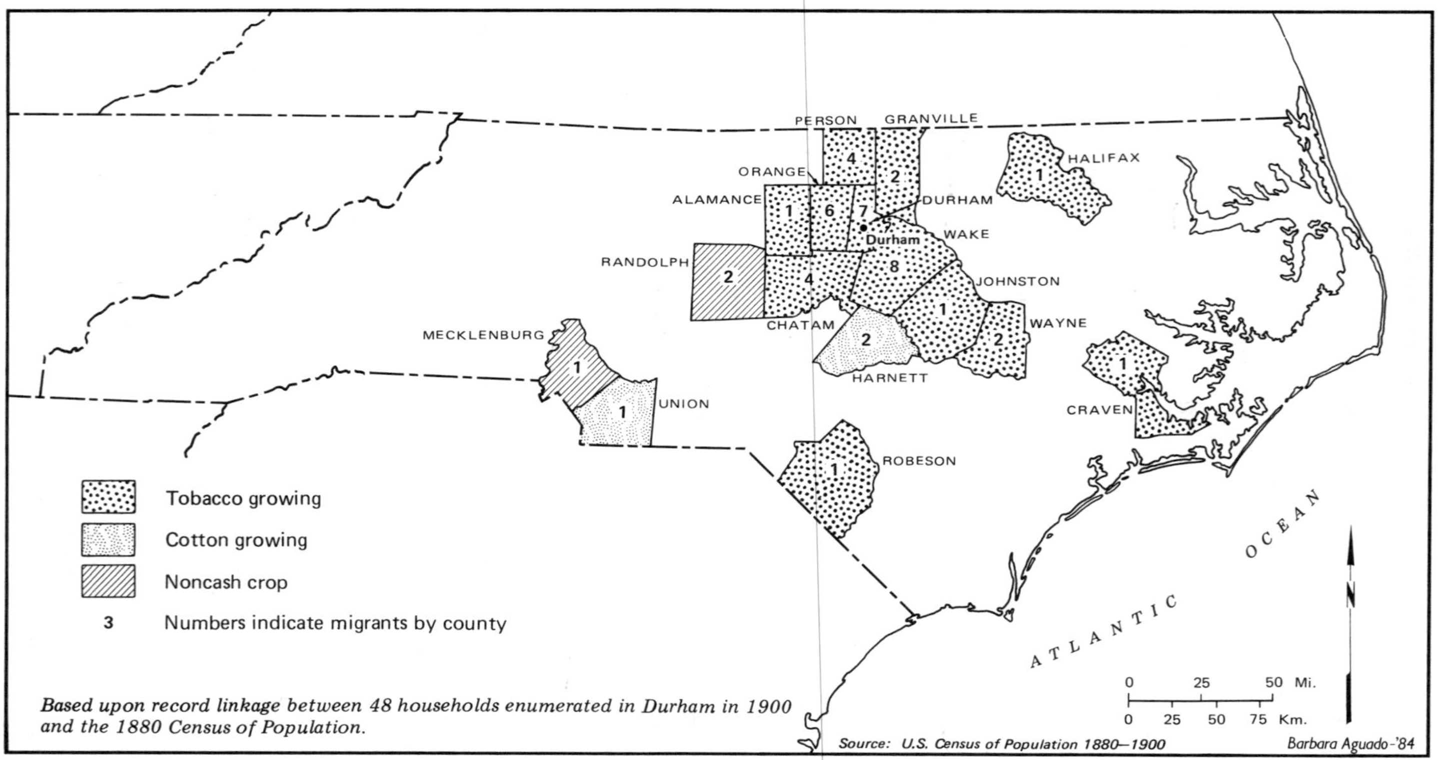

Tobacco growing
Cotton growing
Noncash crop
3 Numbers indicate migrants by county

Based upon record linkage between 48 households enumerated in Durham in 1900 and the 1880 Census of Population.

Source: U.S. Census of Population 1880–1900

Table 10.
Percentages of Female-Headed Households in Rural,* Urban, and Suburban Durham Areas, 1880–1900

AREA	1880		1900	
	WHITE	BLACK	WHITE	BLACK
Rural areas	16.3%	13.8%	16.4%	9.4%
Durham city	18.4	41.0	15.1	37.6
Suburbs†	NA	NA	20.8	18.5

*Rural samples taken from Person, Granville, and Orange/Durham Counties for 1880 and 1900. Figures for Durham County for 1880 from those parts of Orange/Wake County that became Durham in 1881.

†Sample of industrial households in suburbs of Durham.

SOURCE: 10th and 12th Censuses of Population (manuscript) Population Schedules for 1880 and 1900, samples for counties indicated, National Archives, Washington, D.C. (see Appendix for description of sampling techniques).

Whether white or black, most female residents of Durham aged fourteen or older in 1880 or 1900 were living in households headed by their husbands or their parents (see Table 11). Of the less than 15 percent living with nonrelated household heads, 5 to 8 percent were living with relatives. A still smaller group, primarily black women, lived as servants in the homes of their employers. Although women were more likely to migrate and live outside kin-based households in the twentieth century, such women remained a distinct minority. A survey of young white "rural girls" working in Durham in the mid-1920s disclosed that 52 percent were living with their parents, 13.5 percent were living with other relatives, and 33 percent were boarders.[5] Oral history interviews with thirty-three women who came to Durham between 1900 and 1934 showed that 68 percent—including all of the black women—had accompanied other family members in search of economic opportunity. Although the remaining women had traveled alone, they generally lived in Durham with relatives. While households may have taken on a more elastic shape in order to facilitate migration, the data suggest that women remained dependent on kinshp networks to provide emotional support and access to resources unavailable to the solitary female wage-earner.

A major motivation for moving to Durham was the promise of work for women. Families with daughters were more likely to come than were families with sons. Durham either attracted or retained more young women than men between the ages of fifteen and thirty, whereas the sex ratios for younger and older people were more nearly equal. The history of Wilma

Table 11.
Relationships of Women and Girls Aged 14 and Older to Household Heads in Durham, 1880–1900

RELATIONSHIP	1880	1900*	1900†
Head	11.1%	6.0%	6.5%
Spouse of head	17.2	20.3	24.0
Child of head	47.1	45.7	48.2
Other kin	13.2	11.2	9.3
Boarder	8.2	13.3	10.0
Servant	3.2	3.5	2.0
Sample size	273	1,113	321

*1900 for households within boundaries of Durham city in 1900.
†1900 for households involved in industrial employment in suburbs of Durham.

SOURCE: 10th and 12th Censuses of Population (manuscript) Population Schedules for 1880 and 1900 for Durham and Suburbs, National Archives, Washington, D.C. (see Appendix for description of sampling techniques used).

Couch illustrates the interdependence between daughters and the family economy. Born in Alamance County, Wilma Mayfield originally moved to the town of Graham in the late nineteenth century because her injured father could no longer farm and her brothers were too young. The family lived on the earnings of the four Mayfield daughters until the sons grew strong enough to plow. The father, mother, and sons returned to the land while the daughters remained working in the textile mill at Graham until they married. When Wilma Couch was left a widow with four young children, she traveled to Durham to seek better-paying work. Unable to manage a boardinghouse successfully, she placed her two oldest children in the Methodist orphanage in Raleigh and took a job in a Durham tobacco factory to support herself and her youngest child. As her children reached eighteen, they returned to the Couch home in Durham. After Wilma Couch lost her job at the factory because of age, the daughters supported the family until the youngest son had left home. Finally, the Couch daughters married and set up their own households after two successive generations had served as the economic mainstays of the Mayfield and then the Couch households.[6] Other families had similar histories.[7]

Interviews with more than two hundred young women employed in Durham in the mid-1920s revealed the complex forces that impelled so many "rural girls" to come to town. They had journeyed an average of seven miles from their rural origins. Their reasons for leaving home included the narrow range of occupations open to women in rural areas, the endless domestic duties they described as a "cheerless routine," and the stimulation and opportunity available in Durham. Almost 60 percent reported that they had come to find a job, 27.9 percent that their family had decided to stop farming, and 8 percent that a parent's death had led to their decision. Della Thompson, who liked being "independent and free," reported that her family had come to Durham because life was "pretty hard" in the country for a family with ten daughters. Delia Turner's family of thirteen had moved when her father grew too old to operate a two-horse tenant farm. Julia Franklin, an operator in a Golden Belt bag factory, had accompanied her mother and younger siblings to Durham after the death of her father. Her mother found work in a mill; Julia, at fifteen, also went to work. Unlike Della Thompson, Julia regretted the move. She told the interviewer that in "the country a girl can be herself and feel free" and have a "sense of place in the world." Family necessity had forced her to accept a situation that she could not change.[8] Whether or not young women relished the new urban environment, they joined more than 200,000 North Carolinians who moved from farm to town in the 1920s.[9]

Evidence for the 1930s suggests that migration was still an important although decreasing source of labor for Durham's industries. A study of female migration in the latter half of the decade discovered that nearly half of those studied had been born in Durham County or nearby. Almost 87 percent of the white women and 88.5 percent of the black women had come from farming areas, but the distances traveled to Durham differed. More than half of white migrants came from counties near Durham, compared to 38.7 percent of black migrants. The remaining black women came from more distant points with 23 percent from out of state. The percentage of white women from outside the immediate area was 31.4 percent, and only 12.5 percent came from other states.[10]

The survey of Durham tobacco workers conducted by Charles S. Johnson in 1935 reported that employees in the industry were "overwhelmingly rural in origin" and had come primarily from North Carolina. The Johnson study, however, discovered that black women were less likely to conform to this pattern than were other racial and sexual groups. Although more than 60 percent of the black men, white women, and white men working for American Tobacco Company or for Liggett and Myers had come from rural North Carolina, slightly less than 44 percent of black women had originated there. Another 44 percent had grown up in urban areas, 14 percent in Durham itself. Although a slightly greater percentage of white women had originated in Durham, only an additional 7.3 percent had come from other

Table 12.
Origins of Durham Tobacco Workers, 1935

LOCATION	WHITES	BLACKS	WHITE MEN	WHITE WOMEN	BLACK MEN	BLACK WOMEN
North Carolina						
Durham	18.8%	12.3%	18.2%	14.5%	10.2%	13.7%
Other cities	4.7	16.4	6.8	2.4	10.2	20.5
Rural areas	63.5	51.6	63.6	63.4	63.3	43.8
Other states						
Cities	4.7	8.2	4.5	4.9	6.1	9.6
Rural areas	5.9	11.5	9.5	7.3	10.2	12.3

SOURCE: Charles S. Johnson, "The Tobacco Worker: A Study of Tobacco Factory Workers and Their Families," 2 vols. (1935), Division of Review, Industrial Studies Section, NRA/NA, 2:387.

cities. Like the study of female migrants, the Johnson survey reported that blacks traveled from more distant points to reach Durham than did their white counterparts (see Table 12).[11]

A current of migration ran in the other direction, but it is more difficult to measure. Many farmers had forsaken the land only temporarily, and, when prices for farm products began to rise, they returned to their traditional occupations. In 1918 the Mangums, a family whose members worked at American Tobacco and Golden Belt, "went out in the country and started farming" again as sharecroppers. They remained on the land until 1932, "the year nobody made nothing and Daddy lost everything we had." Returning to Durham, the family took jobs at American Tobacco, Erwin Mills, and Golden Belt.[12] Black workers often moved between country and city on a regular basis because their work in the stemmeries was tied to the "green season" when the tobacco leaf was newly harvested and needed to be rehandled, "redried," packed in hogsheads, and aged.

When industrial workers began to acquire automobiles in the 1920s and 1930s, commuting between farm and factory became an option.[13] A black female tobacco worker, married to a small tobacco farmer, hitched a ride to town with a neighbor because she didn't own a car in the late 1930s.[14] A white woman, interviewed in the late 1930s, shared a small farmhouse with two sons in southern Durham County; her four married children had already moved to live "in them little old, dingy factory houses over in Durham." One of her remaining sons was already commuting to work at American Tobacco Company. He planned to move into Durham when he married because "the city has got its hands on me and I can't get loose."[15]

In this fashion, the automobile allowed some to replant themselves in the rural Piedmont, but most migration continued to flow toward the urban comforts of Durham.

■ The testimony of migrants began to be recorded by the late 1870s. A Senate committee investigated the reasons for blacks' leaving the land in 1879, and northern newspapers detailed the abuses perpetrated against black farmers by Democratic authorities. The New York *Times* noted, "White farmers seem to have been able to discover the point at which the laborer may be kept face to face with starvation . . . If he complains, he is turned adrift."[16] By the late 1880s, the plight of white migrants was attracting commentary. An Alamance farmer, giving one reason for the rural labor shortage, declared that the mill operatives in his county fared "much better than the farmers."[17] In Wake County, reported another farmer, many tenants had become "discouraged and gone to the towns, railroads, turpentine districts, etc."[18] A manager in a Durham tobacco factory placed the individual journeys in a broader context:

> I think that we, as a state, are being transformed from an agricultural to a manufacturing people and the inequality of prices paid for the labor by the farmer and the manufacturer is causing his labor to leave the farm and crowd the manufacturing towns and cities with a surplus of labor that is appalling.[19]

About ten years later a white employee at Erwin Cotton Mills Company (Erwin Mills) in West Durham described the predicament of the "unsettled element" who were "moving into our cities and crowding into the factories." T. A. Allen grieved over the fate of the "bold peasant," driven by adversity into mills; there the formerly independent people were "no longer free men and women, but are considered as part of the machinery which they operate."[20] The leader of the first (unsuccessful) Durham textile strike, Allen symbolized the arrival of white men into industry in numbers.

Few black migrants appeared to share Allen's nostalgia for the land, according to their former landlords and the migrants themselves. Writing early in the twentieth century, Piedmont farmers mourned the passing of the "old Negro" who had been "tolerably reliable," whereas the "younger set . . . leave their parents and go to the public works or some town before they are sixteen years old." W. S. Parker of Vance County blamed education for "ruining the negro as a farm laborer. The women work very well by the day but they are not certain."[21] A. M. Walker complained that white tenants or laborers were no substitute for the restless blacks because "nearly all white labor, especially female labor, is now employed by the factories."[22] An Oxford farmer denounced the unfair competition from the "North," the "railroads and the sawmills" that paid "the negro" better wages than farmers could offer.[23] Such commentators opposed education for blacks, believing that learning made them restless; they vigorously condemned "lazy" white men as well, for putting "their wives and children in the factory to work" rather than renting land from landlords like themselves.[24]

Pearl Barbee recalled her mother's decision to make the change:

> I heard my mother said one time that she worked on the farm and the last year . . . she didn't clear anything and so . . . she just decided to leave the country . . . She just moved here and started working for white people, washing, cleaning, doing things like that. I went to work when I was at an early age at the factory.

The daughter approved: she preferred factory life to working in a "hot field all day."[25] Mrs. Hetty Love made the same decision when she realized that there was "nobody left to farm" after her marriage dissolved. In 1914 she arrived in Durham to find work at a tobacco stemmery.[26] Indeed, "nearly a full tenth of the country people of Durham County quit their farms and moved to town" between 1900 and 1910.[27] The low wages paid to farm labor, especially to black women, and the uncertain returns earned by tobacco and cotton growers could not compete with the appeal of the "labor agent" and the hope of an easier life in Durham.

The migrants came in a variety of ways and at different rates. In the early twentieth century, Bessie Taylor, then a young girl, arrived by train with her entire family in the Erwin Mills village in West Durham.[28] About the same time, the first generation of the Jenks family entered a small rural mill at the falls of the Neuse in Wake County. Later, in the 1910s, two generations of Jenkses moved into West Durham and then to mills at Wake Forest and Raleigh.[29] Luther Riley, a more permanent member of the West Durham mill village, remembered the company recruiters who induced his family to forsake its rural home in 1919:

> See, the main reason these people were enticed to come to town was because of having a large family, with a large number of children, and the potential of workers from there. The same thing for the tobacco workers and the hosiery workers. Whether it was good or bad, I'm not going to stand in judgment. I think we have a lot to do with our destiny but there are a lot of things that we can't do anything about.[30]

A few years later, Rose Weeks departed from the family farm in northern Durham County to seek adventure and work in Durham. Her sister soon followed.[31] In the mid-1920s, the Macks began to arrive in Durham from rural South Carolina. Like other future tobacco workers, they sought greater opportunity and less racial and sexual harassment than they had faced further south.[32] Almost ten years later, in 1934, the Jenks family returned to West Durham after Eldred Jenks learned that Erwin Mills was starting a second shift.³³ From the outset, these and thousands of other individual acts merged into a collective transformation of rural folk into industrial workers.

■ Capitalist entrepreneurs followed the same routes to Durham as their less successful contemporaries. With energy, capital, and luck, they created enormous wealth for themselves and (as they saw it) great benefit for other residents. Levi Branson, an admirer, described their role in the first business directory published for Durham in 1887:

> First, they know the value of *undeveloped labor,* and they know how to develop it so as to build the city. They induce thousands of poor people, as well as the rich, to settle in the city. They are set to work and well paid, while superior business skill rapidly turns the product of this labor into cash.³⁴

Julian S. Carr, Washington Duke and his sons, and William A. Erwin relished such praise of their achievements in exploiting the chief asset of the poverty-stricken South — its abundant, cheap labor.

They felt, moreover, that their achievements in setting rural folk to work deserved recognition. As their successors later testified, training an inexperienced labor force was difficult and frustrating. Kemp P. Lewis, a college-educated descendant of some of the first textile manufacturers in North Carolina, came to Durham in 1900 to assist W. A. Erwin in training a textile labor force in West Durham. Nine years later he complained that training "native help to do good work in our mills" was a "tedious" task.³⁵ Julian S. Carr, Jr., wrote extensively on the obstacles to forming an efficient workforce from the black and white workers in the Durham Hosiery Mill chain. Black workers resisted "fixed hours of labor" and forced Carr to allow them to attend marriages, funerals, revivals, and the annual meetings of their churches. White workers, primarily "people who have been raised on small tenant farms," according to Carr, "presented a different problem, just as difficult." They displayed "strong sectional loyalty but no pride of craftsmanship . . . Too many of the general force were content to 'get by.'"³⁶ Creating a brand-name company product, "Durable Durham" hosiery, helped to solve the problem of motivating workers: loyalty to the product gave the rural workers a personal reason to develop industrial work habits. Although Lewis succeeded in disciplining the West Durham mill force, he did not claim final victory until the company's Harnett County employees had also been brought to proper industrial work habits. With this finally achieved to his satisfaction, Lewis took credit in 1931 for the "wonderful civilizing influence" of Erwin Mills that had turned tenant farmers into "self-respecting independent" people attuned to the discipline of the industrial age.³⁷ Indeed, the Dukes, the Carrs, Erwin, and Lewis had directed a process that manufactured not only tobacco goods and cotton cloth but also workers, the common products of the Piedmont soil.

Black entrepreneurs like John Merrick, Aaron M. Moore, William G. Pearson, James Shepard, Charles C. Spaulding, and their associates also traveled to Durham to pursue dreams of success. Having worked in the building and barbering trades in nearby Chapel Hill and Raleigh in the 1870s, Merrick moved to Durham at the request of the Dukes and Julian S. Carr and opened a barber shop in 1880. Eight years later, A. M. Moore followed Merrick and became the city's first black physician. In 1894, C. C. Spaulding, like his uncle, Aaron Moore, came from a free black community in Columbus County to Durham to complete his education. These men, together with Pearson, Shepard, and three other partners, founded an insurance association that became the leading black business in Durham and the South.[38] In addition to practicing their professions—law, medicine, and education—they invested in real estate, banking, stores, newspapers, and a short-lived experiment with a hosiery mill. Except in the unsuccessful attempt to enter manufacturing, the leading black businesses in Durham hired relatively few black workers. College-educated, middle-class blacks flocked to join the staff of North Carolina Mutual and its allied enterprises, but the vast majority of black workers in Durham were employed in white-owned concerns, primarily the tobacco factories that formed the city's industrial core. Consequently, the black entrepreneurs who presided over the social and cultural life of Durham's black community were not major factors in attracting migrants. Rather, the city's sizeable black industrial working class provided these businessmen with their customers, their tenants, and their clients.[39] These black capitalists "grew up with the exploitation of the New South," tolerated by white leaders who could accommodate "black men" who "calculate and work."[40]

Not surprisingly, the white capitalists of Durham reaped the major benefits of the social upheaval that they presided over. Industrialization undermined the independence of the farm population, offered farmers low prices for the crops that they produced, lured displaced farmers into mills and factories, transformed the rural refugees into industrial workers, and turned the products of their labor into profits. According to a historian who studied the relationship between country and city in a global context, a "displaced and formerly rural population moving and drifting towards the centres of a money economy . . . directed by interests very far from their own" was a world-wide phenomenon; cities grew by feeding on the countryside.[41] The "interests" guiding the Piedmont version of this "great transformation" bore the names of a few successful migrants out of the thousands who marched toward Durham. The vast majority, predominately female, supplied the labor that the dominant few required.

V
CAPITALISTS AND PATRIARCHS

> These younger men are truly modern business men. They have adopted the technique of modern business and are saturated with the psychology of the capitalist class. They work hard, not because of necessity but to expand their business and invade new fields . . . They endow charities and schools . . . Above all they want progress . . . The founders of these new enterprises grew up with the exploitation of the New South.[1]

In 1925, Franklin Frazier praised black members of the "new industrial and commercial classes in the South" who resembled their white counterparts in their devotion to productivity, morality, property, and hard work. In celebrating the achievements of the "transformed Negro," Frazier ignored other members of the "new industrial and commercial classes." His brief mention of "the exploitation of the New South" referred only vaguely to the men and women whose labor supplied the basic resource exploited by these "modern businessmen." Eager to prove that black men could succeed on the same turf as white capitalists, Frazier evaded any discussion that might have called the victory into question.

A discussion of the people who were overlooked cannot be written by simply turning Frazier on his head. Two major classes were generated in the industrial process that gave birth to the city of Durham—the capitalists who controlled the lives of the majority and the workers whose labor produced the wealth. Before examining the transformation of rural migrants into industrial workers, we must scrutinize the powerful men who set them to work, persuaded them to accept their authority, and strove to eliminate political and ideological challenges to their power.

■ The entrepreneurs who spawned a few crude factories along the railroad in the vicinity of Durham Station in the 1860s brought the village of Durham into existence. At first the town grew slowly. But in 1868 two tobacco peddlers, James R. Day and William T. Blackwell, arrived in the struggling settlement of fewer than three hundred people and entered into partnership with a local smoking tobacco manufacturer who employed ten workers. Three years later, Julian Shakespeare Carr, son of a prominent local merchant and landowner, took control of a share that his father had bought in the firm. The firm's trademark was the Durham Bull; and at that time it employed "twelve or thirteen hands" making plug and smoking (predominantly pipe) tobacco.

Carr shrewdly built on the original investment made by his father. Technological and marketing innovations transformed the partnership from a local enterprise to a "household word from Maine to the Gulf and from the Atlantic to the Pacific slope."[2] By 1880, the firm's initial capitalization had increased three thousand times, and its rate of profit had soared to 48 percent of its sales.[3] Three years later, the company was reorganized as a corporation that still bore the name Blackwell Durham Tobacco Company, although Blackwell's share had been purchased by Philadelphia investors. Shipping out almost five million pounds of Bull Durham brand smoking tobacco in 1884, the company employed "nearly 1,000 hands, 685 of whom are in the factory and 250 outside, engaged in manufacturing the various sizes of bags in which the tobacco is packed."[4] Meanwhile, the embryo village of 1865 had grown into a small city boasting five thousand people, "palatial buildings devoted to mercantile purposes, huge tobacco warehouses and numerous manufactories of that article that are unexcelled," including "the largest factory in the world for the manufacture of smoking tobacco."[5] The Bull, whose steam-powered factory whistle could be heard for thirteen miles around Durham, had sired a city and an industry.

Carr's chief rival, W. Duke and Sons, began as a small family-run enterprise on the Duke homestead north of Durham. Washington Duke, the nephew of one of the largest landowners in Orange County in the 1850s, had begun peddling tobacco after the Civil War. Successful at selling his own crop, he began to produce pipe tobacco for the retail market. He, his sons Brodie, Benjamin, and James, and his daughter Mary, assisted by black hired hands, processed the smoking tobacco, bagged it, and filled orders in a ramshackle log cabin on the farm. Brodie Duke ventured into Durham and, in 1874, the rest of the family followed, moving to a location near the railroad, where they built a steam-powered factory. The enterprise was then reorganized as a family firm employing a black labor force.[6]

In 1878, Garrard S. Watts, a successful tobacconist in Baltimore, secured an interest in the Duke company for his son, whom he had trained in the family business. The capital brought by George Watts to Durham increased the capitalization of the company, now called W. Duke, Sons and Company, to $70,000.[7] The young Watts became the company's secretary and treasurer, where his financial and commercial training served him well. Confronting a larger, better financed, more mechanized competitor in the smoking tobacco field, W. Duke, Sons and Company entered the 1880s with less than $100,000 invested in its plant and a small work force of forty men and twenty children.[8] A modest success, the company seemed likely to remain a distant second to the Bull, who symbolized Durham's rise to fame and prosperity.

But Carr's slogan, "Let the buffalo gore the buffalo, and the pasture go to the strongest," only fired the Dukes' uncommon ambition. They decided to risk entering a newer branch of the tobacco industry, cigarette making.[9] In 1881 the company enticed skilled cigarette rollers to move from New York City, then the center of the industry. The Carr firm responded by importing its own group of cigarette makers. The Duke company persisted.[10] Dissatisfied with the slow pace of hand-rolling cigarettes, the relatively high labor costs, the difficulties in training additional workers in the skilled tasks, and the stubborn independence of the imported craftsmen, Duke installed James Bonsack's invention, a cigarette-making machine.[11] While the Duke and Bonsack mechanics tinkered with the balky machine, James B. Duke set up a factory in New York City, which was closer to a skilled and cheap labor supply, a large urban market, a national communications network, and sources of capital.[12]

When the Bonsack machine reached efficiency in the mid-1880s, Duke struck a bargain with the inventor. The company would install two Bonsack machines immediately and add other machines more slowly. In this way, Duke said, employees could be discharged gradually "to avoid all possible danger of doing injustice . . . and all risk of collision with labor organizations."[13] Foreshadowing his later exploits, Duke also played the Bonsack company against rival cigarette companies. He prohibited machine sales to the Blackwell firm, strongly advised against sales to the Kinney and Goodwin cigarette companies, but allowed the Ginter and Kimball cigarette manufacturers to purchase the "making" machines.[14] Using the weapons that Carr had pioneered—mechanization, aggressive advertising, reorganization to make cheaper and more efficient use of labor, and an infusion of northern capital—the Duke firm forced its local competitor out of cigarette manufacturing by 1887.[15]

Having vanquished the local rival, James B. Duke confidently wrote to the Bonsack firm, "Nobody can compete with the five largest factories unless they are willing to invest one million in capital." While the Carr firm maintained its superior position in the overall production of smoking (pipe) tobacco, the Dukes, led by the determined younger son, geared up to take on more distant competitors. The upstart firm launched a furious advertising war to force the four major companies to accept its leadership. During the late 1880s, the major cigarette firms were often compelled to spend more for advertising than they took in through sales.[16] Pressured by the brash firm in Durham, Bonsack and the major cigarette companies began to discuss the possibilities of a "consolidated" cigarette industry in 1889.[17] One year later, the American Tobacco Company (ATC) emerged. James B. Duke, the instigator, became its president.[18]

Firmly entrenched in cigarette manufacturing, the company moved to take over other branches of the industry in the mid-1890s. An alleged attempt to capture the Bull Durham Company in 1892 developed into a public controversy. Carr accused the ATC of seeking to persuade him to "enter a trust . . . for the oppression of the already sorely oppressed farmers of North Carolina."[19] Benjamin Duke, a director of the company, indignantly denied Carr's version of the offer. According to Duke, Carr had asked the company to buy his firm and offered to remain as manager.[20] Carr's version of the affair may have been influenced by political ambition in a state whose farm population suffered from low tobacco prices. The controversy became moot in 1899, when the ATC bought the Bull Durham Company and took control of the (pipe) smoking tobacco section of the industry.[21] Carr was thus banished from the local industry that he had dominated and control over Durham's tobacco manufacturing moved north to the American Tobacco Company headquarters in New York City.

Workers and farmers found their lives increasingly shaped by decisions made in corporate offices outside Durham. When company officials decided that cigarettes could be made more profitably in New York, factory workers in Durham were consigned to less skilled and lower paying jobs.[22] Industry employment, a major contributor to the Durham economy, dropped precipitously after the decision to move operations north; similarly, it rose after full-scale cigarette manufacturing returned to Durham after 1911 (see Table 13).

Within thirty-five years, the family labor arrangement at the Duke homestead had developed into a large bureaucratically-run factory system. After his departure in 1884, James B. Duke rarely returned to Durham. Benjamin Duke joined him in New York in 1901. Washington Duke, the last surviving link to Durham, died in 1905. As the company became more embroiled in corporate warfare, finance, and stock manipulations, Durham workers were steadily reduced to impersonal elements of production rather than people whose faces were known to those making the decisions that affected their lives. In his letter to the Bonsack company back in the mid-1880s, James B. Duke had expressed concern for "injustice" to workers. When the U.S. Industrial Commission questioned him about industry conditions in 1903, he seemed only vaguely aware of his employees. Asked about the proportion of female to male labor employed in his factories, he answered, "I do not know. In some factories there is more than there is in others. In the cigarette factories, for instance, where it is all light, easy work, there are, I

Table 13.
Composition of Durham Tobacco Manufacturing Workforce, 1890–1917

COMPANY AND COMPOSITION	1890	1910	1911	1917
Bull Durham*				
Smoking (pipe) total	1,000	677	767	877
% Women	54.0	8.4	9.4	NA
% Children	3.0	24.3	23.7	14.1
Cigarettes total	0	0	0	417
% Women	0	0	0	NA
% Children	0	0	0	17.3
W. Duke and Sons/ Liggett and Myers†				
Cigarettes and Smoking (pipe) total	720	348‡	821	2,305
% Women	41.6	3.0	40.0	44.4
% Children	13.2	14.7	13.0	9.7

*Bull Durham is the nickname for the company that was originally Blackwell Durham Tobacco Company, then a subsidiary of the American Tobacco Company trust, and finally a branch of the new American Tobacco Company after dissolution of the trust in 1911.

†W. Duke and Sons became Liggett and Myers after dissolution of the American Tobacco Company trust in 1911.

‡Smoking only.

SOURCES: North Carolina Bureau of Labor Statistics and North Carolina Department of Labor and Printing, *Annual Reports*, 1890, 1910, 1911, 1917, and Bull Durham statistics for 1917 from U.S. Children's Bureau, Child Labor File, National Archives, Washington, D.C.

suppose, more women than there are men." His guess that ATC employed "15,000 or 20,000 or 30,000" workers betrayed his almost total lack of concern about the labor on which he had built his wealth.[23]

When the U.S. Supreme Court ordered the dissolution of the American Tobacco Company in 1911 on grounds that it illegally restrained competition, the decision did not free Durham from corporate control centered in New York. Nor did it alter the balance of power between tobacco capitalists and the workers in Durham's factories. The court merely divided control between two successor companies, Liggett and Myers (L and M), which took over the W. Duke and Sons plants along with 27.8 percent of the total cigarette production in the United States, and the American Tobacco Company (ATC), which assumed control of the Blackwell Durham properties together with 37 percent of cigarette production. Critics objected to the dominant position assigned to the two companies, along with R. J. Reynolds and

Phillip Morris, but the judges insisted that their plan "disintegrates the combination . . . without a wanton destruction of property."[24]

Although Liggett and Myers, in contrast to American Tobacco, frequently hired Durham men as managers, the decisions made by Clinton Toms, W. D. Carmichael, and other Durham-bred executives were as profit oriented as those of James B. Duke. Cigarette production returned to Durham, but management reinvested the enormous profits in plants, machinery, and capital assets; workers did not share in the corporate gains.[25] Between 1912 and 1923, ATC earned returns on net worth of 16.8 percent and L and M earned 32.2 percent; the companies paid their workers an average annual wage of $600.[26] Productivity increased 120 percent between 1919 and 1931, but wages declined 30 percent. A worker who produced $37,526 worth of products in 1931 received about 2 percent of the value and the companies netted a 16 percent return. Wages declined another 15 percent over the next two years, but the "depression proof" industry's profits remained at an impressive level.[27]

Durham workers thus shared only marginally in the benefits that accrued to the industrialists who owned the machines that they tended.[28] Sustained by the demand for its relatively inexpensive products, the industry maintained its prices while most others slashed theirs. Reaping an additional bonanza from low prices for raw tobacco in the early 1930s, a company like American Tobacco earned 11.1 percent of its net sales while the average U.S. corporation earned only 3.8 percent during the years between 1929 and 1949. The two corporations dominating the Durham economy maintained their positions among the four leading cigarette companies, which together controlled nearly 80 percent of the total U.S. production and sustained their pattern of growth, concentration, and high profits into the 1940s and beyond.[29]

■ As the relentless pressures of the cash crop economy forced large numbers of unemployed people into Durham, tobacco company officials could take their choice from among those competing for jobs. With separate labor markets not only for blacks and whites but for men and women as well, employers could mold their workforce through the recruitment process itself.[30] The tenets of white supremacy, which forbade employing blacks and whites on the same jobs at the same wage levels, worked to the advantage of the tobacco industry. Employers hired black women and men to perform the tasks that their ancestors had performed in an industrial tradition that harkened back to the origins of slavery.[31] Black women, the most likely group to migrate off the land, formed a growing proportion of the industrial labor force because they were hired in the most labor-intensive part of the productive processing—stemming and processing the leaf to prepare it for the mechanized parts of the enterprise. Children or younger brothers and sisters often assisted them, although only the adult women appeared on the company payrolls.³² The companies thus reaped profits by hiring the largest proportion of their work force from the group that—thanks to the combined effects of racial and gender discrimination—could be paid the lowest wages.

Black men, who constituted the overwhelming majority of the labor force under slavery and its aftermath, continued to carry the heavy hogsheads of tobacco, make the barrels, and press and shape the leaf. They also labored in the hottest parts of the process, where the leaf was heated to reduce its moisture content and where the syrups and flavorings were prepared to make the tobacco more appealing to smokers. Hiring black men to work in "bull gangs," the companies adhered to antebellum customs while exploiting a source of cheap local labor.³³ White women, who were hired to operate most of the machines in the factories, could be paid lower wages than white men.³⁴ These policies translated into profits for the company and satisfaction among the white employees, who saw their interests advanced by the subordination of their fellow employees.³⁵

With the enormous capital commanded by a highly concentrated industry like cigarette manufacturing, Durham tobacco factories installed new machinery as soon as prototypes were invented. As the industry moved to the South after the court-ordered dissolution of the American Tobacco Company, the companies constructed more modern plants. The major growth in employment occurred in the leaf departments, where black women continued to prepare the tobacco leaf by hand, but that increase did not alter the drastic impact of mechanization on employment patterns. In 1931, 20,000 workers produced twice as many cigarettes as 24,000 workers had produced in 1919 at wages that averaged about $120 less per year.³⁶ The "extended labor system," fueled by a sophisticated incentive plan for foremen and supervisors, was an accomplished fact in the tobacco industry.

These trends intensified in the 1930s as the tobacco companies took advantage of the crisis that had devastated other industries. Still prospering in the midst of the Depression, managers continued to invest in technological innovations that speeded production. Foremen stepped up pressure on employees, warning them that others would take their places if they objected to management demands. Employees judged careless or negligent were sent home for a week or two without pay. Unless a worker had assiduously cultivated a supervisor, no allowances were made for family illness or personal problems. Riding high on the crest of hard times, management saw no need to cultivate company loyalty among a work force it believed could be easily replaced.

From the beginning, tobacco profits were the "power that created, fostered and . . . dominate [d] all other interests" in Durham.³⁷ The Dukes, the Carrs, and their associates reinvested their gains in textile, hosiery, and bag mills that rose on Durham's eastern and western flanks. Driven by the same motive that led James B. Duke to New York City in the early 1880s ("the determination on riches in his heart"), Durham's industrial entrepreneurs dispensed only a small portion of their proceeds to philanthropic enterprises during their active years.[38] Already by 1884, Carr had begun investing in the Durham Cotton Manufacturing Company to produce cloth for the tobacco bags in which Bull Durham and other smoking tobacco brands were packaged for sale. He also financed the invention of a bag-making machine to eliminate the need to employ women to make bags in their homes.[39] As the Dukes prospered in the 1890s, they invested in textile mills in Mt. Airy, Rocky Mount, and Danville. The family next established its own wholly-controlled textile mills in Durham. They selected William A. Erwin, whose mother had been born into the pioneering Holt textile family of Alamance County, to manage the new Erwin Cotton Mills Company. At the same time, the Dukes and W. A. and J. Harper Erwin assumed control of the Durham Cotton Manufacturing Company as Carr's empire contracted. By 1899 all the major textile mills in Durham—Erwin, Durham, Pearl, Golden Belt, Commonwealth—had come under Duke or Erwin control.[40] As profits from Erwin Mills soared to above 50 percent of the capital stock in the early 1900s, the company expanded to other locations in the state in tandem with Duke investments in mills, banks, hydroelectric power, and railroads.[41]

The sons of Julian S. Carr sought to reestablish the family's fortunes by expanding the small hosiery mill the elder Carr had established on Durham's eastern side in 1898.[42] Securing credit from northern banks and benefiting from a growing demand for seamless hosiery in the early 1900s, the younger Carrs built a chain of fourteen mills for the Durham Hosiery Mills Company.[43] When the Dukes and Watts established a bank, after rejecting an offer from the senior Carr to set up a trust company in Durham, the Carr family set up a smaller bank.[44] In 1917, near the high point of textile prosperity, the hosiery industry in Durham consisted of nine mills ranging in size from the Carr mills, capitalized at $3 million and employing 3,000 workers, to the Knit-Well Hosiery Mill, capitalized at $5,000 and employing 38 workers.[45] The major Durham cotton mills included Erwin Mill No. 1 and No. 4, Pearl Mill, the Durham Cotton Manufacturing Company, and Golden Belt, a bag-making, hosiery, and cloth-making subsidiary of the American Tobacco Company. Although the Duke-Erwin Alliance dominated the economy of Durham, the Carrs had recouped their losses and made their family an important secondary economic power in the city.

Despite a few antebellum experiments with black labor, the textile industry in the New South established labor policies very different from the segmented patterns in tobacco.[46] Excluding black labor almost entirely, the companies recruited white families, who were usually expected to contribute three or more workers. Customarily, a family provided one worker for each room in the house that it rented from the company.⁴⁷ Children, an important but often unrecorded (and unpaid) part of the tobacco labor force, furnished a major portion of the textile labor supply. In the early years of the industry's development in Durham, the 250 textile workers included "about one hundred children—many of them very small children under twelve years of age." Wage data for 1887 indicate the financial incentive: children earned 25 to 50 cents a day, while adults earned 50 to 80 cents. In addition, women and children were more available than men in the 1880s, before the deepening agricultural crisis had convinced many men that there was no future on the land. Gradually the proportion of men in the labor force climbed, but women and children retained a sizable share of the employment. Women began young and generally worked in the mills until marriage, motherhood, or the entry of their children into the factory relieved them of responsibility for wage work as well as housework.⁴⁸

One factory in the Durham Hosiery Mills chain, located in the East End, departed from the prevailing near-exclusion of black labor from southern textile mills. The Carrs founded Durham Hosiery Mill No. 2 at a time of labor scarcity in the early twentieth century. Although disgruntled whites threatened to blow up the building if the Carrs actually began operations with a black labor force, the Carrs proceeded to hire blacks to "knit cheap socks out of cotton that had formerly been sold as waste." That mill and another white-run mill in the Carr chain broke with textile traditions in a different way as well. They lacked the usual cluster of mill village housing, which meant that the mostly female labor force had to walk to work from homes secured independently of their employers. Perhaps the senior Carr's experience in the tobacco industry encouraged the sons to try these innovations. After the mill demonstrated that black women could operate knitting machines, black entrepreneurs launched a short-lived enterprise in which they hired black women to manufacture socks. Although the Carr experiment succeeded in making profits, no other local manufacturers successfully followed their example.⁴⁹

The mill village and family labor system offered benefits that offset the loss of cheaper black labor. Preserving aspects of the farm family economy perpetuated the male head's "marked individualism, bred of having performed most of his work alone with the aid of his family," while easing the family members into an industrial labor force.⁵⁰ Children reared under the watchful eyes of overseers and mill officials could be molded to suit the needs of an industrial labor force. Workers' behavior on and off the job could be scrutinized to punish infringements of company policy, such as gambling, drinking, illicit sexual relationships, or union organizing.

A researcher, investigating the relationship between church and industry, accompanied William A. Erwin on his progress through West Durham: "It is a revelation to see the president walk about the grounds of his Durham plant and hail any passing workers with a cheery, 'good morning,' using his or her first name and asking after the family. Colored or white, man, woman, or child, it is the same."[51] Many employees approved of these policies. Bessie Taylor Buchanan credited Erwin with building "the community up ... If a girl got pregnant, her parents had to leave. It was strict. And if a person came in here and didn't act like he, Erwin, thought they ought to, you'd see them getting out. It was a clean community. We liked it because it was like one big family."[52] Another employee recalled Erwin's nightly habit of riding around the village at 10 o'clock. Every house with lights still burning received a visit from the curious president. A family with a medical emergency might receive assistance if unable to pay for a doctor's visit; a family lacking a valid excuse would receive a lecture.[53] Mill village paternalism, masterfully applied, molded an unlettered, defeated, and preindustrial people into a cohesive, motivated, and stable labor force at minimal cost.

After a series of strikes in 1918 and 1919 called employee relations into question, some firms sought new managerial techniques. Durham Hosiery Mills developed an unusual antidote to "the nefarious influence of the professional agitator."[54] Unwilling to act the "stern parent" as had earlier generations of managers, Julian S. Carr, Jr., decided to create "an organization of independent individuals who delegate their government to those they think are best able to exercise the executive power."[55] He launched his experiment in "industrial democracy" in 1919 with a constitution carefully designed to preserve managerial prerogatives. The Carr family constituted the executive branch with absolute veto power over all legislation. Foremen appointed by the Carrs became the senate. Employees elected their representatives to the house. No judiciary operated to overrule executive decisions.[56]

The plan was never intended to "take final control away from the owners of a business." Instead, it was intended to "provide the form of democracy, but not its essential substance" as a way of inducing restless employees to accept managerial authority."[57] After two years, the Carr experiment in "industrial democracy" collapsed during the general crisis in the industry.[58] Some observers, however, judged the experiment a success because Durham workers had accepted wage cuts and dismissals at the Carr mills without the "strife and turmoil that . . . accompanied efforts to reduce wages elsewhere." The Carr family, particularly after the death of Julian S. Carr, Jr., in 1922, resumed more conventional methods of management that did not try to convince workers that an "equality of purpose" existed between themselves and management.[59]

W. A. Erwin stuck to more familiar methods during the period of labor unrest. According to company official Kemp P. Lewis, Erwin told discontented employees at the Harnett County mill, "We are going to continue running the mill just as they would run their farms if they owned them . . . We want no dissatisfied employees and . . . all who are not pleased with their treatment . . . had better go elsewhere."⁶⁰ In Durham, where subtle appeals to a rural heritage could not evoke the same response, the company distributed bonuses and used an industrial spy to monitor worker discontent.⁶¹ As the textile crisis continued into the mid-1920s, Lewis followed Erwin's example in exhorting the Erwin labor force to greater company loyalty. He employed metaphors more likely to appeal to an increasingly urbanized work force. Calling on workers to engage in "team work," Lewis declared, "There is just as much necessity so far as success goes for co-operation to apply in a cotton mill as in the Army." Yet his homily ended by echoing earlier themes. The company, he said, felt an "intense desire" to produce good cloth but also wanted "to have Mill villages full of good people leading clean and moral lives."⁶² Lewis also enthusiastically introduced "scientific management" that required supervisors to take courses in "modern production methods." This was a major change in the work process. Lewis called it "the extended labor system"; the Erwin workers who bore its brunt labeled it "the stretch-out."⁶³ The end of the 1920s saw a shift "from Daddy to businessman," as the younger Lewis replaced the ailing Erwin in the active leadership of the company.⁶⁴

A prolonged crisis in the textile industry encouraged the shift from paternalism to a more impersonal managerial style. Overproduction, overcapacity, competition from synthetics, and the consequent decline in prices and profits initiated two decades of fierce competition and souring labor relations. As some companies lost the struggle, ownership in the industry became more concentrated.⁶⁵ By 1920 the Carr firm had already absorbed several local mills, including the small black-owned mill. Drawing on its capital reserves, the company sought to protect itself against the deteriorating market for cotton hosiery by establishing a mill in Durham to produce full-fashioned (seamed and shaped to fit a woman's leg) silk hosiery.⁶⁶ Meanwhile, other mills closed. The surviving companies slashed payrolls, cut hours, eliminated shifts, and increased the speed of the machines.

Erwin Mills also improved its productive efficiency in addition to cutting wages and curtailing production. Adding another mill to its operations at Erwin, North Carolina, the company transferred all its denim production to that location and consolidated its sheeting output at the two Durham mills.⁶⁷ As a leading chain, it also joined in the national effort to reach agreements to limit production and maintain prices under the auspices of the Cotton Textile Institute.⁶⁸ The Erwin management joined in discussions with other prominent competitors in the late 1920s about possible mergers—yet another way to restrict competition.⁶⁹ Ultimately, voluntary efforts to curtail production, fix prices, and effect mergers were stymied by the chaotic structure of the industry and by competition among individual managers. Companies met overstocked inventories by slashing prices while producing more cloth and hosiery. Unable to reduce output, Erwin Mills and other firms implemented internal reforms to cut unit costs. In a labor-intensive industry, managers sought to increase productivity while decreasing payrolls. They purchased new machinery that would enable fewer workers to produce more cloth. As individual firms tried to save themselves, their collective actions intensified the general crisis of the industry and undermined the security of textile and hosiery workers.

The onset of the Great Depression buffeted an already weakened industry. Kemp P. Lewis, then vice-president of Erwin Mills, summed up industry ills in a report to stockholders in 1930. Stating that the firm had been unable to sell its goods "when millions are out of work and the farming and labor elements in our population have little purchasing power," he announced that the company had curtailed production 50 percent during the previous six months. The company ended the year with an operating loss of $35,000, but other firms entered the 1930s with more dismal records. The Durham Cotton Manufacturing Company had accumulated an operating loss of $128,239.15 by mid-1931. Its president, W. A. Erwin, told its directors in July 1931 that he could not "advise that the mill be operated further."[70] That same summer, Lewis wrote to G. A. Allen of Liggett and Myers proposing that the tobacco company take over Pearl Mill because the Durham company "can't compete with larger mills."[71] In the following year, Erwin Mills took control of its smaller competitor. The Durham Hosiery Mills closed its large Durham seamless hosiery plant in the mid-1930s.[72] After prolonged efforts to save the Durham Cotton Manufacturing Company, it went into liquidation at the decade's end.[73] Meanwhile, the Erwin firm, despite an $182,566 loss in 1938, managed average net earnings of $407,430 for the last half of the decade.[74] By 1940 Erwin Mills and Golden Belt, sheltered from the full brunt of the economic crisis by their financial resources, were the only prospering survivors of a once thriving industry in Durham.

■ The black men celebrated by Booker T. Washington, W. E. B. Du Bois, and E. Franklin Frazier for their role in the "upbuilding of Black Durham" began their "push upward and onward" in the 1880s and 1890s.[75] According to the myth perpetuated by both black and white scholars, these men thrived in an environment where their possessions were "as fairly protected as are the whites."[76] In reality, as implied by Frazier's observation that their success was due to the "absence of serious competition," the black professionals and businessmen who came to Durham fitted into the niches allowed them by white industrialists.[77] The quintessential city of the New South, Durham lacked white professionals, artisans, and service people to satisfy the needs of its rapidly growing black population. Men like John

Merrick, an enterprising barber; W. G. Pearson, an educator; A. M. Moore, a doctor; and James E. Shepard, a pharmacist and minister, succeeded precisely because the color bar gave them a sheltered market within the black community.

The black entrepreneurial dynasty began with the arrival of John Merrick, a former slave and skilled barber, who eventually established six barbershops in the city, three for whites and three for blacks. He invested his earnings in real estate and the construction of cheap housing for the black workers who came to labor at American Tobacco Company. His ambiguous relationship with his white patrons was suggested by the way he would "tip his hat to the white man and at the same time call him a son-of-a-bitch under his breath."[78] Together with Aaron M. Moore and Charles C. Spaulding, Merrick transformed a tradition of black secret orders and fraternal lodges into a secular enterprise, the North Carolina Mutual Life Insurance Company. Catering to poorer blacks' desperate need for minimal security in case of sickness or death, these members of a tiny black capitalist class presided over an expanding empire in real estate, insurance, and banking.[79]

The narrow economic constraints within which Merrick, Moore, and Spaulding operated were attested by black failures to establish a foothold in the industries that dominated the local economy. Although Richard Fitzgerald, the leading brickmaker in Durham, and Benjamin N. Duke invested in the black-owned W. C. Coleman Mill in Concord, the enterprise employing black workers ended in foreclosure by 1904. Having badgered Duke into investing in the mill, Coleman could not countermand Duke's decision to close the mill when it failed to repay his loan.[80] C. C. Amey's request to learn how to repair the machines and manage the knitters in a Carr factory in Durham was rebuffed. After acquiring the necesary skills in Philadelphia, Amey opened a small mill in Durham employing black women. DuBois and Washington lavishly praised this effort, but the mill soon fell into the Carr hands because limited capital and managerial inexperience restricted its ability to compete.[81] Confined to the sector of the local economy where they did not directly compete with white industrialists, the black capitalists of Durham expanded their businesses with capital extracted from the rent and the premiums paid by black workers.

■ The existence of a few men who controlled "the purse strings of hundreds of men and women" in Durham aroused intense interest and occasional debate.[82] Many Durham citizens agreed with Hiram Paul's early description of their contributions to the city:

> Her Carrs, Blackwells, Dukes and Parrishes, actuated by a lofty State pride, and a sincere desire to advance the best interests of all classes, have freely and unstintingly utilized their energies, brains and money,

elevating Durham to the front rank of the Tobacco Marts of the world . . . Here all classes of honest and industrious mechanics and laborers find profitable employment, kind friends, and are surrounded by the most refined, educational, moral and religious influences and advantages. Durham, to-day, is an asylum for the poor.[83]

The opening of the first textile mill—in the same year that Paul published his history of Durham—was graced by a local Methodist minister and choir. "There is money in these enterprises for the owners, work for our laboring people, and general advantage to the community at large," wrote the editor of *Tobacco Plant*, a newspaper owned by Julian S. Carr, in 1888.[84] Pleading that "Durham needs more enterprise right now," the Durham *Recorder* added, "Let's be like Noah of old: in his great wisdom he entered the ark and was on the safe side."[85] Ten years later the local press was sounding the same anthem to progress, calling Durham the "most progressive town in North Carolina," describing her "public buildings, her leading businessmen, her various enterprises" in enthusiastic detail and insisting,

> This sense of local pride is universal and confined to no one class. They are a busy people, and find no time to repine over misfortunes, or to murmur "what might have been." Their satisfied condition, their exemption from "thoughts for the morrow," might well provoke the envy of many a rich employer, who has learned of these conditions only in theory.[86]

John Merrick, addressing Durham blacks in 1898, praised the opportunities open to industrious members of his race:

> We are here and we are going to stay. And why not stay? We have the same privileges that other people have. Every avenue is open to us to do business there is to any other people. We are allowed to own homes and farms, run farms, do banking business, insurance, real estate business and all other minor business that are done in this Commonwealth. Therefore I claim that the Negro's condition in North Carolina is as good or better than it's been since our Emancipation, if we go ahead and use them in the right direction.[87]

Blacks and whites joined the chorus of praise for the enlightened capitalists of Durham who preached the gospel of faith and work to an integrated congregation.

A few skeptics dissented from the general adulation for Durham's capitalists. Hiram Paul, once a fervent admirer of the Dukes and the Carrs, became an early critic. Discussing the "vast benefit to the manufacturer" promised by the new Bonsack cigarette-making machine, Paul pointed to a paradox of progress. The machine's effect "upon another class of our fellow-citizens will be anything but gratifying to the true philanthropist. Thousands of girls, boys, men and women, and among them worthy orphans, widows, and decrepit old age, will be thrown out of employment."[88] Following this discovery of the contradictory interests of labor and capital, Paul took an increasingly critical view of Duke policies. In 1885 he reported to the national labor press that "the lash is freely used on the backs of helpless little children at the Duke factory . . . The 'poor have a gospel preached into them' in one factory through the glorious (!) 'missionary-box' and lash system." The appearance of Paul's reports in the *Journal of United Labor* and *John Swinton's Paper* brought an anxious James B. Duke to appear before the Knights' General Executive Board and to call on John Swinton in order to mollify the critics. Duke explained to Swinton that "he had to employ many children in his Durham factory in order to get [the] cheap labor" necessary to compete. Duke told the Knights that he would avoid such methods in the future. Paul was unconvinced of Duke's sincerity, but the Knights ordered him to stop his campaign.[89]

Fueling the growing debate was the economic reality that the machinery of the mills and factories ran on cheap labor. Privately, the men who capitalized on the "abundance of cheap white labor" and still cheaper black labor admitted as much.[90] Seeking to encourage investment in a local cotton mill, one Durham industrialist cited attractions that included "girls" who "can be had at from $2.50 to $4.00 per week."[91] Throwing out a similar lure, Benjamin Duke tried to persuade a Lowell manufacturer to join him in establishing a mill in Durham. In the face of northern reluctance, Duke and his associates drew on their own money to utilize the "advantages" that had failed to attract New England capital.[92]

In personal correspondence more than three decades later, Kemp P. Lewis conceded "that a lot of cotton manufacturers in North Carolina, but more South of us, are less generous to their employees than they should be." Writing to an uncle, he defended Erwin wage policies while acknowledging that "they [Erwin employees] are not getting as much money as they need for the high scale of living." But, he wrote, "we are doing everything we possibly can for the people working for us . . . With the cotton mill prices the way they are, it is an impossibility for us to consider a raise in wages that would amount to anything at all." Such frankness Lewis reserved for family members and other manufacturers; he never made such admissions publicly or openly criticized the employers whom he privately described as "full of selfishness."[93]

Wage data available for the tobacco industry proves conclusively that cheap labor played a significant role in its growth, its southward expansion, and its profitability. Indeed, in the 1880s and 1890s, tobacco wages hovered below the notoriously low wages paid to textile workers in North Carolina.[94] Government investigators for the National Recovery Administration in the 1930s discussed the methods by which the tobacco corporations had "successfully met the danger to the industry of being forced to pay a living wage." The officials also pointed out that information about "the miserable annual earnings of the tobacco workers; the gigantic profits of the companies which employ them; [and] the small part which labor costs plays in the total cost" were "well known to the public."[95]

Workers' comments suggested that they recognized the human costs of a cheap labor policy. Addressing an appeal to cigarette makers, Junius Strickland, an employee in the Duke factory, urged his fellow craftsmen to organize because "unorganized you are helpless; your wages are completely at the will of combined and merciless manufacturers, [and are] liable to be reduced at every fluctuation in the market."[96] In 1887, a year after Strickland's unheeded appeal, a stamper in a Durham tobacco factory reported:

> It takes every cent that myself and wife make to meet our expenses and at this, we are not in as bad circumstances as some others in the locality. Of course, we do not expect to look for any heaven to lay up, but we want, when the time comes when one of our family is called away, to be able to go to the furniture store and purchase what we need to bury the dead.[97]

Twenty years later, John Lincoln, a young worker, overheard a conversation between W. A. Erwin and a vistor that revealed his employer's attitudes toward workers:

> They were standing close by me when the strange man glanced over the room and said, Not a very intelligent looking bunch of workers you've got, taking them as a whole . . . Don't want them intelligent, he said. If they have too much sense, they'll realize the difference between their earnings and ours. We have to keep them trod down, you know, trod down.[98]

Dena Coley, a young black woman, supported her two children on the $4 a week she earned in a Durham stemmery in 1919. Unable to attend church because her dresses had gone to clothe her children, she found life to be very tight and very hard."[99] Ozzie Richmond, whose parents worked at L and M in the 1930s, remembered frequent conversations about the family's scanty resources:

> They'd sit down together and try to discuss the decisions they were making. See, my daddy was making about $8 or $9 a week and my momma was making about $6, $6 and a half. You know that was very little income with four children . . . Course things were pretty cheap then but it was still rough. Some people had it worse . . . because some people didn't have no job.[100]

CAPITALISTS AND PATRIARCHS

A machine operator at the American Tobacco Company in the 1930s voiced an unusually strong condemnation of the Dukes:

> Oh, they can make plenty of money—enough while old man Duke was slave-driver so he could give fifty-two million dollars in one whack to a little old college here called Trinity College, to get them to call it Duke University. That's money our people before us sweated to make for him. Duke? Well, just a place where rich men's sons go and live in luxury four years and come back to drive us in cotton mills, mines, in fields and these tobacco plants and work our day-lights out so they can have big, fine buildings like at Duke.[101]

In the mid-1920s Durham capitalists began to face criticism from an unexpected source. Prominent women, including the wives of local manufacturers, Duke professors, and the sisters of men like K. P. Lewis, took up the cause of young working women in their state. The League of Women Voters, the Young Women's Christian Association, and the North Carolina Federation of Women's Clubs encouraged women to investigate conditions in local industries and discuss issues with women workers. Almost as soon as the YWCA began its work in Durham, K. P. Lewis warned its president that the "tendencies of industrial work in the Y was a very dangerous one." Pointing to the "terrible menace" of the "closed shop movement," he advised, "I think the Y should be careful to be conservative and not encourage some of the very harmful and radical views that are now being spread abroad." His warnings apparently were not heeded. Young women, sent by the YWCA to a summer school for women workers, returned to conduct classes for other workers and to raise questions about industrial practices. In 1925 several members of the Durham Industrial Girls Club agreed to testify before the North Carolina legislature in support of an investigation of women's working conditions in the textile industry, a proposal sponsored by a coalition of women's associations.[102] Nell Battle Lewis, K. P. Lewis's feminist sister, vigorously endorsed the movement through her weekly column in the *News and Observer*. This rebellion by female members of their class alarmed Lewis, Benjamin Duke, and other manufacturers.

As the 1920s ended, they faced a still more formidable alliance formed by progressive women like Nell Battle Lewis and Mary O. Cowper, radical professors from Duke and the University of North Carolina, and labor organizers like Alfred Hoffman of the Hosiery and Textile Workers. When Frank Porter Graham, an outspoken champion of the "equal right of the investors of capital" and "the investors of human life and labor to bargain collectively," became president of the University of North Carolina, the university became a battlefield.[103]

Durham's black bourgeoisie did not escape criticism, although its policy of promoting racial uplift as well as business expansion mollified most observers. W. E. B. DuBois praised the black businesses that he observed in Durham, although he voiced reservations about "triumphant commercialism" as a potential destroyer of the "souls of black folk" in a "dusty desert of dollars and smartness."[104] The very caution shown by black businessmen in accommodating themselves to white power could evoke dissent in the black community.[105] Lower-class blacks, who suspected that the "big niggers" were in some sense allies of whites and who doubted that they themselves could achieve wealth without white patronage, felt both pride and resentment toward the small clique that exercised such conspicuous influence over the rest of the black community.[106] They did not fail to observe that the privileged tended to marry within their own circles, to hire their own children, and to favor lighter complexions on their staffs and in the institutions that they established. A young woman, the daughter of a female tobacco worker, noted that "social class and color" were the "primary criteria used in determining status" at the college established by Durham's black elite. The faculty continued to assume as late as the 1960s that "light-skinned students were more intelligent"; the children "of the professional class . . . used to toss their heads and flaunt themselves around the students whose parents were black working class."[107] Resentment, however, did not erupt into open conflict until the 1960s. There was a more important enemy: white men. "Forget all of this class feeling," a black businessman told his audience in the mid-1930s; "We are all in the same boat."[108] Incidents such as one in 1931 in which C. C. Spaulding was beaten by a "little old peckerwood" in a Raleigh drugstore for violating the color line lent credibility to his plea. The common enemy, coupled with friendly relations between employers and employees at black-owned enterprises, worked to minimize friction between classes within the black community.

■ Durham industrialists were aware of the dangers of an open confrontation between capital and labor. They sought to deflect public attention from both the fundamental conflict over low wages and the equally volatile question of workers' rights to organize. Industrial spokesmen strove to convince the public that the "natural instinct of mill management" was always directed toward "the best interests of employees."[109] Wooing the press, which they subsidized, they framed a public discourse that extolled wealth and power as the hallmarks of the Christian gentlemen they represented themselves to be. They appeared regularly in the local press in the guise of pure, disinterested philanthropists, the Noahs who gathered all the worthy, respectable citizenry into the ark of prosperity. Black businessmen adopted a similar strategy. Their publications claimed that "the North Carolina Mutual shows that the race is gradually emerging from under" a "great cloud, a dark night of lost confidence" by teaching "the secret of successful accumulation." Criticisms of high rates for insurance were met by assurances that "many advantages which accrue to our race . . . more than offset this slight difference in rates."[110] The second generation followed the first. The activities of Erwin, Lewis, the younger Carrs, Asa Spaulding, John H. Wheeler, and other associates offered proof of the "constructive philanthropy" of New South businessmen.[111] Donations to charities, to the YWCA and YMCA, to hospitals, schools, and churches demonstated that businessmen adhered to the principles of Christian stewardship.

When criticism was not stilled despite philanthropy and the adulation of the local media, Durham capitalists took sterner measures. Hiram Paul found that ceasing to flatter the "leading spirits" of Durham carried penalties. His printing office began to lose customers. A creditor, "backed, as I learn, by the Dukes," demanded immediate repayment of a loan. "The consequence," Paul reported to the Knights of Labor, "is that I am in very embarrassing circumstances, and, unless matters improve, will be compelled to sell my office at a great sacrifice and leave the city."[112] Embittered, Paul fell victim to the power of the Dukes to silence critics.

The Knights of Labor came under direct attack in the local press. Describing the unequal balance of force between labor and capital, the editor of the Durham *Recorder* warned local members of the order against following Paul's example:

> Now, we would warn these men, for in the first place it is against the law of North Carolina, and then when labor kicks against capital, labor always comes out at the small end of the horn. It is but foolish for labor to kick against capital. Capital can lay back and rest and have plenty to live on, while labor is only dependent upon what is done during the day. Now we ask who can live the longest? Has not capital every advantage?[113]

Simultaneously, foremen in Durham factories threatened to discharge members of the Knights. When the Bonsack machine reached operational efficiency, the Dukes swiftly moved to discharge the cigarette rollers, who had comprised the core of the order in their factory. By 1888, the order had disintegrated in Durham.

Industrialists continued reluctant to bargain with their employees. W. A. Erwin dismissed employees in 1900 when they dared to organize a union. Entire families lost their homes and were reduced to near starvation. Relenting a little, Erwin opened the company store to the starving victims of an industrial war, but they had to seek employment elsewhere. In 1919 the first serious attempt since the Knights' to organize Durham tobacco factories ended when the chief organizer lost his job.[114] Durham Hosiery Mills discharged union members after a strike at the Marvin Carr Silk Mill in the mid-1920s. Industrial spies and paid informers within the union ranks reported in the late 1920s to Lewis of Erwin Mills, Will Carr of Durham Hosiery Mills, and W. D. Carmichael of Liggett and Myers.[115] Making full use of their superior economic resources and the seemingly inexhaustible supply of labor, Durham industrialists provided persuasive evidence that "when labor kicks against capital, labor always comes out at the small end of the horn."

The women in the local YWCA also learned the price of challenging the power of local industrialists. The YWCA's endorsement of a survey of the textile industry in North Carolina produced unexpected results. When the YWCA board tried to raise money to build a dormitory to house working women, the manufacturers rejected their appeals. Benjamin Duke's "turning them down made them very discouraged and bitter." When the women vowed to call off the campaign and blame local manufacturers for its failure, Lewis and other businessmen engaged them in a blunt three-hour discussion. The Durham YWCA thereupon agreed "to co-operate with the manufacturers for the best interest of the City" and Lewis promised to donate to the YWCA building fund.[116]

Elsewhere in the state, officers from other organizations supporting the industrial survey were pressured to resign. The president of the League of Women Voters received an ultimatum from her husband. Unless all publicity were stopped about the campaign, she would have to "resign at once." As the president told Mary O. Cowper, the league's executive secretary and a Durham resident, "Our bread and butter comes entirely from the Mills and there are many families in our Company affected so it's a serious thing for them. It would be better to have a President anyway who is not connected in any way with N.C. Industries, for it is brought back home to them in many ways."[117] In Durham the chastened YWCA refrained from further challenges to the industrial status quo, but industrialists like K. P. Lewis were too quick to claim final victory over their critics.

In the 1930s, Lewis, then a member of the University of North Carolina Board of Trustees, led an undercover campaign to prevent President Graham from allowing the university to serve as a forum for the discussion of industrial and race relations. When Graham failed to respond to warnings in the pages of the *Textile Bulletin* and the regular press, Lewis joined with others in pressing for his resignation. He explained his motives clearly: "I think of the university in a way as I do my church—that it has no business in political or controversial questions."[118] Unable to convince a majority on the board that Graham's devotion to academic freedom and open discussion merited dismissal, Lewis reluctantly abandoned the fight to censor debate at the university. His efforts to silence critics, however, continued in other arenas.

Beyond stifling unfavorable public discourse, Durham capitalists tried to create a positive social image through their piety. Levi Branson, the editor of a local business directory, sketched an idealized portrait in which the industrialists served the best interests of both God and the residents of Durham:

> The leaders are for Durham and they work to the same end. The association spirit is highly developed. The citizens are very much like one family. They help each other and rejoice in each others' success. They are not only a moral but a religious people. They build fine Churches to honor God, and He honors them with success. They work, they pray, they wait, they honor each other—they honor the Master.[119]

Beginning with Washington Duke, Julian S. Carr, and George Watts, Durham manufacturers actively inculcated their belief in an "eminently practical religion" as a sure guide to worldly success. After a conflict-ridden encounter with Jewish cigarette makers imported from New York, the Dukes established a company policy of hiring local whites and worshiping "with those we employ." Washington Duke organized a Sunday school in one room of the Duke factory. There Junius Strickland was converted from a radical Knight to devoted employee and Sunday school teacher. After the construction of the Main Street Methodist Church near the factory, Washington and Benjamin Duke continued to teach Bible classes. An anonymous tobacco manufacturer, probably Julian S. Carr, described a similar approach: "My experience is that we need to educate, elevate, and stimulate our factory labor" and "encourage church-building and church-going." Carr established Sunday schools and churches in East Durham where his hosiery empire had begun, and he conducted a Sunday school class for many years. A devout Methodist, he explained his religious zeal at a banquet in 1912: "Durham's greatest asset is her Methodism . . . doing business every day in the week for Christianity and the uplift of humanity."[120]

George Watts, a Presbyterian, also conducted a Sunday school class. In addition, he chaired an interdenominational mission intended to convert all Durham citizens to active Christianity. W. A. Erwin and John C. Kilgo cooperated with Watts in this campaign.[121] Episcopalians Erwin and Lewis established Bible classes for their predominantly Baptist and Methodist labor force in West Durham. Ambitious workers realized that regular church attendance promised economic as well as spiritual rewards. Yet when asked about the proper relationship between church and industry, Erwin expressed the view common to the Durham capitalists: "The church should not meddle in industrial affairs."[122] Seeing their own motives as pure and disinterested, manufacturers denounced critics like Methodist Bishop James Cannon as "agitators" who were either seeking publicity or were ignorant of actual conditions.[123]

The alliance between church and business was still more pronounced in Black Durham, where the church often served as a recruitment center for Mutual agents. A devout believer that "business and religion will mix," C.

C. Spaulding instructed his agents to use the church as their "most powerful contact."[124] Black ministers in Durham received Christmas gifts from the Mutual and, in turn, discussed "business cooperation" in special services for their congregations. In tribute, Spaulding's portrait hung among those of church leaders at the Nashville headquarters of the National Baptist convention. A skeptical Baptist described the influence exerted by the "town moguls" over the White Rock Baptist Church:

> In this church you meet capitalism undressed and undiluted. In this church capital dominates and I don't mean chicken feed. It is an interlocking directorate . . . When you rise to preach, you look into the faces of people . . . who are connected either by family or business with Shepard, Kennedy, or Spaulding. All of them are officials of the church, Kennedy being the business manager. Now go there and preach a red hot sermon about the proletariat.[125]

Nevertheless, under the skillful and diplomatic leadership of the Reverend Mark Miles Fisher, pastor of White Rock from the 1930s into the 1960s, the church began to espouse "the just cause of labor along with the right claims of capital." Spaulding cautioned Fisher that "those who are in authority and giving employment to our people are watching every move we make," but the pastor opened the church to black tobacco workers' meetings.[126] That action was a conspicuous exception to the generally neutral posture of other black ministers. According to the Reverend John Newsome, a preacher outside the mainstream churches, "If all preachers were like Reverend Fisher, Durham would be a union city and everything would be organized."[127]

Like the Christian patriarchs they conceived themselves to be, Durham's capitalists exercised moral guardianship over their workers. White manufacturers were concerned with the moral reputations of their female workers; black employers concentrated on safeguarding "our young women."[128] Washington Duke demanded that the young women hired in the Duke factory be "self-respecting," "religious," and "chaste."[129] A Durham Cotton Manufacturing official declared, "We have a very moral place. We have no drinking around the mill. They seem very satisfied here; we have had no trouble whatever in regard to strikes." An employee concurred: "The officers are kind and pay close attention to work and sobriety and morality is required of all who work here."[130] Like the cotton mill management, Liggett and Myers enforced chastity among their unmarried white women workers; those who became pregnant or provoked gossip were dismissed. The Erwin Mills policy, as described by one worker, required dismissal for the following infractions: "You couldn't join a labor union or have a party, that was a cardinal sin, and if somebody in your family, like a young girl, if she got pregnant, that girl had to leave that family and go somewhere else or the whole family would be run away from the place."[131] The contract that a worker was required to sign in 1909 prohibited "intemperance, profanity, or obscene language, or fighting on the premises" and "gross misconduct or drunkenness" elsewhere.[132] Indeed, Kemp Lewis justified the company-owned mill village on the ground that it "gives the management a better chance to protect the community from people of low character and dissolute life."[133] These men rarely doubted that their mission was "to uplift and make . . . [their workers] better."[134] Their success was due in part to their confidence in their own righteousness and their employees' willingness to accept their relentless supervision.

■ Good works and faith were not the only instruments wielded by Durham capitalists to dominate the civic life of Durham. Ties of kinship bound the respective racial elites. Six of the first seven presidents of the North Carolina Mutual Company were related. Kinlike ties—presided over by the "patriarch," "moral overlord," and "Papa" of the company—instilled loyalty among the employees.[135] The white business elites used marriage to cement their connections to political figures and business partners. Benjamin Duke married Sarah Angier, a daughter of Durham's first mayor. Later their children would marry the children of the Philadelphia Biddles. Julian Carr and his brother married the Parrish sisters, whose brother ran a major tobacco warehouse in Durham and whose father was a mayor of Durham.[136] Through his mother, W. A. Erwin was linked to the Holt family, the dominant textile interests in Alamance County, where he first learned to manage a business. His close associate at Erwin Mills, E. K. Powe, was also his brother-in-law. J. Harper Erwin, his brother, was the president of other textile mills in Durham.[137] Against the better judgment of his subordinate, K. P. Lewis, W. A. Erwin groomed his son to assume a major role in the company. The young man's death frustrated that plan. K. P. Lewis's mother, Cornelia Battle Lewis, was a direct descendent of the Battle family of Rocky Mount, who had been operating the Rocky Mount Cotton Mills since the early nineteenth century. A grandfather served as president of the University of North Carolina. His brother, Richard H. Lewis, ran the Oxford Cotton Mills, in which the Erwins held an interest.[138] John Sprunt Hill, Durham's leading banker, achieved his position through his marriage to the only daughter of George Watts.[139] Brothers and cousins ran the Durham Hosiery Mills. Although the Carrs claimed that John O'Daniel, the black man who recruited labor for the mill, was only a faithful family servant, gossip in Durham held that O'Daniel was a son of the elder Carr.[140] Bonds, cemented by blood, marriage, and economic interests, helped to create a self-conscious and exclusive ruling class.

The power and the connections formed by Durham capitalists extended beyond the city itself. Membership on the boards of other tobacco, textile, financial, utility, and transportation interests integrated Durham company officials into a national capitalist class. White and black business leaders participated in national organizations to define a common agenda, lobby for favorable treatment from the state and national governments, and devise solutions to their mutual problems. Durham's black capitalists were moving spirits behind the National Negro Business League, which was designed to promote black capitalism.[141] Durham's white capitalists assumed leadership in the manufacturers' organizations in their respective industries and in general organizations like the National Association of Manufacturers. Beginning in 1900, the officers of Erwin Mills took part in the state textile industry's campaign against unions, anti–child labor laws, and other forms of state intervention into employment policies.[142] W. A. Erwin and K. P. Lewis served as directors of the Southern Railway, local banks, and other textile mills.[143] Tobacco manufacturers were more active than their textile counterparts. In a report on Julian S. Carr in 1899, the Durham *Recorder* observed, "There is almost no enterprise in his home city in which he does not bear a leading part." The *Recorder* then listed Carr's activities. He was president of a Durham bank, the electric light company, and the Golden Belt Manufacturing Company. He was vice-president of another Durham mill, treasurer of the local telephone company, and vice-president in a railroad company.[144] The Dukes and Watts filled still more directorships and presidencies. Benjamin Duke, who in 1900 had replaced Carr as president of the Blackwell Durham Tobacco Company, also served as president of one cotton mill, one bank, one lumber company, and one railroad in addition to directorships of eight additional textile mills, two banks, the American Tobacco Company, and two railroads. His close associate, George Watts, was reported to hold directorships in eight textile mills, five of which were in Durham. In addition, he served as a director of three banks, three tobacco companies, and two railroads.[145] John Sprunt Hill, Watts' son-in-law, became Durham's leading banker through the influence of his wealthy father-in-law. These men of the New South had gathered enormous economic power in their hands.

Although the elder Carr nourished political ambitions, culminating in unsuccessful efforts to capture the Democratic Party nomination for senator in the 1890s, most of Durham's capitalist class exercised political influence through donations to candidates and financing of both secular and religious press that defended corporations against populist, socialist, or reform attacks.[146] Ironically, Carr's ambitions spurred him to make rhetorical assaults on "plutocrats," "malefactors of great wealth," and "self-confessed directors of trusts and life-long Republicans" like his crosstown rivals, the Dukes.[147] The Dukes, however, never faced much danger from the conservative, probusiness Democrats who actually controlled the party. The second generation of Durham industrialists avoided even the verbal battles that had pitted the Dukes against the elder Carr. They preferred to lend quiet background support to candidates and causes that defended white supremacy, opposed unions, and created a favorable climate for investment. While Carr was mounting the plantform, W. A. Erwin quietly promoted the passage of black disfranchisement by sanctioning the organization of a White Supremacy Club in West Durham. He addressed a mass meeting intended to whip up voter support for the constitutional amendment and also granted permission for a parade through West Durham. The parade was led by a man carrying a White Supremacy banner, and included a large white float carrying sixteen young women dressed in white and bearing streamers with the slogan, "Protect us with your vote." This was a central motif of the campaign organized by Democratic leaders Furnifold Simmons and Charles Aycock.[148] W. A. Erwin and other textile company officials also led the industry's defense against child labor laws. They tried to persuade the public that "compulsory education" was unnecessary because good manufacturers like themselves "encourage our help all we can to take advantage of their opportunities." When such appeals no longer appeared credible, K. P. Lewis fashioned an updated defense that placed responsibility on the parent who "would apply for work and stipulate that employment would also be given to his children."[149]

Making full use of their economic clout, company officials negotiated deals with local officials that limited the flow of resources to public services. West Durham and East Durham remained outside the Durham city limits through the adroit use of pressure and influence. Even as they resisted incorporation in the city, Erwin officials complained that a law prescribing school attendance for all children could not "be enforced because there are too many children for the schools."[150] In such a context, they did not mention their own reluctance to pay city taxes. Once they had lost the fight to keep their mill villages outside the city, Erwin and Durham Hosiery Mills officials took a more active part in the city government.[151] Lewis served on the school board; W. H. Carr joined the Durham City Council and rose to the mayoralty in the 1930s. Lewis and other businessmen also campaigned for a city manager system, essentially because the electoral system gave too much power to men whose interests might differ from theirs.[152]

While keeping taxes low, these men also used their political power to defend their city against potential threats. An AFL film, for example, was barred from being screened in the city auditorium on the ground that it presented a "fire hazard."[153] In the event of a strike, city police were expected to maintain "order." In short, Durham's leading industrialists made sure that men sympathetic to their interests would control city and state governments. Should local authorities ever prove unwilling to maintain public order, state troopers or militia could be called on to defend the rights of property and the rights of loyal employees to work.[154]

Durham's white business elite developed some informal methods for determining who should have a voice in public affairs. They sponsored the use of racist propaganda in mass meetings, public demonstrations, and local Democratic organs in order to exclude blacks from politics. Agitators were forced to leave town; Edward J. Parrish, brother-in-law of Julian S. Carr, personally accompanied one man accused of inciting blacks in 1888 to the edge of town—before a mob could accomplish the same task. Black men like John Merrick, who asked, "What difference does it make to us who is elected?" were allowed to prosper unmolested. Black men like W. G. Pearson, initially active in Republican Party affairs, learned to accept exclusion from self-government.[155]

It was a lesson that all of Durham's first generation black bourgeosie came to terms with after the violence directed against black political rights during the 1898 and 1900 campaigns. They lived according to the advice that Washington Duke offered in 1890: "Do honest work for an honest dollar . . . at night when you lie down with it under your pillow, the eagle on its face will sing you to sleep."[156] Even so, the Wilmington Race Riot of 1898 and the "Red Shirts" that had terrorized black voters that year and in the 1900 election haunted Charles Spaulding into the 1930s.[157] During the racial upheaval of 1919, when race riots spread across the nation, Spaulding and the other business leaders reiterated the belief that the people of Durham were "too busy" to "have racial differences."[158]

A journalist who came to Durham in the late 1920s described the techniques black businessmen used to protect their economic interests. Taking advantage of the rivalry between the leading industrialists, black businessmen were "able to interlock their business interests and divide their allegiance to the Dukes and Carrs so as to steer clear of any entanglements that could jeopardize the success of their undertakings." They spoke in "most reverent terms of the Dukes and General Carr" while ignoring Carr's frequent political speeches attacking "Duke niggers." One local black leader explained, "We prefer to think of General Carr in terms of his benefactions rather than his politics."[159]

As long as black leaders accommodated themselves to the repressions of white supremacy, Durham's white establishment felt no need to return to the more brutal methods of the 1890s. K. P. Lewis declined an invitation to join the Ku Klux Klan in 1921 because, as he informed his father, "Matters could be very much better handled . . . open and above-board."[160] Lewis's service on the Durham Interracial Commission along with one of the Carrs and W. D. Carmichael of L and M enabled him to prevent the appearance of any semblance of "social equality" in Durham while allowing the black community to be represented by a few spokesmen chosen by whites. In the 1930s, some younger, more radical blacks like Louis Austin who were "disposed to force issues without regard to consequences" brought modifications in the "long-standing institutionalized relationship" but did not transform it into open confrontation. Austin, the editor of the *Carolina Times*, publicly called "white people big apes and fools," but Spaulding continued to use "a little more diplomacy" in his own dealings. He joined with Austin, James E. Shepard, and other leading citizens to form the Durham Committee on Negro Affairs in 1935, an organization committed to regaining political power for black people. Quietly, Spaulding also lent support to the new politics of agitation and legal action under the leadership of the National Association for the Advancement of Colored People (NAACP). Police brutality, unequal pay for black teachers, discrimination in higher education, and inadequate public services to the black community became the subjects of NAACP and Durham Committee concerns. Yet, the old politics of deference still persisted. As Durham's white city manager said in 1937, "We . . . work with their leaders, for the Negroes trust them and fall in line with what they say; that's the way for us to have peace." Black Durham was no longer "too busy" or too intimidated to admit that "racial differences" existed, but its traditional leaders were willing to accept white domination of the political and economic system.[161]

Members of the lower classes in the black community expressed contradictory opinions about the "peace" that was negotiated between the black and white elites. Comparing Durham favorably to the racial climate in states like South Carolina, one tobacco worker declared in the 1930s, "This about the last town going South where the white people ain't so 'rebish' [rebel-like] but from here on down they are as mean as hell." Others did not believe that "race relations are good in this city." A black tobacco worker pointedly distinguished between working-class blacks and the tiny black elite: "I guess things are pretty good for them." The absence of overt racial warfare did not transform Durham into a utopia for its expanding class of black workers despite its reputation as the black Zion of the South. The basic divisions of "caste and class" remained entrenched in the political economy of Durham, enabling the white industrialists to keep "the city under control."[162]

Even so, the power of the dominant white industrialists had been eroded by the shift toward a more aggressive stance in the black community and by rising levels of defiance among Durham workers. By the mid-1920s the subordinate classes no longer deferred to the authority of their superiors as a "matter of course." Women as well as men now professed a belief in their right to a "say-so" about working conditions and openly wondered "what the results would be if we did."[163] Shocked employers cast about for explanations and new ways of dealing with rebellious workers who no longer responded to paternalist actions or appeals for Christian harmony. A new class had begun to define itself in opposition to a class accustomed to unchallenged hegemony. A farmer observing construction of a gothic tower at

Duke University asked a question that was echoed by workers employed in the old Duke factory: "I wonder what part of it he took away from me?" "The modern politics of power and textiles and tobacco corporations" that had grown from Durham's soil had finally led to an open struggle for power.[164]

In Hayti, the center of black life in Durham (named after the black republic but spelled as it is pronounced), the ironies of life in "the capital of the black middle class" had grown too sharp for some to bear. A sensitive observer, Jonathan Daniels, the repentant son of a race-baiting father, noted the contradictory outcomes that sixty years of progress had brought to black Durham:

> There are many such lines even in Durham where the Negro has made money and lifted his pride. Negro insurance men and bankers work in a building in the same business section where the white offices are, but there are wide lines of railroad tracks between where the Negroes work and where they live. Indeed, Hayti . . . is almost the black ghetto complete. I rode across the tracks and by the tobacco factories. The blue and white uniforms for servants, sold everywhere by the chain stores, seem almost the uniform of Negro women in Durham, where they work in the rough preparation of the tobacco while the white girls turn out the endless tubes of Chesterfields and Lucky Strikes.[165]

But as Jonathan Daniels had broken with the white supremacist tradition of his father, so the black women working in "the rough preparation of tobacco" were beginning to deliver themselves from the burdens of their pasts.

If women, black and white, had begun to define themselves as part of a class opposed to the capitalists and patriarchs of Durham, we must turn back again to their journey into town. We must explore their roles as mothers and midwives to a class being born in the workplaces and the streets, their initial entry into the factory system, and their eventual participation in the organization of their class. Yet we must chronicle this process without overlooking the complex social divisions between the "Negro women" and the "white girls." Granny midwives could aid white mothers in delivering their babies while still observing the taboos against whites and blacks eating together; against greater odds, a single class could be incarnated in a world segregated by race and gender.

VI
IN
THE
FACTORY

On arriving in Durham, rural migrants ventured into an urban landscape that bore marks of the same forces that had uprooted them from the land. The railroads curving through the city's heart and the factories bordering its tracks constituted the most prominent landmarks in the man-made environment. Finding work placed the newcomer in the social hierarchy. Bessie Taylor arrived by train in bare feet and a nightgown when she was eight years old and took a position in the Erwin spinning room after her father asked her to choose between work and school. She lived in a mill house in West Durham and grew to womanhood in a tightly controlled community where W. A. Erwin was "like a Daddy" to her.[1] Five days after her arrival in Durham with her two children and mother, Hetty Love stood in line at a tobacco factory gate where black workers were hired "by the number. Some people didn't get on and they have to come back another day . . . I was just lucky like that and got in."[2] Martha Gena Harris, a fifteen-year-old white girl, got a job at American Tobacco through a family acquaintance who worked as a forelady, a common route into the prized jobs in the tobacco factory.[3] Esther Jenks found employment easier to secure in the job-hungry 1930s because her father's skills as a loom fixer gave her family bargaining power with employers. Born, educated, and employed in a succession of mill villages, Jenks never developed the personal loyalty to a single mill manager that was shown by the less transient Bessie Taylor.[4]

The frequent moves made by Mary Burdette in pursuit of better working conditions revealed the economic plight of a young woman who depended on her own earnings to support her family. Leaving one small mill village because some "of the people weren't desirable neighbors," Burdette came to Durham with her sister. Through a friend she found work in a tobacco factory, but "could hardly breathe, the tobacco dust was so thick." "Taking the next job I heard of," Burdette started making bags at Golden Belt before quitting to return to school "with the hopes that I could finish some day." Forced to take a job, she worked at the Golden Belt cotton mill. The wages were lower than the bag mill, and "the people dipped snuff and spit on the floor," a custom begun as a protection against cotton dust but which distressed her. "As soon as they had an opening," Burdette returned to the bag mill, worked for several years, and quit when the overseer ordered her to work at night. Clerking at a jewelry store tided her over the Christmas season; she then found work at the Durham Hosiery Mills as an inspector. Promoted to forelady, she told her interviewer in the mid-1920s, "I expect to keep on working in the cotton mill, but I hope to be able to change the working conditions soon."[5] Prodded by family needs, economic necessity, and the absence of more attractive alternatives, women sought jobs in Durham factories in a process complicated by the biased hiring procedures of the white men who dictated company policy.

■ Whatever their origins, women and men employed in the mills and factories became industrial workers. In that bruising encounter with the power of managers, the relentless pressure of machines, and the discipline of factory whistles and time clocks, workers were produced along with cigarettes, hosiery, and cotton cloth. Managers, foremen, overseers, and second hands translated the abstract reality of capitalist power into factory discipline. Often locally born and bred, they incorporated existing patterns of authority and divisions of labor into the industrial labor process.

Patriarchal authority, the widespread adherence to a sexual division of labor, racial segregation, and black subordination to white authority offered ways to divide and control the labor force. Yet traditional patterns and institutions could not be mechanically reproduced in the factory setting. A textile mill and the surrounding mill village, however superficially they resembled a plantation, differed in purpose and personnel.[6] Subjecting white people, especially adult men, to paternalistic authority subverted longstanding tradition in a society where such subordination had been acceptable only for an inferior race and a submissive sex.[7] Although the traditional allocation of certain tasks as "men's work" and "women's work" appeared suited to factory production, the rationale behind the divisions was weakened by the actual similarity between the jobs and the powerless position of most men as well as all women.[8] The recruitment of young white women into the tobacco industry, where blacks were employed in large numbers, presented risks of a contradictory sort. The potential for racial confrontations was obvious. On the other hand, having blacks and whites work under similar conditions made class-based alliances more possible. Thus, despite divisions already embedded in the work force, managers did not always find it easy to deal with individuals "fresh from rural independence" who could be correctly described as "loyal and tractable" and "at the same time, restive."[9]

Managers never operated in a cultural vacuum. Their strategies were constrained by economic competition, by popular notions of justice and morality, by their own attitudes toward race, gender, and class, and by their exposure to contemporary theories of management, profit-making, and labor relations. Workers' values might concur with managerial views on some issues, but when workers came from a different social milieu, the potential for misunderstandings magnified. For example, the Duke decision to import about 125 skilled Polish cigarette rollers from New York City in the early 1880s led to explosive ideological clashes. The class- and craft-conscious New Yorkers instructed their coworkers in socialist theory and stirred up a public debate about the methods used by the Dukes to discipline employees. They objected to "tyrannous shop rules," child labor, and the whipping of children, and they also resisted efforts to transform or speed up their customary way of production.[10] After the Bonsack cigarette-making machine reached operational efficiency, the Dukes replaced the malcontents with "our own people," who were made to understand "that their situation in the factory depended upon their attendance or membership" in the "fine churches" established by the Dukes.[11] Later episodes, however, suggested that Christian harmony did not always prevail in Durham factories.

Nonetheless, the emphasis on religion was useful in counteracting some of the risks entailed in employing local whites, especially women and children, rather than relying on all-black or all-male labor. The entrance of young white women into the public workplace also proved controversial. Southern society was particularly troubled by the prospect of white women being made vulnerable to predatory males of either race. The sexual behavior of poor whites and blacks had long been suspect, and the mill villages and factory towns were perceived as breeding grounds for promiscuity. "Daily contact" might lead black men in particular to become "bolder and less respectful" to white women.[12] Because Durham employers believed that chastity was linked to the diligence and obedience they wanted in their employees, they pledged to maintain a "moral" work force of "respectable" young ladies only.[13] Strict sexual abstinence for unmarried women became a standard part of factory discipline.[14] Mere suspicion of sexual misbehavior could lead to dismissal, a policy that continued to be enforced into the 1930s.[15] No such anxiety applied to black female employees, who were assumed to lack the purity of white womanhood. This assumption was entirely congruent with antebellum attitudes. Employers not only failed to guard the virtue of their black female employees but tolerated their sexual exploitation by white foremen. Indeed, Ernest Seeman's exposé of Durham and its financial geniuses, whose fortunes "were grounded in low-priced labor," portrays Tysander Warham (Brodie Duke) as consorting with "his high-yellow mistresses up over his factory."[16] Factory morality, like its antebellum predecessor, divided women into pure and impure by color, while striving to convince white public opinion that factory work created no moral stigma for virtuous white women.

Workers sometimes found this paternalist ideology congenial. Many female employees took satisfaction in belonging to a moral community and "a higher class of people."[17] The same code protected white women at L and M from the sexual harassment endured by black women, and even encountered by white women at American Tobacco, where "love birds" received favors from management.[18] Workers sometimes turned paternalism to their advantage. The Erwins, the Carrs, and other officials grudgingly came to accept "local traditions about days on which work could be done."[19] During revivals or church homecomings, God was served before Mammon; on other days, the circus, funerals, or electioneering came before a day's work at the factory. Nor could employers always successfully enforce their rules against drinking, gambling, premarital sex, or other transgressions. Laws requiring two weeks' notice before quitting, or forbidding one mill from enticing another mill's employees, might slow a textile family's ability to move but could not eliminate that method of protest. Indeed, mill managers who wished to keep a stable labor force learned to pay careful attention to employee morale. They invested money and time in schools, playgrounds, milk stations, libraries, recreation centers, and other facilities—but carefully avoided the word *welfare*, whose connotations were disliked by Erwin workers because "they like to feel independent."[20]

There were always ways to avoid authority. Courting couples who wished to violate the Erwin edict against cuddling at the movies could venture into Durham rather than attend free showings at the Erwin Auditorium. Sympathetic coworkers might conspire to protect an unmarried pregnant woman from the Erwin policy that required the expulsion of her entire family from the village.[21] Indeed, as management recognized—by its practice of placing industrial spies in the factories in the 1920s and 1930s—workers were able to disguise their activities and opinions from the most watchful employers.[22] Black workers were particularly adept at this. Schooled by decades of racial oppression, they mystified their supervisors by practicing the ethic of never lying "except to white people."[23] When questioned about the impact of a child labor law on their black employees, for example, the superintendant and foreman for the Imperial Tobacco Company rather helplessly replied, "One can never tell about negroes in that respect." On the other hand, these comments also reflected sheer callousness because they argued that eliminating child labor was an advantage for white children but not for black—even though "there is no future for a child in this business."[24]

Despite minor setbacks, managers successfully used elements in the workers' cultures to adapt them to factory life. Religion was one important tool. Another was white supremacy, which employers catered to by excluding black workers or limiting them to "Negro" jobs, thus making common cause with their white employees on the issue. Although the Carrs, at least in one hosiery mill, defied the edict against allowing blacks to operate machines, most Durham employers honored the "color line."

The belief in clear distinctions between "men's work" and "woman's work" was yet another cultural imperative. Specific industries and companies chose different approaches to the definition of particular jobs as "women's work." Textile managers gave women the "light" work of spinning, weaving, and associated tasks, while men performed the "heavy" work of opening cotton bales and carding, the "skilled" work of fixing the looms and sizing or dyeing the cloth, and the "responsible" tasks of supervising other employees. Hosiery officials believed that "girls can become loopers but they do not make good knitters." Like bag making and sack stringing, looping was believed appropriate for married women in their spare time. As one Durham hosiery manufacturer explained, "They can work at night after their children are put away in bed and their household work is over."[25] Thus the sexual division of labor took account of women's specific responsibilities for reproduction and domestic work, while providing employers with an ample supply of cheap labor.

The leading tobacco companies in Durham differed in the work they assigned men and women, but in each case the division was assumed to be a necessary consequence of the sex's unique characteristics. A policy of employing white women as packers began in the Duke factory in the 1880s and was continued by Liggett and Myers, who took control of operations in 1911. White women continued to operate the packing machines at L and M while white men ran the "making" machines that actually produced the cigarettes. The American Tobacco Company, the successor to the Blackwell "Bull Durham" firm, imposed another division of labor when its officials resumed production of cigarettes in the 1910s. White men ran the making and packing machines, while white women assisted the men by "catching" and "weighing" cigarettes or operating the sealers. In the stemmeries, hand jobs were usually performed by black women, while black men hauled, lifted, and ran the shredding machines and presided over the blending and redrying operations. Such practices gave black women the overwhelming majority of jobs in the leaf and stemming departments, while black men were restricted to work as helpers, odd jobs, "floating gang labor," and cleaners.

Although a few black men broke through the color line during wartime when labor was scarce, employers dismissed them after the war because the "public" opposed the opening of skilled work to blacks.[26] The possibility of employing still lower-paid black women to operate machines did not occur to Durham employers, even though their presence on the same floor with white women might have proved less objectionable to whites. Apparently gender was more important than race in determining who should be allowed to operate machines.

There were important differences in the production processes of tobacco and textiles. The tobacco industry wholly incorporated the racial and gender hierarchy that placed white men on top and black women at the bottom. In textiles, however, production flowed horizontally. The industry lacked sharp distinctions between prefabrication and fabrication or between hand and machine labor; this fostered a less segmented and vertical labor process than in tobacco. While weavers, whose occupation lay at the center of textile production, might be men or women, operators of cigarette-making machines were almost exclusively white men. White women tobacco workers either operated auxiliary machines or assisted the men. Black workers also assisted or worked in prefabrication departments such as the stemmery. In hosiery, men were the knitters and women looped. In all three industries —textiles, hosiery, and tobacco—white men controlled the flow of material either through direct supervision or through work as loom or machine fixers.

Class also shaped the factory hierarchy. Management positions, particularly at the higher levels, were allotted to those with family connections, access to capital, and educational credentials readily available only to members of wealthier families. Although it was possible to rise from the ranks to become second hands, foremen, and supervisors, few men rose higher. The progress of Kemp P. Lewis, a college graduate in 1900, who worked his way up the Erwin organization to assume the presidency in the 1930s, exemplified the career pattern for management in the textile industry.[27] American Tobacco and Liggett and Myers followed a similar model. American's managers, however, unlike those at L and M, often were drawn from outside the South.

A visitor to a typical tobacco establishment in Durham might begin in the redrying plant, where black men fed the leaf into a redrying machine operated by white men. After the leaf was dried and cooled, black men would pack it into hogsheads and store them in warehouses for the two- to three-year ageing process. Aged tobacco was "rehandled" by black women "pickers" who untied the "hands" of tobacco, picked out trash and removed dust, and placed the leaves on a moving belt. Black female "orderers" tied the leaves on racks before steaming added moisture that permitted them to be stemmed without disintegrating. Then "shakers" shook out the leaves, "sorters" arranged them by size, and the leaves were stemmed. Black women usually stemmed the leaves when they were done by hand or fed the leaves into a stemming machine operated by a white man. After machine stemming, the leaves were inspected by black women who looked for ones

IN THE FACTORY

that the machine had missed. Black men presided over the flavoring, blending, and shredding of the leaf. They then transported and perhaps fed the shredded leaf into the hopper of the cigarette-making machine, which was operated by a white man. A white woman, but sometimes a white man, caught the finished cigarettes, placed them in a tray, and sent them to the packing room. Before packing, white women would inspect, weigh, and count the cigarettes. White women or men would run the machines that wrapped the cigarettes in foil, then packed, sealed, labeled, and stamped them.[28] An alert observer would note that the various tasks were assigned in accordance with traditional southern assumptions about gender and racial abilities.

The classification of tasks in the tobacco industry was a long-standing arrangement. Black women filled positions that they had begun to enter in the 1850s, if not earlier (see Table 14).[29] Sketches of the performance of these tasks in 1900 or in 1880 could have been used to illustrate a monograph on antebellum industrial slavery. For that matter, the description in a 1907 U.S. Senate investigation of women and child wage-earners could have applied to Durham workers fifty years before:

> The stemmers or strippers, who are usually women and children, sit at their work which consists of removing the stem and midrib of the leaf by hand . . . In some of the factories it tended to become a family

Table 14.
Division of Labor between Black and White Female Tobacco Workers in Durham, 1900

OCCUPATION	ALL WOMEN (%)*	WHITE WOMEN (%)	BLACK WOMEN (%)
Maker	10.0	14.0	0
Operator	8.0	10.3	0
Packer	39.0	59.0	7.4
Picker	3.0	1.7	0
Bag stringer	3.0	13.8	26.8
Stemmer	24.0	0	53.5
Laborer	4.0	1.7	2.5
Stamper	9.0	0	9.8

*N = 99 women.

SOURCE: 12th Census of the United States, Population Schedules for Durham City and Suburbs of Durham, 1900, samples taken from Manuscript Census, National Archives (see Appendix for description of sampling techniques used).

occupation, mothers bringing their children or young workers, their younger brothers and sisters.[30]

Photographs of black women seated on boxes surrounded by a sea of dried tobacco leaves demonstrated that similar conditions continued into the 1920s, when a survey in Durham and Winston-Salem reported that blacks performed the unskilled labor and whites monopolized the cleaner, skilled machine work.[31]

A more detailed examination of the tobacco industry in 1935 also focused on the central role played by race and gender. The study noted the industry's dependence on female labor and reported that more women than men relied on it for employment. The comparison between the division of labor in 1900 and in 1935 reveals a segmented labor process in which blacks were highly concentrated in a few areas, while white men, with a few rare exceptions, retained the skilled and supervisory work (see Tables 14 and 15).[32]

A range of attitudes about race and gender in the hosiery workplace is revealed by comparing a 1910 photograph of black female hosiery workers in a black-owned mill with descriptions of conditions in other Durham factories. In the black-owned mill, neatly dressed black women stand beside the machines they operated. Neatly, even fashionably dressed women and children sit sorting, turning, and folding the coarse work socks they produced. The black proprietors, dressed in starched wing collars, vests, and business suits, stand in the background, exuding an air of pride and respectability. This vignette from the short-lived black effort to compete with white capitalists portrays black women workers in dignified and self-respecting postures.[33]

The descriptions of black hosiery workers given by white supervisors in a Carr mill were generally negative. As in the black-owned mill, black women, now called "girls," operated the machines that knitted either the tops or the feet of coarse socks. Although the tasks required considerable dexterity to ensure that the pieces could be joined, the foremen disparaged black women's skills. One of the Carrs told a visitor, "Negroes have to be prodded all the time to keep up production and quality. They seem to lack a sense of reponsibility." The supervisors described themselves as "kind but severe"; they took care that their workers would "know who is boss."[34]

Yet the report of a young white woman also employed by the Carrs at another mill in the mid-1920s suggests that racial attitudes weren't the only reason for the management's condescending policy toward employees. The worker described a "horrible place" where women worked eleven hours a day perched on high stools while tobacco-impregnated saliva covered the floor. The women topper had to keep up with the male knitter, "and if you let a machine wait, of course he loses as well as you. I have sat half days at a

Table 15.
Specific Occupations of Tobacco Workers by Race, Sex, and Skill, 1935

OCCUPATION	ALL JOBS (%)	WHITE MALE (%)	WHITE FEMALE (%)	BLACK MALE (%)	BLACK FEMALE (%)
Skilled	5.0	16.0	0	6.0	0
Foreman	1.1	3.5	0	4.3	0
Semi-skilled	95.0	NA	NA	NA	NA
Stemmer, hand	40.0	4.3	9.5	36.7	80.0
Stemmer, machine	5.2	0.7	1.7	1.7	10.3
Machine cutter	4.1	8.6	0	18.8	0
Making machine operator	8.8	43.5	3.0	5.1	0
Cigarette catcher	5.5	0	19.9	0	0
Inspector	7.3	5.8	23.0	0	0
Packing machine operators	5.9	15.1	1.8	2.6	0
Hand packers	3.1	0	10.8	0	0

SOURCE: Johnson, "The Tobacco Worker, A Study of Tobacco Factory Workers and Their Families," 2 vols. (1935), Industrial Studies Section, Division of Review, NRA/NA, 1:26.

time without even getting off my stool for water or anything in order to keep my machines from waiting."[35] According to Mollie Seagrove, who worked in the same mill, "We had a bossman, telling us what to do and what not to do. All men. I got along, the people that I worked with done pretty much like they were told . . . We never did have very much to say, we didn't have much room to talk. We had to work. I just took it and did the best I could."[36] Subjected to the tyranny of machine-paced production and the authority of male managers, women were schooled to obey by employers who were determined to maintain strict factory discipline.

Although numerous studies describe the "average North Carolina textile mill," no account has been found to describe a specific Durham example. In any event, the Durham mills are unlikely to have differed significantly from the ones whose portraits survive. From the picker room to the sewing room, between 25 and 50 percent of the occupations included males and females, but the rest were usually performed by members of a specific sex and age (see Table 16 for a typical division of labor for 1907). In the initial stage, white men and an occasional black man opened bales of cotton. White men then carded the fiber into loose strands. The next processes, performed by men and women, gradually drew the fiber into fine and tauter thread in a se-

Table 16.
Gender and Age Division of Labor in North Carolina Textiles, 1907

OCCUPATION	ADULTS OVER 16 (%)		CHILDREN (%)		TOTAL LABOR FORCE (%)
	MALE	FEMALE	MALE	FEMALE	
Doffers	2.5	0	71.8	0.4	9.0
Ring spinners	0.3	25.2	0.8	68.8	14.1
Scrubbers and sweepers	1.4	0	2.9	0	1.0
Speeder tenders	4.0	2.8	0.4	0.1	2.9
Spoolers	0.1	21.0	0	9.1	6.8
Weavers	1.9	21.6	5.9	8.4	16.7
Exclusively adult male jobs*	63.1	0	0	0	32.5
Others†	10.7	29.4	18.2	13.2	15.8

*Carders, pickers, slash tenders, loom fixers, supervisors.
†Creelers, beamers, spare hands, drawing-in hands, battery fillers, cloth room hands.
SOURCE: U.S. Senate, "The Cotton Textile Industry," vol. 1 in *Report on the Condition of Woman and Child Wage-Earners in the United States*, 61st Cong., 2d Sess. (Washington, D.C.: G.P.O., 1910).

ries of operations called drawing, slubbing, speeding, and roving. Then the yarn, now called roving, arrived in the spinning room where young girls presided in the early twentieth century, although older women gradually took their places by the 1930s. Boys, later replaced by young men, "doffed" the full bobbins of spun thread. Girls or women then ran the spoolers that wound the yarn from several bobbins into a single spool. Some of the spooled thread was moved to beam warpers before being inserted on the looms by females "drawing-in" the threads that would become the warp of woven cloth. Other spools were placed on the looms to supply the threads that would be the woof or filling for the cloth. Weavers, men or women, operated the looms. Subsidiary occupations kept the looms supplied with full bobbins. The loom fixers undertook the important task of keeping the looms in working condition. Then the cloth was inspected, cut, sewed, and packed for shipment. A few black men might work as laborers outside the mill, hauling bales of cotton or bundles of cloth, but only white men and women were employed in the rest of the operation before the Second World War. White male overseers, second hands, and section hands presided over them.[37] But the real power over the company's operations resided above them, in the main office where men like W. A. Erwin and K. P. Lewis worked.

■ Gender and race remained constant organizing principles in the industrial workplace, but the production process itself was continually subject to change. Impelled by the desire to compete and maximize profits, officials often introduced technological or managerial innovations that disrupted established patterns of work. These pressures forced managers to treat employees like "a part of the machinery which they operate," and parts could be changed or discarded as desired.[38] "The paternalistic personal style of management" that characterized factory operations in the 1880s and 1890s was gradually replaced by a "formal disciplined bureaucracy"; this process evolved out of the very success of a corporation as it expanded its production and its labor force.[39] A new generation of officials undermined the paternalist system built by the company founders. Economic crises and consequent layoffs also loosened the bonds between workers and employers.

The initial skirmish in a series of battles over control of the pace of work, job conditions, and hiring practices occurred in the tobacco factories in Durham in the early mid-1880s. The very decision to begin the manufacture of cigarettes necessitated a change in labor, bringing skilled white craftsmen in Durham factories for the first time. To cut costs, the Dukes and Carr tried to use the craftsmen to train local workers, but the slow pace of hand production frustrated their efforts. The Dukes successfully turned to mechanization and thereby solved problems of production and simultaneously eliminated the troublesome craftsmen. White women then entered the industry as a preferred source of labor.

After a period of relative peace, another conflict between workers and managers erupted in West Durham in 1900. Workers who assumed that they had the same right to organize as their employers learned about the realities of unequal power. Having observed the workers' defeat as a boy, the novelist Ernest Seeman later evoked the "bitter feeling of failure and frustration" pervading the crowd of evicted and hungry Erwin workers. The "deep dark shadow-stream of stench and curse" that flowed through the workers' "nights and days of bitterness" darkened his own feelings for the city and its industrial patriarchs.[40] But W. A. Erwin sensed only victory in his relentless crushing of the union. Relative calm once again returned to Durham's industrial communities.

The labor shortages precipitated by the First World War caused another upsurge in worker rebelliousness. Aware of their enhanced bargaining power and determined to force wages to keep pace with inflation, workers again tried to organize in Durham's textile and tobacco factories. When the post-war recession aided employer resistance, the workers fell silent once more. But the silence was soon broken in the mid-1920s when the Marvin Carr silk strike and the arrival of a unionized construction firm to build Duke University gave new impetus to organizing activities in Durham. The renewal of activism was only a prelude to a long period of open and covert battles between workers and managers in all three major Durham industries.

Conflicts in the textile industry were precipitated by management efforts to apply new methods developed in northern industries and business training schools. The prolonged crisis afflicting the industry had persuaded managers that reforms were essential for survival. In the early 1920s, Kemp P. Lewis of Erwin Mills and Julian S. Carr, Jr., tried offering workers incentives, improved recreational facilities, bonuses, and the industrial democracy plan established at Durham Hosiery Mills. As the crisis intensified, they exhorted their employees to give them "absolute cooperation" in a perilous situation that Lewis compared to war. Supervisors took courses in "modern production methods" and psychological techniques to keep workers "satisfied in the mill and in the homes."[41]

After the strike at the Carr Silk Mill in 1925, Durham's leading industrialists also combined in a secret alliance to combat union organizers. A strike at nearby Henderson in 1927 led the three companies to share the same industrial espionage agent in the 1927–1929 period. Beyond spying on workers, the alliance used bribery and an informant within the Tobacco Workers International Union at Winston-Salem fifty miles away to blunt the organizing of tobacco workers in Durham. The flamboyant campaign launched by Alfred Hoffman, an organizer sent by the national hosiery and textile workers unions to Durham in 1927, undoubtedly encouraged the local companies to close ranks.

As the crisis in the textile industry deepened in the late 1920s, K. P. Lewis and other manufacturers turned to modernizing the work process. Soon after a new system was introduced in the weave room at Erwin Mill No. 1, the weavers petitioned the management for the "same prices with the system as we received while the old system was in operation."[42] In effect, they were asking for the same sort of consideration from their employer that their employer had long demanded from them. The company declined the workers' request, which ran counter to the aim of reducing labor costs. By 1931 the new system also increased the workload for loom fixers, although it spared the women who worked as spinners because their low wages made human labor cheaper than new machinery. Such changes and the high-handed way in which they were introduced led to discontent among a previously loyal force.

Given the great financial resources available to the tobacco industry, tobacco workers faced even more rapid changes to accustomed patterns of working. Cigarette companies could afford to introduce new machinery as soon as the prototypes were invented. When the American Tobacco Company built a new plant in Durham in 1929, other companies were forced to invest in new machinery to keep pace.[43] Once again, technological change and managerial strategy affected the labor force. White workers began to be displaced or, if fortunate enough to keep their jobs, were forced to work faster. Black women, on the other hand, saw an increased demand for their labor but found themselves being paid lower wages for more work. Both groups of workers entered the 1930s with a growing distrust of their employers' motives and a deepening resentment over policies that treated them "like a part of the machinery."[44]

Although the economic health of the major Durham industries was strikingly dissimilar after the national economy plunged into the Depression, the companies continued to apply similar managerial methods. Ironically, the reforms implemented under the National Recovery Administration (NRA) accelerated the replacement of human labor with machines. Although the codes set up for the tobacco and textile industries allowed employers to pay southern workers at lower rates than northern workers and to pay lower wages for jobs held by blacks, minimum wage levels and maximum hours for the work week made mechanization attractive. Reacting to these pressures and to the example of Durham firms that collapsed (such as the Durham Cotton Manufacturing Company, the oldest textile mill, and Durham Hosiery Mills), K. P. Lewis insisted that Erwin Mills keep abreast of all technological and managerial trends. If Erwin did not, he warned the company's stockholders, it would have "more trouble fighting competition than ever before in our history." After bringing time-study men into the mills,

Lewis ordered new machinery and reorganized the work process to increase individual workloads. When workers responded with protests and walkouts, Lewis insisted on management's right to control production and issued stern lectures to the now enraged employees.[45]

In addition to the increasing speed of production in the late 1920s, tobacco workers faced employers ready to take advantage of the high rate of unemployment. A company memo issued by American Tobacco instructed its foremen not to "let sympathy" or a worker's long service persuade them to keep on a person "too old to be efficient."[46] Foremen, never known for their genteel language, used more brutal expressions in their efforts to accelerate production. They punished workers who produced flawed products with fines and with temporary or permanent layoffs. Complaints were often met with the suggestion that the dissatisfied could go elsewhere. Whether fueled by desperation or a desire to reap the full benefits of a strong industry in a weak economy, these company policies resulted in rising discontent among workers.

■ Workers' assumptions about their rights influenced the way they adapted to managerial power. Whether they acquiesced, rebelled, or broke beneath the strain depended upon expectations grounded in the past. Some workers, particularly middle-aged white men, could remember a greater "liberty of action" in the rural countryside.[47] Now they had to relinquish to company officials what little independence and control over their families they had enjoyed. Children and women, already accustomed to male control, made the transition to factory labor more easily than could adult men. The image of the thin-skinned, hot-headed, "'pore' but proud" millworker, prone to quit at the slightest infringement of his self-respect, entered the industrial lore side-by-side with an antithetical stereotype, that of the shiftless, broken-down male parasite living off the earnings of his wife and children.[48] Blacks, already innured to limited autonomy, were better prepared for a system in which "white folks are going to always want to be over you." Foremen demonstrated their power by attempting to "fumble your behind," by invading women's restrooms to roust out black women who had lingered too long, and by denying black women a "Miss" or a "Mrs." before their first names. Black women had to "press hard to hold yourself up" against overbearing supervisors and public opinion that classified tobacco workers as a "rough" lower class of people.[49] Defending one's self-respect risked the loss of a job. Some rebels resisted the degradation inherent in working "under a white boss," but they rarely kept a foothold in factories. After a fight with his first supervisor in a Durham tobacco factory, Rufus Mebane suspected that a "blacklist" kept him from securing another "public job." His wife, who accepted her situation at L and M without question or challenge, supported the Mebanes by her earnings.[50] The awareness that their families needed their wages encouraged everyone, even white men, to accept factory discipline. An old woman, recalling her feelings about beginning at Erwin Mills when she was nine years old, said, "Did I like my work? Yes, I liked it! I had to like it. I had to work."[51]

That women who arrived at Durham factories were more accommodating than men was probably an accurate reflection of their powerlessness. Yet some women were able to withhold their labor, thus enhancing their bargaining position. These women could more easily avoid a double or triple day; that is, simultaneous responsibility for wage labor, domestic labor, and reproductive activities. White women worked for shorter periods and with less frequency than black women (see Tables 17 and 18). The higher wages paid to white male workers were obviously an important contributing factor. The effect of cultural inhibitions is more difficult to substantiate but undoubtedly kept some women out of the labor market. Over time, the need for wages to support the family apparently diminished the reluctance to send white females into the labor force, but proportional differences between white and black female labor continued. Moreover, female employ-

Table 17.
Percentages of Females Employed in Durham, 1880–1930

FEMALES	1880	1900 URBAN	1900 SUBURBS/INDUSTRIAL	1930 URBAN*
14 and over	23.3	50.5	55.0	50.0
Black	31.3	67.5	59.3	71.1
White	9.0	41.0	53.8	38.5
Under 14	22.3	13.5	19.6	.6
Black	33.3	16.2	16.1	NA
White	0	11.5	21.0	NA
Household heads	14.8	67.6	23.8	NA
Black	20.0	78.9	60.0	NA
White	8.3	53.3	6.7	NA
Married	5.9	22.3	35.5	38.0
Black	11.1	39.0	50.0	NA
White	2.0	15.4	29.2	NA
N	118	1,111	324	19,574

*1930 figures for females aged 15 and older.
SOURCE: 10th, 12th, 15th Censuses of the United States, 1880 and 1900 sampled from (manuscript) Population Schedules for Durham and Durham suburbs, National Archives; 1930 figures from U.S. Bureau of the Census, *Occupations*, vol. 4 (Washington, D.C.: G.P.O., 1933) (see Appendix for description of sampling techniques used).

Table 18.
Characteristics of Employed Females in Durham and Suburbs, 1900

	AGE GROUPS								
CHARACTERISTICS	1–12	13–14	15–19	20–24	25–34	35–44	45–54	55+	N
ALL FEMALES									
% of each age group employed									
All	7.4	58.6	66.8	65.5	48.0	41.0	30.0	27.5	1,432
Black	10.1	51.9	70.8	75.0	55.2	67.3	53.3	47.6	504
White	5.7	62.8	61.4	62.4	44.3	24.0	20.0	20.3	928
EMPLOYED FEMALES									
% in each age group									
All	5.3	7.2	24.7	25.0	17.1	10.6	5.5	4.4	564
Black	6.6	5.8	21.2	22.4	19.5	13.7	6.6	4.2	241
White	4.3	8.4	27.6	27.6	15.2	8.0	4.3	4.3	323
FEMALE INDUSTRIAL WORKERS									
% of female tobacco workers in each age group									
All	4.0	11.1	33.3	23.2	17.2	5.1	3.0	2.0	99
Black	9.8	12.2	39.0	12.2	12.2	9.8	2.4	2.0	41
White	1.7	12.0	27.6	29.3	20.7	1.7	5.2	1.7	58
% of female textile workers in each age group									
All (white)	9.8	12.5	32.0	32.3	14.3	8.0	1.0	1.0	85

SOURCE: 12th Census of the United States (manuscript) Population Schedules, Samples for Durham and Its Suburbs, National Archives. (See Appendix for description of sampling techniques used.)

ment in Durham exceeded the national averages of 20 percent in 1900 and 23.6 percent in 1930 by more than 20 percentage points even among white women.[52] The "family wage" enabling a male breadwinner to keep his wife out of the labor force did not exist for the majority of Durham women.

In truth, wage levels in Durham were abysmally low. In 1890 the average male operative received an annual wage of $274, adult females $163, and children $93. The presence of large numbers of extremely low-paid black tobacco workers brought the wage levels for that industry still lower: men earned $212 a year, women $111, and children $66. Ten years later the wage levels had declined at both the city and state level; an influx of desperate tenants and indebted farmers had presented employers with enough labor to reduce their payrolls. Now Durham's adult male operatives earned $258, adult women earned $154, and children under fourteen earned $95. At the state level, tobacco wages had fallen to $166 for men, and risen to

IN THE FACTORY

$140 for women and $70 for children. The state's textile workers were receiving $216 for men, about forty dollars less than the average Durhamite and about the same as the Durham wage for women and children. At these levels, the pooling of income became an economic imperative, transforming the family wage into the family wage-earning economy of two, three, or four workers per family.[53]

In the early twentieth century, after industrial expansion had absorbed the readily available labor supply, wage levels rose slightly. Wage schedules for the hosiery, textile, and bag workers employed at Golden Belt in Durham in 1904 averaged $320 per year for adult men, $220 for adult women, and $130 for children under the age of sixteen for a work week of sixty-six hours (see Table 19). Even so, these low wages meant that a family needed at least three members in the mill to achieve a modest income of less than $600 per year.[54]

Although no wage data differentiating the earnings of black and white tobacco workers are available before the late 1920s, black workers always earned less. A black household might send three or four wage-earners into the tobacco factories and still live less well than white textile workers who

Table 19.
Golden Belt Manufacturing Company Wages, 1904

EARNINGS PER WEEK	EMPLOYEE TOTAL	MEN	WOMEN	CHILDREN UNDER 16
Under $3	140	0	60	80
$3–4	65	0	40	25
$4–5	121	24	52	45
$5–6	174	8	92	0
$6–7	145	90	55	0
$7–8	26	5	21	0
$8–9	6	1	5	0
$9–10	15	13	2	0
$10–12	5	2	3	0
$12–15	1	1	0	0
$15–20	1	1	0	0
$20–25	1	1	0	0
$25+	0	0	0	0
Total employed	700	220	330	150
Average weekly wage	$4.69	$6.46	$4.46	$2.60

SOURCE: Manuscript Census Data for Week of 17 Sept. 1904, p. 4. Copy possessed by Southern Oral History Program, Durham Files, Department of History, University of North Carolina. Average weekly wage is calculated from this data.

enjoyed subsidized housing and other amenities available in the typical Durham mill village. Black households, especially those headed by women, found that sending "every hand old enough in the family to work" was an economic necessity.⁵⁵ Despite the rise in wage levels during the early 1900s and the period of war-induced labor scarcity, even more privileged households headed by white males found it difficult to live on the income generated by a single person. As industrial wages spiraled downward in the 1920s and early 1930s, the three- or four-wage-earner household persisted as an economic imperative for many families. Census data for 1930 covering households of all occupational categories in Durham revealed that only 37.7 percent of black households subsisted on one wage-earner's income, compared to 53.7 percent of white households. The same data disclosed that 21 percent of Durham's black households and 15.8 percent of its white families placed three or more wage-earners in the paid workforce.⁵⁶ However, the impact of the prolonged textile crisis and the onset of the Great Depression makes this data harder to analyze. It is impossible to decide whether the households were expressing their preferences or were prevented by low demand from sending more members out to earn wages. In any case, the cost of living, estimated at more than $1,400 for the average family in the early 1930s, could not be reached unless parents and children sought employment and pooled their wages. In August 1932, Erwin workers earned an average of 25 cents per hour, or an annual income of less than $700 if they worked a full fifty-five hour week, fifty weeks a year. Predominantly female job categories varied between the 20 cents an hour paid to spinners and inspectors to the 30 cents an hour paid to weavers; male occupations received from 21 cents an hour for new workers employed as oilers to the 40 cents paid to loom fixers. Many textile and hosiery workers lost their jobs altogether when some Durham companies collapsed during the prolonged crisis of the 1920s and 1930s.

By the mid-1930s, Durham workers employed in the "depression-proof" cigarette industry, who earned the highest average annual wages paid to white men, still required two wage-earners in a household to secure a modest standard of living. Annual incomes for white men reached $726, white women earned $646, black men $543, and black females, more frequently unemployed, $430.⁵⁷ The work assigned to particular racial and gender groups explained the differences. Jobs usually given to black men, such as "pack-up boy," "job hand," "lump capper," or "sacker," paid 30 to 32 cents an hour in 1934, or $600 a year for full-time work. White women's usual jobs as "catchers," "weigh girls," "sealing wrappers," or "relief girls" yielded annual wages of between $600 and $720 a year, while the highest paid woman, the inspector, earned about $800—compared with the $1,000 that a white male inspector took home for similar duties. The white men who ran the making machines took home only slightly less than male inspectors, since at 45 cents an hour, their annual income amounted to $900. Black women, however, in their most typical job category as stemmers, received $375 a year. Since much stemming was seasonal, these wages were subject to more frequent interruptions than in the more stable parts of the production process.[58]

Industrialization affected everyone in Durham, but it seems to have led more white women than black into the labor force. Before tobacco factories began recruiting white females in the 1880s and before textile mills existed, the figures from the 1880 census reported that very few white females worked (see Table 18). By that year, black women had begun working in the local tobacco factories, but the majority were employed elsewhere. By 1900, as traced by the remarkable rise in white female employment, white girls and young women had entered the factories of the Dukes and the Carrs to work as packers, stampers, inspectors, and operators for the now-mechanized production of tobacco bags. White girls and women had also found jobs as spinners, weavers, speeders, creelers, doffers, beamers, spoolers, warpers, and winders in the local textile mills. The manufacture of hosiery also offered work to white women and, after 1904, offered limited employment to black women. Black female employment in the tobacco industry had grown in response to the stepped-up pace of production, which demanded a larger quantity of stemmed tobacco. In addition, other women continued to work at home assembling tobacco bags—a process that had entered the Durham vernacular as "tagging the bulls," because each bag was completed by attaching a Bull Durham emblem to the string. White women and some girls also supplemented their income in this way.

There seems a clear connection between the demographic characteristics of women workers and industrial employment (see Table 18). More than 60 percent of all black female tobacco workers were under twenty, and more than 70 percent of all white female tobacco workers were under twenty-five. White females in the textile industry were still more youthful: almost 90 percent were younger than twenty-five in 1900. When all working women were considered, industrial and nonindustrial alike, the average age began to rise: fewer than 35 percent of all black women workers were younger than twenty; more than 32 percent of white female wage-earners were older than twenty-five. The overall age structure of white working women, however—but not black working women—closely approximated that for industry. Once again, it seems that white women's employment was more influenced by industrial demand. If we compare the percentage of industrial jobs to the total jobs held by female workers, the same result appears: 17 percent of black jobs compared with 44 percent of white. A higher proportion of black women changed occupations over their lifetimes, while white women, after a short period in a textile, hosiery, or tobacco factory, concentrated on their own households.

White women, protected by white male earnings, were employed chiefly between puberty and their mid-twenties. In their old age, even as widows, white women were less likely then black women to seek paid employment. By contrast, black women's employment usually extended from early puberty to old age and was only marginally eased during the childrearing years. For white females, the factory was a relatively attractive way to support themselves or contribute to their family's income before setting up housekeeping with their husbands. Black women also preferred factory work. The combined effect of racial and gender subordination was to reduce their choices to those between back-breaking factory labor or domestic drudgery in white households. A scene outside the American Tobacco plant in the late 1940s captures the reality of white power. A white official emerged to observe the job seekers, who stood in a broiling sun hoping to secure a temporary position. The man, said a young girl who was there to seek her first job in the factory, smiled in satisfaction to behold "the sea of black women struggling forward, trying to get a job in *his* factory" (my emphasis).[59]

Less visible than the exploitation of black women by white employers was the gradual convergence of black and white women's participation in the labor force. True, black women were hired only on the "tobacco side" while white women monopolized the jobs on the "cigarette side," but by the 1930s both groups were more likely to be married women in their middle years. White women as well as black were balancing fulltime occupations as paid workers, housewives, and (in many cases) mothers. The demographic characteristics for both Durham's and North Carolina's female textile and tobacco workers from 1930, 1935, and 1940 reflected the same trend (see Tables 20 and 21). In part this trend represented a shift of wage-earning work from the shoulders of the young, including children, to their mothers. Child labor, under pressure from legislative controls, increased technological complexity, and progressive reform movements, began to disappear from the official payroll records, if not from the actual workplace, by 1919 (see Table 22).[60] As child labor declined, the percentage of females older than fifteen began to rise. Apparently the fall in wage levels after the brief wartime surge encouraged more women to take industrial jobs. In 1900, 40 percent of Durham's female wage-earners had worked in manufacturing; by 1930 that figure had climbed to 55 percent. Although the percentage of Durham's total female employment had not increased by the 1930s (a time of high unemployment, after all), the women who retained their jobs were more mature and experienced (see Table 21). Jobs had become more precious in a time of economic insecurity. In 1934, for example, the average white male tobacco worker had experienced 5.5 weeks of unemployment, the average black male tobacco worker 8.3 weeks, the average white female tobacco worker 8 weeks, and the average black female tobacco worker 11.8

Table 20.
Marital and Age Status of the Female Workforce in North Carolina Tobacco, Hosiery, and Textile Industries, 1920–1940*

INDUSTRY	1920				1930				1940			
	MARRIED	15–24	25–44	45+	MARRIED	15–24	25–44	45+	MARRIED	15–24	25–44	45+
Tobacco	42.0	52.3	38.7	8.9	57.9	43.5	48.0	8.5	66.8	22.9	69.8	6.2
Textile	33.6	65.5	29.7	4.8	48.9	55.8	37.1	7.1	71.8	27.8	63.6	8.6
Hosiery	20.9	62.0	24.8	6.2	43.7	63.5	31.0	5.5	60.8	NA	NA	NA

*In percent.

SOURCE: U.S. Census of Population, 14th, 15th, 16th Censuses, 1920, vol. 4, *Occupations*; 1930, vol. 4, *Occupations*; 1940, vol. 3, *The Labor Force* (see Appendix for publication information).

IN THE FACTORY

Table 21.
Status of Female Tobacco Workers in Durham Factories, 1935

STATUS	ALL	BLACK	WHITE
% Married	48.0	52.0	41.0
% 15–24 years of age	33.0	31.0	39.0
% 25–44 years of age	55.0	58.0	48.0
% 45 and older	11.0	10.6	2.0
Average years employed	12.7	12.3	13.3
Average years in tobacco industry	10.4	9.3	12.4

SOURCE: Charles S. Johnson, "The Tobacco Worker: A Study of Tobacco Factory Workers and Their Families," 2 vols. (1935), Division of Review, Industrial Studies Section, NRA/NA/DC, 1:386, 390–91, 398.

weeks. Less than 50 percent of black workers and 40 percent of white workers believed that their jobs were secure.[61] In this fashion, the 1930s saw the emergence of a biracial, female industrial working class whose commitment to paid employment more closely resembled the male pattern.[62] While black and white women continued to work in different places and assume different family responsibilities, their experience of class relationships in the formal workplace had become increasingly similar. The wage-earning couple was becoming the core of the working-class family economy in Durham.[63] As elsewhere in North Carolina, black and white women traveled

Table 22.
Percentages of Women and Children in the Industrial Labor Force in Durham, 1880–1938

LABOR FORCE	1880	1890	1900	1909	1919	1930	1938
Total workers	943	1,703	4,144	3,699	5,977	11,417	7,813
% Adult female	22.6	19.2	40.0	29.2	28.6	40.3	41.9
% Children	27.3	16.9	13.9	23.5	12.0	6.9	0

SOURCE: 10th, 11th, 13th, 14th, 15th U.S. Censuses of Manufacturing, 1880–1930. Figures for 1880–1900 are for Durham County; figures for 1909–1938 are for Durham City (see Appendix for publication information). 1938 figures from North Carolina Departments of Conservation and Development and of Labor, *Industrial Directory and Reference Book of the State of North Carolina* (Washington, D.C.: Works Project Administration, 1938).

daily between their paid and unpaid workplaces. Perhaps their journeys had finally brought them to a common destination.

■ Measured against any objective criterion—occupation, income, workplace, economic position, actual or potential husbands—working women in Durham had been members of an industrial working class since the 1880s. If they earned wages only for brief periods, they lived off the wages of husbands, fathers, brothers, or children while caring for present and future workers. Owning no property, not even the houses in which they lived, they embodied the classical definition of an industrial proletariat. They lived by selling their labor power or by sharing in the income generated by other workers' sales of their only valuable commodity. Employers paid them considerably less than the value of their product, and profited from their unremunerated labor in the household, which kept down the cost of subsistence.[64] Exploitation in Marxist (and some non-Marxist) senses was clearly their lot.[65]

Moreover, these women lived in relatively close contact with their employers. They could see, in the words of one child worker at Erwin Mills, that the "mill officials didn't live as we did, that there were different standards of living, and that, although wages were not raised, the mill was making money." They experienced the snobbery of "certain people because they had money and we had none."[66] Some inhabitants of West Durham found a way to ridicule such snobbery. "Monkey Top" was their name for the Erwin mansion that their employers called "Hilltop." Towering over West Durham and the hollow area called "Monkey Bottoms," where the outcasts of the mill village were exiled, "Monkey Top" signified both awareness and disdain for the powerful men who controlled their lives. Some workers, particularly those employed by Erwin Mills, were subject to the "sedative effects of paternalism," which sought to transform "power relationships" into "moral" obligations between benevolent superiors and deferential subordinates.[67] The sting in the subordinates' humor suggested that even industrial paternalism could not stifle a knowledge of the "boundaries between them and us."[68] If so, then Durham possessed the raw materials for an "active and conscious conflict" between the classes.[69]

Yet, "raw material" does not by itself create class consciousness.[70] When the issue concerns black and white working-class women in the South, the complications multiply. These women's identities were rooted in three coexisting sets of relationships: sex, race, and class. Each relationship conditioned the others and, as a consequence, the boundaries between "them and us" were elastic. Inequality between the sexes, the races, and the classes was usually portrayed as the natural result of moral, biological, or racial differences.[71] The prevailing exchange between the social groups was often defined as legitimate—"free and fair."[72] In this context, black and white working-class women had difficulty perceiving the parallels in their common situation.⁷³ Although manufacturers generally exploited racial antagonisms, the peculiar history of the South aided their efforts. Furthermore, women's domestic responsibilities tended to isolate them from formal or informal discussions that can create a sense of common identity. Women remained closely tied to the private, "natural" household headed by a male who served as his family's intermediary with the public world.⁷⁴

Workers' comments about factory life afford us glimpses into how they perceived their experiences. In some cases, these exercises in "self-discovery" (a term borrowed from Karl Mannheim) led them to embrace one or another form of group consciousness (e.g., class, race). Sometimes the worker defined her identity by membership in some other group, such as the respectable, God-fearing people—or the converse. Others, avoiding social categories altogether, emphasized their identity as wives, daughters, parents, pragmatic survivors, or solitary rebels. Unfortunately, the historical record before the practice of oral history records little of women's perceptions. The available sources from the 1880s to the turn of the century reveal the sentiments of male workers but not those of young white or black women. Thereafter, the records become more inclusive, but are still weighted toward the male perspective. Even oral histories, despite earnest efforts, sometimes fail to topple the social barriers between interviewer and subject. Black people and white women demonstrated particular reticence in interviews conducted by comparative strangers, particularly if the stranger also differed in race or sex.⁷⁵ Nevertheless, oral history adds immeasurably to sometimes skimpy written sources.

Although women do not speak for themselves in sources from the 1880s and 1890s, the documents disclose the conflicts that enveloped workers as they dealt with the disruption imposed by mechanized production. In the mid-1880s the skilled handworkers imported from New York and their like-minded Southern colleagues sent bulletins northward warning about the "horrors of the Bonsack cigarette-making machine" that "takes the bread out of our mouths."⁷⁶ By the late 1880s, other male craftsmen joined in protest over the "condition of working people" in Durham, which was "rapidly growing worse on account of the rapid introduction of labor-saving machinery." Another man, who condemned the system that put "women and children of many families" to work "while the men are unemployed," revealed the contradictions of the crisis. Other statements added a new dimension. A black brickmason referred to the "despotism on the part of those mechanics who like to employ all white men and not give the colored mechanic a fair showing"; a white man lamented that "the laboring people are at war with each other."⁷⁷ This man added his hope that workers would eventually recognize their common interests, although the bulk of testimony into the twentieth century suggests that they never did.

IN THE FACTORY

By the early twentieth century, the record began to reveal the opinions of women. Their observations offer clues concerning the absence of worker rebelliousness. Survival itself often absorbed all their energies; one black man recalled his early childhood:

> The winter was so bad, they couldn't get no wood and coal in, so she'd go way back yonder where that hosiery mill used to be and work. We children would be wrapped up in bed, and she'd come back with a great pan of food and stuff. There used to be a hosiery mill right there on the corner of Duke Street. They worked night and day. She'd work over there and come in at night.[78]

The reactions voiced by some Durham mothers and children to the child labor law in 1918 conveyed a matter-of-fact understanding of their economic situation. A white mother told a government investigator:

> When you're raisin' children you ought to work them all you can. Heap of them marry before they're 14 . . . A child of 10 or 11 years old ought to work in [the] mill—raised myself to work ever since I was 9 years old. It's no more harm to work in the mill than loaf on streets.[79]

Mary Mebane described the way her mother adapted to factory life:

> This was her routine—fixed, without change, unvarying. And she accepted it. She more than accepted it, she embraced it; it gave meaning to her life, it was what she had been put here on this earth to do. It was not to be questioned. To Nonnie this life was ideal; she saw nothing wrong with it. And she wondered in baffled rage why her daughter didn't value it but rather sought something else, some other rhythm, a more meaningful pattern to human life.

Other children more readily complied with their parents' wishes—believing, as Theotis Williamson did, that "people just should be satisfied with what they get."[80] Having accustomed themselves to limited choices, many women instilled the same resignation in their children.

Women who never learned as children that they were "bound to work or starve to death" could acquire that knowledge as adults. Annie Mack Barbee, the child of a family who came to Durham out of rebellion against white racial domination in rural South Carolina, felt that entering into a Durham tobacco factory had led her into a trap from which she never escaped:

> But a young woman going in a place like that to work, you never get anywhere in your goals, you just get up there and work and then it becomes habit forming. You just work, work. A lot of 'em did . . . It's all right to go there and get some money for awhile but once you get there and get stuck, you don't try to go nowhere, you just stay there.[81]

IN THE FACTORY

The "urgency of livelihood" and the fear of reprisals led many to censor their thoughts in order to keep their jobs. Soon, the acceptance of "humbling" became second nature.[82] Factory life tended to reinforce parental lessons concerning the dangers of rebellion or anger. Resentments, if allowed to surface, could lead to arguments between workers or to open defiance of a supervisor. Intense heat and humidity in the mill or factory did not help. Fights broke out. Sometimes knives were drawn. Jessie Ervin described an incident that began with a dispute between a female weaver and a battery hand, and ended when the battery hand "cut another man that wasn't even involved in it." She added, "It didn't happen very often, [but] sometime a very small incident like that will trigger a big bang." Fighting sometimes cost women their jobs and, as one woman remarked, "the times would be very tight then."[83] Some workers harassed their own subordinates as a way to relieve frustration. Others chose an approach that allowed them to vent their feelings and also win favors. They were the "white man niggers," "stool pigeons" who told management about the transgressions of their fellow workers; some of these "thought the overseer was a little tin god." These workers helped management "keep tabs," and "tended to your morals and everything else."[84] Claiborne Peavey recalled how supervisors used high unemployment in the 1930s to silence discontented workers: "If you went up to the foreman, he'd fire you, if he wanted to. When I sued to try to get a raise, he'd tell me, there's people out there in the street who'll work for less than I'm paying you."[85] A still more vulnerable black stemmer, after calling her foreman "as fine a white man as I ever seen to work for," added, "I'm looking to be laid off any time. I certainly am worried 'cause I ain't got nobody, not a soul in the world. They liable to tell you to go home any time. I been lookin' for it." Since doing what you were told and working for a white man offered the only job security, it was not surprising that many workers accepted "their ill fortune when it came as lamentable but unavoidable."[86]

The popular belief that tobacco and textile workers deserved their fate because they lacked the character or intelligence to do anything else increased the difficulties of developing pride or group solidarity. Some workers separated themselves from others by stressing their superior morals, their better education, or some other symbol of prestige. A black schoolteacher, working at American during the green season, "earned the wrath of the whole floor" by her airs and threats to inform on "one of the 'girls' for not doing her job properly." Other black workers responded to a negative stereotype by fulfilling it. They boasted about their sexual prowess and carried themselves in such a way that coworkers and bosses alike understood that they weren't to be "messed" with.[87] Although the sheer numbers of workers in Durham sheltered them from some of the snobbery prevalent in a city like Raleigh, where "the people . . . in town didn't have anything to do with the textile people," ranking systems still persisted. One white daughter hated the summer she worked beside her mother at L and M because "some people who knew that you worked in a factory might look down on you."[88] She took advantage of the high school education she had received in the Methodist orphanage to become a clerical worker. Similarly, a woman who resented the snubs of townspeople looked down on the "low-grade people" who lived in Monkey Bottoms.[89] White women at L and M described themselves as a "higher class" of people than those who worked at American, where a few women were rumored to trade sexual favors for better treatment on the job.[90] Workers thereby assuaged their own humiliations while reinforcing the power of their employers.

Racial antagonisms drew white workers toward their employers while teaching black workers to distrust all whites, regardless of class. Men were involved in the most explosive episodes. Charlie Decoda Mack, a black worker at L and M in the late 1920s, remembered working "with a cracker and they loved to put their foot in your tail and laugh. I told him once, 'You put your foot in my tail again *ever* and I'll break your leg.'" Yet blacks did not maintain a united front in the face of white oppression. "We have a lot of white man niggers up there. You do something in the street and he know it Monday what you done out there. That's Uncle Tom folks."[91] But women did not avoid racial conflicts. Constantly abused verbally by a white coworker, a black woman at American finally responded to her attacker, "You'd be a son-of-a-bitch if your feet matched." Laughter silenced her antagonist. A white woman who betrayed her sisterly regard for her black coworkers earned the epithet of "nigger lover" and learned to keep her heretical views to herself.[92] Black workers in one Durham factory believed that white workers had conspired to get one of their number fired because he owned a later model car than whites liked for a black man to own. Whites expressed satisfaction with black workers as long as they weren't "impudent" and "did what they were told" without argument. White feelings of superiority were reinforced by factory etiquette that forbade the use of titles before a black worker's name, approved the use of "boy" and "girl" to address them, assigned them separate and usually inferior facilities, and gave them menial jobs in any area where they might coexist with whites. The general white insistence on keeping blacks firmly beneath them taught most blacks to "know white people—and the best way is to have nothing to do with them."[93]

Even so there were developments that countered the tendency toward fragmentation on the basis of race or other competing loyalties. Despite all attempts to deflect workers' attention from their class identity, discontent continued to produce an awareness of class inequities. In the early years, desires among white male workers to "do something and be somebody" could be satisfied by promoting them to the managerial ranks, but the new emphasis on hiring college-educated men set limits on that solution. Education might offer some working-class children an escape from the factory but few parents could afford the sacrifice. Shifting from one mill to another was a way "to get away from the sordidness of things," but the move offered more novelty than dramatic improvement.[94] As paternalist bonds began to fray during the economic crises of the 1920s and 1930s, workers discovered that they were expendable in the eyes of a more distant management.[95] The sale of mill village houses, a practice begun by the financially troubled Durham Hosiery Mills, made visible the erosion of personal ties between company and employee.[96] In West Durham the death of "daddy" Erwin and the accession of "businessman" Lewis symbolized the growing estrangement between restless, discontented workers and an anxious management determined to survive the economic crisis. Finding that maintaining the "personal element" imposed too many restrictions on their freedom to act, Durham's managerial class placed their faith in mechanization and bureaucratic controls.[97]

The passing of industrial paternalism coincided with growing restrictions on migration as a way for workers to improve working conditions. As layoffs, wage cuts, and short work weeks undercut job security, white workers shared in the insecurity previously reserved for black workers. Those who had jobs considered themselves lucky. Quitting, once a bold gesture of defiance, now verged on the suicidal. Aware of their new power, supervisors became increasingly abusive. Even when curse words, "bawling out," and occasional kicks were not company policy, the relentless pressure of faster-paced machinery forced workers to meet steadily rising production quotas. Blacks continued to endure more rigorous supervision. One embittered white worker observed, "They like the nigger better, pay him less, treat him worse, kick and curse him around, and the nigger'll take it."[98] The painful irony of the Depression meant that the white worker in the 1930s faced a similar deterioration and she was also expected to "take it."

Government sponsored minimum wages and maximum hours favored the replacement of human labor by machines. A black stemmer at L and M reported on changes in her factory:

> They put in all them automatic jacks and things since I been there. That's why they cuts off so many people. They got machines there, I don't know their names, but I hear them say they got machines there that do as much stemming as twenty people. I'll tell you, don't write this down, I don't think it's right to put in them machines to take work away from us poor people.[99]

The faster work speed increased tensions. According to a fixer, the pressure wracked up the nerves of the white female packers at L and M: he reported that "they jump all to pieces" when spoken to unexpectedly. Another fixer, employed in a Durham stemmery, described black women "pressed to make $10 a week":

> This 12,000 an hour on No. 1 bright tobacco is compulsory. They have got to produce that or find out why. And, if that machine was properly fixed and properly adjusted, and I O.K. it, she has got to do it or she has one more hour to hold her job, one hour. That is a fact. Any time that any woman is supposed to perform her duties does that, they do not argue. They are out the door.[100]

Remembering the same era, a white woman expressed the anguish she felt as a male coworker sobbed while being reprimanded harshly by a supervisor. He couldn't reply to the foreman because he needed his job. A supervisor threatened a cigarette inspector at L and M, "Damn your soul, if you don't watch your work, I'll kick your fanny off," in the presence of her shocked coworkers and her husband.[101] Although the level of personal invective was lower in the textile industry, workers grappled with demands of the "stretch-out system," which increased the workload without increasing the pay. Petitions described the "load they have on them and the speed with which the machinery runs" and asked Lewis to "meet us half way," but there were no positive changes. If the death of W. A. Erwin had represented the end of paternalism, the Depression blew away the last lingering faith in that system.[102]

While employers might have been able to suppress employee protest by exploitation of the labor surplus and the skillful use of reprisals, they faced yet another source of danger. Now, as the public lost faith in business leaders, an activist administration had taken control of the federal government and sought to balance the interests of workers against those of management. Durham workers seized the chance. A cutter at L and M wrote a letter directly to President Roosevelt complaining about managerial practices:

> And if we don't run good, they are ready to bless us out. They are putting in some new improved machinery and speeding that. Please help us if you will for they are making millions and millions of clear profit every year. They tear machines up and put them back down in the same place so as to keep from paying so much income tax. Please do not let any one see this letter for if they found out I wrote you, they would fire me before dinner tommorrow. Burn this letter up after you have read it. If you don't think that I am telling the pure facks, let one of your men investigate it. This is at Liggett and Myers. Please forgive bad writing and spelling. H. C. Hall[103]

Disgruntled black women, disappointed in the inadequacies of the National Recovery Administration code for the tobacco industry, directed their complaints to researchers sent by the NRA into Durham in 1935:

> NRA or no NRA, they are not going to give us the money we earn. The firm would do anything to keep you from getting that $14.00 a week. Do you know you're subject to get fired for any little thing? They will send you home for 10 days or three weeks if you stem over 20 pounds ... If you are doing more than they want to pay you for, the boss will come around and find all manner of fault and act just as hateful as he can. That makes you nervous and scared and then you naturally can't do as well and that naturally makes you slower.[104]

More ominous in the eyes of the Durham employers was the section in the NRA act that pledged government protection for the right of workers to organize. If workers began to believe that the law of the land supported them, what could stop them from bargaining for higher wages and even skimming a share of decision-making power?

Growing estrangement induced even once loyal workers to devise schemes against their adversaries. The repertoire of sly tricks, mutual self-protection, and subtle defiance helped them to resist the bullying supervisor or the relentless pace of the machine. As Jessie Ervin observed, Erwin workers found ingenious ways to "beat the clock" used to time their movements:

> Believe you me, they learned ways to beat. They could do something to the clock to make it go as fast as all get out. Run that loom without a warp on it, and make the clock run, different gimmicks. I never did go in for that sort of thing myself, much. It was too much trouble for one thing; for another, I was usually on an hourly job.[105]

Humor could serve as a weapon for the quick-witted. Reprimanded for having shut down her machine to go to the toilet, a white American worker told her boss, "If the Lord had intended me to ask permission, he'd have put a stop watch on my you-know-what."[106] The thrill of that moment remained with one worker who'd heard the retort more than forty years before. Explaining how her coworkers would "carry" a slower colleague, Mary Bailey recalled one moment of triumph:

> My bossman called me one night when we were going out to supper. He said, "Mary, you know some of them people you're working with ain't doing nothing. You're doing their work and yours, too. How come you don't tell me?" I said, "Listen, you didn't hire me to tell you who was working and who wasn't working. You hired me to work. Now if you want to know about them people not working, you look and see for yourself, cause I ain't telling you nothing." He told all the rest of the bossmen, "You needn't ask Mary nothing, cause she ain't gonna tell you nothing." I laughed and he laughed and went off.[107]

Black workers had also learned to set limits on the abuse they would take from white colleagues. One black tobacco worker would "cuss them out" if whites "start calling me 'boy'." A black woman recognized that "if you don't stand up and demand respect, they won't give you nothing. You have to demand it. And let 'em know you willing to pay the price to get it."[108] As the interests of workers and employers came increasingly into conflict, acts of individual resistance might inspire a search for more collective methods of demanding "respect."

It would not be easy to unite. The same black woman who insisted on keeping her self-respect also knew that "white folks is mean and nasty." Her experience at L and M had etched that understanding deeply in her mind. "You're over here doing all the nasty dirty work. And over there on the cigarette side . . . The white women over there wear white uniforms . . . And you're over here handling all that old sweaty tobacco . . . There's a large difference."[109] White women, dressed in clean white uniforms, believed just as firmly that there was a "large difference" between themselves and black women, a difference that must be preserved. They clung to their privileged status without doubting their moral and racial superiority. One of their number, unselfconsciously, spoke about seeking a way "out of slavery" for white workers without a thought about her more downtrodden sisters.[110] The bitterness of one woman and the complacency of the other were consequences of the system that divided them. Each in her own way stood up for herself, but they remained estranged.

Another Durham woman, the daughter and the neighbor of many tobacco workers, eloquently summarized the internal barriers that reinforced the external obstacles to the formation of a conscious and cohesive class:

> The constrictions, the restraints, the hidden threats that we lived under, that were the conditions of our lives, inevitably produced mutations in the natural human flowering. To me we were like plants that were meant to grow upright but became bent and twisted, stunted, sometimes stretching and running along the ground, because the conditions of our environment forbade our developing upward naturally.[111]

According to Mary Mebane, too many victims preyed on each other or repressed their own anger in order to survive.

Ernest Seeman, another sympathetic observer, saw only "dull anger and despair" coming out of workers' futile efforts to refuse "to work on the mill owners' terms." In his bleak vision, Durham's factories would "forever fabricate and roll out from the workers' sweat and toil . . . the dividends for their absentee owners." He saw them as the helpless victims of the greed and cunning of their employers, "snapped-up and tumbling into the hopper's trembling vortex" that fed "the gigantic machine process" that had created Durham. These workers could only remain "spellbound by all the clatter and technological din" while progress and prosperity remained the possession of a tiny few.[112]

Bessie Buchanan recalled a dream that echoed Seeman's nightmarish vision. In the dream she was seized by a group who threatened to throw her into a "lions' pit":

> I asked them, "Why are you doing this to me? I never joined a union in my life." And so, one of the girls said, "Can you prove that . . . There's a gang of men with these knives . . . going this way, and if you can walk down that line and not get killed, I'll let you out of here." I just said, "Lord, go with me." And I went down. I never heard so many people hollering at you . . . You could see the women on the outside just hollering at you. But I walked down that line and I was not harmed. And when I got out, I was the only person out, 'cause I hadn't joined a union . . . I never joined and I always felt like it was a vision that the Lord gave me.[113]

Her dream placed salvation on one hand, solidarity on the other. The class-conscious members of her community became the malevolent harpies of her nightmare. A picket line, perhaps remembered from the 1934 strike, was transformed into a gauntlet from which she was the only survivor because she "hadn't joined a union." The implications of that dream could chill the hope of the most optimistic believer in working class resistance.

Any organizer attempting to mobilize Durham workers had to transform their "silent acquiescence" into "intelligent discontent."[114] Workers had to be convinced that salvation was possible through collective effort. Racial fears and hostilities had to be overcome. Considering the large numbers of female workers, an organizer had to convince his feminine listeners that class-based organizations led by white men could advance their interests without threatening their respectability. He had to pursue the allegiance of these women by going into the communities and the households where they labored after their stint in the public workplace. Like this imaginary organizer, we must enter the segregated neighborhoods of working-class Durham so that we can listen to the voices of Durham women speaking about their hopes and fears. Only then can we begin to understand the forces that were creating a class that was beginning "to grow upright."[115]

VII
THE
OTHER
WORKPLACE

> The womenfolk of [Durham's] mill villages, however—of its cotton-mills and tobacco mills, of the niggertowns, in the "City of Opportunity"—went on, of driven necessity, amusing themselves at the washpot and the cooking pot. Hacking the dull blade of a hoe into their leisure time from the loom or the long hours in the stemmeries. Weeding in the bean vines and collard patch to hold the wolf away a little longer from their scuffed and broken doors. Dropping their clothes to quench their squalid menfolks' lust; having also the tugging pap-lust of their too-fast-arriving excrementitious young to dance attendance upon.[1]

The "driven necessity" that Seeman refers to was the product of the class, racial, and sexual subordination of Durham's working women. Once a staunch believer in the "Foremost City of the New South," Seeman turned heretic as he observed the yawning gap between rich and poor. Moreover, Seeman understood the economic imperatives that impinged on women's lives both in the formal workplace and in the "poverty-struck and stenchful" neighborhoods surrounding the factories.[2] As Seeman makes clear, there were other workplaces in Durham besides the red brick buildings crowned with gothic arches. Before the morning whistles beckoned factory hands to work and after the machines had ceased for the evening, women labored in small frame houses, shacks, and rows of identical mill housing. Black women and girls, when the factory didn't require their labor, often performed "day's work" in homes of more affluent white tobacco or textile workers. On Sundays and after their household chores were completed, some women carried on the "Lord's work"—which was understood to be women's work: attending services, teaching Sunday school, collecting money for missions and charity, visiting the sick and the dying, converting sinners, and offering spiritual counsel. On Saturdays and evenings they did their shopping; "toting the pocketbook" had become women's work in an urban world where household needs were mostly purchased. Women's leisure hours often involved the tasks that connected family and friends: visiting on the front porch, gossiping, preparing festive meals, nursing sick relatives, sheltering needy kin, adopting orphaned children, and overseeing births, weddings, and funerals. Some women also found time to catch a movie downtown or listen to a blues musician on the street. As Seeman suggested, however, "leisure time" was scarce.

While carrying on these essential but generally unpaid tasks, Durham women also assumed major responsibility in the birth and rearing of children.[3] Through interaction with their children, they taught skills and values to the next generation of workers. Others, primarily females, assisted in the child-minding and socialization. Most childcare was conducted on an unwaged basis, but sometimes mothers without willing relatives or neighbors would pay another woman for those duties. Women thus oversaw major social relationships in which personal identities were formed.[4]

Men—fathers, husbands, and employers—vied for the right to control female sexuality. Some women, primarily young unmarried women, were required to remain chaste. Shotgun marriages were one method for forcing sexually active couples into respectability; gossip acted as another check. Sexually-experienced girls and women were labeled "bad" or "fast." It was a rare person who, like Ernest Seeman, left any sympathetic record of the plight of women who earned their living in Durham streets. Meeting a young black prostitute, Johnny Anders (Ernest Seeman's fictional self) "saw in his mind's eye the devil that was driving her" and understood that she'd been "sent out to bring back some money or take a beating . . . And he knew there were many other young skinny girls, wilding things, and not all of them black, out in [Durham] tonight trying to bring back a little money." Gangs of young men exercised informal controls over female sexuality by their regulation of courtship. Young men from a different neighborhood would be "rocked" if they dared to call on a local girl.[5] To be considered respectable, a female had to become the exclusive sexual property of her husband; men's sexual behavior was never equally restricted. Men often seduced females without assuming responsibility for their partners or offspring. White men claimed sexual access to black women both inside and outside the factory; employers ignored or condoned the sexual exploitation. The rape of a black woman by a white man was rarely treated as a crime. In general, then, cities recreated the sexual values of the rural South.

There were other parallels between the rural past and the urban present. Although urban women were more likely to be the family purchasing agents (consumers, in the modern sense) and to bear fewer children, their identities remained crucially linked to their household duties. The household also supplied one of the few acceptable areas for encounters between women of different races: the black maid or washerwoman relieved her white female employer (possibly a wage-earner like herself but better paid) from some burdens of housework. White women thus shared in the privilege of exploiting black labor.[6]

The sheer hours that a working-class female passed in the household and surrounding community influenced her understanding of the world and her place in it. The socialization that she acquired as a child occurred within an environment that tangibly expressed the configurations of power and wealth. Segregation by race and class was a central organizing principle. The earliest maps recorded the tobacco manufactories scattered along the railroad tracks, identified the location of the small houses of black tobacco workers, and listed the white farmers who shared ownership of the land with the manufacturers. Later maps of the 1880s and 1890s depicted mill villages rising on the eastern and western flanks of a small city. An artist who drew a "Bird's Eye View of Durham" in 1891 graphically captured the dominance of the railroad tracks that carved paths through Durham's heart. In one corner of the map, he sketched a scene that exemplified the relationship between industry and city. An enormous mill loomed above rows of tiny, neatly aligned houses that appeared to prostrate themselves before the god that begat them.[7] The image speaks volumes about the reverence accorded industry and its capitalist entrepreneurs. The physical contours of the city's ridges, hills, flats, and creek "bottoms" enabled wealth to occupy the "high ground and poverty . . . the low," after a brief period when the mansions of the Dukes and Carrs had lined the railroad tracks.[8] Seeman described the higher ground, the "large houses and well-groomed lawns, where several of its richest and most righteous rajputs and masters of machinery lived." He also described the "undesirable and disreputable edges, dumping brinks and smelly sewage brooklets" where black washerwomen and factory workers clustered.[9] In this setting, women located themselves spatially and socially.

The neighborhoods of working-class Durham mirrored the differences in wage levels based on race and gender, the contrasts between mill village housing and rental dwellings purchased on the open market, and racial segregation. Where a person lived also symbolized her respectability in a society that believed that success was a reward for the virtuous and failure a punishment for the dissolute. A low-lying area populated by bootleggers and gamblers, Buggy Bottom was known as a dangerous place after dark. Living precariously between Monkey Top and Monkey Bottoms, West Durham residents prided themselves on their position among the respectable. One Erwin worker mused in 1938, "A person don't ever know what they'll be brought to in this life, but I sure hope I'll never have to move to Monkey Bottom."[10] Pauli Murray, the granddaughter of once-prosperous black brickmakers, lived on "a hill just above the Bottoms," but "of course, my family would never admit we lived in the Bottoms. They always said we lived 'behind Maplewood Cemetery,' but either choice was a gloomy one." Observing the shacks that housed her neighbors, often tobacco workers, Murray described West End as "an odorous conglomeration of trash piles, garbage dumps, cow stalls, pigpens and crowded humanity."[11] With quiet irony, Murray described her family as trapped between the Bottoms and a "whites-only" cemetery—despite her aunts' education, her grandmother's connections to a wealthy planter family, and her grandfather's former success. Millworkers lived in West Durham, East Durham, and Edgemont—in descending order of prestige and according to the company that employed them. By virtue of their higher wage levels, white tobacco workers, particularly in households that pooled incomes, could live in neighborhoods intermingled with middle-income and lower-income residents. Black tobacco workers lived in separate areas. Most lived in Hayti, the largest black community, which was located across the railroad tracks from the American Tobacco Company and the Durham Hosiery mill that employed black workers. Other blacks lived in the small pocket ghettos of Hickstown, West End, East End, Lyons Park, and Walltown. A few workers commuted from rural areas. Yet the expense of automobiles meant that most workers, white and black, lived within walking distance of their workplaces into the 1930s.[12]

By the 1920s and 1930s, the impact of class and race on access to housing was clear. A study of black life in Durham in the late 1920s contrasted the well-kept homes of the businessmen and clerical workers with the inadequate housing stock of the "laboring class." The survey noted "rough, unpaved streets," unpainted houses, drainage "so bad that it constitutes a considerable health hazard," the lack of garden space, the inadequate facilities for heating and lighting, and primitive or nonexistent plumbing.[13] Another study conducted ten years later judged about 60 percent of Durham's housing stock to be "substandard." The worst of it was located in black areas like Hayti, East End, West End, and Hickstown, but the mill village housing in Edgemont and East Durham (by then privately owned) had also deteriorated. In a comparison of white and black rental housing, only 12 percent of the 4,725 black dwellings, but 45 percent of the 6,235 white dwellings, were considered adequate. With an average income of less than $20 a week—the combined wages of a black tobacco workers couple—black families could afford rents only in ramshackle duplexes erected perhaps forty years before. White tobacco workers were more often able to pay the $25 per month that promised satisfactory housing. But even when blacks and whites paid the same rent, the blacks received inferior housing. Unemployed mill workers and residents of areas once owned by the failing Durham Hosiery Mills, the bankrupt Durham Cotton Manufacturing Company, and parts of West Durham like Monkey Bottoms, added to the large numbers of the poorly housed. Overall, one-fourth of Durham's children lived in buildings "unfit for use."[14] The children of black and white tobacco workers fared better; only 8 percent of black households and 2 percent of white households were classified as "unfit for occupancy" in a comparison done in 1935. Although black tobacco workers were less likely to live in houses labeled "good" (39 percent of white houses compared with 18 percent of black), they were better off than other "laboring class" blacks.[15]

■ Inadequate housing made domestic labor and the care of a family more difficult. Insufficient heat during winter, poor sanitation, inadequate diet, and overwork contributed to malnutrition, tuberculosis, typhoid, pneumonia, diarrhea, and great susceptibility to influenza, measles, and other contagious diseases. These, coupled with the dust, heat, and humidity in areas of the tobacco factory where most blacks worked, contributed to a black death rate nearly double that of white Durham. Death and sickness exerted an additional toll on women who nursed the ill and suffered the emotional consequences of losses. As housekeepers, women found that dust and mud from unpaved streets made cleaning an endless chore. In West Durham a black employee cleaned out the village privies in the early twentieth century until indoor bathrooms were installed in the mill village; the majority of black tobacco households, however, lacked bathtubs, inside toilets, modern utilities like electricity and gas, and all "essential equipment" for modern living except running water into the mid-1930s. It was left to housewives and relatives to substitute their labors for the modern technology that was available to more privileged members of society.[16]

In the late nineteenth century, an increasing number of mothers with children under five years of age began to enter the paid labor force (see Table 23). Perhaps the added pressures were responsible for declining rates of fertility. Between 1900 and 1940, rates of employment for married women rose as the rates of births declined. By 1940, black and white women resembled one another in their wage-earning and maternal activities. Obviously, women took advantage of both more reliable information and techniques to control fertility (see Table 24). The rising costs of childcare (influenced by the declining demand for child labor, laws requiring school attendance, and the need to purchase food, clothing, and shelter) probably encouraged this trend. Rather than struggling with three jobs—paid employment, domestic labor, and childrearing—Durham women increasingly were occupied with only the first two.

Another factor that may have contributed to a declining fertility rate was the decreasing opportunity for women to earn money at home. Black women were accustomed to taking in "a little laundry," but the introduc-

Table 23.
Percentage of Women Employed Having Children under Five Years of Age for Durham and Industrial Suburbs, 1880–1900

MOTHERS*	1880	1900 URBAN	1900 SUBURBAN
All	11.4	27.7	43.9
White	5.2	15.3	31.6
Black	18.8	51.1	36.0

*N = 245.
SOURCE: 10th, 12th Censuses of the United States, 1880, 1900 (manuscript) Population Schedules for Durham City and Its Suburbs, National Archives, Washington, D.C. (see Appendix for description of sampling techniques used).

Table 24.
Number of Children under Five Years of Age per Woman of Childbearing Age* in Durham, 1880–1940

WOMEN	1880	1900	1920	1930	1940
All	.33	.59	.35	.34	.22
Housewives	.47	.60	NA	.47	NA
White	.52	.53	.37	.38	.22
Black	.16	.72	.28	.15	.23

*Women between 14 and 45.
SOURCE: 10th, 12th, 14th, 15th, 16th Censuses of the United States, 1880, 1900 figures from (manuscript) Population Schedules for Durham, National Archives; 1920, 1930, 1940 figures from U.S. Census of Population, published volumes, for Durham (see Appendix for description of sampling techniques and publication information for published volumes).

tion of appliances and the impact of the Depression limited that alternative. Caring for boarders was another way to increase family income (see Table 25), but the limited returns for the amount of work required made it unattractive:

> My mother cooked for boarders. Gave them a hot dinner. A lot of people would come out of the mill and have dinner with us, and they'd pay

THE OTHER WORKPLACE

Table 25.
Durham Households Keeping Boarders by Race of Household, 1880–1930

HOUSEHOLDS	1880	1900 URBAN	1900 SUBURBAN	1930
All (%)	18.8	23.0	19.0	21.0
White (%)	9.1	19.1	NA	NA
Black (%)	27.8	30.7	NA	NA
N	68	301	100	11,478

SOURCE: 10th, 12th Censuses of the United States, 1880, 1900 figures sampled from the 1880 and 1900 (manuscript) Population Schedules for Durham, National Archives, Washington, D.C.; 1930 figures from 15th Census of the United States, U.S. Census of Population, published volume, for Durham (see Appendix for description of sampling techniques).

my mother a little something. 'Course it wasn't much because we weren't making much . . . She cooked on a wood range where you could burn coal. The mothers had a hard time. When we were in the country, she did all our knitting for us, stockings and things. We didn't know what it was to have a storebought pair of stockings. Even carded the cotton, spinned. In town she just bought material and made them. I never had the opportunity to sew. My mother always had a big garden, cows, chickens.[17]

Health codes and the growth of the city restricted a woman's ability to keep cows, chickens, or pigs to feed her family.

From the 1880s to the end of the 1930s, a unique form of domestic production enabled some women to work at home. In 1884 about 250 women took up the sewing of bags to hold Bull Durham smoking tobacco. After bag making was mechanized in the Golden Belt Manufacturing Company, women carried on subsidiary tasks. Bessie Buchanan occupied herself tagging bags for "spending money" the year she nursed her dying mother. A young and curious boy watched his poorer neighbors work at this occupation in the mid-1920s on his Durham street:

The Bull Durham tobacco was packed in sacks and used to sell for a nickle, and it was famous. The cowboy and pictures with a cowboy sack. But the round tag had a hole in it and you had the two loops, the strings that came out of the sack and the way they fastened it was to put one of those loops through that hole and then you looped it around . . . I guess elderly women or maybe women who had to work at home. I'm very conscious of this because we had a woman who lived a few houses up from us, a Mrs. Vickers . . . We would sit and she, just like people knit, would have a big croaker, a big burlap sack, full of the tobacco bags and another bag full of the tags. Like knitting, you could do it without thinking . . . It was sort of a pleasant occupation. You sat and talked. [Do you know how much she was getting paid?] I'm sure it was very little because I do recall when the minimum wage came in, the tobacco companies said that they couldn't afford to guarantee the minimum wage on this sort of thing. My recollection was that they said this was to keep older people occupied and it probably was.[18]

He was referring to the controversy over the impact of the Fair Labor Standards Act of 1938 that imposed a minimum wage and ended most forms of household production in the United States. After mechanization and the law eliminated this means for supplementing wages, rising numbers of Durham women entered the public workplace.

Many Durham women struggled through a "double" or even a "triple" work day. The rate of female employment among married and single women in Durham was substantially higher than the national average, and the numbers of employed women with primary responsibility for housework must have been equally high. Less than 40 percent of Durham's female working-age population were full-time housewives in 1900, and these numbers probably concealed many who were stringing sacks, keeping boarders, or otherwise earning wages (see Table 26). Nevertheless, male notions of what constituted women's work did not alter because more women

Table 26.
Distribution of Women's Employment in Durham and Industrial Suburbs, 1900*

SECTOR	URBAN	SUBURBS
Unpaid housework	39.2%	31.2%
Domestic service	21.4	9.5
Manufacturing	29.0	56.0
Other jobs†	10.4	3.0

*N = 802 women above age 12 and not attending school.

†Including seamstresses, teaching, clerical, sales, boarding, housekeeping, bag-making, and stringing.

SOURCE: 12th Census of the United States, 1900 (manuscript) Population Schedules for Durham City and Its Suburbs, National Archives, Washington, D.C. (see Appendix for description of sampling techniques).

earned wages. Even single female textile workers completed forty-five minutes of housework after an eleven or twelve hour day in 1907, and married women spent nearly three hours in the 1920s. A study of black tobacco workers in the 1930s discovered that 65.9 percent were "responsible for the provision and care of homes" while another 27 percent "had distinct home duties . . . to be performed after the heavy strain of the workday."[19] On a typical day, a black female tobacco worker rose at 5:30 A.M. to prepare breakfast, pack lunches, and get her family ready for work and school. After returning from the factory, "the mother has the night meal to cook, the laundry, cleaning, and care of the children to do; which, if she is conscientious, will take well towards midnight before it is completed." Another study reported that the "children were neglected because father and mother" struggled "daily to supply elemental wants."[20]

As a young girl, one woman remembered looking at the faces of weary tobacco workers trudging home with "the dust on their clothes":

> I would think how hard they had worked . . . for cheap prices . . . In the face of some, joy; in the face of some, distress. That was in the depression years . . . I knew some of them would be hurrying home . . . Some of those women after working all day had to go home to take care of families. It always bothered me to see that some had to work so hard to make a living. It didn't place a desire in my mind to work in a factory.[21]

Another observer identified the interplay between age, sex, and marital status that sent some Erwin employees home after "closing time," but allowed others to linger on street corners and sidewalks:

> The quiet streets become alive with crowding humanity. The young girls come in clusters, talking and laughing gaily. They are bareheaded, buoyant with youth and the love of living. A group of young men join them. There is more laughter, several pair off in couples and drop behind, walking slowly and the laughing chatter continues. The older women walk quickly, anxious to get home where the evening meal must be prepared and the ironing must be finished before they can sit down to the quietude of closed doors and the comfort of a rocking chair where they can sit and rest their work-weary feet—feet that all day have been standing beside the clacking looms. The older men linger on the street corners talking and smoking. Someone tells a joke and bass laughter mingles with the staccato voices of the girls further down the street.[22]

What awaited the women who hurried home was more work. Young girls began to contribute their labor to the household at an early age. Bessie

Taylor Buchanan, who started working at Erwin Mills at the age of eight, described what she did after the hours in the mill:

> I don't know, we just never had the chance to walk around and play. We was never idle. And then when we went home, we had a chore to do at home. We had to scrub the house and a whole lots of time we had a cow and chickens ... At that time there were hogpens in this section ... and we had to slop the hog and clean out the hogpen after we did all that work. We just didn't have time to do anything.[23]

Allie Ennis, who helped her mother "wash for white people" as a young girl, cleaned house, ironed, and cooked while her brothers worked in the garden that fed the eleven members of her family. When her father died, she left school to work full-time at domestic and occasional factory work.[24] To support herself and her youngest child, Wilma Couch carried on "light housecleaning" to supplement the low wages paid to white tobacco workers in the 1920s. Scanty resources caused the Couches to operate "on a shoestring with a bare minimum of furniture and appliances." Mrs. Couch cooked on an oil stove with a movable wick, kept food in a "primitive ice box," and washed clothes "by hand in a zinc tub" in the evening after work. Continually in search of cheaper accommodations, mother and son lived from "week to week." On special Sundays they visited her three older children at the Methodist orphanage in Raleigh.[25]

Mrs. Dena Coley, also a widow, attempted to support her two children on the still lower wages paid to black women by the same company that employed Wilma Couch. Earning $4 a week in 1919, she rose at 5 A.M. to carry her children across town to a woman who watched them for 50 cents a week. After a ten-hour work day, she returned home to wash, iron, and do other housework. A day might end after midnight as Mrs. Coley washed the windows.[26] Another black woman told an interviewer,

> All of the women who worked in the factories had to do the same thing ... They worked out all day long, then they would come home and look after their families, and looked after their houses. [So they had to work really hard?] Oh, yes, that's all some of us knew, most of us, hard labor ... All we knowed was hard labor and not much pay.[27]

It was no wonder that a visitor to black Durham detected a "tenseness" among its residents.[28]

Having children old enough to be useful did not always provide relief. After preparing her own breakfast, Nonnie Mebane left her only daughter in charge:

> My job after she left was to see that the fire did not go out in the wood stove, to see that the pots sitting on the back didn't burn—for in them

THE OTHER WORKPLACE

was our supper, often pinto beans or black-eyed peas or collard greens or turnip salad . . . The other pot would have the meat, which most often was neck bones or pig feet or pig ears, and sometimes spareribs. These could cook until it was time for me to go to school; then I would let the fire die down, only to relight it when I came home to let the pots finish cooking . . . After I got older we sometimes had meat other than what had to be prepared in a "pot." It would be my duty to fry chicken or prepare ham bits and gravy. After supper, she'd read the Durham *Sun* and see that we did the chores if we hadn't done them already: slop the hogs, feed the chickens, get in the wood for the next day . . . Saturdays were work days, too, the time for washing, ironing, going to the garden, preparing Sunday dinner . . . and always on Friday she went to the A & P on Mangum Street and bought her groceries . . . That was her routine—fixed, without change, unvarying.

And that routine led to quarrels between mother and daughter about "scorched food." The real issues, however, were the mother's exhaustion and the daughter's resentment of endless drudgery that left the young little choice but to "accept your lot just like the rest of us."[29]

If "sheer drudgery" drained the energies of many young women, it also taught them to accept the traditional divisions between the sexes. Children in these households accepted as natural a clearcut division between men's work and women's work. An observer who interviewed many former residents of Carrboro described the mill child's view of work:

They knew that there were some things men did and some things women did; there was no uncertainty. Women washed and ironed. Women sewed. Women cooked. Women preserved food for winter. Women were in charge of boarders. Men might cook, but they did not wash dishes, or wash clothes, or sweep or make beds. Men tended the livestock and worked in the garden. Men butchered the hogs. Men could milk; but it was the women's job to churn. Men did not wash children, but they could take them swimming in the creek. Men chopped wood and brought it into the house for the stove. Men went to the company pile to buy coal. Men trapped in the woods and fished to supplement the family's food supply . . . Small children tended the garden behind the house. But it was the boys, eight, nine and ten, who cut the grass. They chopped the firewood and brought the water from the well. Both boys and girls (five years old and up) watched younger brothers and sisters in the yard. Both boys and girls were sent to the store to shop for their mothers. Girls, eight years old and olde , washed the dishes and the clothes. Girls swept and dusted the inside of the house. They helped with canning and preserving. They learned to sew and cook . . . Women and girls made all of the family's clothes and sewed for other people. If there was an extra bed in the house, they took in a boarder.

Expending considerable ingenuity in "making things work and making things do," girls modelled themselves after their hardworking mothers and accepted the sexual division of labor as inherent in the natural scheme of things.[30]

While females remained tied to the household, the streets and other public spaces were male territory. Men patrolled, negotiated, and altered the social boundaries that demarcated neighborhoods, racial communities, and the middle places in which different groups mingled or fought. Men were more likely to "cross" or trespass into other men's territory. Older men conducted the formal negotiations: interracial discussions, political contests, petitions to employers, and the other meetings between different groups within the city. Young men were more likely to be involved in informal encounters, sometimes violent, that carved the urban space into enclaves, neutral ground, or contested areas. "Rocking" was one method of defending turf:

> People used to be clannish. A guy from one section didn't travel through the other sections, or he'd get his head whupped, get it tore up. They all kind of had a thing for guys from Hayti. You couldn't hardly go into North Durham, East Durham, or West Durham, unless you carried your soldiers with you. If for any reason they didn't like you, you'd come out of there hauling potatoes. White and black were the same way . . . You had to be good with your fists, throwing big bricks, or fast on foot, or you'd get a hole knocked in your head. I never had any trouble except going over here to the park, when the white boys and the black boys always tangled, because we had to go through their community . . . That was white versus black, in East Durham.[31]

In the 1920s, white men revived the Klan to control the public spaces of Durham. As elsewhere, the Klan arranged a march through the main streets of Durham in full regalia. The police, as one black woman suspected with fear, "were mixed up in them."[32]

There were lighter sides to male-dominated street life. The "hustles"—bootlegging, prostitution, panhandling—were important leisure activities in black Durham. Women who participated, however, would be criticized and could earn reputations for being "bad" or "fast."[33] The street was a place of male prerogative. In white sections, white women rarely ventured into the barber shops, the illegal bars, or other male haunts. Whether the street was a battlefield, a place to exchange jokes or ogle women, or an opportunity for illicit pleasures, it was no place for a virtuous woman.

Although men monopolized the positions of authority in Durham churches, the church belonged to the female world. Congregations usually included more females than males. Religion, moreover, was used by women as a way to woo men from the streets. The juxtaposition between the secular blues and sacred gospel music was one manifestation of the conflict between male and female views of the world. The small churches that attracted worshipers from the poor black community frowned on street life, house parties, and the music that flowed from both. According to a scholar of the Piedmont blues, the distinctive style in Durham, "There was no way that you could sing blues and be in the church. Some churches would throw you out . . . The blues were 'Devil music.'" In interviewing many blues players, he discovered that many of their mothers had adamantly opposed their music:

> There were a lot of children, people tell me that when they were being raised, they couldn't listen to blues in the house. None of the guitarists would play blues for their mother. It's almost a universal. If you ask them about how their parents felt about their being blues musicians, they'll start by telling you their parents were church-goers. Often the father, though a church-goer, would encourage his son, the mother would not. The mother would often not let him play blues in the house. Very often there would be a dominant female figure who was adamantly opposed to the music coming up in the early life histories of the musicians. A lot of people, when they join the church, either stop singing the blues, or switch . . . It was a cultural thing that women were more strongly involved in the church, I think. The blues and the church are two opposing world views. They could never get together.[34]

The existential realism of the blues ("the only one that is going to do anything about [my problems] is me") and the religious reliance on God's inexplicable will as the answer to suffering were weapons in a war between the sexes that was waged on the battleground of street and church. A study in nearby Chapel Hill noted that black women would seize the opportunity when men were sick or despondent to "save" them from sin.[35] "When God put a halter on them," declared a Durham woman active in a local church, men were ripe for conversion from the culture of the streets to the sanctity of home and church.[36]

Although no scholar has focused on the way in which white women used the church to domesticate errant males, the church's denunciation of drinking, gambling, and extramarital sex obviously aided women with unreliable husbands. Men who were "saved" were more faithful husbands, better providers, and more diligent employees, which was desirable for women, employers, and churches alike. In part, Erwin Mills' policy of monitoring employees' moral behavior was intended to impose industrial discipline on people accustomed to agrarian life. By firing a man who "stepped out" on his wife, dismissing young women who became pregnant out of wedlock, and routing bootleggers and other undesirables from West Durham, Erwin Mills formed a tacit alliance with women.[37] Sanctions for nonconformity were severe; a man's drinking, petty thievery, or sexual immorality could consign his family to Monkey Bottoms.[38] Alternatively, marriages might shatter because the woman continued to serve the Lord while her man preferred the Devil. Such was the experience of Martha Hinton, a boardinghouse keeper in East Durham. Through the debacles of a sexless marriage with a drinking, philandering husband, the premarital pregnancy of her rebellious daughter, and a grim struggle to raise her grandchildren in the strict code that she herself had embraced, Hinton took satisfaction in never having "failed the Lord."[39] Whether they cheerfully accepted their men's lapses, attempted to reform them, or resignedly pursued their duty, women could grasp religion as a weapon or a consolation.

Residential segregation marked the estrangement between racial groups. Black and white workers shared no common meeting places: churches, schools, clubhouses, parks, and athletic facilities were separate. Blacks entered white homes only in subordinate roles. While there, they were expected to honor all the taboos against common meals, use of white persons' first names, or any suggestion of challenge to a white decision. A white tobacco worker, seeking a suitable metaphor to describe how a foreman had treated her, said, "He treated me cooler than I'd treat a nigger in my house."[40] Another worker fondly remembered her family's black help:

> We had a relationship with the black families that lived nearby that was just great. They'd come over and help my mother with the washing and ironing . . . There was never no trouble. They stayed in their place. They'd help my mother cook and clean, but never would they sit down and eat with us. They would go and eat after.[41]

A less enthusiastic woman would not hire a cook because she "couldn't abide niggers in my house."[42] A textile worker was also reluctant to employ help when her mother was ill becase low-paid black domestics were reputed to "hit" their employers' groceries.[43] Whether these complaints were expressions of blind racism or practical recognition of the structural deceit built into racial relations, the attitudes accurately reflected the distance between the two groups.

White insistence that blacks never appear as equals created many tense situations. When the Durham Cotton Manufacturing Company sold its mill village, the real estate speculator who purchased the houses decided to rent to black tenants, who would pay higher rents than white textile workers had been used to. The sudden shift in racial boundaries rankled white sensibilities. Four white boys jumped a black youth outside a store. The victim's father returned to the scene of the incident with a gun. Four white men grabbed their guns and chased the black man. A white neighbor averted violence by calling police, telling an observer later that he bore "no hard feelings against the niggers for moving in. My feelings are against the white man that moved them in."[44] His rational attitude was unusual in the neighborhood during the summer of 1939. Having lost their jobs when the mill closed, the white men were even more determined to protect their cherished racial superiority symbolized by segregation. The landlord lived elsewhere; the blacks were on the scene and handy targets for white rage.

A mere bus journey between white and black parts of Durham could provoke violent encounters. In the late 1930s, a black man refused to move to the back of the bus and was beaten by a policeman. Mary Mebane heard about another dispute between a black soldier and a white bus driver in which the soldier was shot; a warehouse in Durham mysteriously burned down later that night. Mebane always feared trouble when she rode a bus. Once a black man refused to surrender the seat between the black and white sections to a white man. A middle-aged black woman defended the defiant black man when the bus driver tried to make him move: "These are niggers' seats! The government plainly said these are the niggers' seats!" screamed the little woman in rage. Mary Mebane was "embarrassed by the use of the word 'nigger' but I was proud of the lady. I was also proud of the man who wouldn't get up." The bus driver backed down. This incident later assumed particular importance for Mebane: "One minute we had been on a bus in which violence was threatened over a seat near the exit door; the next minute we were sitting in the very front behind the driver. The people who devised this system thought that it was going to last forever." Yet, as her autobiography demonstrates, she never completely freed herself from "the psychological terror of segregation."[45] Nor did many of her friends, neighbors, and relatives.

The segregation of churches, a continuation of rural practices, was never confronted:

> I reckon it was just the times we were living in. It hadn't been integrated. We'd just been raised up that way. It wasn't that we thought anything against them because a lot of colored people we loved. I know a lot of times my sister would take her lunch and give it to colored people on the way to school. It wasn't because we didn't like them. It was because we just wasn't raised up to do things with them like that. They was their nationality and we was our nationality. It was like the Jews and the Gentiles today.[46]

Most ministers, black and white, refused to address racial issues. In their view, religion was concerned with personal sin and salvation, not the evils of secular society. Yet indirectly the church strengthened black women's ability to cope in a white-dominated society. They joined a community of the respectable people who were loved by God and by one another. They organized in circles, "agencies for mutual self-help" that provided care for the sick and needy. Winning new members to the church and participating in church-related clubs, schools, and governing bodies helped women to "escape from the repressions . . . of daily existence" and gain skills in meeting "the practical affairs of life."[47] If religion taught black and white women to accept a white-dominated society and a male-controlled church, it also taught them self-confidence. Unintentionally, the churches were preparing women to take active roles in movements for social change.[48]

The inferior facilities offered to black residents made it more difficult for their children to receive a decent education or proper health care. Pauli Murray, the granddaughter and niece of devoted teachers, talked about the conditions that eventually led her to leave Durham:

> Our seedy run-down school told us that if we had any place at all in the scheme of things it was a separate place, marked off, proscribed and unwanted by the white people . . . We came to know that whatever we had was always inferior. We came to understand that no matter how neat and clean, how law abiding, submissive and polite, how studious in school, how churchgoing and moral, how scrupulous in paying our bills and taxes we were, it made no essential difference in our place.

Like other black Durhamites, Murray noted the mysterious fires that burned down three black schools during her childhood. Later, determined to acquire an equal education, she headed north.[49] Other Durham children, unable to follow her example, dropped out of schools that offered only lessons in inferiority. According to a Durham school board report in the late 1920s, 90 percent of the pupils of either race dropped out before completing high school. White students, however, "forced by economic stress," left gradually; black students lost half their number between the first and second grades. When asked by the school board to explain these dramatic losses, black teachers reported that many black children "shift about from place to place in the city"; "little children stay at home because of inadequate clothing against inclement weather"; other children were kept at home "to help with the home work"; factory workers who left home before the school day began could not monitor their children's attendance; and "little negroes" had problems with "reading and writing." In response, the school board urged that black education should become "more largely industrial and vocational" and thus even more differentiated from white education. Its members, representatives of dominant economic interests, including Kemp P. Lewis of Erwin Mills, offered no acknowledgment of the pervasive economic problems that propelled nine out of ten pupils from the school system.[50]

The rapid disappearance of black children from school reflected a hard-bitten realism: education would not necessarily lead blacks to better-paying jobs. Even a black person with a high school education might find no better job than a tobacco factory offered. Black girls found that community pressure to form a heterosexual attachment in their early teens made it more difficult to concentrate on education.[51] Pearl Barbee later regretted declining an opportunity for advanced schooling:

> Ah, there was a doctor that my mother worked for. He offered to send me to school. And I got hooked at the factory and wanted to help her out. And I just stayed on at the factory . . . [But didn't you think, maybe if you had gone to school, you would have earned more money?] Well, I couldn't think that way then, but I see now what a mistake I made, because I could have. Now this doctor, this doctor my mother worked for, now he wanted to give me schooling. He said I was so billiant about waiting on people, sick people. Like my brother was sick. He give me some kind of plaster to stay sixty minutes and told me after sixty minutes were up to put a needle in there. And I did it perfectly. And from that day he told my mother he wanted to give me schooling 'cause I would be a brilliant nurse. Now I would have liked to be a teacher, but I just got hooked and then I jumped up and married and messed up everything. Just messed up everything.[52]

One black child, after overhearing anguished discussions between his parents about financial matters, tried to help the family and still continue school. Evenually he abandoned the effort:

> It was pretty tough back in Depression times. I was small so I didn't have to worry but I realized it was tough. When I got a quarter it was like twenty-five dollars. They'd sit down together and try to discuss the decisions with what they were making. See, my daddy was making about eight dollars or nine dollars a week and my momma was making about six dollars [or] six dollars and a half. You know that was very little income with four children 'cause I was holding my end up. 'Course things were pretty cheap then but it was still rough. Some people had it worse . . . because some people didn't have no job.

In this case "holding my end up" meant starting "to work before I quit school, odd jobs, helping clean school to start with. I gave my money to my parents. Children didn't keep their money then, that wasn't the style." The boy quit school at fifteen to work in the Duke Hospital kitchen, where "you wasn't making nothing." His pay was docked for every dish he broke and his food was carefully rationed so that he never got enough to eat.[53]

Giving wages to parents was indeed the style. Allie Ennis, for example, began working at home. She and her siblings strung and turned tobacco sacks, assisted their mother with chores that included hauling water from the well, making lye soap, tending the family garden, boiling clothes in an iron pot, and ironing them with heavy flatirons. When she reached eleven, she began working part-time at the Durham Hosiery mill turning socks. Before and after school, she also washed dishes and cared for white people's children. All the children in the Ennis family gave their mother at least one dollar from their wages to keep the eleven-member household together. After her "father passed in 1918," she was forced to leave school. At the age of fifteen, this young black girl became one of the family's major breadwinners, together with her older brother who worked in a tobacco factory.[54]

Black females grew to an adulthood that offered few options. Black women competed for factory jobs because wage levels, though very poor, exceeded those paid for domestic work. The lucky ones joined the processions of tired tobacco workers who marched homeward at night to do domestic chores. On Sundays they attended segregated churches in their respective parts of town. Even if they remained above street battles and apart from racial negotiations between the white and black leadership, they could not remain uninfluenced by the issues at stake. They suffered from the irresponsibility of men who were themselves overwhelmed by circumstances. After discussing their problems related to black men, a group of black women concluded, "You know what's the problem with black men? It's the white man."[55] Some men, and occasionally women, drank their troubles away. Marital violence, child abuse, murder, suicide, and acute depression all claimed victims. Some women abdicated their family responsibilities. Others vented their frustrations on fellow victims by "being mean and fighting," engaging in street "hustles," depriving their children of affection, or participating in racially or sexually inspired violence.[56] Both men and women deserted their children. Disease inflicted other casualties. An investigation into juvenile delinquency, sickness, and childhood accidents in the late 1930s discovered that the highest rates for each occurred in the deteriorating neighborhoods of East Durham, where unemployment was high, "self-supporting" poor people were congregated, and many mothers worked outside the home.[57] Families headed by women struggled for a livelihood. Heightened racial tensions often accompanied these ordeals. The Ellis family, whose sons left school early to help the family, later produced a local Klan leader who saw blacks as the "cause" of his deprivations.[58] His anger exacerbated the difficulties faced by black families who, despite his perceptions, were still more victimized than his. Reared in such a world, Annie Mack Barbee and her sisters learned that "there is a time for meekness and humbling," for such was their daily experience. To humble yourself, to repress justifiable anger, to mind your tongue so that you could continue to provide for yourself and your family—these were essential for survival in black Durham.[59]

Durham's households and neighborhoods were shaped by the same economic forces that created its factories. The resources that women had available, the likelihood that they would have to earn wages, the opportunities open to their children, and the quality of life they would enjoy all depended on their access to property, to capital, and to the men who controlled both. While some farm girls and small-town women like Sarah Angier, Nannie Parrish, and Mary Duke might become the wives or sisters of successful industrial entrepreneurs, their numbers were few. Most were white. Class also determined the chances of success. The son of a Durham optometrist described the effect of attending an economically diverse (white) elementary school:

> It resulted in me going to school, all the way through grade school with kids, two-thirds of the class were poor people, working people, tobacco or cotton mills . . . I found it very educational. We had a situation in which most of the kids were working class, but we also had Anne Lewis in my class. Her father [K. P. Lewis] was superintendant of Erwin Mills. We had several doctors' daughters in class. And my first day of school, I remember her very well. I sat next to Mary Duke Lyon, a grandniece of Buck Duke . . . So we actually had some of the richest and the poorest and then ones like myself. I knew or sensed very early that some of my class would not go past the eight grade . . . You just knew. I think one of my closest friends, I knew perfectly. He lived with his grandfather who sawed wood. He went barefoot most of the year . . . You could almost know who would make it. Out of 30, there were maybe 5 or 6, who, just because you knew who their parents were, would go through. I think one of the status symbols was if you bought your books . . . But you just knew that some of them would drop out soon . . . I guess the Depression came along and some of them had to quit . . . Growing up in the school that I did, I had the strong feeling that there but for the grace of God go I 'cause there were some kids in our school who were as smart as any one of us but they were simply in those days not going to get ahead.[60]

Later this man took a demanding white collar position; his fellow students from the lower classes entered the factory or found other ways to survive.

Some children of "the poor people, the working people" later recounted how they dealt with the realization that "they were simply . . . not going to get ahead." Sometimes they accepted their fate cheerfully. As Theotis Williamson said, "I had to like it. I had to work." Love for her widowed mother was a primary reason for her cheerful acquiescence: "She raised us, her and all the rest of us together raised all the kids. She had three or four that were old enough to go to work when my father got killed. And there weren't no welfare; there weren't nothing like that then. She made the decisions for us."[61] Another child described a bribe of a stick of candy that brought him into the mill at the age of eleven; his voice was tinged with bitterness. One black man was determined to do better for his children:

> Well, I treat my children better than my parents treated me, because I was better able to do for them than my parents were for me. I could give them what they wanted but my parents couldn't give me what I wanted. And then I had a different belief, a different mind toward children than my parents did. In the time my parents came up, parents didn't believe in giving children too much and my parents was about like they came up. But when I came up I believed in giving children most anything they wanted . . . That's the difference between me coming up and them coming up.[62]

Louise Couch Jenkins appeared to accept the necessity that forced her mother to "ship three of us off" to an orphanage, but there was regret in her voice. Although she got along "pretty well," her hot-tempered younger sister had a harder time, because "many of the people who worked at the orphanage didn't understand how to raise children." She could hardly miss the irony that kept the youngest child with his mother: that child, largely because the older children supported the mother after they left the orphanage, was the only one to finish college. Explaining that her mother was forcibly retired in her early fifties, the daughter added, "The big corporations would just put people off when they got a little gray so they wouldn't have to retire them. I think it happened in her case, but it didn't happen just to her." Dismissed from L and M, Wilma Couch depended on her older children for support because "there wasn't Social Security then which might have given her more independence and pride."[63]

Pride was a factor in persuading one young resident of East Durham to leave school. In the late 1930s, she told an interviewer, "It's awful to have to sit in a room where most of the people have on good clothes and you are so ashamed of your own. It's awful to see your teacher get up with a list in her hand and to know that in a minute, she'll be reading out your name as one that hasn't paid the book rent." Her father was working only part-time and the family couldn't afford the 85-cent book rental fee in Durham high schools. The girl helped her mother "tag bulls for two hours after I got home from school . . . That'll help to buy bread."[64] Nonnie Mebane's education was cut short because of racial discrimination and economic pressures—there was no high school for black young people in her part of Virginia. She came to Durham, found a job, and eventually married. Her daughter Mary, fortunate to be born in the 1930s rather than in earlier decades, was able to finish school and graduate from college despite embittered relations with her mother.[65] Unlike children of tougher times, Mary Mebane could escape the life lived by her parents. The change from their spare, uncomplaining acceptance to her fiercely successful rebellion marked the passing of a world whose disappearance occasioned little regret.[66]

The "driven necessity" that sent children to work produced the Durham version of the "proletarian" family, that is, the family with only its children (or proles) as its assets. Child labor enabled hard-pressed families to survive, as many of its victims understood. In the absence of welfare, retirement benefits, or disability insurance, families relied on their members. Asked by a government investigator in 1918 about the effects of the federal anti-child labor law, a black Durham mother asked, "But what's the poor widow gonna do?" Another black woman suggested that the law should raise her wages if the legislators sincerely wanted better opportunities for her children.[67] Federal intervention seemed to make things worse, especially for black households headed by women. Many parents believed that the price of survival demanded the sacrifice of their children's hope "to do better."[68]

■ Instead of vain ambitions or gnawing regrets, women were encouraged to accept their unsolved problems and take pride in small victories. They prided themselves on clean homes, clean clothes, and food on the table. Indeed, their self-respect was demonstrated through the unpaid labors they performed at home or in their communities. Dena Coley always housed her children in a one-family house rather than a duplex. That marked a small victory over the forces that tried to crush her spirit. Theotis Williamson and Allie Ennis reared their younger brothers and sisters through hard work and self-sacrifice. Wilma Couch kept her children together by the expedient of placing some in an orphanage. Rose Weeks taught Sunday School while her husband helped with the housework: "If he stayed with me, he had to."[69] Annie Mack Barbee had her baby the way she chose: she paid for the best obstretrician she could find despite her husband's objections. As she explained, "Being married don't mean that your husband controls your whole life. You all work together."[70] Having seen her mother's life as a dependent housewife, Esther Jenks never married: "I didn't want to ask somebody for what I got."[71] Bessie Buchanan lived a moral, upright life in a community of respectable people. Louise Couch Jenkins and Mary Mebane avoided permanent employment in the factory, unlike their mothers. Hetty Love switched when her original church refused to allow her to preach.[72] Fannie Jenks won numerous skirmishes with her father over bobbing her hair, shortening her skirts, and dating men he disliked. Her successes made life easier for her younger sisters.

But there was often an unbridgeable gap between personal resistance and collective rebellion. Many of the influences impinging on women's consciousness opposed or conveyed ambiguous messages about workers' rights to engage in conflict with their employers. Most churches refrained from advocating unions or discussing economic issues. As one black worker observed, the church concentrated on the "inner man" while neglecting the "outer man." Economic contributions from black and white businessmen discouraged ministers from endorsing social protests, even if they were so inclined.[73] Moreover, an emphasis on heaven favored acquiescence to the world of "hard work at low wages" in this "vale of misery and tears."[74] Mark Miles Fisher and John Newsome spoke about the rights of workers but other black ministers remained silent.[75] In West Durham the Pentacostal minister counseled his congregation against taking part in secular conflicts, the Baptist minister kept silent lest he split his congregation, and only the minister of the local Christian Church earned a reputation as "an out-and-out labor man." When questioned, most Durham ministers would probably have concurred with the views of the leading Episcopal minister, the brother of an assistant manager at Erwin Mills: "In my opinion the Church should not commit itself, either to unions or to employers' associations."[76]

The Lord also appeared to straddle the fence. He spoke to Bessie Buchanan in a dream telling her that she would be saved because she "never joined a union in my life." But, in reference to the strike that Buchanan refused to join, the Lord sent a contradictory message to Esther Jenks. Discussing the Erwin Mills strike in March 1940, Jenks recalled:

> It was in March. The reason I remembered it so good, I had joined the church up here. We were out those two weeks and naturally we didn't get an Easter outfit. And I went to church that Sunday. I had on my old winter coat, you know and all. It was snowing just as pretty on all those new outfits. I said I knowed the Lord was looking.

Jenks also sought the Lord's help to sustain her through the year's unemployment that followed. She responded to the church's request to tithe: "So, I thought I would give it a try, so I did and it worked . . . They had to put me back to work in 1941."[77] The same God sustained Buchanan in her opposition and Jenks in her activism, while allowing both women to heed their own inclinations in good conscience.

Nor did the organs of public opinion often discuss the conditions faced by working people. When they did, they usually praised the benevolence of the factory owners and the harmony that prevailed in Durham workplaces. "Outside agitators" received a less than enthusiastic welcome. The selection of a unionized company to build the east campus of Duke University was denounced by local business leaders. A pro-union film was denied a showing in the Durham City Auditorium, as we have seen, "because of the increased fire insurance rate."[78] Reared in such an atmosphere, workers displayed understandable caution in openly discussing views opposed by their employers. An investigator discovered that it was difficult "to get a single direct answer" from the mill workers whom he questioned. He ascribed their unwillingness to a "double fear. In the first place, southern workers naturally distrust outsiders, and over and beyond that many have learned by experience that it is not to their personal interest to 'talk too much to snoopers.'" Discussions were held in private places and secret locations. Only knitters were allowed to join one secret organization of hosiery workers because "expansion to include toppers and menders would be sure to destroy its secrecy." This policy also effectively excluded women.[79] Moreover, as several investigators learned, women felt particularly ignorant about the purposes of a union. Katherine Norman, then a seamer at Golden Belt's hosiery mill, tried to explain the reasons for low union membership: "Some people take the religious viewpoint that they should 'not oppose them that have rule over them'" but "other would join if they understood." Black women, "laboring under the double disadvantage of being marginal workers because of their sex and race," exhibited the greatest reticence in discussing collective action and usually claimed that they were ignorant of the issues involved.[80] Advised by black business leaders against taking risky actions, offered little encouragement from their church, and disillusioned by past experience with unions, many black women shared Roxanne Clark's opinion: "I thought it was foolish . . . for them to do that when that was how they was making their living."[81] Well acquainted with unemployment because of the seasonal nature of their work, black women were more reluctant than their colleagues to court additional disasters. Whether people were silent out of apathy, caution, fear, or conviction, they reinforced the pressures from above that hindered them from devising collective solutions.

Censorship could not screen out all challenges to employers, but the "masters of machinery" were protected by their relative inaccessibility. Also, there were more convenient targets for workers' frustrations. According to a lawyer who was experienced in defeating southern union drives, "The inherent conflict between the white Southern industrial worker and the colored worker . . . in keeping with the human need of having somebody of lower status than we are . . . has a great deal to do with the so-called antiunion sentiment in the South."[82] Black workers, for their part, were likely to distrust any movement in which whites participated.[83] Although gender differences rarely produced such intense hostility, the sexual wars also claimed victims and provided villains. The inadequancies of a spouse or father sometimes focused a woman's resentment at home instead of at the exploitative conditions under which she worked. Indeed, a woman could blame her man for her having to work at all. Alternatively, some men found it easier to physically mistreat their wives and children than to challenge their employers. Drinking and sexual conquests were other forms of transitory relief. Violence and petty crimes often set members of an oppressed group against one another. Still other victims blamed themselves for their own poverty. Somehow they had failed to build a better life. Self-blame could turn destructive, leading to irrational actions and an abandonment of all efforts to improve a person's life.[84] An environment with so many possibilities for internal conflicts within the working-class community and also between racial groups impeded the formation of a common front. Such were the "trade secrets" that anti-union strategists offered their clients in the battle to keep workers internally divided.

But the increasing demand for anti-union "trade secrets" in the 1920s and 1930s suggested that a maturing working class contained many members who were defining themselves as a distinct group in opposition to their employers. The creation of working class neighborhoods and institutions were bringing "together people and movements which historically had been divided and apart" in cities like Durham.[85] Employer vigilence and "trained confidential agents" were no longer preventing "professional agitators" from attempts "to inject costly restlessness into southern labor." Indeed, the growth of tightly-knit communities around a core of permanent inhabitants could shield "persons who may be agitators . . . . or 'have an ax to grind.'"[86] Living closely together, workers began to develop cultural institutions: separate churches, social organizations, family and kinship networks, recreational activities, consumption patterns, moral sensibilities, and distinct vocabularies that separated "them from us." The separation of "lint-heads" in mill villages from the respectable townspeople was particularly conducive to a growing self-consciousness, but that awareness could emerge among other working people in a place like Durham.[87] By the late 1920s in the Durham area, workers could listen to speeches by men "trying to tear down the industrial life of the State," in the view of Kemp P. Lewis, who was engaged in a losing battle to silence such critics. Although Lewis and other manufacturers considered these "outside agitators" and their local supporters to be "dangerous dreamers or vicious propagandists," he could not suppress all discussion of "the union doctrine" even in his own mill village.[88]

The arrival of a more militant younger generation of black leaders prodded Durham's conservative elite to champion "the just cause of labor along with the right claims of capital."[89] C. C. Spaulding and a leader of the organized tobacco workers eventually served together on the Board of Deacons of the White Rock Baptist Church—a tangible expression of the accommodation by black capital to black labor. Indeed, to retain influence, the black elite had to abandon its old strategy of silencing protests against inequities.[90] Durham had become a "Hot Spot," according to two anti-union activists, where "some eloquent radical can stir up unrest if the opportunity and time are given."[91]

The Durham elite never faced a radical feminist movement, but the growing concentration of working women did produce a milder social feminism.

Unlike rural households, working-class women in Durham were frequently in contact with women outside their families. Also, they were bringing money into the family economy and "toting the pocketbook." Their numbers drew the attention of more privileged women in the city. Cooperation between sympathetic upper-class women and working women to study and then reform working conditions created a potential crisis for the industrialists. Even though K. P. Lewis and his associates forced the officers of the Durham YWCA to apologize for their enthusiastic support of working women's causes, the danger remained that female empathy might overcome class interests.[92] The YWCA sponsored an Industrial Girls' Club and sent female wage-earners to the Southern Summer School for Women Workers, where they learned about the labor movement and their own economic position.[93] Mary O. Cowper, an active participant in the cross-class alliance of Durham women, continued to support labor organizing, childcare, and discussions with workers about their situation.[94] For the most part, however, the social feminists confined their activities to white women, a serious limitation in a city like Durham. Ultimately the timid women's groups in Durham offered little real help to their female constituency, but there was a growing awareness that men could not always protect women. Some Durham women had learned to think and act for themselves.

The journey from field to factory, then, presents a complicated mixture of continuity and change. By many objective measures, women's lives were the better for it. Their labors lightened; their consumption levels rose; their childbearing declined; and some were able, by the end of the period, to live outside the patriarchal family economy. The battle between the sexes now involved combatants who were more equally matched. Moreover, women's common experiences in the city and workplaces, however hedged in by racial barriers, tended to draw them together. Whether they could submerge their differences and unite as women and workers was a question that could now at least be posed. Judged by the lives they led in the workplace and the household, black and white women qualified as sisters "under their skins."

VIII
BEYOND
THE
FRAGMENTS

> [Women] are the background to history. Our present situation imposes fragmentation and isolation. Divided inside and against ourselves and one another we lack both physical and class solidarity . . . The family maintains us in the interior world and the class of our man gives us status in the exterior . . . This puzzles us and means it is harder for us to begin to experience our own identity as a group.[1]

So might a Durham worker, had she been versed in feminist theory, have articulated her situation: "Breaking silence." "Becoming visible." "Creating a language that will translate what we have experienced into a plan for collective action." "Healing the divisions." "Moving beyond the fragments." These phrases capture the dilemma posed by class exploitation, racial domination, and gender subordination. But at that time no theory had emerged that linked these experiences of oppression, as inextricably as they were bound together in daily life. Instead, women dealt with their problems in partial ways.

The labor movement was the central arena into which the women of Durham channeled their energies. It offered working women a public space to discuss the problems they shared with working men and with working people of both races. It taught women a language that connected their economic plight to that of other workers, and it called them to collective action—although it demanded that its participants use a language conceived in the masculine gender and constructed in a white idiom. Still, a fragmented reflection of the real situation faced by black and white working women took shape. By examining women's experiences in the labor movement, we can better appreciate the impediments to their emergence as a unified class. At the same time we can recognize their achievements as we witness their struggles to go beyond the fragments.²

Before the 1930s Durham workers and employers rarely clashed in organized fashion. When they did, men took the lead. In contrast to the leadership of women in some southern strikes, Durham women were passive observers or silent victims in a struggle waged by men.³ The dismissal of two women from the Duke factory in the mid-1880s typifies their early role. According to the *Journal of United Labor*, the two cigarette makers lost their jobs merely because their father belonged to the Knights of Labor.⁴ In fact, black and white women joined the Knights in Durham and its vicinity but they never took a central role in its losing battles.⁵ During the 1900 strike at Erwin Mills, women again appeared as passive victims. According to a local newspaper, the strike sent "one lady into spasms."⁶ After summoning the "heads of families" to a meeting closed to the "young men who were the leaders of the organization," W. A. Erwin announced that all union members and their families would be dismissed. The guilty were evicted from their homes.⁷ Women then appear in the accounts as homeless victims of a battle of wills between a benevolent patriarch and his rebellious sons.⁸

During the next flurry of organizing activity in 1918 and 1919, the tobacco and textile unions invited "the ladies to enlist." This time, however, the unions hoped to avoid defeat by refraining from provocation. Instead, Local 153 of the Tobacco Workers International Union (TWIU) pledged that "members will discourage and prevent any strife," "render a good honest day's work every day," and if discharged, "submit without protest."⁹ Aiming to win the confidence of the employers, the union was left defenseless when American Tobacco refused to reciprocate. After offering bonuses to workers, promoting a few blacks to operative positions, and firing the TWIU organizer, the company successfully disrupted the union without disrupting production.¹⁰ Similarly, W. A. Erwin refused to bargain with the members of a textile union that claimed one thousand members from "all sections of the township."¹¹ Sending a confidential agent to spy on his employees, Erwin rejoiced to learn that the "union had just about gone to the bad." Content with their promised bonuses, the Erwin workers ceased making complaints against their employer. Like the men, the "ladies" appeared to be "satisfied."¹²

Women do not appear among the active combatants of the labor wars during the 1920s. There was "no union of any kind for women workers in Durham," although skilled male knitters employed at the Marvin Carr Silk Mill organized a local of the American Federation of Full-Fashioned Hosiery Workers in the mid-1920s. After the Carrs ordered union members to train new workers (who were required to sign a pledge against joining the union as a condition of employment), a strike resulted. Having lost the strike, the union members left Durham to seek jobs in cities like Philadelphia, where their union offered them help.[13] By the late 1920s the remnants of that union existed "entirely sub-rosa due to the fact that when the worker's affiliation is discovered . . . he is soon laid off and usually discharged, 'if he doesn't take the hint,' as one member of the knitters' union put it." For the rest of the decade the battles often were conducted underground as the Carrs, Lewis, and Carmichael of L and M marshalled their forces against "the threatened invasion of radical unionism."[14] Alfred Hoffman, the dynamic organizer for the Hosiery Workers, the United Textile Workers, and the American Federation of Labor, came to Durham in 1927 to lead the union side. Trained at Brookwood Labor College in "economics and social psychology," prepped in "journalistic requirements," and able to "analyse labor problems intelligently," Hoffman initially predicted that southern workers "will go along just so long and then they will explode." A year in Durham dampened his optimism. Emphasizing the "need for patient work," he told the convention of hosiery workers that employers used a blacklist, "a very fine spy system," the mill village, and direct threats to intimidate union activists. Innovative methods, such as a motor parade by the former Durham workers who had found jobs in Philadelphia, the organization of a Piedmont Organizing Council, and extensive publicity in the union press, generated excitement, but employers still retained the upper hand.[15]

Although Hoffman never explicitly addressed his appeals to women, another Durham activist was quietly probing into reasons for the unpopularity of unions among Durham women in the 1920s. Mary Cowper talked with young women whom she'd met through the YWCA Industrial Girls' Club and learned that most knew little or nothing about unions. They eased their discontent by frequently changing jobs and companies. One young woman, whose father knew about unions, offered a disturbing response: "There weren't many [unions] in this part of the country," she said, "because people are afraid there will be trouble and they will lose their jobs. They also said that leaders are lacking and that people won't stick together and it only makes trouble to try to better conditions." Other young workers appeared too frivolous to think seriously about their working conditions, or thought that they could "help change the working conditions soon" if they became supervisors.[16] Had Alfred Hoffman and other labor organizers learned the results of the Cowper survey, it would have confirmed their conviction that men, not women, should remain the primary target of unionization.

Yet the experiences of some Durham women suggested that a male-oriented strategy overlooked many opportunities. Nellie Carter, along with other Durham women, attended a summer school for working women in the late 1920s where she studied economics, history, and labor issues.[17] The brief period at the Southern Summer School for Women Workers offered these women a "social space . . . to talk to one another, to reflect upon their lives, and obtain a fundamental sense of their worth."[18] But disappointment followed Carter's return home. Durham's male activists ignored her suggestions. She denounced them, declared that she knew more than they about union organizing, and withdrew from active participation. On her own, without the aid of other enlightened women, Nellie Carter could not overcome the resistance of men who had never been encouraged to consider women's leadership.[19] She found it impossible to believe that an alliance between women and the labor movement was "a natural one." In the harsh environment of Durham, some dreams died.[20]

White women were not alone in their frustrations. Aware since 1900 that blacks must be brought into the TWIU, the union's national leadership urged that "the interest of both whites and colored are locked up in the success of the union," but local leaders found it difficult to act on that advice. Any violation of racial taboos led to fierce attacks against unions in the regular and industrial press. Nor did many union activists wholeheartedly endorse racial equality, as the pages of the *Union Herald*, an AFL organ published in Raleigh, made evident. Having defended the Ku Klux Klan, the paper also declared that "the organization of the colored workers does not mean, in any sense of the word, social equality," and it opposed the extension of the vote to black women.[21] Whether the paper was opportunistically protecting the local AFL from attacks by manufacturers or expressing honestly felt racial beliefs, such comments could only encourage prejudice in its white readership. Black workers in Durham recalled persistent discrimination by organized labor that dated back to the refusal of the Knights to give black workers a fair chance for a job. Similar practices continued in Durham into the 1920s:

> One morning I came to work and saw my men standing around with their coats on looking at a cloth sign stretched across the front of the house we were building. In the middle was a skull and crossbones and large red letters saying, 'Run, Nigger, Run.'" I told my men to tear it down and go to work. I complained to the Mayor and was no further molested on that job.[22]

Black workers recognized that the rise of trade unions was often accompanied by their exclusion from skilled trades. White trade unions did not protest when a construction firm refused to hire a black mason. In fact, union leaders blamed black reluctance to "make temporary sacrifices for the sake of future gains."[23] The arguments made by black Durham businessmen that "labor agitators only create mutual suspicions between blacks and whites" expressed the convictions of many Durham workers. Black women, having been generally ignored by organized labor and seeing the discrimination against black men, responded with still greater skepticism. Even as late as 1935, less than 10 percent of the black female tobacco workers interviewed in Durham endorsed unionization, compared with 20 percent of black men and white women, and 40 percent of white men. Any local activist who wished to bring blacks into the labor movement had a long history of betrayals to contend with.[24]

Moreover, the labor movement was too weak to be appealing. Unions had not won a strike against a Durham employer into the late 1920s. Durham workers had also witnessed the traumatic defeats inflicted on workers in other cities and in mill villages across the Piedmont. As a young girl, Jessie Ervin watched the eviction of a union leader at Pilot Mill in Raleigh. A wave of strikes near Charlotte in 1919 resulted in the jailing of the man who had organized the Durham union on a charge of incitement to riot.[25] Many Durham workers knew about the failed Henderson strike of 1927, Alfred Hoffman's first experience after coming to the South.[26] When Hoffman was arrested during the Marion strike in 1929, Durham workers lost their charismatic leader. The mass firing of 3,000 R. J. Reynolds employees in Winston-Salem, seventy miles west of Durham, served as a warning to Durham tobacco workers. The eviction of textile organizers in Greensboro in 1930 by the Cones, close allies of K. P. Lewis, reinforced the lesson in employer power.[27] A new decade began with the long and bitter Danville, Virginia, strike in winter 1930–1931. North Carolina workers may well have concluded, "Folks can talk all they want about their right to join the union, but right don't count much when money is against you."[28] Indeed, there seemed no end to defeat.

But many of the defeated were not discouraged. Some Danville workers came to Durham still determined to unionize. They joined with Durham workers who believed that "right" was more important than the "might" of employers. By the late 1920s, they had begun to consider the proper relationship between themselves and their employers as a question of ethics: "a conception of justice for 'us' as opposed to 'them.'"[29] James Evans, the Cone organizer, remained faithful to his vision even as he eked out a living on the tenant farm to which he'd been exiled. He clung to his hope "that in not so many years the laboring man will actually have justice."[30] Teachers at the Southern Summer School for Women Workers believed that their students were sharing in the general awakening of working-class consciousness in the South. As they expressed it, their students were "beginning to wonder why they suffer from poverty although they spend their lives working from dawn to dark." Although there were no visible signs that the schism between black and white workers could be healed, once confident employers were beginning to fear that "no one knows the workers as they know themselves."[31]

■ A sullen interlude followed the defeats of the late 1920s and early 1930s. Workers confronted an economic crisis that devastated the textile industry, crippled the hosiery industry, and left only tobacco unscathed. Jobs vanished. Wages plunged. The stretch-out speeded the pace of work for those fortunate to have jobs. Cocky foremen intimidated disgruntled employees by threatening to replace them with one of the hordes of unemployed. As some workers understood it, the supervisors were telling employees, "You'll do what we tell you. You'll shut your mind up and let us think for you or we'll starve you to death."[32] Unwilling to risk their jobs, women and men sometimes wept as they were browbeaten by supervisors.[33] While textile overseers drove their remaining employees harder in order to ride out the economic storm, tobacco foremen speeded up the machines and spurred anxious employees to increase productivity.

The sullen mood began to lift in summer 1933. Taking advantage of a sympathetic administration in Washington, workers sought to extend "the meaning of freedom" into the workplace.[34] Suddenly they were not alone. Their notions of justice had acquired the stamp of legitimacy, the sanction of law. Latent energies began to stir. The pledge of federal protection "in the exercise of the workers' right to organization," a promise embodied in Section 7A of the National Industrial Recovery Act, was eagerly embraced by the white men who greeted an organizer sent by the TWIU.[35] E. L. Crouch arrived in Durham the day the Blue Eagle of the NRA took flight. The next day seven workers from L and M gathered at the home of Sam Latta, a longtime union activist. During July and August they gathered in increasing numbers in E. L. Crouch's hotel room to debate strategy. The core group pressed for a mass meeting in early August, but Crouch advised them to wait "so that we may have all the workers around, women, the colored, and those in smoking tobacco." Somehow, in their eagerness to redress injustices, the male vanguard had forgotten the majority of the tobacco workers in their city.[36]

Yet the discussions in the hotel room revealed something more than simple eagerness among white men and hesitation among all the other tobacco workers. They revealed a deep attachment to patriarchal and white supremacist values. These men—fixers, machine operators, and other employees in the cigarette departments—complained because L and M gave each cigarette-making machine operator a can to "catch" the cigarettes. They demanded that they be "given girls" to catch cigarettes, as was the practice at American.[37] W. R. Culbreth particularly objected to TWIU proposals that the NRA code for the tobacco industry include a 35-cent minimum wage. Writing to E. Lewis Evans, president of the TWIU, he complained that the minimum wage would mean "an increase in negro pay of about 100% and increases my pay none." He added, "I can not ask a white man to join an organization having gone on record for such a thing."[38] Evans replied that "the Negro . . . is a strong competitor in our industry and, if we do not travel with him economically, the BOSSES will use him to defeat our general purpose." This reasoning apparently convinced Culbreth, although black workers remained lumped together as "the colored" or "the Negro."[39] Thus the TWIU began a campaign to recruit all of Durham's tobacco workers but remained biased toward white men.

When Duby Upchurch arrived in January 1934 to replace E. L. Crouch, the white workers at L and M had already formed Local 176 and the white employees at American had formed Local 183. Black workers were only beginning to meet. Aided by a mass meeting at the black YWCA that was addressed by Louis Austin, the editor of the *Carolina Times*, Local 194 at L and M soon attracted more than three thousand workers, primarily black women.[40] Despite the impressive gains, Upchurch believed that black workers were "not reliable" recruits. He also discovered that some black ministers had "denounced the union from their pulpits."[41] Talks by Henry Addams, an organizer dispatched by the Hosiery Workers to Durham, and R. R. Lawrence of the North Carolina State AFL failed to change the ministers' stance. Upchurch and Evans then decided that the ministers had been bribed by white employers and black businessmen.[42] By the end of 1934, the membership of Local 194 had shriveled; Local 193, established for black workers at American, was almost moribund. Nevertheless, the TWIU continued its emphasis on white workers and expected that black workers would eventually fall into line.

Just as the TWIU was addressing itself to its reluctant black recruits in spring 1934, the United Textile Workers (UTW) and the Hosiery Workers resumed their efforts to organize Durham textile workers. An industrial espionage agent hired by Erwin Mills surveyed the attitudes of the workers. Disguised as a radio salesman, the spy noted that the women he spoke with either opposed the union or remained silent; he found that men were evenly divided.[43] Two months later, a rabidly anti-union journalist, who had interviewed Albert Beck of the UTW, wrote K. P. Lewis some reassuring news. Although Beck had made good progress in organizing workers at Golden Belt in East Durham, he had more limited success at Durham Hosiery Mills and had found it "impossible to do any real work" in West Durham.[44]

During summer 1934, however, the opinion of Durham workers shifted in favor of the unions. The national campaign orchestrated by the UTW for recognition, the elimination of the "stretch-out," and the establishment of the thirty-hour week evidently spoke to workers' needs. By August 1934 Beck had created Bull City Local 2155, which included seven separate locals in the mill villages of Durham. At a mass meeting that month, two thousand Durham textile workers gathered to plan a general textile strike for September if the textile industry did not accept its demands.[45] It appeared that

BEYOND THE FRAGMENTS

Alfred Hoffman's prophecy had finally come to pass: Durham textile workers would go "along just so long and then they will explode."[46]

White tobacco workers also responded to the rising current of labor militancy. Having reached "near the perfect organized state," Durham workers at L and M pressed for action. Upchurch proposed that the campaign be extended to other L and M plants in Richmond, Toledo, Chicago, St. Louis, and San Francisco.[47] Some white activists, convinced that "they must have the colored workers or else they will never get anywhere themselves," plunged into a campaign to reach black workers. The appointment of Charles Parrish, a Durham native holding "advanced views on the Negroes," renewed the attempt to get "hold of the leaders of both men and women among the colored race."[48] Meanwhile, white male union activists from Durham journeyed to Washington to testify in favor of the TWIU's proposals for the code governing industry conditions. Although cautioned "not to advertise the trip to Washington as no colored worker was invited," they appeared at the hearings as spokesmen for all the tobacco workers of Durham.[49]

The workers' desire for action was beginning to strain the cautious framework established by the TWIU. Yet Evans, after more than forty years in the TWIU leadership, remained convinced that persuading employers to accept union labels was a better policy than pressuring them to make concessions through workers' actions. Furthermore, he distrusted rank and file initiatives. Despite a warning from a long-time associate that the new locals "are going to demand a voice and a say-so in how the organization [is] run," Evans insisted on running the union his way.[50] The agitation subsided as workers' attention turned to the tobacco code and local organizing, but the possibility remained that workers' demand for a "say-so" would undermine the authority of heavy-handed union officials. The sources of discontent had not been eliminated.

Inspired by the excitement of the August mass meeting and armed with pledges of support from black and white tobacco workers' locals, Durham began preparations for the general textile strike on Labor Day. A large motorcade carried local workers to Pine Hill Cemetery. There the president of the Hosiery Workers spoke over the grave of Clem Norwood, one of the employees dismissed from the Marvin Carr Silk Mill, who had later found work in the Philadelphia area. Killed during a hosiery strike in Philadelphia, Norwood symbolized the solemn commitment Durham workers were being asked to make. Four thousand men and women listened as the union official spoke:

> We men and women of labor, gathered at the grave of Clem Norwood who died that our cause might triumph, do hereby pledge ourselves to

carry on this great fight against the evils of poverty amid plenty, oppression in democracy, and against all social greed, selfishness . . . bigotry . . . and class discrimination."[51]

Later, white Durham workers gathered at a park to listen to speeches and express their solidarity. No longer uncertain about voicing their opinions, women exhibited the same enthusiasm as men.[52]

The next day the determined strikers shut down all the cotton mills in Durham. Within a week the hosiery locals, after an unsuccessful attempt to gain recognition from the Carrs, joined the strike. Local merchants supplied food, credit, and tents to shelter the striking members of their community. Kemp P. Lewis found it "galling . . . to have a mob refuse to allow him entrance into his office," but did not call in the police in order "to keep Durham from being torn up with bitter antagonisms, leading to disorder and crime." Durham, as he told his stockholders, was a city "permeated with a union sentiment."[53] Golden Belt officials endured a similar humiliation.[54] Disciplined but feisty, Durham workers joined the "flying squadrons" that carried the call to strike to communities where union fever had not reached the same intensity. After three weeks, the UTW ended the strike when Franklin Roosevelt promised an investigation of conditions in the industry. Many of the more than seven thousand strikers paraded from Five Points up Main Street to the Durham Hosiery Mills in East Durham, shouting "Victory is Ours" and "We Killed the Stretch-out."[55]

But the victory soon turned to ashes. According to one striker, the workers never understood the "reasons for striking." According to another: "The government will make the next move . . . the workers gained in the strike but . . . the Union lost a lot of ground and friends." A West Durham woman concluded that "they had not gained anything as they are going back to work the same as before the strike." A scholar endorsed the pessimistic assessment of the strike after interviewing numerous union officials. "The UTW really had no southern strategy," he wrote, "or any other strategy for that matter."[56] In the aftermath of the inconclusive strike and a governmental report that failed to offer concrete improvements to the textile workers, the UTW collapsed.[57] Although the size of the strike protected Durham workers from wholesale firings that punished workers in more divided communities, local activists shared the doubts about the UTW. The imprisonment of the local's treasurer for embezzling $500 from the strike fund further disillusioned members.[58]

Vengeful employers, unable to vent their frustrations through mass dismissals, pledged that the strike would cause no changes in their operations. The Carrs told the union at Durham Hosiery Mills, "We will not let you folks represent the whole crowd."[59] One hundred workers at Durham Cotton Manufacturing Company lost their jobs, after which J. Harper Erwin

BEYOND THE FRAGMENTS

assured the remaining employees that the company would "show no partiality between union and non-union employees."[60] Six watchmen at Durham Hosiery Mill No. 6, the black-run mill, lost their jobs because they had allowed strikers to enter the mill at night. When pressed by the federal mediator to rehire the watchmen, the Carr spokesman refused. The lesson of the strike, he told the official, "is that we have been too sympathetic."[61] Kemp P. Lewis expressed a similar determination to continue the company strategy of installing new machinery, increasing workloads, and eliminating unnecessary workers.[62] Never again would unions in Durham's textile industry draw such an enthusiastic and united constituency as the UTW attracted—and misled—in the general textile strike of 1934.

Tobacco workers had witnessed both the strike's exciting beginning and its disillusioning aftermath. The defeat clearly discouraged many potential union members, especially among black workers. The majority opinion was that unions were "ineffectual or too radical or too costly to the workers in the matter of fees, or . . . placed their jobs in jeopardy." One worker at L and M combined many strands of workers' pessimism:

> One wouldn't work here now because colored have been deceived too much. A dollar to join and twenty-five cents a week is too much to let somebody run away with . . . It would be a pretty hard job to get a union in this town because colored people have been treated so dirty. It takes a lot of money to run a union—to buck capital. If 7 or 8 hundred hands in any of these factories went on a strike there's enough people here to keep the factories running. When they had the hosiery mill strike, the union lost, and many of those that lost their jobs are out in the street right now.[63]

A white woman who caught cigarettes at American expressed a similar disbelief:

> They had a union but I don't know what become of it. No one ever goes any more. I'll tell you, when you put your money into a thing you want to get something out of it. I was re-instated once, but it's no use.[64]

A black woman, a member of Local 194 at L and M, described the reasons for the emormous expansion and contraction of the local's membership:

> The white man said it was good to join the union cause they would see we would have a job. We ain't ever been in nothin' like that. Durham never had nothing like that, so we was scared to mess with it. They told us, "Well, if you don't join somethin' or 'nother is going to happen next week." So I jumped up there and joined. He told us at one time they was goin' to have a strike at Liggett and Myers and if you didn't

> belong to the union, you would be put out. I didn't believe much in it, but everybody was talkin' so I joined. I didn't see where it did the hosiery mill no good. When they had a strike they had, they all had to get relief. I hear that white man done took all the money and left . . . When we got the last raise since Christmas, the white man [of the union] says, "You see what the union done? We got a raise." Course I don't believe the union done nothing. We got that raise cause the boss man gave it to us.[65]

The solidly established local among the white workers at L and M was only slightly hindered by the defeat. But support for the black locals and the white local at American was less deeply rooted and the strike's failure confirmed the doubts of many workers. Some had been frightened into the union or carried along on a wave of enthusiasm. Now they decided that the union "ain't mounted to nothin' here" and never would.[66] At L and M, the local for black workers saw its membership plunge to fewer than two hundred members, a tenth of its former size.[67] Black Local 193 at American disintegrated.

There were positive notes buried within the general disillusionment. One woman, fired for inviting another worker at American to join Local 183, reported on the discussion with her former supervisor:

> I went to see him with some plain talk. He just wouldn't talk. Treated me cool. He just said No. He treated me cool, I noticed, at least three weeks before he laid me off . . . His niece, the one I got to join the union, went with me. The niece bawled him out.[68]

The report suggested that even the relatives of foremen might be drawn into the union—and side with a coworker against an uncle. In fact, women sometimes acted more forcefully than survey data suggested, perhaps because they tended to answer questions posed by a stranger with reserve. Ella Faucette, for instance, was a black woman who put aside her doubts to "get it existing." She persuaded other workers to join.[69] Rose Weeks joined Local 183 at the first meeting she attended:

> One of the women asked me if I'd be interested. "We have a meeting tonight, would you be interested?" I said, "I sure would." I saw that somebody had been doing a lot of talking, the hall was full. The waves of enthusiasm lasted about six months and then some of the women started dropping out, getting behind with their dues . . . The union had only forty paid members and I was one of them. It was mostly women dropping out and some of the men. I thought it would be wonderful if everybody that worked could stick together and back each other up and love each other that much.[70]

A white woman at L and M eagerly embraced the union because it offered a chance for workers to live "more like God would have us live." She and other women members had concluded that the only way "you can survive was through organization."[71] Their experiences had convinced them that the risks were preferable to the costs of passive submission.

The success achieved by TWIU locals in Durham varied in direct proportion to the cohesiveness of the membership. Local 176, the original white union in Durham, forced L and M to sign the first collective bargaining agreement in Durham history in 1935.[72] Because many American employees had been newly hired in the early 1930s, its white labor force lacked a similar cohesion. Its management also mounted a more vigorous resistance to unionization. Yet, after establishing a common front with white locals at American plants in Reidsville, North Carolina, and Richmond, Virginia, Local 183 signed a contract in 1936.[73] Meanwhile, black locals floundered. Local 194 repeatedly risked losing its TWIU charter as its membership fell below the required number of dues-paying members; the newly chartered Local 204 for black American workers performed similarly. Only Local 208, formed by black manufacturing employees who split from Local 194 in 1937, succeeded in negotiating with employers. Its membership, primarily male and more securely employed than were the female stemmers who comprised the majority of Local 194, became the first black local in Durham to sign a contract—and only a year after its founding. During that same year the locals enrolling black women pleaded for help from the TWIU leadership. Daisy Jones, the corresponding secretary for Local 194, asked Evans to "please have a little more patience with us." She reported that "our members . . . are being unusually changed from one department to another, from one shift to another. It is very difficult to keep in touch with them or them with the local."[74] After scolding her, Evans granted an extension beyond the dues-paying deadline. When the local asked for a black organizer, however, Evans refused. "The supervision of Local 194," he informed the local's president, "is entirely in the hands of T. L. Copley and H. A. McCrimmon."[75] In December 1938, the executive board of Local 204 addressed the same request to Evans, asking for "a part-time organizer" because "we do feel like a colored organizer can get closer to most of our people."[76] Evans again responded negatively. These unions, unlike their white counterparts or Local 208, could boast no accomplishment after three or four years beyond mere survival.

Although some tobacco workers made gains through quiet but steady pressure on employers, Durham's textile workers confronted the dispiriting results of a failed strike and a deteriorating local industry. The Carrs justified wage cuts, layoffs, and the installation of new machinery by declaring that Durham Hosiery Mills had operated at a loss during the first six months of 1935. Nonetheless, these moves precipitated a strike in July 1935.[77] A. F. Carr, then Durham's mayor, played a significant role when police escorted non-striking workers across picket lines. Non-striking workers attacked two union officers, including Bonnie Glenn, the local's president, on the strike's first day.[78] Other fights erupted between strikers and non-strikers. After a month, the strike was broken and the union destroyed. Three months later, the company closed down its No. 1 plant. Four hundred and fifty white workers lost their jobs; the white spinners from No. 1 moved to No. 6 to start working on the night shift.[79] Economic crisis thus brought black and white hosiery workers into the same mill, but they continued to work separately.

Textile organizing then centered on Golden Belt and Erwin Mills, companies that were surviving the industrial crisis by substituting the latest technological advances for "worn-out machinery," by constantly reorganizing the labor process, and by keeping a tight rein on the payroll.[80] These policies enhanced productivity but also heightened tensions in the work force. Luther Riley, long active in the union drive, described the interaction between company pressure and union activism:

> It would swell up to a certain size and then it would reduce. Each time it would never reduce to the first nucleus . . . And then it would expand even greater and then it would draw back again . . . The company would realize what they were doing and would let up, then the thing would cool off . . . They would start putting pressure on again and finally it got to where it just wouldn't recede. It just stayed there and that's when the Textile Workers Union of America came.

The "pressure" that finally impelled Erwin workers to organize was the "Bedaux" version of the "time study system," which Erwin used "to stretch people out."[81] The union that Riley referred to was the Textile Workers Organizing Committee (TWOC), which had been established under the auspices of the Committee for Industrial Organization (CIO) to sponsor an organizing drive among southern textile workers. Equipped with seasoned organizers from the ranks of the Amalgamated Clothing Workers and other unions, the TWOC officially arrived in West Durham in November 1937 when a committee paid its first call on Kemp P. Lewis.[82] Three months later, the TWOC won an overwhelming electoral victory in an election held under the auspices of the National Labor Relations Board.[83] For the next four years, the company and the union engaged in fierce but indecisive combat.

Maintaining a "calm and pleasant attitude" while refusing to negotiate with his employees, recognize the union, or consult about company policy, Lewis insisted on the managerial prerogative to run the company as he saw fit. When the local threatened a strike in July 1938 to protest the company's refusal to discuss a contract or an announced wage cut, management prepared by shipping out finished cloth, shutting down the bleachery, removing the books from the office, and taking the weights off the looms. A strike by the women in the sewing room over a workload issue in June 1939 produced an Erwin offer to "bring in engineers to study not only sheet tearers' jobs, but all the jobs in the bleachery and sewing room"—a proposal that the company had planned even before the strike and therefore not a meaningful concession to the workers.[84] Furthermore, the company hired Carl R. Harris, an industrial engineer, to handle labor relations. Harris, in the view of the employees, frequently went "overboard" in his quest for increased production, placed impossible workloads on their shoulders, and neglected human relationships in the process.[85] By reducing labor relations to a technique, Erwin Mills lost the loyalty of its workers, who felt that they were being treated like moving parts.

Although repeated defeats had cooled the ardor of many Erwin workers, recurrent layoffs, wage cuts, and workload changes aroused others. According to Esther Jenks, the sewing room was a perpetual "hot spot." The women who sewed, inspected, and folded sheets became "really upset about the way they got laid off" and the favoritism shown in decisions to call them back to work. Workers like Jenks, a battery-filler, had problems with workload changes. Because she worked on the second shift, she also suffered occasional days off when the overseers gave a day's work to the spare hands. Combined with the general increase in the pace of work and the requirements for workers to keep up production, Jenks concluded that the company had deliberately moved "away from their people." Managers had grown so obsessed with "all these technical things" that they had forgotten "the human element." Feeling abused and manipulated, women like Esther Jenks welcomed the opportunity to join an organization that offerred them a voice.[86]

The rise of the CIO, its presence in Durham's textile worker communities, and its efforts to develop a new form of militant industrial unionism, widened existing cleavages in the AFL-affiliated TWIU. White activists, chafing under Evans' heavy-handed, personalistic authority, resumed their campaign for union democracy. Durham leaders were attracted by the drama of the CIO-sponsored challenges to industrial giants and defended their textile colleagues against the purges the AFL demanded of all its affiliated bodies.[87] Black workers, gradually learning about a labor movement that placed "social equality" on its agenda, began to question TWIU practices that catered to white prejudice.

Aware that a majority of his southern constituency was attracted to the "Lewis way of organizing," Evans toyed briefly with bringing the TWIU into the CIO under John L. Lewis's charismatic leadership.[88] But fearing the loss of the union label, which AFL members honored, and possible raiding by the International Association of Machinists, who were pursuing machine fixers, Evans decided to stick with the AFL.

A series of letters between Evans and Durham correspondents suggested an additional motive for Evans' decision: the greater racial egalitarianism promised by the CIO. Endorsing H. A. McCrimmon's decision to prevent the former president of a black local from addressing a meeting because of his suspected radicalism, Evans gave McCrimmon the power "to make them do what they should do and never give them any free right to do as they think they should."[89] A month later, in June 1937, an exchange of letters with Sam Blane, a local leader, gave Evans the reassuring news that neither CIO nor "Communist" activity was brewing in Durham. Evans responded by launching an attack on "communistic-social equality" and accused the former leader of the black local of expounding that philosophy.[90] Undoubtedly worried by the CIO's support for successful campaigns among tobacco workers in Richmond, Evans continued to express suspicion of local black leaders in Durham while trying to prevent a white rank and file revolt.[91] Responding to the competition from the CIO, local whites redoubled their efforts to organize black workers while steadfastly resisting "social equality."[92] For their part, black workers had several choices: they could accept the TWIU as it existed under Evans' paternal dictatorship, forge an alliance with white activists to remove Evans from power, or pin their hopes on a distant CIO which, thanks to the local strength of the TWIU among white workers, never came into Durham in force. Workers like Oliver Harvey, who refused to abandon their belief that "'union' means together," stayed outside the labor movement that reached Durham in the 1930s.[93] A two-sided struggle for control over the TWIU ensued between local rebels and the Evans clique.

The April 1939 strike against L and M, the first strike by tobacco workers in Durham history, occurred during the internal battle within the TWIU. Having formed connections with other white locals at L and M plants in Richmond and other cities, Local 176 broke with Evans' conservative tradition by having "an honorable, peaceful strike" for a preferential shop. Local 208 took an active part in the work action, which succeeded in closing L and M factories across the nation. Lacking the exuberance of the 1934 textile strike, the TWIU locals picketed the closed plant for eleven days before the company capitulated to their demands.[94] The new contract, signed in June 1939, informed employees that L and M preferred that they join the union and also established collective bargaining as a permanent fixture in company labor relations.[95] This achievement, based on interracial cooperation between the two TWIU locals, strengthened the alliance between rank and file dissidents. A new generation appeared to have overcome the barriers to class-based unity that employers had depended upon to keep workers divided. Nervously, Evans and prescient employers like Kemp P. Lewis awaited the next stage in the creation of a united working class.[96]

For black women in the stemmery, the L and M strike served as another demonstration of their impotence, or, to the disaffected, the irrelevance of the union to their welfare. Active supporters of Local 194 excused the organization's absence from the picket line, saying the local was "too weak" to strike. Chester Clarke, who believed that "times commenced getting a little better" after the union was organized, remembered the reasons other black workers didn't join as readily as he did: "I joined when they commenced organizing. A whole lot didn't join; they said the union wasn't no good. They found out what was good . . . later after they got straightened out like they wanted! I mean the white folks and all joined . . . The white and colored went in then and he gave them that nickel raise." Yet even Chester's wife wasn't convinced. Roxanne Clarke explained her decision to give up her job at L and M during the strike: "Then when they had the strike—we was in the union—they said that all them that went up and marched wouldn't have their jobs back, so I went down to Robertson, at the factory down there, and worked. I said I wasn't gonna march out there." Later she regretted her decision ("I didn't see into it like I do now"), but she never returned to L and M.[97] Annie Mack Barbee's version was much more cynical:

> The black people had no choice when the white people closed down on their side . . . I don't say that the black people did it 'cause they didn't have no voice, no how. And that was oneness. But they did it. I've said, as poor as black folks is, you know they won't stay home. No, that was their bread . . . The white people did it . . . I guess they got what they wanted.[98]

Although many employees at L and M and American developed positive attitudes about the union, the deep-seated mistrust felt by many black women was an important factor in the union's feeble beginning.

In fall 1939, the white locals and the black male leadership of Local 208 joined with other southern locals in forcing the TWIU to hold its first convention in over thirty years. The convention's decision to sever the presidential office from the office of secretary and treasurer struck a blow at Evans' monopoly of power.

The victory over L and M and Evans' loss of two of his offices did little to ease the problems facing black stemmers. Locals 194 and 204 continued their uphill battle for survival. Now, as indicated by Daisy Jones in another letter pleading for a dispensation from dues payments, the local faced a massive threat to its existence. The tendency for the company to replace stemmers with machines had accelerated after the passage of the Fair Labor Standards Act in 1938. Writing to Evans, Jones reported:

> L & M has and is still installing machinery that is taking the jobs from the workers and laying them off rapidly, sometimes as many as twenty-five in one day. For this reason everyone has become alarmed. They are watching to see just what will be best for them. The second reason: we have not been working but four days per week. That makes the money hard to get for dues or anything.[99]

The plight of the local was intensified by the terms of the contract negotiated by the TWIU for Local 194 in October 1939: these displaced workers enjoyed seniority rights only "among women by various occupations in the stemmery."[100] No matter how long they had worked for L and M, they could not bid for jobs held by black men in the stemmery, the cigarette department, or for jobs held by white workers in any of the departments. L and M proceeded to cut its stemmery labor force in half during the late 1930s unimpeded by the TWIU or the other locals who protected their positions in the factory hierarchy.

While black women were being "cut off" from their livelihood, white workers and their black allies were triumphing over Evans and the old guard.[101] In late 1940 the coalition chased Evans from office altogether and placed a Louisville man in the presidency. Durham activists like Sam Blane assumed official positions as vice presidents and paid organizers. Roy Trice, the president of Local 208, narrowly lost the chance to join George Benjamin from Winston-Salem as the TWIU's first black vice president.[102]

While Durham tobacco workers were celebrating victories and enduring layoffs, the torturous course of labor relations in West Durham continued. Frustrated by the stalemate in contract negotiations, Local 246, soon to be a local of the newly formed Textile Workers Union of America (TWUA), broke off negotiations for an indefinite period.[103] Instead of attempting to negotiate, the local focused its energies on representing workers in meetings with management over shop-floor problems. Following company policy, however, supervisors listened to complaints but refused to yield on any issue. When a shop committee pressed a complaint from loom fixers concerned about the discharge of "a boy" from the third shift, the supervisor told the union representatives: "We always expected in the future to handle these things as we saw fit and we never expected to take these matters up with them as it was a matter entirely in our jurisdiction."[104]

After the inclusive strike by about 250 employees in the sewing room, the Erwin management felt confident that the union represented "a few hotheaded and dissatisfied employees" rather than "the more substantial, the more intelligent, and the most highly respected and best paid type of our employees (many of our loom fixers, weavers, etc)."[105] Accordingly, the management decided to implement the advice of Carl Harris to alter the workload assigned to loom fixers. Eliminating four of the fourteen loom fixers assigned to the weave room, the management told the disgruntled fixers that they could take a demotion to become weavers, be laid off if they felt too old, or be sent to overhaul looms. To emphasize their determination, an Erwin official told the loom fixers that the company contained an inventory sufficient to survive a strike.[106] Similar complaints from women in the sewing and spinning departments about increased workloads, which "meant throwing some out of work," received the same adamant response. The Erwin management had resolved to eliminate the irritation of constant discussions with discontented employees. The local, for its part, could not avoid the challenge posed by the company. Both sides geared up for a decisive battle.

On March 11, 1940, the loom fixers walked out. Fifty per cent of the Erwin employees from the No. 1 plant initially joined the striking fixers.[107] Another half of the labor force tried to cross the picket lines to work and fights broke out. Esther Jenks and a non-striking employee were involved in one battle. As Jenks recalled the encounter: "In fact, this lady said I pulled her hair. She made the brag that her overseer would give her anything she wanted. She didn't have to join the union. But I didn't hear of her bragging after that. And, she joined the union, this girl did."[108] Arrested, Jenks appeared in court, where she was particularly angered by non-strikers who lied on the witness stand against their fellow workers. But the refusal to change company policy gradually wore down the strikers. By March 26, Lewis reported to one of the Carrs that the company was "running nearly all the machinery and [had] replaced a great many strikers."[109] Sensing victory, Lewis credited "our having proper police protection" for the company's ability to "keep our gates open and gradually build back our operations until . . . the strikers voted to go back to work." He wrote the governor of North Carolina on the day after the vote to applaud his stand that "people who want to work should be allowed to work."[110] Although he expressed regret that many strikers "had to lose their jobs," a franker letter to an Erwin director claimed that the dismissal of some three hundred union supporters had cleared "the atmosphere" in West Durham for good. Confident that the union had now grown "very unpopular," he planned to move in for the kill by calling for another election to recertify the union before resuming contract negotiations.[111]

The three hundred Erwin workers who had lost their jobs now faced their severest test. They were out of work and had suffered a resounding defeat. Eldred Jenks, who had not broken ranks because his daughters had threatened to kick him in the head if he did, soon returned to work as a warper because his skills were still in demand. The oldest Jenks sister also was called back to work, but Esther and her sister Ethel remained unemployed. Esther could find nothing for the next eleven months.[112] Luther Riley was out of a job for six months and his brother Lester was out for a year. While their right to be rehired at Erwin Mills was being appealed to the National Labor Relations Board, the unemployed strikers "helped one another the best we could until we got us something to do."[113] Religious faith sustained women like Esther Jenks. Other workers found odd jobs.[114] "Share and share alike," the old motto of the family economy, offered the social security that workers could not find through their own efforts.[115]

Sure that he held the upper hand, Kemp P. Lewis tried to consolidate his gains. The TWUA counterattacked by charging that the strike concerned not only a change in work assignments but Erwin's failure to bargain in good faith. Lewis insisted the company had always been willing to sign a contract if it contained a clause that the "union would not coerce or intimidate non-union" employees.[116] He followed his attorney's advice and refused to reinstate the dismissed employees, because to do so would risk a return to "union domination."[117] Pursuing the policy that had brought on the strike, the Erwin management proposed in July 1940 to install "the new work arrangement in No. 4 similar to the one . . . that caused the strike." In the face of renewed employee protests, Lewis insisted that managers "do our duty." He wrote to an Erwin director, "It would be fatal if it should get out that we are afraid to take action when the necessity arises."[118] When Local 246 began to press for negotiations in September 1940, Lewis replied that the company would insist on "a proviso in the contract that an election must be held, and that the fair way to vote would be for only those that worked to vote." He also warned the union delegation that the company would not "stand for anything like insubordination or impudence or anything of that kind." As he told W. R. Perkins, an Erwin director and former associate of the Dukes in the American Tobacco Company, "We are trying to hold a firm grip on the discipline of the mill." Lewis's optimism did not last. "A great many of those who are still unemployed because of the strike are very bitter," he told Perkins six months later and assured him that he would be kept "advised of any developments."[119] Final victory seemed to be eluding his grasp.

Although the local lost some membership in the aftermath of the strike, the nucleus remained. The shop stewards and general shop committee representatives resumed the tedious battles with a recalcitrant management. Sending an experienced organizer into Durham in late 1940, the TWUA launched a new membership drive in the Erwin chain.[120] The union also won its appeal before the NLRB; the board held that the fired workers deserved reinstatement. Esther Jenks and the other union stalwarts finally returned to work, living testimony to persistence and federal support for the union position. Bitter feelings lingered. Jenks and other union supporters ostracized those who had betrayed their fellows. When a woman who had given false testimony against a striker reproached Jenks, she exploded: "I'm going to tell you exactly how I feel about you. If you get on that stand and swear a lie against one of my fellow workers, you'll lie on me. I don't want no part of you."[121] Aided by workers' renewed anger over changes in work assignments and by the favorable decision of the NLRB, Jenks and her allies brought more workers back into the local. When the National Defense Mediation Board ruled in March 1941, one year after the strike, that Erwin Mills must sign a contract with Local 246 in order to sell cloth to the military, the workers who had borne the costs of the strike savored the moment of victory.[122]

■ As the preparations for war created a new climate for labor relations, the women who had embraced labor activism could enjoy the fruits of their efforts. A favorable conjuncture of people and events had transformed Durham into the best organized city in the state. Although women never assumed leadership roles in union activities, their participation, given their numbers, was crucial to success. They served as shop stewards, corresponding secretaries, financial secretaries, and the like, and generally the men in the unions recognized their contributions.

Decades later, many women still spoke proudly about their activities. They mentioned the tangible benefits that had been achieved—seniority, pensions, improved wages, job security—and also the intangible rewards of greater dignity, respect, and the right to a "say-so" about work conditions. Esther Jenks described her union as a "basic freedom." Dena Coley mentioned increased salaries, access to "different kinds of jobs," and seniority; she added, "We had to come so far." Pearl Barbee declared that "the union did a lot" for her by forcing L and M to allow her to sit down after she got too sick to stand. Joe Daniels remembered that "all of us pulled up together, white and colored. One didn't get more than the other." Horace Mize revelled in his old comradeship with Sam Blane; the two had traveled through Durham neighborhoods inviting black workers to join the union. Rachel Medlin exuded pride in her years as a union officer. Ada Scoggins claimed that the "union made a whole lot of difference. You could get better satisfaction. If a thing went wrong, you could tell your head official and he'd straighten it out."[123] These survivors of a harsher time relished the power that came from having a voice in their working conditions.

The shift in the balance of power between employers and workers was reflected in the political system. An alliance of trade unionists, the liberal professional middle class, and the Durham Committee on Negro Affairs wrested control of local government from the old conservative coalition of manufacturers and their business allies. The Durham Committee on Negro Affairs, once the exclusive domain of the black business elite, welcomed black labor leaders to active membership. A labor paper bound the new working-class constituency together while promoting the liberal political program favored by the national labor movement. The Durham *Labor News* and the CIO-affiliated Industrial Union Council supported civil rights legislation being debated in Congress. Education sponsored by the TWUA locals taught workers to extend their vision of their rights to include political activity and support for pro-labor candidates.[124] When a new generation of Second World War veterans assumed leadership of the local labor unions, they found that Durham's labor, racial, and liberal coalition offered a unique environment. Wilbur Hobby rose from the Local 183 to become a prominent leader at the state level. When younger blacks took control of Local 208, they began to press their demands for equal treatment in the union and in the larger society. Brown vs. the Board of Education of Topeka seemed to create the momentum for a great transformation similar to the passage of the NRA thirty years before.

The urban contours of Durham offered visible evidence of the shifting balance of economic and political power. The Erwin mill village was an early casualty. No longer willing to subsidize housing for ungrateful employees, Erwin Mills began to sell its houses in the 1940s. Esther Jenks, aided by her sisters, became the owner of a home in West Durham. Some houses were sold to buyers who didn't work in the mills—to the distress of Bessie Buchanan, who missed the old, homogeneous community. Tobacco workers, black and white, acquired automobiles and took advantage of postwar housing policies to purchase homes far from their workplace. Conversely, the decaying mill villages in East Durham became slums surrounding abandoned mills. Only Golden Belt survived in that section of Durham. Pearl Mill and its village gave way to an apartment complex that retained only the mill tower to mark its former identity. Other apartments, single family houses, and duplexes disrupted the former coherence of industrial neighborhoods. Some disappeared altogether. Urban renewal, roadbuilding, and the expansion of Duke University and its medical complex eliminated Monkey Bottoms, Buggy Bottom, a major section of Hayti, and parts of West Durham. As working-class communities surrendered their territorial integrity, many of their inhabitants moved into segregated suburbs. Unlike the railroad that had attracted people and industry to Durham, the new roads encouraged the population to drift away from the city's industrial heart. Apparently Durham's organized working class had realized its share of the American dream. The industrial city dissolved into the endless suburbs of the post-war South.[125]

Yet a person seeking former industrial workers to interview quickly discovers that not all are living in ranch-style houses or refurbished mill tenements. Interviews confirmed that not everyone had shared in the prosperity. The same interviews also elicited some criticism and indifference toward union achievements. Black workers and some of the older textile workers were more likely to express dissatisfaction, while white tobacco workers and younger textile workers were more positive. Ella Faucette, an ardent early supporter of Local 204, remarked, "It was unfair" that "black jobs never did come up to the white."[126] Pearl Barbee mentioned that she had been "cut off" like other black women. Oscar Scoggins, referring to his aunt Ada and other black women, spoke bitterly about the policies that displaced so many black workers from the industry. When asked what happened to the women "cut off" he answered, "Nothing, except die."[127] His aunt, however, returned to domestic service. Other women joined the public form of that occupation by entering the dormitories and endless corridors of the university they called Duke's. Annie Mack Barbee spoke more caustically about the union. She recalled a female shop steward's intervention in a dispute between a black worker and the foreman who had called him "boy." After the steward prevented the angry worker from throwing the supervisor out the four-story window, the worker cursed her and the "union mess" that offered him no support in his battle to be addressed by name. Barbee clearly endorsed his sentiments. She also remembered her last day of work at L and M:

> The very day we quit working up there, here come the machines . . . Here come the machines and the white man was up there putting up signs for the bathrooms—"White Only." That's up there at Liggett and Myers. So the white women went up there and they didn't need to put no signs . . . I didn't get anything from Liggett and Myers . . . The mass of black women didn't get a whole lot of nothing from them.[128]

By implication, her indictment encompassed both union and company. Neither had opened new areas of the factory to displaced black women, despite their seniority. Both Theotis Williamson and Bessie Buchanan agreed that work had been easier and community life better in the old pre-union days. When asked whether the union had brought improvements to West Durham, Buchanan replied: "Not a bit in the world. In my opinion, it made it harder and harder. Now they have upped the wages a lot, but it's killing the people. So what has been gained by it?"[129] Other retired textile, hosiery, and tobacco workers, clustered in the subsidized housing that Durham offered its impoverished elderly poor, were clear evidence that the benefits of unionization had not lifted everyone out of poverty.

Interviews with the men who had led Durham's unions offered some clues to the mixed reviews. Wilbur Hobby, a product of Edgemont, the Second World War, and Local 183, spoke about the impact of the 1954 U.S. Supreme Court decision on the labor-liberal-black alliance in Durham. Heightened racial tensions had split the alliance, allowing conservative whites to regain control. These tensions, moreover, had weakened the tobacco worker unions; some whites joined the Klan and some blacks became civil rights activists.[130] The internal dissention made it extremely unlikely that white tobacco workers would open their positions to displaced blacks. Oscar Scoggins felt that the union and ultimately the federal government had betrayed black workers. The union had allowed the dismissal of most black workers, so that a majority in the 1930s became a minority in the 1950s. Beginning in the late 1940s, Local 208 had pressed for equal treatment from the union. Their lawyer in the 1960s, Floyd McKissick, spoke in their name: "We want a chance to get any job that we have laid down our blood and guts all through these years and inhaled all of that tobacco dust down there."[131] Yet in 1964 the federal government combined forces with the TWIU and L and M and required a merger between black and white workers. There had been little pressure for integration until the blacks were effectively outnumbered. Some members left the TWIU after that defeat in the courts, and its memory still rankled them decades later.

Another former union official spoke about the fratricidal conflict that had engulfed the TWUA after its failures to continue the southern offensive. A walkout at the 1952 TWUA Convention had led the Durham local to become affiliated with the remnants of the UTW. Other battles against "red hots," or radicals, who attempted to move the union leftward also left their marks in suspicious attitudes toward outsiders.[132] By the 1960s, the Burlington chain had accepted the Durham local into its mostly non-union plants because the union posed little risk. Its isolation and inward-looking character displayed little potential for a membership drive in the rest of the Burlington empire. Although veterans remained loyal to the union, its spirit had aged with its membership.

Some problems were beyond the ability of union or membership to overcome. The national drift toward conservatism after the Second World War, anti-union legislation like Taft-Hartley, and the decline in union militancy were felt with special force in the South, always the weakest area for the movement. The decline of some local companies, particularly textiles, and L and M, decreased the demand for labor, thus undermining labor's bargaining position. Durham, like the nation itself, was shifting from industry toward service. Duke University and the health industry replaced manufacturing as the major employer in Durham, thereby creating a two-tiered labor force of low-waged custodial and cafeteria workers and high-salaried professionals. The dispersal of workers during the Second World War was accentuated by the post-war dissolution of the working-class communities.[133] Resembling the rest of the nation, Durham's decline as an industrial center after 1940 was a major factor in undermining the power of organized labor.

Labor's successes came at a particular historical conjuncture when the nation had lost faith in its business elite and the federal government smiled on the industrial working class. The movement lost its vitality when that moment passed. The civil rights and the feminist movements stirred after the labor movement had begun its retreat. The ideologies of these three movements, unfortunately, never merged into a single coherent vision. Lacking a feminist analysis, the unions never fully mobilized their female constitutents. Warning restless black members against creating a "division between black and white," the unions achieved a partial solidarity that denied racial antagonisms instead of dealing with them.[134] Similarly, the civil rights movements' insistence on the primacy of racial injustice masked gender and class conflicts within the black community. Each movement might have benefited from the insights of the others.[135] The working-class women of Durham thus lost an opportunity to hear challenges to pervasive assumptions about women's place and work.

The comments of Durham workers must be seen in a particular perspective. These workers, after all, belonged to the most successful unions in the state. Durham's white tobacco unions were the most active in the TWIU and the most earnest in their efforts to enlist black workers. Together with the CIO-affiliated unions in Richmond and Winston-Salem, the TWIU transformed the tobacco industry into the most unionized sector in the South.[136] Similarly, compared with the difficulties experienced elsewhere by union organizers in textiles, Durham was a rare success story. Durham unions survived in both industries from the peak of labor militancy in the 1930s and 1940s through the decline in the post-war period. Still, the victories were flawed by the stubborn persistence of racial conflicts and gender inequalities. Annie Mack Barbee's sarcastic reference to "oneness" on white terms was echoed in Ozzie Richmond's assessment of the TWIU's record after the 1939 victory at L and M: "It kept on going the same when the union came in. I think because the majority of the whites seek to overrule the black. It stayed that way. Some on the committees would say they weren't going to let those blacks take white folks' jobs."[137]

Most white tobacco workers believed that blacks had received their just rewards. Rose Weeks insisted that blacks "had no desire to run that machinery after civil rights," despite black agitation.[138] Martha Harris had worked for decades in rigid separation from blacks. She responded to the changes that brought blacks into all parts of the factory by avoiding any return visits. She also opposed the practice of women taking "men's jobs."[139] The former president and one of the organizers of Local 176 blamed declining productivity and workmanship on equal opportunity legislation:

To keep women on the job, management relinquished certain requirements . . . and it has a tendency to bring down the overall efficiency . . . Whenever you're paying two people identical and one is less efficient than the other, it's easier for the one who's more efficient to fall down.

It takes a strong person to say that I'm going to do a good job. Now this doesn't just apply to the sexes. It relates more clearly to the color line. We find that, in most instances, due to integration, that quality has diminished a great deal.

His belief that only white men were "strong" and "efficient" enough "to do a good job" revealed the divided loyalties of a privileged white worker who identified with the company at the same time as he spoke for the workers.[140] Although a few white workers welcomed the movement of blacks into better jobs, most regretted the passing of a time when everyone knew their "place" and kept to it.

As their comments make clear, class solidarity for the vast majority of tobacco workers was subordinate to caste solidarity. Yet the overwhelming significance of race must not obscure evidence of everything else. Even as junior partners, black leaders felt that they were making gains for their people. They viewed their union with pride and were willing to fight for it against the more radical CIO-affiliate.[141] Indeed, their bitterest statements concerned their forced integration with a white-controlled local, not their struggles during the segregated years. Similarly, the competing claims of class and race must not obscure the issue of gender. The leadership in the locals and the partnerships between local leaders involved black and white men. The same local of black male workers that broke away from the stemmers in the late 1930s to forge an alliance with the white L and M local served to champion the interests of black workers in the post-war decades. Male bonding and male jousting set the tone of the new relationship. Women, however, remained isolated from one another and from power on either side of the color line. The balance of power began to shift visibly between the classes and the races, but sexual politics showed almost no change.

The flaws that undermined support for unions among Durham's textile workers are also easy to identify. The very process that sparked the union, the "stretch-out," continued despite the union's presence. Indeed, Bessie Buchanan accused the union of major responsibility for the faster pace of work that was "killing the people."[142] Control over the workplace remained firmly in management's hands while Durham unions concentrated on bargaining for better wages and benefits. The passage of a "right to work" law contributed to the weakening of the union. Now workers no longer had to belong in order to gain union representation. As the TWUA gave way to the revived UTW, the weaknesses in the union became more evident. When the movement for workers' health gained momentum in the 1970s, the Durham local remained on the sidelines of activity sponsored by the successor to the TWUA, the Amalgamated Clothing and Textile Workers Union. Although the Durham local clung to life as other locals disappeared, it was only a ghost of its once vibrant self.

The historical legacy of the Durham unions, then, is a mixture of achievements and setbacks, a record that gives credibility to both their supporters and their detractors. The achievements of individual workers, on the other hand, deserve a more positive assessment. The desperate rural refugees who trekked into Durham made considerable progress in only a few decades. They had been set to work in a divided work place and molded into a segmented labor force. Domestic labor and childcare, more segregated and isolated than labor in the factory, tied the family's female members to their households. Economic exploitation also encouraged women's dependence on male breadwinners. Already divided into antagonistic racial groups, they colluded in their own fragmentation; even so, they managed to overcome some of the distance between black and white. And as one generation succeeded the other, the working-class communities matured. The typical female industrial worker shifted from a young unmarried woman to a married woman who perceived herself as part of a permanent wage-earning class. Greater commitment to improving job conditions underlay a willingness to ally with the other racial group. Married women in the Erwin sewing room led the walkouts that forced managers to consider their needs. Without their female membership, neither the TWUA nor the TWIU could have established a foothold in Durham.

■ Let us briefly consider women apart from their identity as workers and union members. Such an approach is essential, because working-class history all too unwittingly adopts a male-defined measure by which women are found wanting. The question is often posed: Why are women so hard to organize? But if we adopt a perspective that allows for women's needs, the question becomes: Why are class issues defined in male terms? And more specifically: Why are unions irrelevant to so much of women's lives? Recast in this form, the answers come more easily. Unions almost never link the personal and the political, the private and the public work places. Instead, they accept the conventional definition of work, politics, economics, and organization. A union becomes a formal, bureaucratic structure, an instrument for collective bargaining, an organization apart from daily life. This narrow vision essentially ignores the validity of other important community institutions, such as church, school, and household. Shallow-rooted in the workers' communities because of estrangement from the churches, the unions survived but did not flourish among women, the most attentive and ardent churchgoers. Without proper nourishment, the union as a living entity wilted in the long southern summers. Its narrow definition of class, which did not incorporate an understanding of culture and community, left the movement vulnerable when its opponents mustered their forces against it.

Women can never be wholehearted participants in a movement premised on their continued exploitation. A "movement culture" (to borrow a phrase from Lawrence Goodwyn) must infuse new, egalitarian values and ways of seeing to replace the hierarchical patterns imposed by the dominant culture. Men must yield control over women's reproductive capacities, labor, and persons. Releasing black women's potential, moreover, requires a reformation in racial as well as sexual attitudes. Rather than accepting racial and sexual hierarchies as natural or God-ordained, women and men must recognize them as flawed social conditions that can be changed.

No cultural transformation of major proportions took place in Durham. The legacy of the past, the constrictions of the present, and the limited vision of the movement that recruited Durham workers into formal bargaining with their employers offered only reform. The timid TWIU accommodated itself to the prejudices of its white members and sacrificed its black female constitutency. The more daring TWUA faltered before it could welcome black workers into its midst. Black and white women—"sisters under their skins"—never fully realized their kinship in a society where skin color blinded them to their common interests.

Measured against what might have been, the journey into Durham factories and urban households fell short. But if women's subordinate position, as many theorists argue, is a result of their primary responsibility for household labor and childcare, then Durham women steadily gained greater freedom. Almost entirely unpaid in the countryside, they now claimed a share of society's resources through wage-earning. Formerly isolated in rural homesteads, they now enjoyed daily social contact in the workplace and the surrounding community. Once politically disfranchised, they had become active in the public realm of shop-floor, church, community, and city-wide politics. Through their own efforts, aided by federal legislation and the power of their unions, they achieved a living wage by the 1940s. Families headed by women, despite their limited resources, could more readily survive in the city than the country. They had demonstrated their ability to organize in the church, the community, and the work place, and had gained a precious sense of their own power and entitlements. Their pride in having survived the hard times and tribulations was well deserved. With gritty determination, they had done "women's work" and "men's work" for women's wages. They had arrived at a better place.

Appendix

ORAL HISTORY SOURCES AND METHODOLOGY

The present study is based on ninety oral history interviews, including sixty-four conducted by the author. Of the twenty-nine others, nineteen were done by scholars associated with the Southern Oral History Program at the University of North Carolina. The core interviews were fifty-five life histories of industrial workers employed in Durham between 1900 and 1950 (see Table 27). Other interviews were conducted with agricultural workers, teachers, manufacturers, domestic workers, and other residents of Durham in the period between 1880 and 1940. The interviews posed a series of questions about family background, work experience, involvement in union or other community activities, family relationships, and work-related contacts with coworkers and employers. There was no direct attempt to elicit attitudes toward race, gender, or class, and no attempt to force the informant to follow the outline of topics drawn up by the interviewer. Among other interviews are more than two hundred oral histories contained in the North Carolina Federal Writers' Project collection, excerpts from surveys conducted by Emma Duke of the U.S. Children's Bureau in 1918, by Margaret Hagood among tenant farm women in the 1930s, by Orie Latham Hatcher among young employed women in Durham in the mid-1920s, and by investigators under Charles S. Johnson, who interviewed tobacco workers in Durham in 1935.

Although oral history is an irreplaceable tool in a study intended to discover the ways in which women experience and perceive their lives, it has certain limitations. The gender, race, and class of the interviewer shape the informant's responses in ways difficult to measure. For example, black in-

APPENDIX

Table 27.
Background of Durham Industrial Workers Interviewed, 1900–1950*

	BY AUTHOR					BY OTHERS				
INDUSTRY	WM	WF	BM	BF	TOTAL	WM	WF	BM	BF	TOTAL
Tobacco	4	11	5	6	26	6	11	11	14	42†
Textile	5	6	0	1	12	8	9	0	1	18†
Domestic	0	0	0	5	5	0	0	0	5	5
Rural inhabitants	2	10	2	8	22‡	3	11	4	11	29‡

*N = 55; WM = white males; WF = white females; BM = black males; BF = black females.
†These figures include 5 workers who moved between textile and tobacco occupations.
‡These figures include 7 people also in the tobacco and textile worker groups.

formants were far more likely to express anger about racial injustice to black interviewers. White informants, however, displayed less hesitation in discussing their racial views. The interviewer also sensed that the format of the interviews, which involved one or two formal sessions, was less productive with women than men. Studies by anthropologists and sociologists indicate that women are more likely to reveal their views in intimate settings, whereas men are more accustomed to public presentation of their opinions. Each interview, moreover, involved an encounter between a historian and an industrial worker, two people of vastly different backgrounds. Despite the intentions of the interviewer, it was harder to reconstruct patterns of daily life in the household and domestic labor than it was to retrieve memories of the public workplace. Moreover, the data were shaped by all these factors because the informants were conscious of speaking to a particular audience. There is no way to estimate how the result might have differed given another approach, another interviewer, or another setting.

APPENDIX

INTERVIEWERS AND INFORMANTS

Some of the informants and interviewers who contributed to this study include the following:

Interviewer	Informant	Affiliation/Occupation
Non-industrial workers		
Dolores Janiewski	Solomon Barkin	TWUA official (interviewed by mail)
	James Cavanaugh	TWUA historian (interviewed by mail)
	William R. Currin	L and M vice president
	Frank DeVyver	Erwin Mills official
	W. C. Dula	Author of local history on Durham
	Stuart Kaufman	TWIU historian
	George Lougee	Local historian and journalist
	Leonard Rapport	Participant in Federal Writers' Project, former Durham resident
	William H. Ruffin	Former Erwin Mills president
	Earlie Thorpe	Black historian, Durham resident, son and nephew of Durham tobacco workers
Lanier Rand, Southern Oral History Program	George Parks	Golden Belt president

Industrial workers (interviews from the Southern Oral History Program Collection)

Interviewer	Informant	Affiliation/Occupation
Bill Finger	Wilbur Hobby	Tobacco worker
Glenn Hinson	Mary Bailey	Tobacco worker
	Chester and Roxanna Clarke	Tobacco workers
	Thomas Burt	Tobacco worker
	John Patterson	Tobacco worker
	Sallina McMillon	Tobacco worker
	Reginald Mitchener	Tobacco worker
Dolores Janiewski	Esther Jenks	Textile worker
	Martha Gena Harris	Tobacco worker
Beverly Jones	Annie Mack Barbee	Tobacco worker
	Charlie Decoda Mack	Tobacco worker
	Dora Scott Miller	Tobacco worker

APPENDIX

Interviewer	Informant	Affiliation/Occupation
Industrial workers (interviews from the Southern Oral History Program Collection)		
Valerie Quinney and Brent Glass	Carrboro textile workers	
Lanier Rand	Bessie Taylor Buchanan	Textile worker
	Ernest Latta	Tobacco worker
	Obie Richmond	Tobacco worker
	Ozzie Richmond	Tobacco worker
	Luther Riley	Textile worker
	Theotis Williamson	Textile worker
Industrial workers (interviews by unaffiliated scholars)		
Linda Daniel	*Mollie Seagrove	Hosiery worker
Linda Guthrie	*Pearl Barbee	Tobacco worker
	*Hetty Love	Tobacco worker
History 101	*Nellie Carter	Tobacco worker
	*George Ferndale	Hosiery worker
Stuart Kaufman	*Horace Mize	Tobacco worker
George McDaniel	*Anna Ruffin Whitted	Tenant
	*Annie Holman Green	Tenant
Peggy Rabb and Chris Potter	Senior citizens resident in Oldham and Henderson Towers	

*Pseudonym.

QUANTITATIVE SOURCES AND METHODOLOGY

The quantitative analysis presented in this study was based on samples taken from the 1880 and 1900 manuscript census at the National Archives for Orange/Durham, Person, and Granville Counties. When the sampling was underway, the 1910 manuscript census was not yet open to researchers. The counties sampled were selected as typical of the areas from which women migrated into Durham. The urban samples represent one-fifth of all the households containing a female aged twelve and over in the city of Durham and its surrounding suburbs for those census years selected. The rural samples represent a one-fiftieth sample of rural households containing a female aged twelve and over in rural Orange/Durham, Person, and Granville Counties. Orange County, from which Durham was created in 1881, was the unit of analysis in the 1880 sample. The sampling procedure involved taking every fifth or fiftieth household that met the criteria without random sampling because there was little risk of any recurrent pattern in this data base. In addition, a smaller, one-eighth sample was taken of suburban

APPENDIX

households containing textile, tobacco, or hosiery workers that also included a female aged twelve and over. Thus, the essential basis for selecting the households was the presence of a woman old enough to be working or bearing and caring for children in the chosen household.

After selection, the sample households and the members of the households were organized in a series of files and coded in a system developed by the author. Only the simpler statistical programs were run to analyze the data because its categorical nature did not justify elaborate programs such as regression analysis. Cross tabulations and frequency distributions were the major statistical tests used to explore women's working experiences in the rural Piedmont and in Durham. These were used to process 832 total housholds, including 262 rural households and 570 urban households for the years 1880 and 1900.

Other sources for the quantitative analysis included the studies undertaken by Charles S. Johnson for the National Recovery Administration, the investigations completed in 1907 for the U.S. Senate Report on the condition of working women and children, and published studies done by agricultural economists.

The major source of data, however, was the published volumes of the U.S. Department of Commerce, Bureau of the Census, for the years from 1880 through 1940. These included for general population data the following: 1880, Tenth Census, *Statistics of the Population of the United States* (Washington, D.C.: G.P.O., 1881); 1890, Eleventh Census, *Report on the Population of the United States* (Washington, D.C: G.P.O., 1895); 1900, Twelfth Census, *Population of the United States* (Washington, D.C.: G.P.O., 1901); 1910, Thirteenth Census, *General Population and Analysis* (Washington, D.C.: G.P.O., 1913); 1920, Fourteenth Census, *Number and Distribution of Inhabitants* (Washington, D.C.: G.P.O., 1921); 1930, Fifteenth Census, *Population* (Washington, D.C.: G.P.O., 1931); and 1940, Sixteenth Census, *Population* (Washington, D.C.: G.P.P., 1942). For agricultural data, the following agricultural censuses were used: 1880, Tenth Census, *Report on Production of Agriculture* (Washington, D.C.: G.P.O., 1883); 1900, Twelfth Census, *Agriculture* (Washington, D.C.: G.P.O., 1902); 1910, Thirteenth Census, *Agriculture: Reports by States* (Washington, D.C.: G.P.O., 1910); 1920, Fourteenth Census, *Agriculture: Reports by States* (Washington, D.C.: G.P.O., 1923); and 1930, Fifteenth Census, *Agriculture: Type of Farm* (Washington, D.C.: G.P.O., 1932). For manufacturing and occupational data the following publications were used: 1880, Tenth Census, *Report on the Manufacturing of the United States* (Washington, D.C.: G.P.O., 1883); 1890, Eleventh Census, *Report on Manufacturing Industries in the United States* (Washington, D.C.: G.P.O., 1895); 1900, Twelfth Census, *Manufactures: States and Territories* (Washington, D.C.: G.P.O., 1902); *Occupations at the Twelfth Census* (Washington, D.C.:

APPENDIX

G.P.O., 1904); Thirteenth Census, *Manufactures: Reports by States* (Washington, D.C.: G.P.O., 1909); *Census of Manufactures, 1909* (Washington, D.C.: G.P.O., 1910); 1920, Fourteenth Census, *Occupations* (Washington, D.C.: G.P.O., 1923); *Manufactures, 1919: Reports by States* (Washington, D.C.: G.P.O., 1923); 1930, Fifteenth Census, *Occupations by States* (Washington, D.C.: C.P.O., 1933); *Families: Reports by States* (Washington, D.C.: G.P.O., 1933); *Unemployment* (Washington, D.C.: G.P.O., 1933); *Manufactures: Reports by States* (Washington, D.C.: G.P.O., 1933); Sixteenth Census, *Manufactures, 1939* (Washington, D.C.: G.P.O., 1942); *The Labor Force* (Washington, D.C.: G.P.O., 1942); North Carolina Bureau of Labor Statistics, First to Twelfth Annual Reports (Raleigh, 1887–1898); North Carolina Bureau of Labor and Printing, Thirteenth to Twenty-First Annual Reports (Raleigh, 1899–1907); North Carolina Department of Labor and Printing, Twenty-Second to Thirty-Second Reports (Raleigh, 1908–1919).

Notes

KEY TO ABBREVIATIONS

AFL	American Federation of Labor
AVC	Arthur Vance Cole papers (PL/DU)
BND	Benjamin N. Duke papers (PL/DU)
CB	Children's Bureau record group (NA/DC)
DC	District of Columbia
DU	Duke University
ECMC	Erwin Cotton Mills Company papers (FD/PL/DU)
FD	Frank DeVyver papers (PL/DU)
JBD	James B. Duke papers (PL/DU)
JSC	Julian S. Carr papers (PL/DU)
KPL	Kemp P. Lewis papers (SHC/UNC)
ML	McKeldin Library (UM)
MOC	Mary O. Cowper papers (SHC/UNC)
NA	National Archives (DC)
NCFWP	North Carolina Federal Writers Project papers (SHC/UNC)
NLRB	National Labor Relations Board
NRA	National Recovery Administration record group (NA/DC)
PL	Perkins Library (DU)
SHC	Southern Historical Collection (UNC)
SOHP	Southern Oral History Program (SHC/UNC)
TWIU	Tobacco Workers International Union papers (ML/UM)
UM	University of Maryland
UNC	University of North Carolina
WB	Women's Bureau record group (NA/DC)

CHAPTER I

1. Quotations from Durham *Morning Herald*, 4, 5, and 23 Sept. 1934.
2. The phrase comes from a poem by Rudyard Kipling, "The Ladies," in *A Choice of Kipling Verse* (Garden City, N.Y.: Doubleday, 1962). The phrase, which I

NOTES TO CHAPTER I

remember from a poem encountered in my school days, refers to the kinship "under their skins" of an Irish washerwoman and the "Colonel's lady" and argues for the sisterhood of women across class and ethnic lines.

3. Like C. Vann Woodward, who first employed the term in his pioneering study, I agree that a "New South" began to emerge in places like Durham, although surrounded by the legacy of the old. See C. Vann Woodward, *Origins of the New South, 1877–1913* (Baton Rouge: Louisiana State University Press, 1951).

4. Edward Palmer Thompson, *The Making of the English Working Class* (New York: Vintage, 1966), 9–10.

5. For discussions of the connections between southern racial and class relationships, see Edmund S. Morgan, *American Slavery, American Freedom: The Ordeal of Colonial Virginia* (New York: W. W. Norton, 1975); Steven Hahn, *The Roots of Southern Populism: Yeoman Farmers and the Transformation of Georgia's Upper Piedmont, 1850–1890* (New York: Oxford University Press, 1983); Barbara J. Fields, "Ideology and Race in American History," in *Region, Race, and Reconstruction: Essays in Honor of C. Vann Woodward*, ed. J. Morgan Kousser and James M. McPherson (New York: Oxford University Press, 1983), 143–78; Roger L. Ransom and Richard Sutch, *One Kind of Freedom: The Economic Consequences of Emancipation* (Cambridge: Cambridge University Press, 1977); Jonathan M. Wiener, *Social Origins of the New South: Alabama, 1860–1885* (Baton Rouge: Louisiana State University Press, 1978); J. Morgan Kousser, *The Shaping of Southern Politics: Suffrage Restrictions and the Establishment of the One-Party South, 1880–1910* (New Haven: Yale University Press, 1975); Jay R. Mandle, *The Roots of Black Poverty: The Southern Plantation Economy after the Civil War* (Durham: Duke University Press, 1978); Roger W. Shugg, *Origins of Class Struggle in Louisiana: A Social History of White Farmers and Laborers during Slavery and After, 1840–1875* (Baton Rouge: Louisiana State University Press, 1972); and Harold D. Woodman, "Sequel to Slavery: The New History Views the Postbellum South," *Journal of Southern History* 43 (1977): 523–54.

6. Whether females are universally subordinated within the family and the private sphere and universally isolated from public power is an issue that I do not wish to discuss; I do not know enough about other societies and there are problems with the available data and with appropriate measurements of female subordination. Those interested in this issue should consult: Sherry B. Ortner and Harriet Whitehead, *Sexual Meanings: The Cultural Construction of Gender and Sexuality* (Cambridge: Cambridge University Press, 1982); Sandra Harding and Merrill B. Hintikka, eds., *Discovering Reality: Feminist Perspectives on Epistemology, Metaphysics, Methodology, and Philosophy of Science* (Dordrecht: D. Reidel Publishing, 1983); and Carol P. MacCormack and Marilyn Strathern, eds., *Nature, Culture and Gender* (Cambridge: Cambridge University Press, 1980).

7. For a discussion of the ways in which societies undergoing change fear pollution and strive for purity, see Mary Douglas, *Purity and Danger: An Analysis of Concepts of Pollution and Taboo* (London: Routledge and Kegan Paul, 1979). See also Carroll Smith-Rosenberg, "Sex as Symbol in Victorian Purity: An Ethnohistorical Analysis of Jacksonian America," in *Turning Points: Historical and Sociological Essays on the Family*, ed. John Demos and Sarane Spence Boocock (Chicago: University of Chicago Press, 1978), 212–47. Douglas's discussion of the

NOTES TO CHAPTER I

pollution rituals in the Hindu caste system offers some possible explanations of similar taboos in the southern racial system; see especially 124–27.

8. See the Appendix for a fuller discussion of the oral history and quantitative evidence used in this history.

9. See, for example, Jonathan Prude, *The Coming of Industrial Order: Town and Factory Life in Rural Massachusetts, 1810–1860* (Cambridge: Cambridge University Press, 1983); Daniel J. Walkowitz, *Worker City, Company Town: Iron- and Cotton-Worker Protest in Troy and Cohoes, New York, 1855–84* (Urbana: University of Illinois Press, 1981); Alan Dawley, *Class and Community: The Industrial Revolution in Lynn* (Cambridge: Harvard University Press, 1979); Bruce Laurie, *Working People of Philadelphia, 1800–1950* (Philadelphia: Temple University Press, 1980); Anthony F. C. Wallace, *Rockdale: The Growth of an American Village in the Early Industrial Revolution* (New York: W. W. Norton, 1978); Thomas Dublin, *Women at Work: The Transformation of Work and Community in Lowell, Massachusetts, 1826–1860* (New York: Columbia University Press, 1979); Leon Fink, *Workingmen's Democracy: The Knights of Labor and American Politics* (Urbana: University of Illinois Press, 1983); Michael H. Frisch and Daniel J. Walkowitz, eds., *Working-Class America: Essays on Labor, Community and American Society* (Urbana: University of Illinois Press, 1983); Peter J. Rachleff, *Black Labor in the South: Richmond, Virginia, 1865–1890* (Philadelphia: Temple University Press, 1984); and Melton A. McLaurin, *The Knights of Labor in the South* (Westport, Conn.: Greenwood Press, 1978). With the welcome but rare exceptions of Fink, Rachleff, and McLaurin, recent explorations of working-class communities rarely have ventured outside the Northeast and Midwest and almost never have integrated gender and race in their analysis of class formation. In this respect, the present study diverges from the usual practice in labor historiography.

10. All too often, southern historians have celebrated the family as a harmonious unit buffeted by the malevolent forces of the market, while ignoring conflicts within the family or in the communities of independent producers. By evading the issue of gender, they have also failed to demonstrate that harmony and interdependence were the prevalent values in the remote countryside. For varying perspectives on rural life before and during the emergence of commercial agriculture and industrialization, see Steven Hahn, "Common Right and Commonwealth: The Stock-Law Struggle and the Roots of Southern Populism," in *Region, Race, and Reconstruction*, ed. Kousser and McPherson, 51–88; Hahn, *The Roots of Southern Populism;* David Alan Corbin, *Life, Work, and Rebellion in the Coal Fields: The Southern West Virginia Miners, 1880–1922* (Urbana: University of Illinois Press, 1981); Ronald Eller, *Miners, Millhands, and Mountaineers: Industrialization of the Appalachian South, 1880–1930* (Knoxville: University of Tennessee Press, 1982); Crandall A. Shifflett, *Patronage and Poverty in the Tobacco South: Louisa County, Virginia, 1860–1900* (Knoxville: University of Tennessee Press, 1982); and Elizabeth Rauh Bethel, *Promiseland: A Century of Life in a Negro Community* (Philadelphia: Temple University Press, 1981). All these studies acknowledge racial and class conflicts in rural areas where blacks and whites lived close to one another, but only the exceptional study like Eller's and Bethel's deals with patriarchal domination and women's unequal position inside the independent, property-holding family economy. Harmony and interdependence may accurately describe interactions within the

household unit whose head relied on "family labor," but the case is not proved unless the issue of gender has been addressed.

11. Although Lawrence Goodwyn, the author of one of the most powerful explorations of the Farmers' Alliance in the South, repeatedly attacks the "received culture" of racial and class domination for hindering farmers from a full realization of their democratic potential, he gives the Farmers' Alliance organizers too much credit for creating a "movement culture" free of the old "habits of domination" (my phrase). In fact, class and racial conflict prevented the Farmers' Alliance from incorporating the entire farm population in their movement. See Lawrence Goodwyn, *Democratic Promise: The Populist Moment in America* (New York: Oxford University Press, 1976). Goodwyn's condemnation of the "received culture" constrasts oddly with Steven Hahn's emphasis on the "habits of mutuality," independence, interdependence, and ownership of productive resources that Hahn described as "linked intimately in this rural culture" (Hahn, "Common Right and Commonwealth," 55). Although the differences may stem from Goodwyn's attempt to survey the entire South and Hahn's examination of a few primarily white upcountry Georgia counties, a synthesis of their approaches could well describe the culture of the nonplantation South as combining "habits of domination" and "habits of mutuality."

12. For a discussion of the neglect of southern women and recent efforts to redress that omission, see Anne Firor Scott, "Historians Construct the Southern Woman," in *Sex, Race, and the Role of Women in the South,* ed. Joanne V. Hawks and Sheila L. Skemp (Jackson: University Press of Mississippi, 1983), 95–110; and the forthcoming essay by Anne Firor Scott and Jacquelyn Dowd Hall in the revised edition of *Writing Southern History,* ed. Arthur Link and Rembert Patrick (Baton Rouge: Louisiana State University Press, forthcoming). Anne Firor Scott and Jacquelyn Hall are leaders in the effort to place women in southern historiography.

13. Although no scholar has yet developed a fully integrated analysis of the interplay of race, gender, and class in the lives of women (or men), see Elizabeth Fox-Genovese, "Placing Women's History in History," *New Left Review* 133 (May-June 1982); 5–29; Gloria Joseph and Jill Lewis, *Common Differences: Conflicts in Black and White Feminist Perspectives* (Garden City, N.Y.: Anchor Books, 1981); Lydia Sargent, ed., *Women and Revolution: A Discussion of the Unhappy Marriage of Marxism and Feminism* (Boston: South End Press, 1981); and the work now underway by Bonnie Thornton Dill, Elizabeth Higginbotham, Cheryl Townsend Gilkes, and Evelyn Nakano Glenn, tentatively titled "A Way Out of No Way: The Impact of Racial Oppression on Women of Color in the United States." Among the growing list of books dealing with the intersection of gender and class in the lives of working women, I would include Alice Kessler-Harris, *Out to Work: A History of Wage-Earning Women in the United States* (New York: Oxford University Press, 1982); Barbara Melosh, *"The Physician's Hand": Work Culture and Conflict in American Nursing* (Philadelphia: Temple University Press, 1982); Leslie Woodcock Tentler, *Wage-Earning Women: Industrial Work and Family Life in the United States, 1900–1930* (New York: Oxford University Press, 1979); and Christine Stansell, "The Origins of the Sweatshop: Women and Early Industrialization in New York City," and Susan Porter Benson, " 'The Customers Ain't God': The Work Cul-

NOTES TO CHAPTER II

ture of Department-store Saleswomen, 1890–1940," in *Working-Class America,* ed. Frisch and Walkowitz, 78–103, 185–211.

14. Sara Evans, *Personal Politics: The Roots of Women's Liberation in the Civil Rights Movement and the New Left* (New York: Vintage, 1980), uses the term "redemptive" or "beloved" community. Barbara J. Fields, "Ideology and Race," writes about the rituals and slogans of white supremacy. I disagree with Fields's attempt to distinguish between race and class; she argues that "class is a concept that we can locate both at the level of objective reality and at the level of social appearances," while "race is a concept that we can locate at the level of appearances only" (151). As the rest of this study will demonstrate, race operated as something more than an ideological cover for class in the southern context.

CHAPTER II

1. Frank Tannenbaum, *Darker Phases of the South* (New York: G. P. Putnam, 1924), 144–45.

2. Raymond Williams, *The Country and the City* (New York: Oxford University Press, 1973), 284–87. Scholars now working to extend our knowledge of agriculture in the post–Civil War South include Harold D. Woodman, *King Cotton and His Retainers: Financing and Marketing the Cotton Crop of the South, 1800–1925* (Lexington: University of Kentucky Press, 1968); Steven Hahn, *The Roots of Southern Populism: Yeomen Farmers and the Transformation of Georgia's Upper Piedmont, 1850–1890* (New York: Oxford University Press, 1983); Eric Foner, *Nothing but Freedom: Emancipation and Its Legacy* (Baton Rouge: Louisiana State University Press, 1983); Michael Wayne, *The Reshaping of Plantation Society: The Natchez District, 1860–1880* (Baton Rouge: Louisiana State University Press, 1983); Charles L. Flynn, Jr., *White Land, Black Labor: Caste and Class in Late Nineteenth-Century Georgia* (Baton Rouge: Louisiana State University Press, 1983); and various other authors discussed in Harold D. Woodman, "Sequel to Slavery: The New History Views the Postbellum South," *Journal of Southern History* 43 (no. 4, 1977): 523–44.

3. Cameron support for the NCRR is discussed in Jean B. Anderson, "Fairintosh Plantation and the Camerons," North Carolina Division of Archives and History, June 1978, p. 63. The general impact on the local area is discussed in Durward T. Stokes, *Company Shops: The Town Built by a Railroad* (Winston-Salem, N.C.: John F. Blair, 1981), 2–7.

4. For a description of the beginnings of the bright tobacco culture, see Joseph Clarke Robert, *The Tobacco Kingdom: Plantation, Market and Factory in Virginia and North Carolina, 1800–1860* (Gloucester, Mass.: Peter Smith, 1965), 20–23; Nannie May Tilley, *The Bright Tobacco Industry: 1869–1929* (Chapel Hill: University of North Carolina Press, 1948); J. D. Cameron, *A Sketch of the Tobacco Interests in North Carolina* (Oxford, N.C.: W. A. Davis, 1881); and Samuel Thomas Emory, "Bright Tobacco in the Agriculture, Industry, and Foreign Trade of North Carolina" (Ph.D. diss., University of Chicago, 1939).

5. The creation of the crop lien system was a southwide phenomenon, and its

NOTES TO CHAPTER II

impact on the cotton-growing regions is discussed by Gavin Wright, *The Political Economy of the Cotton South: Households, Markets and Wealth in the Nineteenth Century* (New York: W. W. Norton, 1978); Roger L. Ransom and Richard Sutch, *One Kind of Freedom: The Economic Consequences of Emancipation* (Cambridge: Cambridge University Press, 1977); and Harold Woodman, *King Cotton*. For tobacco conditions in a Virginia county, see Crandall A. Shifflett, *Patronage and Poverty in the Tobacco South: Louisa County, Virginia, 1860–1900* (Knoxville: University of Tennessee Press, 1982).

6. As discussed in Robert, *Tobacco Kingdom*, and in Ronald L. Lewis, *Coal, Iron and Slaves: Industrial Slavery in Virginia, 1715–1865* (Westport, Conn.: Greenwood Press, 1979).

7. North Carolina Bureau of Labor Statistics, *First Annual Report for the Year 1887* (Raleigh, 1887), 91, 97, 128.

8. North Carolina Bureau of Labor Statistics, *Fifth Annual Report for the Year 1891* (Raleigh, 1892), 82.

9. See Table 1.

10. North Carolina Bureau of Labor Statistics, *Fifth Annual Report*, 33; *First Annual Report*, 136; *Fifth Annual Report*, 104, 134.

11. S. H. V. and M. W., Local Assembly 10, 699, to Editor, *Journal of United Labor*, 24 Dec. 1887; J. H. M., *Journal of United Labor*, 9 June 1888.

12. This figure was calculated by W. E. B. DuBois for his study of blacks in Farmville, Virginia, and was used for the same purpose by Shifflet, *Patronage and Poverty*, 43. George A. White, "Agriculture and Agricultural Labor," testimony in *Hearings before the Industrial Commission* 10 (Washington, D.C.: G.P.O., 1901), 422.

13. This history originally appeared in the Raleigh *News and Observer*, 25 Sept. 1921, and later in Rupert Vance, *Human Factors in Cotton Culture* (Chapel Hill: University of North Carolina Press, 1929), 259–66.

14. The authors are discussed by Harold D. Woodman, "Sequel to Slavery," whose perspective I generally share. For economic historians with whom I disagree, see Robert Higgs, *Competition and Coercion: Blacks in the American Economy, 1865–1914* (Cambridge: Cambridge University Press, 1977), and Stephen J. DeCanio, *Agriculture in the Postbellum South: The Economics of Production and Supply* (Cambridge: Cambridge University Press, 1974).

15. Quotations are from North Carolina Bureau of Labor Statistics, *First Annual Report*, 125; North Carolina Bureau of Labor and Printing, *Twenty-first Annual Report* (Raleigh, 1908), 51. The discussion about the tendency of black women to withdraw from agricultural labor includes Roger L. Ransom and Richard Sutch, *One Kind of Freedom*; Noralee Frankel, "Workers, Wives, and Mothers: Black Women in Mississippi, 1860–1870" (Ph.D. diss., George Washington University, 1982); and Bell Hooks, *Ain't I a Woman: Black Women and Feminism* (Boston: South End Press, 1982).

16. J. A. J., Statistician, Local Assembly 10, 585, *Journal of United Labor*, 24 Dec. 1887.

17. Vance, *Human Factors in Cotton Culture*, 259–66.

18. For descriptions of the difficult lives faced by women in tobacco tenant families, see Shifflett, *Patronage and Poverty*, and Margaret Jarmon Hagood, *Mothers*

NOTES TO CHAPTER II

of the South: Portraiture of the White Tenant Farm Woman (1939; reprint, W. W. Norton, 1977). For the contrasting improvements in the lives of women in landowning families, see Elizabeth Rauh Bethel, *Promiseland: A Century of Life in a Negro Community* (Philadelphia: Temple University Press, 1981).

19. For discussion of the Knights of Labor, see Melton A. McLaurin, *Knights of Labor in the South* (Westport, Conn.: Greenwood Press, 1978); Leon Fink, *Workingmen's Democracy: The Knights of Labor and American Politics* (Urbana: University of Illinois Press, 1983), 149–77; and Philip S. Foner and Ronald L. Lewis, eds., *The Black Worker during the Era of the Knights of Labor*, vol. 3 in *The Black Worker: A Documentary History from Colonial Times to the Present* (Philadelphia: Temple University Press, 1978). For discussions of the Farmers' Alliance and Colored Farmers' Alliance, see Lawrence Goodwyn, *Democratic Promise: The Populist Moment in America* (New York: Oxford University Press, 1976); Robert C. McMath, Jr., *Populist Vanguard: A History of the Southern Farmers' Alliance* (New York: W. W. Norton, 1977); Bruce Palmer, *"Man over Money": The Southern Populist Critique of American Capitalism* (Chapel Hill: University of North Carolina Press, 1980); Theodore Saloutos, *Farmer Movements in the South, 1865–1933* (Lincoln: University of Nebraska Press, 1960); John D. Hicks, *The Populist Revolt: A History of the Farmers' Alliance and the People's Party* (Lincoln: University of Nebraska Press, 1961); and Gerald H. Gaither, *Blacks and the Populist Revolt: Ballots and Bigotry in the "New South"* (University, Ala.: University of Alabama Press, 1977).

20. *Journal of United Labor*, 11 July 1889. See also McMath, *Populist Vanguard*, 74; Goodwyn, *Democratic Purpose*, 47–51, 58–60, 85–86, 88–94, 107–8, 111–22, 125–45, 307–86; and Fink, *Workingman's Democracy*, 225.

21. The first quotation is from *Tarboro Farmers' Advocate*, 3 June 1891, in Palmer, *"Man over Money,"* 9, the most thorough and useful analysis of Populist ideology. The second quotation is from the Declaration of Principles of the Knights of Labor, originally quoted from George McNeill, *The Labor Movement: The Problem of Today* (Boston, 1887), 485, by Fink, *Workingmen's Democracy*, 23. For a fuller discussion of the Knights' analysis, see Fink, 9–15, and the introduction to Gregory S. Kealey and Bryan D. Palmer, *"Dreaming of What Might Have Been": The Knights of Labor in Ontario, 1880–1900* (Cambridge: Cambridge University Press, 1983). For comparisons of the Knights' and the Populists' visions, see the introduction to Hahn, *Southern Populism*, and Robert C. McMath, Jr., "The 'Movement Culture' of Populism Reconsidered: Cultural Origins of the Farmers' Alliance in Texas, 1879–1886," in *Southwestern Agriculture: PreColumbian to Modern*, ed. Henry C. Dethloff and Irvin M. May, Jr. (College Station: Texas A & M University Press, 1982). According to Fink, *Workingmen's Democracy*, 16, "The 'cooperative commonwealth' was one among many variants of the contemporary labor ideal; 'commonwealth of toil,' 'commonwealth of labor,' and the 'association of producers' were also popular." See Goodwyn, *Democratic Promise*, xi–xv, 536–55, for a sympathetic discussion of Populist versions of the "cooperative commonwealth" and the consequences of its defeat.

22. The first quotation comes from Fink, *Workingmen's Democracy*, 162. For further discussion of racial equality in the Knights of Labor, see Fink, 169–72, and McLaurin, *The Knights of Labor in the South*. On the subject of women in the or-

NOTES TO CHAPTER II

der, see Susan Levine, "Labor's True Women: Domesticity and Equal Rights in the Knights of Labor," *Journal of American History* 70 (1983): 323–39, and Fink, 12. For the racial attitudes of the Farmers' Alliance and the Populists, see Palmer, *"Man over Money,"* 50–68. The second quotation is from Palmer, 57, and Gaither, *Blacks and the Populist Revolt*. For discussions of the activities of women in the Southern Farmers' Alliance, see Julie Roy Jeffrey, "Women in the Southern Farmers' Alliance: A Reconsideration of the Role and Status of Women in the Late Nineteenth-Century South," *Feminist Studies* 3 (1975): 72–91. The remaining quotations are from Jeffrey. See also Lu Ann Jones, "'The Task That Is Ours': White North Carolina Farm Women and Agrarian Reform, 1886–1914" (Master's thesis, University of North Carolina, 1983).

23. *Journal of United Labor,* 11 June, 27 Aug. 1887.

24. Ibid., 7 Nov. 1889.

25. The Durham *Tobacco Plant,* a Democratic organ in the city, frequently attacked the Knights by reporting on the gains made by blacks since the election of the order's candidate to Congress in 1886.

26. For example, see "The Farmers and the Knights," *Journal of United Labor,* 5 Dec. 1889.

27. *Progressive Farmer,* 18 Aug. 1887.

28. As argued by McMath, *Populist Vanguard*.

29. See Robert D. McMath, Jr., "Southern White Farmers and the Organization of Black Farm Workers: A North Carolina Document," *Labor History* 18 (Winter 1977): 115–19.

30. *Journal of United Labor,* 12 Nov. 1887; 2, 30 Aug. 1888.

31. McMath, "Southern White Farmers," 115–19.

32. *Progressive Farmer,* 4 Dec. 1888.

33. H. H. Perry to Elias Carr, Elias Carr papers, East Carolina University, quoted in Foner and Lewis, *The Black Worker,* 294.

34. Foner and Lewis, *The Black Worker,* 330–64, and Gaither, *Blacks and the Populist Revolt,* 11. A comment by the editor in the *Progressive Farmer* concerning black migration out of the state suggested the racial constraint on the alliance between black and white farmers: "The Negro is and will ever remain, so long as he stays, a running, festering sore on our body politics"; the editor offered to "pray God's blessing to attend him" in his departure from North Carolina; quoted in Frenise A. Logan, *The Negro in North Carolina, 1876–1894* (Chapel Hill: University of North Carolina Press, 1969), 129.

35. VCF [Vance County Farmer], *Gold Leaf,* 1 Dec. 1887; McMath, *Populist Vanguard,* 50–54; Tilley, *Bright Tobacco Industry,* 406–21; Michael Schwartz, *Radical Protest and Social Structure: The Southern Farmers' Alliance and Cotton Tenancy, 1880–1890* (New York: Academic Press, 1976), 212.

36. Lawrence Goodwyn, *Democratic Promise,* 115–17, 152–53, 166–72.

37. The most complete discussion of the growing racial and economic conservatism of the North Carolina Populists is in Palmer, *"Man over Money,"* 143–54. Quotations from *Progressive Farmer,* 18 July 1893, in Palmer, 149; North Carolina People's Party platform quoted in Goldsboro *Caucasian,* 2 Aug. 1894, in Palmer, 34–35.

38. Jeffrey J. Crow and Robert F. Durden, *Maverick Republican in the Old*

NOTES TO CHAPTER III

North State: A Political Biography of Daniel Russell (Baton Rouge: Louisiana State University Press, 1877), 49, 79–80, 109; quotation from Raleigh *News and Observer*, 23 Nov. 1898.

39. J. Morgan Kousser argues that the decline was the object of the campaign to reduce the poor white and black vote directed by southern elites. See Kousser, *The Shaping of Southern Politics: Suffrage Restriction and the Establishment of the One-Party South, 1880–1910* (New Haven: Yale University Press, 1975), 238–66. For his discussion of the North Carolina campaign of 1900, see 183–95; for discussion of the decline in voting participation, see 240–42, 245–46.

40. Tilley, *Bright Tobacco Industry*, 354.

41. *Southern Tobacconist and Manufacturers Record*, 29 Sept. 1903, quoted in Tilley, *Bright Tobacco Industry*, 423.

42. Tilley, *Bright Tobacco Industry*, 94–95.

43. Ibid., 354, 356, 386–91.

44. Thomas J. Woofter, Jr., *The Plight of Cigarette Tobacco* (Chapel Hill: University of North Carolina Press, 1931), 26–40; Pete Daniel, "The Crossroads of Change: Tobacco, Cotton, and Rice Cultures in the Twentieth Century," paper delivered at the Woodrow Wilson International Center Colloquium, Washington, D.C., 13 July 1982.

45. Rupert B. Vance, *The Human Geography of the South: A Study in Regional Resources and Human Adequacy* (New York: Russell and Russell, 1934), 177–204.

46. Anthony J. Badger, *Prosperity Road: The New Deal, Tobacco, and North Carolina* (Chapel Hill: University of North Carolina Press, 1980), 11.

47. C. Horace Hamilton, "Recent Changes in the Social and Economic Status of Farm Families in North Carolina," North Carolina Agricultural Extension Station *Bulletin*, no. 309 (Raleigh, May 1937).

48. Badger, *Prosperity Road*, 59, 95, 271, 183–96, 201, 227; see also George Tindall, *The Emergence of the New South* (Baton Rouge: Louisiana State University Press, 1967), 396–407, 414–15; and Charles S. Johnson, Edwin R. Embree, and W. W. Alexander, *The Collapse of Cotton Tenancy* (Chapel Hill: University of North Carolina Press, 1935), 41–57.

49. Jonathan Daniels, *Tar Heels: A Portrait of North Carolina* (Westport, Conn.: Negro Universities Press, 1941), 80–81.

CHAPTER III

1. Alice Schlegel, an anthropologist, discusses these social relations as important components of the hierarchical relationship between men and women cross-culturally. See Alice Schlegel, ed., *Sexual Stratification: A Cross-Cultural View* (New York: Columbia University Press, 1977), 3–25.

2. Although the southern racial system resembled the Indian caste system in certain respects, I use the term *race* because the two systems were not identical. The southern racial system was a considerably cruder and simpler arrangement that divided southerners into two racial communities rather than a series of ascending castes defined by occupation and other characteristics.

3. Richard H. Whitaker, *Reminiscences, Incidents and Anecdotes* (Raleigh:

NOTES TO CHAPTER III

Edwards and Broughton, 1905), quoted in Michael Schwartz, *Radical Protest and Social Structure: The Southern Farmers' Alliance and Cotton Tenancy, 1880–1890* (New York: Academic Press, 1976), 66.

4. In contrast to some scholars, I use the term "family economy" to specify a type of agricultural household production that involves family labor rather than wage labor, slave labor, or other variants. For discussions of these issues, see Louise Tilly and Joan W. Scott, *Women, Work, and Family* (New York: Holt, Rinehart and Winston, 1978); Rayna Rapp, Ellen Ross, and Renate Bridenthal, "Examining Family History," in *Sex and Class in Women's History*, ed. Judith L. Newton, Mary P. Ryan, and Judith Walkowitz (London: Routledge and Kegan Paul, 1983), 232–58; Michael Merrill, "'Cash Is Good to Eat': Self-Sufficiency and Exchange in the Rural Economy of the United States," *Radical History Review*, Winter 1977, 42–71; and Harriet Friedman, "Household Production and the National Economy: Concepts for the Analysis of Agrarian Formations," *Journal of Peasant Studies* 7 (January 1980): 158–83. In the rural Piedmont the units of household production included independent commodity producers using family labor, plantation production using tenant and sharecropping family households as the units of production, and relatively independent tenant households that rented the land while owning some of the tools of production.

5. This patriarchal ideal apparently existed in the rural Piedmont, according to J. A. Dickey and E. C. Branson, "How Farm Tenants Live in Mid-State Carolina," *North Carolina Year-Book, 1921–1922* (Chapel Hill: University of North Carolina Press, 1922), 86. That it still existed as a cultural ideal into the 1930s is clear from the interviews conducted by Margaret Hagood with white tenant farm women, in Margaret Jarman Hagood, *Mothers of the South: Portraiture of the White Tenant Farm Woman* (Chapel Hill: University of North Carolina Press, 1939; reprint, New York: W. W. Norton, 1977). For a discussion of the same ideal among black rural families, see Elizabeth Rauh Bethel, *Promiseland: A Century of Life in a Negro Community* (Philadelphia: Temple University Press, 1981).

6. Share tenants were legally considered to own the crop and paid a share of the crop in lieu of rent to the landlord; sharecroppers were legally considered to be laborers who earned a share of the crop in exchange for their labor. Although one writer was still describing the tobacco farmer as the "best remaining example of the Jeffersonian ideal of an independent yeomanry" as late as 1981, the realities of tobacco marketing, tenancy, and federal price supports had long since deprived small tobacco producers of economic independence. See William R. Finger, ed., *The Tobacco Industry in Transition* (New York: D.C. Heath, 1981).

7. As discussed by William H. Fisher, bright tobacco was one of the most-highly labor-intensive crops, with labor accounting for 80 percent of the total costs. See William H. Fisher, *Economics of Flue-Cured Tobacco* (Richmond, Va.: Federal Reserve Bank of Richmond, 1945), 71.

8. Harvesting took 257 hours of labor per acre of tobacco before mechanization in the 1970s cut the demand to 58 hours per acre. See Finger, *Tobacco Industry in Transition,* 48.

9. Hagood, *Mothers of the South,* 36, 160–62, 218. Frances Sage Bradley and Margetta A. Williamson, *Rural Children in Selected Counties of North Carolina,* reprint of U.S. Children's Bureau *Bulletin* (New York: Negro Universities Press,

1969), 49–51, 54, discusses male control and greater male mobility in cotton-growing counties where, as in tobacco areas, the family financial transactions took place in town.

10. The use of *he* and *his* to refer to farmers was universally applied in the sources. The surveys of farmer opinion published by the North Carolina Bureau of Labor Satistics and its successors were conducted exclusively with men. The residents of Chatham County in the early 1920s distinguished between tenants and croppers by saying that a cropper is a "tenant 'run by the landlord' while a renter 'run himself'" (Dickey and Branson, "Farm Tenants," 64). T. J. Woofter described tobacco cultivation as "merely a device for the farmer to use his land and sell his labor rather cheaply and occasionally make a small profit" (Thomas J. Woofter, Jr., *The Plight of Cigarette Tobacco* [Chapel Hill: University of North Carolina Press, 1931], 21).

11. Jonathan Daniels, *Tar Heels: A Portrait of North Carolina* (Westport, Conn.: Negro Universities Press, 1941), 90–92. Bethel, *Promiseland*, 157–58, describes relatively greater economic and social equality between black men and women, but identifies the assumptions that men have "dominance" over women and that women should be loving "helpmates" to their husbands who were the "heads" of the household.

12. *Harriet Suitt Umstead, interview by Dolores Janiewski, personal holding. Here and below, names marked with an asterisk in these notes are pseudonyms chosen to protect the privacy of the person interviewed.

13. *Bertie Loman, interview by Dolores Janiewski, personal holding.

14. Hagood, *Mothers of the South*, 89–90. Sherry B. Ortner and Harriet Whitehead, anthropologists, argue that the "social organization of prestige is the domain of social structure that most directly affects cultural notions of gender and sexuality" and that "in every known society men and women compose two differentially valued terms of a value set, men being as *men*, higher." They also assert the near universality of male control of the "'public domain' where 'universalistic' interests are expressed and managed"; women are "nearly universally . . . located in or confined to the 'domestic domain,'" and their concerns are seen as more "particularistic" and encompassed within the male-controlled realm. See Sherry B. Ortner and Harriet Whitehead, eds., *Sexual Meanings: The Cultural Construction of Gender and Sexuality* (Cambridge: Cambridge University Press, 1981), 16, 7–8. Certainly women appeared to have recognized that "men's work" in tobacco, the crop that was their link to the public world of the marketplace, carried more prestige and value than the private work of women.

15. Quotations from the *Progressive Farmer*, in Julie Roy Jeffrey, "Women in the Southern Farmers' Alliance: A Reconsideration of the Role and Status of Women in the Late Nineteenth Century South," in *Our American Sisters: Women in American Life and Thought*, ed. Jean E. Friedman and William G. Shade (Lexington, Mass.: D. C. Heath, 1982), 361, 358.

16. This discussion is based on the work of Lu Ann Jones and Julie Roy Jeffrey: see Lu Ann Jones, "'The Task That Is Ours': White North Carolina Farm Women and Agrarian Reform, 1886–1914" (Master's thesis, University of North Carolina, 1983), and Jeffrey, "Women in the Southern Farmers' Alliance," 348–71.

17. Bradley and Williamson, *Rural Children*, 35–41.

18. Dickey and Branson, "Farm Tenants," 74–75. Another description of household equipment is given in Arthur F. Raper, "A Case Study of Democratic Procedures in Rural Development—A Personal Account," paper in possession of Peter Wood, Department of History, Duke University, Durham, North Carolina.

19. Hagood, *Mothers of the South*, 93–107, 91. In addition, I gathered information on housekeeping methods and equipment in interviews with *Harriet Suitt Umstead, *Anna Ruffin Whitted, *Rachel Medlin, *Ella Lassiter, and *Vera Rowan, personal holdings.

20. Charles B. Loomis, "The Growth of the Farm Family in Relation to Its Activities," North Carolina Agricultural Experiment Station *Bulletin* no. 298, June 1934, 25–27. On average, the tenant farm family consumed more of its income in food and clothing and less in investment in either the farm or the household than did the typical landowner.

21. Raper, "Case Study." Merrill discusses "swap work," under the rubrics of "cooperative work," "changing work," or "neighborliness," as a characteristic of the "household mode of production." See Merrill, "Cash Is Good to Eat," 57–58. Steven Hahn designates such practices as "habits of mutuality," which, together with slavery, limited "the development of directly exploitative, market relations between whites." See Hahn, *The Roots of Southern Populism: Yeoman Farmers and the Transformations of Georgia Upcountry, 1850–1890* (New York: Oxford University Press, 1983), 50–85. Yet, rather than representing a distinctive type of economy or mode of production, such patterns may simply have represented the response of those who lacked other resources. For example, the contemporary poor continue to rely on kin and friends for services and access to resources, while the middle class "substitute commodity forms." See Rapp, Ross, and Bridenthal, "Examining Family History," 178–80; and Carol B. Stack, *All Our Kin: Survivial Strategies in a Black Community* (New York: Harper and Row, 1974).

22. An ugly incident resulting from this pattern of racial etiquette, which forbade the two races to eat together and insisted on the greatest social distance between white women and black men, was observed by Margaret Hagood while accompanying photographer Marion Post Wolcott in the Durham vicinity. See Hagood, "Corn Shucking," 16 Nov. 1939, in Subregional Laboratory Records, Howard W. Odum papers, SHC/UNC.

23. This explanation of the sexual division of labor in a patriarchal system comes from Heidi Hartmann, "The Unhappy Marriage of Marxism and Feminism: Toward a More Progressive Union," in *Women and Revolution: A Discussion of Marxism and Feminism,* ed. Lydia Sargent (Boston: South End Press, 1982), 1–42.

24. Clarence Poe, the editor of the *Progressive Farmer,* noted that "throwing brickbats at the men" seemed to be a favorite pastime of the women writing letters to his journal (8 Mar. 1906).

25. As revealed in my interviews. Only interviews with *Laura Turrentine Markham and *Helen Ball Riggsbee betrayed any women's resentment toward husbands or fathers. In both cases, the men were failures as farmers. Schlegel, *Sexual Stratification,* 335, posits that the economic partnership between men and women within the family economy might mitigate sexual dominance. Thus women might have correctly seen their needs as being better served in a prosperous family economy under an enterprising head than in a poorer and more egalitarian household.

NOTES TO CHAPTER III

Hagood, *Mothers of the South,* recorded that white tenant farm women identified their interests with those of the family as a whole without questioning the "rightness of male dominance" or the conventional belief in "innate sexual difference in ability." Yet, as she observed, "Patriarchy prevails in form but not always in practice" (162–65, 168–69). Quotation from Jones, "'The Task That is Ours': White North Carolina Farm Women and Agrarian Reform, 1886–1914," paper given at the Organization of American Historians convention, Los Angeles, 7 Apr. 1984, p. 10.

26. For the use of the courts to control poor white and free black women's sexuality, see Victoria Bynum, "Court Control over Poor White and Free Black Women in North Carolina: The Effects of the Civil War and Reconstruction," paper given at the Organization of American Historians convention, Los Angeles, 7 Apr. 1984. For the discussion on childbearing, see Hagood, *Mothers of the South,* 108–27; for child raising, see 128–56. Quotations from Hagood, 143, 147, 200.

27. See John Patrick McDowell, *The Social Gospel in the South: The Woman's Home Mission Movement in the Methodist Episcopal Church, 1886–1939* (Baton Rouge: Louisiana State University Press, 1983) for a discussion of feminism in a white southern church. The unpublished work of Cheryl Townsend Gilkes on the activities of black women in the Church of God in Christ illustrates the struggles of women for leadership in a black church.

28. Bethel, *Promiseland,* 33–36, reveals that women in landowning families worked outside the household less often than women in tenant families. Loomis, "Growth of the Farm Family," 59, reports the same relationship between tenure status and women's work outside the household. Bradley and Williamson, *Rural Children,* report that black women worked in the fields more often than did white women. The migration data comes from W. A. Anderson and C. P. Loomis, "Migration among Sons and Daughters of White Farmers in Wake County," North Carolina Agricultural Extension Station *Bulletin,* no. 275 (June 1930).

29. C. Horace Hamilton, "Recent Changes in the Social and Economic Status of Farm Families in North Carolina," North Carolina Agricultural Experiment Station *Bulletin,* no. 309 (May 1937), 129; Loomis, "Growth of the Farm Family," 48.

30. Hagood, *Mothers of the South,* 168. Wage data from North Carolina Bureau of Labor Statistics, *First Annual Report for the Year 1887,* (Raleigh, 1887); North Carolina Department of Labor and Printing, *Thirty-Second Annual Report (1919–1920).*

31. See B. W. C. Roberts and Richard F. Knapp, *John Thomas Dalton and the Development of the Bull Durham Smoking Tobacco* (Durham: Solar Plexus Enterprises, 1977), and an unpublished study by Sherlock Bronson, "Tobacco Bag Stringing" (Richmond: Virginia-Carolina Service Corporation, 1939). The company that distributed bags to rural workers sponsored Bronson's study to prove that the Fair Labor Standards Act, which eliminated home work that didn't pay a minimum wage, should not be applied to bag stringers. The study argued that such action would "take supplemental income" from poor rural women.

32. Although there is no single source for these ideas about the interconnections between gender and race in southern productive and reproductive systems, see Mary O'Brien, *The Politics of Reproduction* (Boston: Routledge and Kegan Paul, 1983); Jacquelyn Dowd Hall, "'The Mind That Burns in Each Body': Women, Rape, and Racial Violence," in *Powers of Desire: The Politics of Sexuality,* ed. Ann Snitow,

NOTES TO CHAPTER III

Christine Stansell, and Sharon Thompson (New York: Monthly Review Press, 1983), 328–48; Randall Collins, "Stratification by Sex and Age," in his *Conflict Sociology: Toward an Explanatory Science* (New York: Academic Press, 1975); Bertram Wyatt-Brown, *Southern Honor: Ethics and Behavior in the Old South* (New York: Oxford University Press, 1982); Mary Douglas, *Purity and Danger: An Analysis of the Concepts of Pollution and Taboo* (London: Routledge and Kegan Paul, 1966), 124–27, 162; Frigga Haug, "Morals Also Have Two Genders," *New Left Review* 143 (1984): 51–68; Rosalind Coward, *Patriarchal Precedents: Sexuality and Social Relations* (London: Routledge and Kegan Paul, 1983); Sue Gronewold, *Beautiful Merchandise: Prostitution in China, 1860–1936* (New York: Institute for Research in History, 1982); and Ortner and Whitehead, *Sexual Meanings*, 1–28.

33. Otto H. Olsen, "North Carolina: An Incongruous Presence," in *Reconstruction and Redemption in the South*, ed. Otto H. Olsen (Baton Rouge: Louisiana State University Press, 1980), 156–97; Governor Jonathan Worth to William Clark, 16 Feb. 1868, in Olsen, *Reconstruction*, 167; and Allen W. Trelease, *White Terror: The Ku Klux Klan Conspiracy and Southern Reconstruction* (New York: Harper and Row, 1971), 196, 197.

34. Pauli Murray, *Proud Shoes: The Story of an American Family* (New York: Harper and Row, 1978), 224, 221.

35. Raleigh *Standard*, Oct. 1869, quoted in Trelease, *White Terror*, 196. For discussion of the ending of Reconstruction in North Carolina, see Trelease, 209, 224, 336–37, 347, 408–9; and Olsen, "North Carolina," 170–97.

36. Frenise A. Logan, *The Negro in North Carolina, 1876–1894* (Chapel Hill: University of North Carolina Press, 1969), 125–29.

37. George White is quoted in Eric Anderson, *Race and Politics in North Carolina, 1872–1901* (Baton Rouge: Louisiana State University Press, 1981), 255.

38. North Carolina Department of Labor and Printing, *Fifteenth Annual Report* (Raleigh, 1902), 59, 70. Both quotations were from farmers in counties bordering on Durham. See Clarence Poe, "Rural Land Segregation between Whites and Negroes: A Reply to Mr. Stephenson," *South Atlantic Quarterly*, 13 July 1914, pp. 207, 212.

39. *Christian Recorder*, 31 July 1888.

40. Raper is quoted in Jay R. Mandle, *The Roots of Black Poverty: The Southern Plantation Economy after the Civil War* (Durham: Duke University Press, 1978), 29.

41. *James Lester, interview by Dolores Janiewski, personal holding.

42. *Anna Ruffin Whitted, interview.

43. U.S. Department of Commerce, Bureau of the Census, *Negroes in the United States* (Washington, D.C.: G.P.O., 1935), 379, 413–15, 782–85.

44. Bradley and Williamson, *Rural Children*.

45. *Zina Riddle, interview by Dolores Janiewski, personal holding.

46. Annie Mack Barbee, interview by Beverley Johnson, SOHP/UNC.

47. *Annie Holman Green and *Anna Ruffin Whitted commented about the sexual exploitation of black women while discussing slavery.

48. *Anna Ruffin Whitted, interview.

49. *Zina Riddle, interview.

50. *Mamie Gray, interview.

NOTES TO CHAPTER III

51. *Zina Riddle, and *Anna Ruffin Whitted interviews.

52. Bethel, *Promiseland*. See also John Wesley Hatch, "The Black Rural Church: Its Role and Potential in Community Health Organization and Action" (Master's thesis, University of North Carolina, 1974), and Dale Newman, "Work and Community Life in a Southern Textile Town," *Labor History* 19 (1978): 220–21, which suggest that similar patterns existed in the areas around Durham as well.

53. Tenure status also affected longevity. It contributed to higher death rates among black women, who came primarily from tenant and laboring households.

54. Jacqueline Hall, *Revolt against Chivalry: Jessie Daniel Ames and the Women's Campaign against Lynching* (New York: Columbia University Press, 1979), presents the most developed discussion of this issue in the chapter, "Strange Fruit."

55. Rufus B. Spain, *At Ease in Zion: A Social History of Southern Baptists, 1865–1900* (Nashville: Vanderbilt University Press, 1967), 101.

56. For Methodist views on racial issues, see Harold Fair, "Southern Methodists on Education and Race, 1900–1920" (Ph.D. diss., Vanderbilt University, 1971).

57. Hagood, *Mothers of the South*, 177, 178–79, 141.

58. Hall, *Revolt against Chivalry*, describes women who "revolted" against the practice.

59. Arthur F. Raper, *The Tragedy of Lynching* (Chapel Hill: University of North Carolina Press, 1933), 107–24, 114, 124.

60. *Anna Ruffin Whitted, interview.

61. Annie Mack Barbee, interview.

62. E. Franklin Frazier, "Durham: Capital of the Black Middle Class," in *The New Negro: An Interpretation*, ed. Alain LeRoy Locke (1925; reprint, New York: Arno Press, 1968), 333–40.

63. Hatch, "Black Rural Church."

64. See Hortense Powdermaker, *After Freedom: A Cultural Study in the Deep South* (New York: Viking Press, 1939), 223–85, for a provocative analysis of the black church. Powdermaker argues that there was a reciprocal influence on the church: "The Negro God exhibits more maternal characteristics" than does "the stern patriarchal God of the white Protestants" (247).

65. Based on a comparison of patterns in the interviews that I conducted.

66. See the analysis by Bruce T. Grindal, "The Religious Interpretation of Experience in a Rural Black Community," in *Holding On to the Land and the Kinship, Ritual, Land Tenure and Social Policy in the Rural South*, ed. Robert L. Hall and Carol B. Stack (Athens: University of Georgia Press, 1982), 92–100. See also Powdermaker, *After Freedom*, 253–60, for a comparison of religious beliefs and practices among poor whites and poor blacks.

67. This emphasis on consciousness as a negotiated response comes from my reading of Edward P. Thompson, *The Making of the English Working Class* (New York: Vintage, 1966); Sarah Eisenstein, *Give Us Bread but Give Us Roses: Working Women's Consciousness in the United States, 1890 to the First World War* (London: Routledge and Kegan Paul, 1983), 37–54; and Ortner and Whitehead, *Sexual Meanings*, 1–27.

68. The "democratic moment" that was Populism is the subject of Lawrence Goodwyn, *Democratic Promise: The Populist Moment in America* (New York: Ox-

NOTES TO CHAPTER III

ford University Press, 1976), and of Bruce Palmer, *"Man over Money": The Southern Populist Critique of American Capitalism* (Chapel Hill: University of North Carolina Press, 1980). Quotation from Tarboro *Farmers' Advocate,* 23 Sept. 1891, in reference to the cotton pickers' strike of 1891 supported by the black Farmers' Alliance, in Palmer, *"Man over Money,"* 65. See Palmer, 50–68, 144–54, and Goodwyn, 276–306, for contrasting assessments of the Populist response to black farmers.

69. Quotations in Jeffrey, "Women in the Southern Farmers' Alliance," 364, 358; Hahn, *Roots of Southern Populism,* 286.

70. Frederick A. Bode, *Protestantism and the New South: North Carolina Baptists and Methodists in Political Crisis, 1894–1903* (Charlottesville: University Press of Virginia, 1975), 53, 55–56, 45, 79, 117.

71. Jessie Jeffrey, interview by W. O. F., 10 July 1939, NCFWP/SHC/UNC; Hagood, *Mothers of the South,* 181; *Zina Riddle, *Anna Ruffin Whitted, and *Laura Turrentine Markham interviews.

72. Hagood, *Mothers of the South,* 183–92.

73. *Anna Ruffin Whitted, interview.

74. Ortner and Whitehead, *Sexual Meanings,* 6–13.

75. Loomis, "Growth of the Farm Family," 38–41, 55–56. Bethel notes, however, that leadership in the black church was "vested within the kinship systems of the original landowners in the community" (*Promiseland,* 144), and her general discussion of "God and power" suggests that class distinctions were present although less developed than in white society.

76. See Rapp, Ross, and Bridenthal, "Examining Family History," 236–38, for discussion of this issue.

77. Gerda Lerner, in a forthcoming work tentatively titled "The Sexual Foundations of Western Civilization," is tracing back this mediated form of women's class identity to ancient Babylonia and Mesopotamia. She also traces the division of women into the "veiled" and the "unveiled"—the sexually controlled and respectable versus the sexually uncontrolled and disreputable—to ancient Assyrian law. The tendency to describe women by their relationships is discussed by Gayle Rubin, "The Traffic in Women: Notes toward a Political Economy of Sex," in *Toward an Anthropology of Women,* ed. Rayna Reiter (New York: Monthly Review Press, 1975), 157–210, as based in the male exchange of women that gives me "certain rights in their female kin" and denies women "full rights to themselves" and thus defines women in relationship to men (177). See also Ortner and Whitehead, *Sexual Meanings,* 8.

78. *Harriet Suitt Umstead, interview.

79. There is a similar tendency in Samoa, according to Bradd Shore, "Sexuality and Gender in Samoa: Conceptions and Missed Conceptions," in Ortner and Whitehead, *Sexual Meanings,* 192–215. See also Bethel, *Promiseland,* 157–60, for a discussion of the sexual double standard in a rural black community.

80. *Laura Turrentine Markham, interview. Mary Douglas, *Purity and Danger,* 124–27, describes a similar connection between types of occupation and social status in the Indian caste system, which designated some occupations as polluting and others as fit for the pure and higher castes.

81. Ortner and Whitehead, *Sexual Meanings,* 5; more fully developed by Jane F.

NOTES TO CHAPTER IV

Collier and Michelle Z. Rosaldo, "Politics and Gender in Simple Societies," in Ortner and Whitehead, 275–329. Collier and Rosaldo extend their analysis of the political importance of sexuality to rape as an expression of "three culturally salient themes" in simple societies (i.e., nonclass societies)—"sexual intercourse, male violence, and male solidarity"—intended to punish "women who wander beyond male control—through promiscuity, assertions of undue independence, and/or refusals to marry" (297). Compare this analysis with Jacqueline Hall's examination of rape, "The Mind That Burns the Body," in the more complex and racially divided society of the South. Here lynching for the crime of rape expressed white male solidarity and control over the bodies of white women and black men, while black women were offered no such "protection."

82. Rapp, Ross, and Bridenthal, "Examining Family History," characterize the split "between public and private, workplace and household, economy and family," as a false dichotomy that disguises the fact that "household activities are continuously part of the 'larger' processes of production, reproduction, and consumption" (233–34).

83. Household Account Book, Cameron Family papers, SHC/UNC.

84. Margaret Hagood, "Corn Shucking."

85. *Laura Turrentine Markham, interview. Hagood reported that tobacco-farm women like Markham considered cotton-growing to be "back-breaking work, fit only for 'niggers,'" and too low-paying compared with tobacco" (*Mothers of the South*, 80).

86. *Anna Ruffin Whitted, interview.

87. *James Lester, interview.

88. For a complex discussion of black attitudes toward "white people," see Powdermaker, *After Freedom*, 325–53.

89. Mary E. Mebane, *Mary* (New York: Fawcett Junior, 1981), 220–24. See also E. Franklin Frazier, *The Negro Family in the United States*, 2d ed. rev. (Chicago: University of Chicago Press, 1966), 89–101, 190–208; and Charles S. Johnson, *Growing Up in the Black Belt* (Washington, D.C.: American Council on Education, 1941), for comparisons of sexual mores between lower-class and middle- or upper-class rural blacks. Bethel discusses how the churches dominated by black landowners dealt with unwed mothers; they were "turned" out of the church as soon as the pregnancy became obvious, isolated within their homes during a period of social disgrace, and then reintroduced into the church and society after acknowledging guilt and giving birth to the baby (*Promiseland*, 157–59). See also Powdermaker, *After Freedom*, 143–74, for another comparison of sexual attitudes and marriage patterns among blacks of different classes.

90. Hagood, *Mothers of the South*, 37, 130, 152, 177–78, 180–82.

CHAPTER IV

1. Based on Hugh Penn Brinton, "The Negro in Durham: A Study of Adjustment to Town Life" (Ph.D. diss., University of North Carolina, 1930); Charles S. Johnson, "The Tobacco Worker: A Study of Tobacco Factory Workers and Their Families," 2 vols. (1935), Division of Review, Industrial Studies Section, NRA/NA;

NOTES TO CHAPTER IV

Orie Latham Hatcher, *Rural Girls in the City for Work: A Study Made for the Southern Women's Educational Alliance* (Richmond: Garrett and Massie, 1930); C. Horace Hamilton, "Rural-Urban Migration in North Carolina, 1920–1930," North Carolina Agricultural Extension Station *Bulletin*, no. 295 (Raleigh, February 1934); and Irwin Dunsky, "The Excess Female Population in Durham, N.C.: A Study of Migration and Urbanization" (Master's thesis, Duke University, 1939).

2. See the discussion of the "great migration" in Elizabeth Rauh Bethel, *Promiseland: A Century of Life in a Negro Community* (Philadelphia: Temple University Press, 1981), 171–94. Sex ratios are based on comparison of population figures for Durham, Person, and Granville Counties with Durham, 1900–1930.

3. This is due, in part, to the practices of the Bureau of the Census, which recorded no location more specific than the state of birth for the period in question.

4. Durham *Negro Observer*, 4 Aug. 1906, quoted in Walter B. Weare, *Black Business in the New South: A Social History of the North Carolina Mutual Life Insurance Company* (Urbana: University of Illinois Press, 1973), 27.

5. Hatcher, *Rural Girls,* 211.

6. *Calvin Couch and *Louise Couch Jenkins, interviews by Dolores Janiewski, personal holding. Calvin and Louise were the children of *Wilma Mayfield Couch. Here and elsewhere in these notes, names marked with an asterisk are pseudonyms chosen to protect the privacy of the person interviewed.

7. Esther Jenks, interview by Dolores Janiewski, SOHP/UNC.

8. Hatcher, *Rural Girls,* 10, 14, 25.

9. Hamilton, "Rural-Urban Migration."

10. Dunsky, "Excess Female Population in Durham."

11. Johnson, "The Tobacco Worker," 2:387.

12. *Rowan Mangum, interview by Dolores Janiewski, personal holding.

13. Harriet Herring, *Passing of the Mill Village: Revolution in a Southern Institution* (Westport, Conn.: Greenwood Press, 1977). Herring reports that the mill village began to pass away during the wartime boom when mill managers allowed some workers to live outside the mill village. Later, the construction of paved roads in the 1920s allowed others to commute from homes in the "stringtowns" that began to line North Carolina highways. Herring reports that this trend was most pronounced in North Carolina; two of its leading industries—tobacco and furniture—never established company housing, and a third—hosiery—had never housed all its employees. Durham Hosiery Mills began eliminating company housing for its employees and Erwin Mills began the deliberate sale of its houses in the 1940s.

14. Mary E. Mebane, *Mary* (New York: Fawcett Junior, 1981), 96. According to interviews conducted for the Johnson survey, white workers resented the ability of black tobacco workers to buy automobiles (Johnson, "The Tobacco Worker," 2:428).

15. Mrs. John Gates, interview by W. O. F., NCFWP/SHC/UNC.

16. New York *Times*, 23 Sept. 1879.

17. North Carolina Bureau of Labor Statistics, *Annual Report for 1887* (Raleigh, 1887), 86.

18. North Carolina Bureau of Labor Statistics, *Annual Report for 1887*, 136.

NOTES TO CHAPTER V

19. North Carolina Bureau of Labor Statistics, *Second Annual Report* (Raleigh, 1888), 302.
20. North Carolina Bureau of Labor and Printing, *Fifteenth Annual Report* (Raleigh, 1901), 301–2.
21. North Carolina Bureau of Labor and Printing, *Twenty-first Annual Report* (Raleigh, 1907), 52; North Carolina Bureau of Labor and Printing, *Seventeenth Annual Report* (Raleigh, 1903), 53.
22. North Carolina Bureau of Labor and Printing, *Seventeenth Annual Report*, 45–46.
23. North Carolina Bureau of Labor and Printing, *Fifteenth Annual Report*, 81–82.
24. North Carolina Bureau of Labor and Printing, *Seventeenth Annual Report*, 241.
25. *Pearl Barbee, interview by Linda Guthrie, personal holding.
26. *Hetty Love, interview by Linda Guthrie, personal holding.
27. William Merriman Upchurch and M. B. Fowler, *Durham County: Economic and Social*, April 1918 (Chapel Hill: Department of Rural Economics and Sociology, University of North Carolina), 13.
28. Bessie Taylor Buchanan, interview by Lanier Rand, SOHP/UNC.
29. Esther Jenks, interview by Dolores Janiewski, SOHP/UNC.
30. Luther Riley, interview by Lanier Rand, SOHP/UNC.
31. *Rose Weeks, interview by Dolores Janiewski, personal holding.
32. Annie Mack Barbee and Charlie Decoda Mack, interviews by Beverly Jones, SOHP/UNC.
33. Esther Jenks, interview.
34. Levi Branson, *Directory of the Business and Citizens of Durham City for 1887* (Raleigh: Levi Branson, 1887), 13.
35. Kemp P. Lewis to the Commissioners of Harnett County, 2 Mar. 1909, KPL/SHC/UNC.
36. Julian S. Carr, Jr., "Building a Business on the Family Plan," *System* 35 (July 1919): 301–5.
37. Kemp P. Lewis to J. O. Bailey, 19 Dec. 1931, KPL/SHC/UNC.
38. Weare, *Black Business*, 50–59, 29, 34, 36–49.
39. Weare, *Black Business*, 44–45, 101–2, 114–16.
40. Edward Franklin Frazier, "Durham: Capital of the Black Middle Class," in *The New Negro: An Interpretation*, ed. Alain Locke (New York: Albert and Charles Boni, 1925; reprint, New York: Arno Press, 1968), 339.
41. Raymond Williams, *The Country and the City* (New York: Oxford University Press, 1973), 284, 287.

CHAPTER V

1. Edward Franklin Frazier, "Durham: Capital of the Black Middle Class," in *The New Negro: An Interpretation*, ed. Alain Locke (New York: Albert and Charles Boni, 1925; reprint, New York: Arno Press, 1968), 338–39.
2. This chapter draws on the work of C. Vann Woodward, *Origins of the New*

NOTES TO CHAPTER V

South: 1877–1913, vol. 9 (Baton Rouge: Louisiana State University Press, 1974), principally 107–41, 291–320, 369–428. For additional information about Blackwell and Carr, see *U.S. Tobacco Journal*, 17 Nov. 1883; Nannie May Tilley, *The Bright-Tobacco Industry: 1869–1929* (Chapel Hill: University of North Carolina Press, 1948); Hiram V. Paul, *History of the Town of Durham, N.C.* (Raleigh: Edwards, Broughton, 1884); William K. Boyd, *The Story of Durham: City of the New South* (Durham: Duke University Press, 1927); and Peter Burke Hobbs, "Plantation to Factory: Tradition and Industrialization in Durham, N.C., 1880–1890" (Master's thesis, Duke University, 1971). Quotation from *U.S. Tobacco Journal*, 17 Nov. 1883, quoted in Paul, *Durham*, 134.

3. U.S. Bureau of the Census, 10th Census, (manuscript) Census for Manufacturing, 1880, Orange County, North Carolina/NA.

4. Paul, *Durham*, 105.

5. Ibid., 27, 104.

6. The firm's history is described in Robert F. Durden, *The Dukes of Durham* (Durham: Duke University Press, 1975); Dwight B. Billings, Jr., *Planters and the Making of a "New South": Class, Politics, and Development in North Carolina, 1865–1900* (Chapel Hill: University of North Carolina Press, 1979); Jonathan Daniels, *Tar Heels: A Portrait of North Carolina* (Westport, Conn.: Negro Universities Press, 1941); and Richard B. Tennant, *The American Cigarette Industry: A Study in Economic Analysis and Public Policy* (Hamden, Conn.: Archon Books, 1971).

7. Durden, *Dukes of Durham*, 18–19.

8. U.S. Bureau of the Census, (manuscript) Census for Manufacturing, Orange County, 1880.

9. *U.S. Tobacco Journal*, 17 Nov. 1883.

10. Joseph C. Robert, *The Story of Tobacco in America* (Chapel Hill: University of North Carolina Press, 1967), 141.

11. Tennant, *American Cigarette Industry*, 17–21.

12. In New York City, James B. Duke canvassed the retail trade selling goods and conducting a vigorous advertising campaign. See Tennant, *American Cigarette Industry*, 23, and *Manufacturers' Record*, 28 Aug. 1886.

13. James B. Duke to D. B. Strouse, 16 Mar. 1888, JBD/PL/DU.

14. James B. Duke to D. B. Strouse, 2 Apr. 1886 and 19 July 1887; and D. B. Strouse to Duke, Ginter, and Allen, 8 Feb. 1888, JBD/PL/DU.

15. Don Maby Lacy, "The Beginnings of Industrialism in North Carolina" (Master's thesis, University of North Carolina, 1935).

16. James B. Duke to D. B. Strouse, 19 July 1887, JBD/PL/DU.

17. James B. Duke To D. B. Strouse, 27 Mar. 1889, JBD/PL/DU.

18. Tennant, *American Cigarette Industry*, 24–5; Durden, *Dukes of Durham*, 48–55; Meyer Jacobstein, "The Tobacco Industry in the United States," *Columbia University Studies in History, Economics, and Law*, vol. 26, no. 3 (1907), 102–5.

19. Durham *Weekly Globe*, 8 June 1892. See also A. W. Hayward to Benjamin N. Duke, 10 May 1892, BND/PL/DU.

20. Benjamin N. Duke to Stonarch, 12 May 1892, BND/PL/DU, and Durham *Weekly Globe*, 8 June 1892.

NOTES TO CHAPTER V

21. Benjamin N. Duke to Julian S. Carr, 11 Nov. 1899, BND/PL/DU. By this time, Carr apparently was in financial difficulties because Benjamin Duke asked him to repay a loan a week later. See Benjamin N. Duke to Julian S. Carr, 20 Nov. 1899, BND/PL/DU.

22. Jacobstein, "Tobacco Industry," 97.

23. James B. Duke, testimony, 7 May 1902, U.S. Industrial Commission, *Trusts and Combinations* (Washington, D.C.: G.P.O., 1903), 317–37.

24. William H. Nicholls, *Price Policies in the Cigarette Industry: A Study of Concerted Action and Its Social Control, 1911–1950* (Nashville: Vanderbilt University Press, 1951), 31–32.

25. Tobacco manufacturing rested on a foundation of cheap labor, according to Robert C. Weaver, "The Tobacco Industry in North Carolina," n.d., an unpublished study in the Tobacco Code Section, NRA/NA/DC. Weaver reports that labor's share in the proceeds of the industry declined steadily after 1899, which means that the decline coincided with the growing monopolization of the industry and its move to the South.

26. Industry profits are recorded in Nicholls, *Price Policies*, 42–43; wages are found in Paul H. Douglass, *Real Wages in the United States, 1890–1926* (Boston: Houghton Mifflin, 1930), 610–13.

27. I. M. Osbreen, President, Cigar Makers International Union of America, Memorandum to National Recovery Administration, Code of Fair Competition for the Cigarette Industry, Tobacco Code Section, NRA/NA.

28. Durham workers, however, fared better than workers in northern plants whose factories were closed as the industry moved south to take advantage of lower wage rates. The American Tobacco Company, for example, closed its Brooklyn plant in 1930 and moved its operations to Durham. See Survey Materials for *Bulletin* No. 100, Women's Bureau record Group, WB/NA. The subject is also discussed in Charles S. Johnson's 1935 study, "The Tobacco Worker: A Study of Tobacco Factory Workers and Their Families," 2 vols., Division of Review, Industrial Studies Section, NRA/NA.

29. Tennant, *American Cigarette Industry*, 4–5.

30. This is described by radical economists as "labor market segmentation" and by Marxist-influenced scholarship as "colonized labor," in which racial-ethnic workers are confined to the most labor-intensive and least remunerative parts of the economy. See the articles in *Labor Market Segmentation*, ed. Richard C. Edwards, Michael Reich, and David M. Gordon (Lexington, Mass.: D. C. Heath, 1975), especially those by Harold M. Baron and Alice Kessler-Harris, for examples of the first approach. See Robert Blauner, *Racial Oppression in America* (New York: Harper and Row, 1972), for an example of the second.

31. A tobacco employer quoted in Emma L. Shields, "A Half-Century of the Tobacco Industry," *The Southern Workman*, 22 Sept. 1922, p. 420.

32. This also happened in textile mills.

33. These basic divisions of labor in the tobacco industry are described in Johnson, "The Tobacco Worker."

34. In Richmond, white women had been hired by Allen and Ginter in the late 1870s and early 1880s to roll cigarettes by hand, but by the late 1880s they had al-

NOTES TO CHAPTER V

most no employment in Durham except for bag making. After mechanization, they usually ran the packing rather than the making machines.

35. A few women became foreladies, but Johnson's survey of the industry in the mid-1930s found that no women, black or white, occupied the foreman's level in the industry: Johnson, "The Tobacco Workers," 1:26.

36. Harriet A. Byrne, "The Effects on Women of Changing Conditions in the Cigar and Cigarette Industries," U.S. Women's Bureau *Bulletin*, No. 100 (Washington, D.C.: G.P.O., 1932), discussed the effects of the move south. Herbert R. Northrup, *The Negro in the Tobacco Industry* (Philadelphia: University of Pennsylvania Press, 1970), discusses the employment trends in the industry.

37. Durham *Recorder*, 19 Jan. 1899.

38. Daniels, *Tar Heels*, 113. The Durham example contradicts the version of southern industrialization presented in works such as Broadus Mitchell, *The Rise of Cotton Mills in the South* (Gloucester, Mass.: Peter Smith Publishing, 1906), in trade journals such as the *Manufacturers' Record* and the *Southern Textile Bulletin*, or in the local histories by Hiram Paul, William K. Boyd, and Robert Durden. These sources place undue emphasis on the philanthropic and public-spirited motives that fostered the growth of industry in communities like Durham. The Durham example also contradicts the thesis presented by Dwight B. Billings, who tried to make a clearcut distinction between the social origins and managerial behavior of textile and tobacco manufacturers in Dwight Billings, Jr., *Planters and the Making of a "New South."* Claiming that textile manufacturers sprang from the planter class and tobacco manufacturers from the yeoman class, Billings ascribed structural differences in the industries to the origins of the entrepreneurs who built them. In the Durham case, however, the men he called *planters* and the men he called *yeomen* cooperated in building both textile and tobacco enterprises.

39. Hobbs, "Plantation to Factory," 17. Using the machine invented by William H. Kerr, Carr was able to increase bag output almost six times.

40. See BND/PL/DU, 1892–1902, for extensive discussions of the Duke involvement in the textile industry. See also Durden, *Dukes of Durham*, 124–33.

41. W. A. Erwin to B. N. Duke, 3 Jan. 1901, BND/PL/DU; Durden, *Dukes of Durham*, 139.

42. J. S. Carr, Jr., "What Made Our Business Grow," *System* 35 (2 Feb. 1919), 201–5.

43. J. S. Carr, Jr., "Building a Business on the Family Plan," *System* 35 (7 July 1919), 47–50.

44. J. S. Carr to B. N. Duke, 4 Jan. 1898, BND/PL/DU, and J. S. Carr, Jr., "What Made Our Business Grow."

45. North Carolina Department of Labor and Printing, *Annual Report for 1917* (Raleigh, 1917).

46. See Allen Heath Stokes, Jr., "Black and White Labor and the Development of the Southern Textile Industry, 1800–1920" (Ph.D. diss., University of South Carolina, 1977); John Curtis Barstenstein, "The Exclusion of Black Workers from N.C. Textile Industry, 1880–1910" (B.A. thesis, Harvard University, 1976); Holland Thompson, *From the Cotton Field to the Cotton Mill: A Study of Industrial Transition in North Carolina* (New York: Macmillan, 1906), 248–65; and Daniel A. Tompkins, *Cotton Mill, Commercial Features* (Charlotte: the author, 1899), for

discussions of the reasons for the exclusion of black workers from the mills. By the late 1840s the exclusive use of slaves in southern textile mills began to decline. The ready availability of white labor on the land undoubtedly contributed to the policy. By the late 1880s and 1890s, white workers defeated attempts to introduce black labor into the mills. Meanwhile, industrial ideologues like Daniel A. Tompkins were arguing that the exclusion of black labor would "reestablish respectability for white labor," which had been demoralized by the unsuccessful competition waged by poor whites with slave labor and then black labor. Had there been a serious labor shortage, manufacturers would have copied the Carr experiment despite threats from white workers, but the agricultural crisis eliminated the need of taking that risk.

47. See Jennings J. Rhyne, *Some Cotton Mill Workers and Their Villages* (Chapel Hill: University of North Carolina Press, 1930); Marjorie Potwin, *Cotton Mill People of the Piedmont: A Study in Social Change* (New York: Columbia University, 1927); Thompson, *From the Cotton Field to the Cotton Mill;* Lois MacDonald, *Southern Mill Hills: A Study of Social and Economic Forces in Certain Mill Villages* (New York: Alex L. Hillman, 1928); Paul Blanshard, *Labor in Southern Cotton Mills* (New York: New Republic, 1927); Tom Tippett, *When Southern Labor Stirs* (New York: Jonathan Cape and Harrison Smith, 1931); and Jeannette P. Nichols, "Does the Mill Village Foster Any Social Types?" *Social Forces* 2 (1923): 350–57, for descriptions of mill villages.

48. North Carolina Bureau of Labor Statistics, *First Annual Report for the Year 1887* (Raleigh, 1887), 149–50, 142. Census reports in North Carolina and a U.S. Senate study reported the following percentages of female textile workers under the age of 21: 1900, 68.2%; 1907, 68.2%; 1920, 36.4%; 1930, 33.7%. As the age of the women workers rose, the same sources also recorded a rise in the numbers of married women employed in the industry: 1900, 16.7%; 1907, 6.9%; 1920, 32.2%; 1930, 48.9%. All the figures come from the U.S. Census of Manufacturing except for the 1907 figures, which come from the Senate report. See U.S. Senate, "The Cotton Textile Industry," vol. 1, in *Report on the Conditions of Women and Child Wage-Earners in the United States,* 61st Cong., 2d Sess. (Washington, D.C.: G.P.O., 1910).

49. Carr, "Building a Business"; Walter B. Weare, *Black Business in the New South: A Social History of the North Carolina Mutual Life Insurance Company* (Urbana: University of Illinois Press, 1973), 45, 82–83.

50. R. W. Henniger, "What the South Offers Industry," *Factory and Industrial Management* 77 (4 Apr. 1929); the author was listed as Professor of Industry, North Carolina State College, Raleigh.

51. Spencer T. Miller, Jr., and Joseph E. Fletcher, *The Church and Industry* (New York: Longmans, Green, 1930), 201. Although blacks did not work in the mills, they cleaned the village privies and worked in the yards.

52. Bessie Taylor Buchanan, interview by Lanier Rand, July 1977, SOHP/SHC/UNC.

53. Luther Riley, interview by Lanier Rand, July 1977, SOHP/SHC/UNC.

54. H. R. Fitzgerald to the Southern Textile Association, *Southern Textile Bulletin,* 30 Oct. 1919.

55. Carr, "Building a Business."

NOTES TO CHAPTER V

56. Durham *Morning Herald,* 18 July 1919.

57. "A Doctor of Industrial Relations," *Southern Textile Bulletin,* 22 Jan. 1920. See also 10 July, 24 July, 14 Aug., 2 Oct., and 30 Oct. 1919.

58. J. F. Sturdivant, "Employee Representative Plan of Durham Hosiery Mills," *Journal of Social Forces* 4 (3 Mar. 1926): 625–28.

59. Obituary for Julian S. Carr, Jr., in the Greensboro *Daily News,* 18 Mar. 1922.

60. Kemp P. Lewis to Hayden Clement, 10 Aug. 1920, KPL/SHC/UNC.

61. Harry Preston, Railway Audit and Inspection Company, to K. P. Lewis, 11 and 18 Aug. 1919, KPL/SHC/UNC; "Report of Operative No. 230," 22–23 Jan. 1920, ECMC/FD/PL/DU.

62. Kemp P. Lewis, "Need of Cooperation for Our Company's Good," speech given in 1925, KPL/SHC/UNC.

63. A. L. Agner, report on his course, "Modern Production Methods," taught by the Business Training Corporation, 8 Feb. 1921; there are similar reports in 1922 and 1923 (KPL/SHC/UNC); K. P. Lewis to W. A. Erwin, 27 Feb. 1931, refers to the "extended labor system." "The Petition of the Weavers and Fixers of the No. 1, Weave Room," 8 Apr. 1929, refers to the "stretch-out" (KPL/SHC/UNC).

64. Luther Riley, interview, uses this formulation. So did one of the West Durham merchants interviewed by Richard Franck concerning the 1934 textile strike at Erwin Mills (personal holding).

65. Based on a comparison of the listings for Durham mills in *Davison's Textile "Blue Book"* for 1920–21, 1925–26, and 1935 (New York: Davison Publishing, 1921, 1926, 1935).

66. See Durham *Morning Herald,* 26 Sept. 1929, and Durham *Sun,* 26 Apr. 1939, for descriptions of how the Carr firm survived.

67. Erwin Cotton Mills Company reports, Aug. 1925 and Jan. 1926, KPL/SHC/UNC.

68. Numerous letters in the Lewis correspondence for 1928 deal with the efforts led by the Cotton Textile Institute (KPL/SHC/UNC).

69. Correspondence concerning the merger began in January 1928 and continued intermittently until 1 Jan. 1929 when the Erwin Company officially rejected the proposal. See correspondence in 1928–1929, KPL/SHC/UNC.

70. Kemp P. Lewis to the Stockholders and Directors of the Erwin Cotton Manufacturing Company, 29 July 1931, KPL/SHC/UNC.

71. K. P. Lewis to G. A. Allen, 26 June 1931, KPL/SHC/UNC.

72. Durham Hosiery Mills report to the Stockholders, 26 Nov. 1935, KPL/SHC/UNC.

73. Report of the liquidation proceedings for the Durham Cotton Manufacturing Company, 1 May 1940, KPL/SHC/UNC.

74. Kemp P. Lewis memorandum, 1940, KPL/SHC/UNC.

75. Frazier, "Durham," 338–39; Booker T. Washington, "Durham, North Carolina: A City of Negro Enterprise," *Independent* 70 (30 Mar. 1911): 642–50; and W. E. B. DuBois, "The Upbuilding of Black Durham," *World's Work* 33 (Jan. 1912): 334–38.

76. Paul, *Durham,* 49. Frazier, for example, describes white business as showing "respect" for black businessmen's achievements ("Durham").

77. Frazier, "Durham," 338–39.

NOTES TO CHAPTER V

78. Walter Weare, "Charles Clinton Spaulding: Middle-Class Leadership in the Age of Segregation," in *Black Leaders of the 20th Century,* ed. John Hope Franklin and August Meier (Urbana: University of Illinois Press, 1982), 171.

79. See also William J. Kennedy, Jr., *The N.C. Mutual Story: A Symbol of Progress, 1898–1970* (Durham: North Carolina Mutual Publications, 1970), and Weare, *Black Business.*

80. Allen Edward Burgess, "Tar Heel Blacks and the New South Dream: The Coleman Manufacturing Company, 1896–1904" (Ph.D. diss., Duke University, 1977).

81. DuBois, "Upbuilding of Black Durham," 335–36. Weare, *Black Business in the New South,* 41, depicts a more supportive attitude on the part of the Carrs toward the black-owned mill, but the DuBois article seems the more credible assessment since its author was generally pleased with the way in which white Durham was treating black Durham.

82. T. A. Allen, North Carolina Bureau of Labor and Printing, *Fifteenth Annual Report* (Raleigh, 1902), 415–16.

83. Paul, *Durham,* iv, 99.

84. *Tobacco Plant,* 14 Sept. 1888, quoted in Durham, *Dukes of Durham,* 125.

85. Durham *Recorder,* quoted in Durden, *Dukes of Durham,* 126.

86. Durham *Recorder,* 19 Jan. 1899.

87. John Merrick, "A Speech to Durham Negroes in 1898," quoted in Robert McCants Andrews, *John Merrick: A Biographical Sketch* (Durham: Seeman Printery, 1920), 158–61.

88. Paul, *Durham,* 207.

89. *John Swinton's Paper,* 8, 22 Nov., 13 Dec. 1885; Hiram V. Paul to editor, *Journal,* 15 July 1887; *Journal of United Labor,* 6 Aug. 1887.

90. Benjamin N. Duke to Charles F. Lovering, 4 Feb. 1893, BND letterbook, PL/DU, quoted in Durden, *Dukes of Durham,* 128.

91. R. H. Wright to A. C. Watts in London, 11 Aug. 1891, Wright letterbook, PL/DU, quoted in Durden, *Dukes of Durham,* 128.

92. Duke to Lovering, Durden, *Dukes of Durham,* 131.

93. Kemp P. Lewis to Kemp D. Battle, 4 Feb. 1930; K. P. Lewis to William J. Battle, 30 July 1929; and K. P. Lewis to J. Spencer Love, 18 Oct. 1932, KPL/SHC/UNC.

94. Harry Mortimer Douty, "The North Carolina Industrial Worker, 1880–1930" (Ph.D. diss., University of North Carolina, 1936).

95. Richard Eldridge, memorandum to Labor Advisory Board, n.d., Tobacco Code, NRA/NA/DC.

96. Junius Strickland, "Wake Up! Cigarettemakers," Appeal of Master Workman Strickland, Office of Master Workman, Progressive Assembly No. 4105, Knights of Labor, Durham, N.C., 9 Mar. 1886, published in *John Swinton's Paper,* 14 Mar. 1886.

97. North Carolina Bureau of Labor Statistics, *Fifth Annual Report for 1891,* p. 300.

98. *John Lincoln, interview by Travis Jordan, 9 Jan. 1939, NCFWP/SHC/UNC. Here and elsewhere in these notes, an asterisk before a name indicates a pseudonym.

99. *Dena Coley, interview by Dolores Janiewski, personal holding.

NOTES TO CHAPTER V

100. Ozzie Richmond, interview by Lanier Rand, SOHP/SHC/UNC.
101. Johnson, "Tobacco Worker," 2:419.
102. K. P. Lewis to Mrs. Brooks, president of Durham YWCA, 6 May 1921, KPL/SHC/UNC. See also Marion W. Roydhouse, "The 'Universal Sisterhood of Women': Women and Labor Reform in North Carolina, 1900–1932" (Ph.D. diss., Duke University, 1980), which covers this episode and others in extensive detail. For a thorough discussion of reformers and the "Mill Problem," see David L. Carlton, *Mill and Town in South Carolina, 1880–1920* (Baton Rouge: Louisiana State University Press, 1982), 129–214.
103. The Corporation Industrial Auxiliary Company sent K. P. Lewis frequent reports on reform meetings in the late 1920s; these are available in his papers. *The Southern Textile Bulletin* also covered the meetings, which included Broadus Mitchell, Mary O. Cowper, Frank P. Graham, and Nell Battle Lewis. See "Our Greatest Menace," *Southern Textile Bulletin*, 5 Jan., 2 Feb. 1928; and "The Drive against Southern Cotton Mills," *Manufacturers' Record*, 28 Oct. 1909. The statement from which the quotations were taken was circulated by Graham in 1930 before he became president of the University of North Carolina. Its signators included Kemp. D. Battle, K. P. Lewis's cousin. See correspondence for January-February 1930, KPL/SHC/UNC.
104. Compare W. E. B. DuBois, "Upbuilding of Black Durham," with his *The Souls of Black Folk: Essays and Sketches* (London: Archibald and Constable, 1903), 50, and see the discussion of DuBois's views in Weare, *Black Business*, 16–18.
105. Weare, *Black Business*, 32–37.
106. Harry J. Walker, "Changes in Race Accommodation in a Southern Community" (Ph.D. diss., University of Chicago, 1945), 83, quoted in Weare, *Black Business*, 33–34.
107. According to Weare, *Black Business*, 116, the typical official at North Carolina Mutual was a "light-brown man . . . who almost without exception possessed a college degree," the son of "upper-class professionals or middle-class craftsmen, and almost always property-owners." Portraying the black-owned institutions in Durham as the "black middle-class Zion," Weare described the complex links of kinship between its officials (138–39). The pictures illustrating his book also demonstrate the generally light complexions of the Mutual's staff and officers. Mary Mebane, daughter of a Durham tobacco worker, entered North Carolina College in 1951; the quotations in the text are her characterization of attitudes prevalent at the college "since the beginning"—in 1910. See Mary E. Mebane, *Mary* (New York: Fawcett, Junior, 1981), 218–24, 229–32. According to Mebane, "For people who wonder why segregation lasted so long without effective protest against it, one answer might lie in the notion of a 'privileged' class among oppressed people," a class she identified with the Durham elite and their children (230). Weare, *Black Business*, 227–32, describes the founding and growth of the college as resulting from collaboration among its president, James E. Shepard, C. C. Spaulding, and influential whites like the Dukes.
108. Quotations from Walker, "Changes in Race Accommodation," 219–20, from a discussion at a Durham Committee on Negro Affairs meeting that probably occurred in 1938, quoted in Weare, *Black Business*, 241. Weare's discussion of the assault on Spaulding (153, 236) was based on a folder of correspondence and clip-

NOTES TO CHAPTER V

pings in the Charles Clinton Spaulding Papers, North Carolina Mutual Life Insurance Company archives, Durham, N.C. The incident occurred on 3 August 1931.

109. *Manufacturers' Record*, 28 Oct. 1909.

110. National Negro Business League, *Proceedings*, Sixteenth Annual Meeting, Boston, 1915, p. 118, quoted in Weare, *Black Business*, 99. C. C. Spaulding was the person quoted.

111. The phrase was taken from William P. Few, "The Constructive Philanthropy of a Southern Cotton Mill," *South Atlantic Quarterly*, Jan. 1909.

112. Paul's charges were contained in letters published in Knights of Labor, *Record of the Proceedings of the Ninth Regular Session of the General Assembly*, held at Hamilton, Ontario, 5–13 Oct. 1885, p. 30–35.

113. Durham *Recorder*, J. F. Crowell scrapbooks, PL/DU (as reported in Hobbs, "Plantation to Factory," 64).

114. Raleigh *News and Observer*, 18 and 26 Aug. 1900. Arthur Vance Cole was the organizer. See Arthur Vance Cole papers [AVC], 1917–1920, PL/DU.

115. This is apparent in the correspondence among W. D. Carmichael, K. P. Lewis, and W. H. Carr, 1926–1928, KPL/SHC/UNC.

116. K. P. Lewis to J. T. Thorne, 23 Feb. 1926, KPL/SHC/UNC.

117. Mary Belle McMahon to Mary O. Cowper, n.d., MOC/PL/DU.

118. K. P. Lewis to Burton Craige, 20 Jan. 1936, KPL/SHC/UNC. The precipitating issue was Graham's decision to eliminate football scholarships, as Lewis reported to David Clark on 23 May 1936, but the underlying conflict lay in the profound disagreement between industrialists and Graham about the purpose of the university. K. P. Lewis also protested campus events such as Langston Hughes's visit, a lecture by Bertrand Russell, Graham's offer of bond for a student arrested in a bombing episode at a Burlington mill, and a UNC professor's lunch with James Ford, a Communist Party black activist. See 1929–1936, KPL/SHC/UNC.

119. Levi Branson, *Directory of the Business and Citizens of Durham City* (Raleigh: Levi Branson, 1887), 13.

120. Raleigh *News and Observer*, 6 Apr. 1896. See Costen Harrell, *The Methodist Church in Durham* (Durham: Durham City Board of Extension, 1915), and Frederick Bode, *Protestantism and the New South: N.C. Baptists and Methodists in Political Crisis, 1894–1905* (Charlottesville: University Press of Virginia, 1975), for opposing views about the relationship between the Dukes and the Methodist Church in Durham. North Carolina Bureau of Labor Statistics, *Fifth Annual Report*, 300; Julian S. Carr, speech to Methodist banquet, Apr. 1911, JSC/SHC/UNC.

121. Durham *Recorder*, 5 Mar. 1896.

122. St. Joseph's Episcopal Church, *The Life and Service of St. Joseph's Episcopal Church: Fifty Years in the West Durham Community, 1908–1958* (Durham, 1958). Miller and Fletcher, *Church and Industry*, 207.

123. See *Southern Textile Bulletin*, 16 Feb. 1928, for the standard industrial and conservative religious rebuttal to Cannon's letter. Cannon had objected to the institution of the mill village, advocated the right of workers to organize, and called for a living wage in the textile industry. See also *Manufacturers Record*, 21, 28 Apr., 12 May 1927, for similar opinions.

124. C. C. Spaulding, speech at Howard University, 4 Apr. 1943, quoted in Weare, *Black Business*, 185.

NOTES TO CHAPTER V

125. Undated clipping, *Natural Baptist Voice*, quoted in Weare, *Black Business*, 189.

126. According to Weare, *Black Business*, 193, Rev. M. M. Fisher even wrote speeches for Spaulding that included this new emphasis on the rights of labor. Second quotation from C. C. Spaulding to Miles Mark Fisher, 24 Apr. 1939, in Weare, 194.

127. John Donald Rice, "The Negro Tobacco Worker and His Union in Durham, N.C." (Master's thesis, University of North Carolina, 1941), 62. Fisher's role is also revealed in Miles Mark Fisher, *Friends: A Pictoral History of the Ten Years Pastorate: 1933–1943* (Durham: White Rock Baptist Church, 1943), and *Horace Mize, interview by Stuart Kaufman, in possession of Stuart Kaufman, Department of History, University of Maryland, College Park, Maryland.

128. C. C. Spaulding, quoted in Weare, *Black Business*, 142, referring to the residence he established, the North Carolina Mutual Clerks Home, for single women employees.

129. Raleigh *News and Observer*, 6 Apr. 1896.

130. North Carolina Bureau of Labor Statistics, *Annual Report for 1887*, 149–50.

131. *Henry Laws, interview by Dolores Janiewski, personal holding.

132. Contract between "the Erwin Cotton Mills Company and the Undersigned Employee," 13 Sept. 1909, KPL/SHC/UNC.

133. Miller and Fletcher, *Church and Industry*, 208.

134. Quoted from Erwin's obituary, Durham *Morning Herald*, 27 Feb. 1932.

135. Weare, *Black Business*, 139–40.

136. Biographical information from Paul, *Durham*.

137. Durham *Morning Herald*, W. A. Erwin obituary, 29 Feb. 1932.

138. *Cotton*, May 1939, clipping contained in KPL/SHC/UNC, as was other information concerned with the relations between Erwin, his son, K. P. Lewis, and his relatives.

139. Durham *Recorder*, 16 Apr. 1900.

140. The official Carr version of the relationship is contained in Julian S. Carr, Jr., "Building a Business on the Family Plan." The title itself may contain inadvertent support for local gossip among black (and some white) Durhamites that Carr had sired black sons who helped his "legitimate" white sons carry the coffin at his funeral in 1924. Walter Weare mentioned this gossip to me in a telephone conversation about Carr, the personification of the "divided mind" of the South, according to Weare. See also Weare, *Black Business*, 39–42. Ernest Seeman's *American Gold*, a roman à clef about Durham, contains a Carr-like figure, General Eugene Pericles Owsley, who dons a Confederate uniform, as Carr did, and was known for his "way with colored ladies" (Seeman, 235–36).

141. Weare, *Black Business*, 144–52.

142. In May 1900, leading North Carolina textile manufacturers met in Greensboro to formulate a common labor strategy. They decided not to hire union members or workers from struck mills. The agreement, dated 10 May 1900, was signed by men from Erwin Mills, Pearl Mill, and the Durham Cotton Manufacturing Company. A copy of the agreement is contained in the North Caroliniana Collection, UNC.

143. As revealed in KPL/SHC/UNC.

NOTES TO CHAPTER V

144. Durham *Recorder*, 19 Jan. 1899.

145. Durham *Recorder*, 16 Apr. 1900.

146. See Durden, *Dukes of Durham*, 100–104, 154–55, for discussions of the Dukes' devotion to the Republican Party and Daniel L. Russell, Republican-Fusion governor from 1896 to 1900. The use of the press to counter Populist criticisms by members of the Durham elite is also discussed in Bode, *Protestantism*, and Josephus Daniels, *Editor in Politics* (Chapel Hill: University of North Carolina Press, 1941).

147. Phrases such as these frequently appeared in Carr's speeches, which have been preserved from 1890 to his death in the mid-1920s, JSC/SHC/UNC. The sharpest attack on the Dukes appeared in the Durham *Weekly Globe*, 8 June 1892. Carr's bombast made it easier for historian Nannie May Tilley to dismiss Populist arguments as self-serving, as she declared in a letter to Leonard Rapport, in possession of Leonard Rapport, Archivist, National Archives, Washington, D.C. Where Georgia Populism gave way to the rantings of Tom Watson and South Carolina's Populism produced Cole L. Blease, the death of Leonidias L. Polk led to the eventual rise of Julian S. Carr, Populist, leader of the Confederate Veteran's Association and tobacco and hosiery entrepreneur.

148. Durham *Daily Sun*, 21 July 1900, and Oliver H. Orr, Jr., *Charles Brantley Aycock* (Chapel Hill: University of North Carolina Press, 1961), 123–28, 132, 174.

149. North Carolina Bureau of Labor and Printing, *Seventeenth Annual Report* (Raleigh, 1903), 141, contains this discussion by E. K. Powe, brother-in-law of W. A. Erwin; K. P. Lewis quoted in ECMCO report, Child Labor file, U.S. Children's Bureau, CB/NA/DC.

150. K. P. Lewis, ECMCO report, Child Labor file, CB/NA/DC.

151. See the Kemp P. Lewis correspondence for Apr.–Aug. 1924, SHC/UNC.

152. This is revealed by letters in the Lewis papers. See for example K. P. Lewis to Victor S. Bryant, 22 Mar. 1935, in which he opposed constitutional changes that would give more power to the city council; it would be "unfortunate to throw away what we have gained by adopting the managership plan of operation" (KPL/SHC/UNC).

153. The incident is described in the K. P. Lewis papers for 1926 and from the labor point of view in Miller and Fletcher, *Church and Industry*, 210–11.

154. This was the case in the 1940 strike at Erwin Mills. Lewis sent a letter to Governor Clyde R. Hooey thanking him for his "stand that people who want to work should be allowed to work" (K. P. Lewis to Clyde R. Hooey, 28 Mar. 1940, KPL/SHC/UNC). An earlier letter from Presiding Judge Samuel E. Shull, Court of Common Pleas, Stroudsburg, Pa., suggests that Lewis's influential connections extended beyond North Carolina. Apparently Shull and Lewis had been classmates at the University of North Carolina and Lewis had commented on Shull's conviction of Alfred Hoffman, the textile and hosiery organizer, on a "charge of conspiracy" arising from a strike in Pennsylvania. According to Shull, "his conviction met with universal satisfaction . . . and at least for the next two years, neither North Carolina nor Pennsylvania will be annoyed by his activities." "Mike" Shull to Kemp P. Lewis, 30 Nov. 1931, KPL/SHC/UNC.

155. For examples of the attacks on W. G. Pearson, see *Tobacco Plant*, 20 Oct. 1886 and 5 Oct. 1888. For the Parrish episode, see the same paper, 14–21 Nov. 1888. In addition to Pearson, four of the seven founders of the North Carolina Mu-

NOTES TO CHAPTER VI

tual had been active in Republican Party politics, but eventually they heeded the warnings of men like Julian S. Carr that "if the negro is to continue to make politics his chief aim . . . there can be but one ending" (Weare, *Black Business*, 23, 40).

156. Quoted in Durham *Recorder*, 16 Apr. 1900.
157. Weare, *Black Business*, 232–33.
158. Durham *Morning Herald*, 20 June 1919.
159. Albion L. Holsey, "Pearson: The Brown Duke of Durham," *Opportunity*, Apr. 1928, pp. 116–17.
160. K. P. Lewis to R. H. Lewis, 18 Jan. 1921, KPL/SHC/UNC.
161. James E. Shepard in Robert Cannon, "The Organization and Growth of Black Political Participation in Durham, N.C.: 1933–1958" (Ph.D. diss., University of North Carolina, 1975); C. C. Spaulding quoted in Walker, "Changes in Race Accommodation," 306. According to Weare, *Black Business*, 225–27, Spaulding and Austin "functioned well as a team, one rocking the boat, the other stabilizing it, their reciprocal actions maintaining movement without upheaval" (225), but Cannon's interpretation, based on reading NAACP records, emphasizes conflict between the two men and portrays Spaulding as always striving to keep the lid on protests from the black community. For information on the Durham Committee on Negro Affairs, see Weare, 240–64; Cannon, "The Organization and Growth of Black Political Participation"; Walker, "Changes in Race Accommodation"; and William R. Keech, *The Impact of Negro Voting* (Chicago: Rand McNally, 1968). Durham city manager quoted in Weare, 244.
162. Weare, *Black Business*, 252, 259, 263, 261, 45.
163. Naomi Brooks, "A Southerner's Point of View about Bryn Mawr," Bryn Mawr Day, 1922, Hilda Worthington Smith papers, Box 3, Schlesinger Library, Radcliffe College, Cambridge, Mass.
164. Daniels, *Tar Heels*, 107, 116.
165. Ibid., 134.

CHAPTER VI

1. Bessie Taylor Buchanan, interview by Lanier Rand, SOHP/SHC/UNC.
2. *Hetty Love, interview by Linda Guthrie, personal holding. Here and elsewhere in these notes, an asterisk before a name indicates a pseudonym.
3. Martha Gena Harris, interview by Dolores Janiewski, SOHP/SHC/UNC.
4. Esther Jenks, interview by Dolores Janiewski, SOHP/SHC/UNC.
5. Mary Burdette, interview by Mary O. Cowper, MOC/PL/DU.
6. Even when industrial slavery was the major form of labor control in antebellum factories, planters found that slaves could be rendered unfit for agriculture after exposure to the greater freedom of factory slavery and town life. See Robert S. Starobin, *Industrial Slavery in the Old South* (New York: Oxford University Press, 1970).
7. This is another instance of my disagreement with Dwight Billings' comparison of the textile industry with the plantation. Placing whites instead of blacks under direct supervision was an innovation rather than a continuation of antebellum traditions. Furthermore, the textile mill village was not a uniquely southern invention but

NOTES TO CHAPTER VI

closely resembled the company towns erected in New England and the Middle Atlantic states. See Dwight Billings, Jr., *Planters and the Making of a "New South": Class, Politics, and Development in North Carolina, 1865–1900* Chapel Hill: University of North Carolina Press, 1979), and Anthony F. C. Wallace, *Rockdale: The Growth of an American Village in the Early Industrial Revolution* (New York: W. W. Norton, 1978) for comparisons between northern and southern examples of the mill village system.

8. Theoretically, one might refer to this transition as a shift from a private or familial to a public patriarchy in which increasing numbers of white men were becoming subject to the public patriarch embodied in a mill village system. See Carol Brown, "Mothers, Fathers, and Children: From Private to Public Patriarchy," in *Women and Revolution: A Discussion of the Unhappy Marriage of Marxism and Feminism*, ed. Lydia Sargent (Boston: South End Press, 1981), 239–68, for a discussion of these issues in feminist theory. See Elizabeth Fox-Genovese, "Placing Women's History in History," *New Left Review*, no. 133, May–June 1982, pp. 19–25, for efforts to link changes in gender relationships to changes in the political economy. As expressed by Fox-Genovese, "[gender] difference became an ideological justification for collective male and class dominance in a society that claimed to draw its identity from the freedom of individuals . . . In this respect, the representations of gender difference came to dominate the most fundamental representations of the social order." Racial differences, although Fox-Genovese does not include them in her discussion, serve a similar ideological purpose by masking the differences in power between classes of white men. The experience in the mill village, however, calls for a modification of Fox-Genovese's assertion that industrial capitalism strengthened private patriarchal power; clearly, the patriarchal authority of men who entered the textile mill was eroded by their permanent subordination to the authority of mill management. In effect, they became perpetual adolescent "sons" to a patriarch who would never relinquish his authority.

9. Holland Thompson, *From the Cotton Field to the Cotton Mill: A Study of Industrial Transition in North Carolina* (New York: Macmillan Company, 1906), 207.

10. The cigarette makers made these complaints in the pages of *Progress*, the journal of the Cigar Makers Progressive Union (CMPU), in which they were the only southern local. The reports of Local 27 began appearing on 26 Sept. 1884, shortly after the local was founded on 14 July "as a benevolent and protective association with fourteen members" (*Progress*, 26 Sept. 1884). "Tyrannous shope rules" were denounced in *Progress*, 13 Jan. 1885. In the 24 Apr. 1885 issue, Junius Strickland, the corresponding secretary for Local 27, proposed that the CMPU constitution read: "Workingmen of all countries unite and prepare yourselves for the coming battle, you have nothing to lose but everything to gain." He warned members against spending money to support electoral candidates, and advised them to "use the money they contemplated spending on election humbugs in buying weapons and preparing for the coming revolution." When the CMPU altered its constitution to replace the work *tobacco* (describing the trade of its members) with *cigars*, Local 27 disappeared from the organization; it continued to exist, however, as a local assembly in the Knights of Labor.

11. Hiram Voss Paul, a local printer recruited into the Knights of Labor, di-

NOTES TO CHAPTER VI

rected these charges against the Dukes in the *Journal of United Labor*, 6 Aug. 1887. According to Paul, a few local workers, including two women, were also discharged by the Dukes because two knights "happened to speak of some of the hardships and unchristian acts" in the Duke factory.

12. Thompson, *From Cotton Field to Cotton Mill*, 249. Thompson, however, made this explanation for the exclusion of blacks from the textile mills. Like most commentators, he never explained the discrepancy in policy between the textile and tobacco industries, which calls into question his statement that a "fixed belief" underlay the exclusion of blacks from the mills. Charles S. Johnson, who did not avoid this issue, suggested that the labor-intensive textile industry needed a more cohesive labor force, while greater mechanization in tobacco made this less important. Both industries evolved a particular tradition, possibly without a thought-out reason for so doing. Charles S. Johnson, "The Tobacco Worker: A Study of Tobacco Factory Workers and Their Families," 2 vols. (1935), Industrial Studies Section, Division of Review, NRA/NA.

13. Washington Duke, quoted in Raleigh *News and Observer*, 6 Apr. 1896. By 1886, the *Tobacco Plant* reported that the Duke firm employed 120 "young ladies" as packers (22 Dec. 1886).

14. Harriet L. Herring, *Welfare Work in Mill Villages: The Story of Extra-Mill Activities in North Carolina* (1929; reprint, Montclair, N.J.: Patterson Smith, 1986), 270–71. Herring's book, based on interviews with representative mills, including Erwin and Durham Hosiery Mills, explains that mill housing was "essential to get rid of undesireable families." By threatening to evict families that violated their moral code, mill owners could make sure that they retained a virtuous, chaste, and temperate work force. This policy also involved a strict monitoring of girls' sexual behavior and reputation but did not require that management be "equally strict with the boys and men." Interviews with Bessie Taylor Buchanan, Esther Jenks, Luther Riley (interview by Lanier Rand, SOHP/SHC/UNC), and *Henry Laws (interview by Dolores Janiewski, personal holding) discussed the moral controls in the Erwin mill village. Interviews with *Rose Medlin, *Lona Oakey, *Maude Foushee (interviews by Dolores Janiewski, personal holding) discussed the moral code for the L and M factory, the successor to W. Duke and Sons.

15. *Lona Oakey interview. Oakey prided herself on meeting this requirement, which signified that she belonged to a "higher class of people" than her counterparts at the morally indifferent American Tobacco Company.

16. Ernest Seeman, *American Gold* (New York: Dial Press, 1978), 256, 69. The historical record offers some evidence to support Seeman's fictionalized portraits of the two men: Brodie Duke was married four times and was known to have a problem with alcohol; Julian S. Carr was rumored to have had black mistresses and "several Negro sons" as Seeman also alleges (166).

17. *Lona Oakey, interview.

18. Annie Mack Barbee, interview by Beverly Jones, SOHP/SHC/UNC, describes the foremen who tried to "fumble your behind." *Clara Jeffries, interview by Dolores Janiewski, personal holding, described the "love birds" who offered sexual favors to the visiting officials sent by American Tobacco from New York. They received benefits, such as being able to rest while others were working.

NOTES TO CHAPTER VI

19. Julian S. Carr, Jr., "Building a Business on the Family Plan," *System* 35 (7 July 1919): 301–5.

20. E. K. Rowe and K. P. Lewis (then executive assistant to the treasurer), ECMCO, interview by Emma Duke, 11 Apr. 1918; Child Labor Law File, CB/NA/DC.

21. *Jessie Ervin interview, Dolores Janiewski, personal holding.

22. Reports of these operatives or letters concerning their activities are contained in KPL/SHC/UNC.

23. This quotation, taken from the memoirs of a white woman who went south to teach in a black school in Wilmington, epitomizes the creation among blacks of a separate morality for dealings with whites. See Lura Beam, *He Called Them by the Lightning: A Teacher's Odyssey in the Negro South, 1908–1919* (Indianapolis: Bobbs-Merrill, 1967), 11.

24. W. Izard and A. D. Turrentine, interview by Emma Duke, 11 Apr. 1918, CB/NA/DC.

25. W. C. Cole and Son, interview by Emma Duke, 6 Apr. 1918, CB/NA/DC.

26. C. Tinsley Willis, "Negro Labor in the Tobacco Industry in North Carolina" (Master's thesis, New York University, 1931). As suggested by the example of the Carr mill, which employed black workers during the wartime labor scarcity, "public sentiment" could be altered to suit managerial necessity.

27. The Kemp P. Lewis papers are the basic source for this data on Lewis's career, KPL/SHC/UNC.

28. Charles S. Johnson, "The Tobacco Worker"; Willis, "Negro Labor"; and Meyer Jacobstein, *The Tobacco Industry in the United States*, in the Columbia University *Studies in History, Economics, and Law*, 24:3 (New York: Columbia University Press, 1907), are among the sources for this description.

29. This date for the entrance of black women in significant numbers into the tobacco industry comes from Joseph Clarke Robert, *The Tobacco Kingdom: Plantation, Market, and Factory in Virginia and North Carolina, 1800–1860* (Gloucester, Mass.: Peter Smith, 1965). Robert states that the percentage of women employed rose from 10 percent in 1850 to 17 percent by 1860 but varied in tobacco centers from 1 percent in Richmond to 33 percent in Petersburg (197). The same decade saw the first introduction of white women into a few Virginia factories because the cost of male slaves had risen too high for manufacturers making plug tobacco (208).

30. U. S. Senate, "Women and Children in Selected Industries," vol. 13 in *Report on the Condition of Women and Child Wage-Earners in the United States*, 19 vols., 61st Cong. 2d Sess. (Washington, D.C.: G.P.O., 1910), 13:314. Earlier the study describes a factory in which the workers were "very old, others crippled," seated on low benches "without backs or rests of any kind; the floors are very dirty, the light is poor, and the women have to lean over their work" (13:79).

31. Emma L. Shields, "A Half-Century in the Tobacco Industry," *Southern Workman* 52 (1922): 419–25.

32. I am drawing on the theoretical work of labor historians like Alice Kessler-Harris as well as labor economists. For the latter, see Michael Reich, David Gordon, and Richard Edwards, eds., *Labor Market Segmentation* (Lexington, Mass.: D.C. Heath, 1975). I also drew on many scholars who study "dual labor markets" and

NOTES TO CHAPTER VI

"segmented labor processes." See, for example, Eva Gamarnikow, "Sexual Division of Labour: The Case of Nursing," in *Feminism and Materialism: Women and Modes of Production,* ed. Annette Kuhn and Ann Marie Wolpe (London: Routledge and Kegan Paul, 1978), 96–121. My own work suggests a segmentation by gender, class, and race that would render the term *dual labor* market inadequate. The notion of hierarchy must also be incorporated into the center of the theory to make it correspond with some precision to the actual case of women in Durham.

33. The photograph illustrated the article by W. E. B. DuBois (written after a visit to Durham), "The Upbuilding of Black Durham," *World's Work,* Jan. 1912, pp. 334–35. The clothing may have been specifically worn for the photograph, but such posturing would only strengthen the message that the image was meant to convey.

34. Hugh P. Brinton, "The Negro in Durham: A Study in Adjustment to Town Life" (Ph.D. diss., University of North Carolina, 1930), 134–35, describes the labor process in a hosiery mill employing an all-black labor force. The description is also based on an interview with *Ada Scott by Peggy Rabb, personal holding.

35. Mary O. Cowper, "Cotton-Cloth: A Type Study of the Community Process," unpublished paper (1925), p. 82, MOC/PL/DU.

36. *Mollie Seagrove, interview by Linda Daniel, personal holding.

37. Thompson, *From Cotton Field to Cotton Mill,* 118–33, describes the labor process in a typical North Carolina mill.

38. T. A. Allen, quoted in North Carolina Bureau of Labor and Printing, *Fifteenth Annual Report,* 301–2.

39. David Moberg, "A Familiar Story of Changing Times," *In These Times,* 3:15 (14-20 Feb.), 1979. See Daniel Nelson, *Managers and Workers: Origins of the New Factory System in the United States, 1880–1920* (Madison: University of Wisconsin Press, 1975); Harry Braverman, *Labor and Monopoly Capital: The Degradation of Work in the Twentieth Century* (New York: Monthly Review Press, 1974); and Alfred D. Chandler, Jr., *The Visible Hand: The Managerial Revolution in American Business* (Cambridge: Harvard University Press, 1977), for a more thorough analysis of these issues.

40. Seeman, *American Gold,* 174, 273, 251.

41. Kemp P. Lewis, "Need of Cooperation for Our Company's Good," 1924; A. L. Agner, report on his course, "Modern Production Methods," taught by the Business Training Corporation, 8 Feb. 1921, KPL/SHC/UNC. Other reports are contained in the same papers for 1922 and 1923. K. P. Lewis continued to turn to outside experts for advice on managing the labor force at Erwin Mills. For example, in 1938 the Charles E. Bedaux Company, a firm of industrial engineers who specialized in "human power measurement," advised the company not only on the introduction of new machinery but on the scientific way to manage "laying off and rehiring of employees." Citing a series of factors to be considered, including seniority, skill, productivity, health, and family, the Bedaux company insisted that "in all cases their rating should be amenable to mathematical, precise, evaluation rather than personal judgment," an obvious contrast to paternalist managerial practices. See Albert Rauoud to Carl R. Harris, 16 Aug. 1938, EMC/FD/PL/DU. Rauoud was chairman of the Charles E. Bedaux Company, according to its letterhead.

42. KPL/SHC/UNC, 1925–1929, contain correspondence dealing with these is-

NOTES TO CHAPTER VI

sues, including an unsigned petition to K. P. Lewis from the Weavers and Fixers of the No. 1 Weave Room, dated 8 Apr. 1929. Alfred Hoffman's activities were covered in the Raleigh *Union Herald*, 1927–1929, and in reports from the Corporation Auxiliary Company, KPL/SHC/UNC. After leaving Durham, Hoffman became embroiled in the famous Marion textile strike of 1929. The Corporation Auxiliary Company sent secret observers to the meetings of the Piedmont Organizing Council and also to meetings of its supporters, who included Frank Graham, Nell Battle Lewis, Mary O. Cowper, and women associated with the workers' education movement.

43. According to the survey materials used by Caroline Manning and Harriet A. Byrne, "The Effects on Women of Changing Conditions in the Cigar and Cigarette Industries," U. S. Women's Bureau *Bulletin* No. 100 (Washington, D.C.: G. P. O., 1932). The closing of the Brooklyn plant brought the Turkish and special brand production to Durham in Jan. 1930. This led to the employment of 500 new workers, bringing the total work force at the Lucky Strike plant to 1,431, including 757 white women and 54 black women, WB/NA/DC.

44. Manning and Byrne, "Effects on Women," and Caroline Manning, "Hours and Earnings in Tobacco Stemmeries," U. S. Women's Bureau *Bulletin* No. 127 (Washington, D.C.: G.P.O., 1934), and survey materials for both reports, WB/NA/DC. W. B. Mitchell, American Tobacco Company, quoted in NRA "Hearings on Code of Fair Competition in the Cigarette, Smoking Tobacco, Snuff, and Chewing Tobacco Industries," Aug. 1934, NRA/NA/DC.

45. Kemp P. Lewis, "To the Stockholders and Directors of the Erwin Cotton Mills Company," 26 Jan. 1935, KPL/SHC/UNC. The K. P. Lewis papers for 1935–1941 cover this long series of conflicts between Erwin workers and management over work rules and workloads.

46. W. B. Mitchell, NRA, "Hearings on Code of Fair Competition," NRA/NA/DC.

47. Thompson, *From Cotton Field to Cotton Mill*, 207.

48. Ibid., 206. Paul Wheeler, a Durham manager, presented the second stereotype: "There are lots of lazy men in this country that move to town and put their wives and children in the factory to work for them so they can sit around on the street corners and dry goods boxes and tell yarns and cry hard times" (North Carolina Bureau of Labor and Printing, *Seventeenth Annual Report* [Raleigh, 1903], 240–41).

49. *Pearl Barbee, interview by Linda Guthrie, personal holding; Annie Mack Barbee interview; Dora Scott Jones, interview by Beverly Jones, SOHP/SHC/UNC.

50. Mary E. Mebane, *Mary* (New York: Fawcett Junior, 1981), 98–99, 125.

51. Theotis Williamson, interview by Lanier Rand, SOHP/SHC/UNC.

52. U.S. Bureau of the Census, *The Statistical History of the United States from Colonial Times to the Present* (Stamford, Conn.: Fairfield Publishers, 1965), 71.

53. Harry Mortimer Douty, "The North Carolina Industrial Worker, 1880–1930" (Ph.D. diss., University of North Carolina, 1936).

54. The North Carolina Commissioner of Labor established $560 as a modest standard of living. It included $34 for fuel, $94 for clothing, and $247 for food. A textile worker's lower housing costs (figured at the average rent of 25 cents per room per week or about $3 per month) reduced the total budget by $20 from the average

NOTES TO CHAPTER VI

presented in the North Carolina Bureau of Labor and Printing, *Eighteenth Annual Report* (Raleigh, 1904), Table 3, "Cost of Living and Retail Price of Food, 1903," p. 335. Jerome Dowd, a professor of economics and sociology at Trinity College in Durham, collected statistics on the cost of living in Durham in 1899 and published them in "Cheap Labor in the South," *Gunton's Magazine*, Feb. 1900, pp. 113–21.

55. As discussed by Frank H. White, "The Economic and Social Development of Negroes in North Carolina since 1900" (Ph.D. diss., New York University, 1960). To some extent the Durham example differs from comparisons in Boston presented by Elizabeth Pleck, "A Mother's Wages: Income Earning among Married Italian and Black Women, 1896–1911," in *A Heritage of Our Own: Toward a New Social History of American Women*, ed. Nancy F. Cott and Elizabeth H. Pleck (New York: Simon and Schuster, 1979), 367–92.

56. U.S. Department of Commerce, Bureau of the Census, 1930, Fifteenth Census, *Families: Reports by States* (Washington, D.C.: G.P.O., 1933).

57. Based on wage data contained in ECMCO/FD/FL for Erwin workers, and Johnson, "Tobacco Worker," 2: 434–38, for Durham tobacco workers.

58. Evidence gathered by the Industrial Studies Section of the NRA contained this wage and occupation data which were included in the records included with the NRA, "Hearings on a Code of Fair Competition," NRA/NA/DC.

59. Mebane, *Mary*, 166.

60. Some children "helped" their older relatives by working in the stemmery or hosiery mill, according to interviews with *Dena Coley and *Robert Thompson, D. Janiewski personal holding.

61. Johnson, "Tobacco Worker," 2: 401–3.

62. This refers to the arguments made by Leslie Woodcock Tentler, *Wage-Earning Women: Industrial Work and Family Life in the United States, 1900–1930* (New York: Oxford University Press, 1979), and Sarah Eisenstein, *Give Us Bread but Give Us Roses: Working Women's Consciousness in the United States, 1890 to the First World War* (London: Routledge and Kegan Paul, 1983), that the impermenence of working women's presence in the labor force made wage labor "secondary to, and indeed structured by, the expectation of marriage and motherhood" (Eisenstein, 48). By the 1930s, Durham women had moved beyond this short-term commitment to paid employment.

63. Brinton, "The Negro in Durham," 244, noted that 42 percent of the black laboring class in Durham in the late 1920s depended on the earnings of an employed couple, compared with 26.9 percent supported by an adult male. The increasing numbers of married women in the paid labor force suggested that the same trend applied to white households.

64. There is, of course, a debate among Marxist and socialist feminists whether it is employers alone who benefit from women's domestic labor or whether working-class male relatives share the benefits. See Natalie J. Sokoloff, *Between Money and Love: The Dialectics of Women's Home and Market Work* (New York: Praeger, 1980), 112–80.

65. By *non-Marxist*, I refer to the definition of "economic exploitation" presented by Roger L. Ransom and Richard Sutch, *One Kind of Freedom: The Economic Consequences of Emancipation* (Cambridge: Cambridge University Press, 1977), 3, which defines the phrase as the "expropriation of the product of labor

NOTES TO CHAPTER VI

without compensation." These authors also cite Joan Robinson's definition of *exploitation* as a worker's being "paid less than the value of his marginal production" (Joan Robinson, *The Economics of Imperfect Competition* (London: Macmillan, 1969), 281–83. See Ransom and Sutch, 317. While Ransom and Sutch are willing to assume that the market assigns a fair return to labor and capital, which would mean that only unpaid labor is exploited, Marxists assume that the returns are dictated by unequal power between the two classes based on their different relationship to the means of production. Thus Marxists might more readily describe women as "exploited" in their wage-earning work, while Ransom and Sutch would more readily see exploitation in women's unpaid domestic labor. However, I feel that both areas of work involve women's exploitation.

66. *John Lincoln, interview by Travis Jordan, NCFWP/SHC/UNC.

67. Howard Newby, Colin Bell, David Rose, and Peter Saunders, *Property, Paternalism, and Power: Class and Control in Rural England* (Madison: University of Wisconsin Press, 1978), 28.

68. David Metza and David Welham, "The Ordeal of Consciousness," *Theory and Society* 9 (1980): 7.

69. E. P. Thompson, "Patrician Society, Plebeian Culture," *Journal of Social History* 7 (1973–74): 393. See the discussion by Hans Medick, "Plebeian Culture in the Transition to Capitalism," in *Culture, Ideology and Politics*, ed. Raphael Samuel and Gareth Stedman Jones (London: Routledge and Kegan Paul, 1982), 84–112.

70. E. P. Thompson, "The Long Revolution, I," *New Left Review*, no. 10 (1961), 33.

71. This emphasis on inequality as "natural" is the other side of the American emphasis on "natural rights" and was emphasized in the South in part to justify slavery.

72. Newby et al., *Property, Paternalism, and Power*, 29.

73. In the words of Karen Brodkin Sacks, "Labor: White Coats and Pink Collars," *Women's Review of Books* (July 1984): 6–8, "class consciousness has plural foundations" because a gender-specific and racially-specific identity is the take-off point for consciousness (7).

74. Eisenstein, *Give Us Bread*, 39.

75. See Appendix for a fuller discussion of this issue.

76. "Durhamite," Letter to the Editor, *Journal of United Labor*, 23 Aug. 1888.

77. North Carolina Bureau of Labor Statistics, *Second Annual Report* (Raleigh, 1888), 81–83.

78. Chester Daniels, interview by Glenn Hinson, SOHP/SHC/UNC.

79. Child Labor File, Durham Extracts, CB/NA/DC.

80. Mebane, *Mary*, 98–99, 108; Theotis Williamson interview.

81. Annie Mack Barbee, interview.

82. Metza and Wellham, "Ordeal of Consciousness," 6; Annie Mack Barbee interview.

83. *Jessie Ervin, interview by Dolores Janiewski, personal holding; *Pearl Barbee interview.

84. Charlie Decoda Mack, interview by Beverly Jones, SOHP/SHC/UNC; Jessie Ervin, 2d interview; Johnson, "Tobacco Worker," 2: 415.

85. *Clairborne Peavey, interview by Dolores Janiewski, personal holding.

NOTES TO CHAPTER VII

86. Johnson, "Tobacco Worker," 2: 420.
87. Mebane, *Mary*, 173–74.
88. *Louise Couch Jenkins, interview by Dolores Janiewski, personal holding.
89. Bessie Taylor Buchanan, interview.
90. *Lona Oakey, interview.
91. Charlie Decoda Mack, interview.
92. *Clara Jeffries, interview.
93. Johnson, "Tobacco Worker," 2: 427–28.
94. *John Lincoln, NCFWP/SHC/UNC, tried to use education and a promotion to a clerk's position as a way out of the mill; Mary Mebane also chose education. Pauli Murray left Durham. *Ada Scott left but returned at her daughter's request, to her ultimate regret, and *Louise Couch Jenkins secured a white collar job on the basis of her college training.
95. Newby et al., *Property, Paternalism, and Power*, 26–27.
96. Herring, *Welfare Work in Mill Villages*, 275.
97. Luther Riley, Theotis Williamson, Bessie Taylor Buchanan, interviews.
98. Johnson, "Tobacco Worker," 1: 126.
99. Ibid., 2: 420.
100. K. B. Wheeler, NRA, "Hearings on a Code of Fair Competition," NRA/NA/DC.
101. Johnson, "Tobacco Worker," 2: 421.
102. Petition of the Weavers and Fixers of No. 1 Weave Room, KPL/SHC/UNC; Petition of Shop Committee of Bull City Textile Local Union No. 2155, 24 Sept. 1935, KPL/SHC/UNC.
103. H. C. Hall to President Roosevelt, 9 Aug. 1933, Correspondence in support of the Code of Fair Competition for the Cigarette, Snuff, Chewing, and Smoking Tobacco Industry, NRA/NA/DC.
104. Johnson, "Tobacco Worker," 2: 421.
105. *Jessie Ervin, interview.
106. *Clara Jeffries and *Tillman Jeffries, interview by Dolores Janiewski, personal holding.
107. Mary Bailey, interview by Glenn Hinson, SOHP/SHC/UNC.
108. Johnson, "Tobacco Worker," 2: 428; Annie Mack Barbee interview.
109. Annie Mack Barbee, interview.
110. *Lona Oakey, interview.
111. Mebane, *Mary*, 177, 178.
112. Seeman, *American Gold*, 174, 173, 251, 274, 273, 279.
113. Bessie Taylor Buchanan, interview.
114. Phrase from George Gunton, "Factory Labor in the South," *Gunton's Magazine*, Apr. 1898, pp. 227–28.
115. Mebane, *Mary*, 177.

CHAPTER VII

1. Ernest Seeman, *American Gold* (New York: Dial Press, 1978), 259.
2. Ibid., 274, 283, 7.

NOTES TO CHAPTER VII

3. See the provocative study of reproduction by Mary O'Brien, *The Politics of Reproduction* (London: Routledge and Kegan Paul, 1981).

4. This clarification of the complicated levels of meaning for the term *reproduction* is based on the discussion by Lourdes Benería, "Reproduction, Production, and the Sexual Division of Labour," *Cambridge Journal of Economics* 3 (1979): 205–6.

5. Seeman, *American Gold*, 173. For a useful comparison to the Durham ritual, see Natalie Zemon Davis, "The Reasons of Misrule," in her *Society and Culture in Early Modern France: Eight Essays* (Stanford: Stanford University Press, 1975), 97–123, esp. 105–9.

6. The word "economy" is used in these two formulations in its twofold meaning as a system of producing, distributing, and consuming wealth and as the management of that system. "Sexual economy" refers to the distribution or exchange and utilization of women's reproductive capacities, one of the most important forms of wealth and wealth-gaining assets in most societies. Natalie Z. Davis uses this term in her introduction to Georges Duby, *The Knight, the Lady and the Priest: The Making of Modern Marriage in Medieval France* (New York: Pantheon, 1983), ix. She discusses the connection between changes in marriage and kinship relations and changes in property and political relationships. In the first, gender is constructed; in the second, class and race.

7. "Bird's Eye View of the City of Durham" (Madison, Wis.: Ruger and Stoner, 1891), Map Collection, North Carolina Department of History and Archives, Raleigh.

8. Coy T. Phillips, "City Pattern of Durham, North Carolina," *Economic Georgraphy* 23 (Oct. 1947): 233–47.

9. Seeman, *American Gold*, 7.

10. Ida L. Moore, "Description of a Mill Village," West Durham, 17 Sept. 1938, NCFWP/SHC/UNC.

11. Pauli Murray, *Proud Shoes: The Story of an American Family* (New York: Harper, 1978), 26–27.

12. According to Charles S. Johnson, "The Tobacco Worker: A Study of Tobacco Factory Workers and Their Families," 2 vols. (1935), Division of Review, Industrial Studies Section, NRA/NA, 25.8 percent of the white tobacco workers interviewed and 8.8 percent of the black workers owned automobiles in 1935 (2:445). At that time, second- and third-hand autos could be purchased for $25–$75.

13. Hugh P. Brinson, "The Negro in Durham: A Study of Adjustment to Town Life" (Ph.D. diss., University of North Carolina, 1930), 222.

14. U.S. Works Project Administration, "Real Property Survey," W.P.A. Project 3833 (Washington, D.C.: G.P.O. 1939).

15. Johnson, "Tobacco Worker," 2: 440–42. According to the Johnson survey, the median weekly earnings of white families in Durham were $20.83; black families received $14.11. Using the rule that families should pay about 25 percent of their monthly income for housing, it is clear that far more white than black workers could afford the higher-priced housing.

16. North Carolina Bureau of Vital Statistics, *Annual Report for 1934* (Raleigh, 1934), and U.S. Bureau of the Census, *Negroes in the United States* (Washington, D.C.: G.P.O., 1933).

NOTES TO CHAPTER VII

17. Theotis Williamson, interview by Lanier Rand, SOHP/SHC/UNC.

18. Bessie Taylor Buchanan, interview by Lanier Rand, SOHP/SHC/UNC; Leonard Rapport, interview by Dolores Janiewski, personal holding.

19. U.S. Senate, "The Cotton Textile Industry," *Report on the Conditions of Women and Child Wage-Earners in the United States*, vol. 1, 81st Cong. 2d Sess. (Washington, D.C.: G.P.O., 1910); U.S. Women's Bureau, *Bulletin* No. 52, "Lost Time and Labor Turnover in Cotton Mills" (Washington, D.C.: G.P.O., 1926); U.S. Women's Bureau, *Bulletin* No. 70, "Negro Women in Industry in Fifteen States," (Washington, D.C.: G.P.O., 1929).

20. Brinton, "Negro in Durham," 118; C. Tinsely Willis, "Negro Labor in the Tobacco Industry in North Carolina" (Master's thesis, New York University, 1931).

21. Quotation from a series of interviews conducted by Peggy Rabb and Chris Potter with the residents of Henderson and Oldham Towers, two senior citizens centers in Durham in fall 1977 and spring 1978. The residents, aided by Rabb and Potter, put together a slide show of their remembrances, which included this quotation.

22. Travis Jordan, "Life in Erwin Village," Durham, N.C., 21 Nov. 1938, NCFWP/SHC/UNC.

23. Bessie Taylor Buchanan, interview.

24. *Allie Ennis, interview by Dolores Janiewski, personal holding. Here and elsewhere in the notes, an asterisk indicates a pseudonym.

25. *Calvin Couch, interview by Dolores Janiewski, personal holding.

26. *Dena Coley, interview by Dolores Janiewski, personal holding.

27. Quotation from a series of interviews conducted by Dolores Janiewski with people at the Lyons Park Senior Citizens Center in Durham, personal holding.

28. Brinton, "Negro in Durham," 119. Brinton continues: "An attitude of physical tenseness and helplessness is bred which is disorganizing to family stability and sustained efforts at adjustment, social or economic."

29. Mary E. Mebane, *Mary* (New York: Fawcett Junior, 1981), 96–98, 107.

30. Valerie Quinney, "Childhood in a Southern Mill Village before World War I," unpublished paper, 16–17, later revised as "Farm to Mill: The First Generation," in *Working Lives: The Southern Exposure History of Labor in the South* (New York: Pantheon, 1980).

31. A blues musician, interview by Glenn Hinson, SOHP/SHC/UNC.

32. Lyons Park Senior Citizens Center interviews. The Klan march was also discussed by Leonard Rapport.

33. Mebane, *Mary*, 128, 144–50, 173–74, 177–201, discusses how her views of "bad" or "fast" women altered; Brinton, "Negro in Durham," 206, discusses "the loafing places, affording an opportunity for demoralizing contacts with baser elements," in the business district of Hayti. The white male haunts are described by the special operatives hired to spy on Durham workers. For example, see the report for 13–17 Sept. 1919 in W. A. Erwin papers, PL/DU, and also the reports of Special Operative No. 1357 for 27, 28, 31 Mar. 1934; R. L. Roscoe to K. P. Lewis, 21 Mar. 1934: and Frank L. Dobbs to K. P. Lewis, 25 Sept. 1934, KPL/SHC/UNC.

34. Glenn Hinson, interview by Dolores Janiewski, personal holding.

35. Helen L. Phillips, "Shouting for the Lord: A Black Rite of Modernization" (Master's thesis, University of North Carolina, 1969).

36. Brinton, "Negro in Durham," 305.

NOTES TO CHAPTER VII

37. According to Jessie Ervin (interview by Dolores Janiewski, personal holding), women complained to their supervisors when men violated their marital vows. The official Erwin employment contract, as exemplified by one dated 13 Sept. 1909 and signed by C. D. Carter, declared that "no intemperance, profanity, or obscene language or fighting will be tolerated on the premises, nor will gross misconduct or drunkenness be tolerated off the premises . . . Any hand failing to comply with these rules subjects him or herself to discharge without notice," KPL/SHC/UNC.

38. The Dunnes, interview by Ida L. Moore, West Durham, 12 July 1938, NCFWP/SHC/UNC, discusses one family who ended in Monkey Bottoms because they took coal from the village coal pile and because the husband occasionally drank too much. Bessie Taylor Buchanan, interview, and Luther Riley, interview by Lanier Rand, SOHP/SHC/UNC, discuss the Erwin policy of dismissing families with unwed mothers.

39. *Martha Hinton, interview by Travis Jordan, 9 Dec. 1938, East Durham, NCFWP/SHC/UNC.

40. Johnson, "Tobacco Worker," 2: 415.

41. *Nellie Carter, interview by students in History 101, holding of Professor Sydney Nathans, Department of History, Duke University.

42. *Martha Hinton, interview.

43. *Jessie Ervin, interview.

44. *Clarence Byrd, interview by Ida L. Moore, East Durham Mill Village, 29 July 1939, NCFWP/SHC/UNC.

45. Walter B. Weare, *Black Business in the New South: A Social History of the North Carolina Mutual Life Insurance Company* (Urbana: University of Illinois Press, 1973), describes the beating and the shooting of the black soldier as two separate events. In the version circulated in Mebane's community, the events were combined. See Mebane, *Mary*, 32, 158, 159–65.

46. Bessie Taylor Buchanan, interview.

47. Brinton, "Negro in Durham," 298, 303–5.

48. For other assessments of the role of religion in stimulating southern women's social activism and organizing skills, see Sara Evans, *Personal Politics: The Roots of Women's Liberation in the Civil Rights Movement and the New Left* (New York: Vintage, 1980), 33–37; Anne Firor Scott, *The Southern Lady: From Pedestal to Politics, 1830–1930* (Chicago: University of Chicago Press, 1970), 134–63; Jacqueline Jones, *"To Get Out of This Land of Suffering": Black Migrant Women, Work, and the Family in Northern Cities, 1900–1930* (Wellesley, Mass.: Wellesley College Center for Research on Women, 1982); and Mary E. Frederickson, "Shaping a New Society," in *Women in New Worlds: Historical Perspectives on the Wesleyan Tradition* (Nashville: Abington Press, 1981), 345–61.

49. Murray, *Proud Shoes*, 270; Pauli Murray, "The Fourth Generation of Proud Shoes," *Southern Exposure* 4 (Winter 1977): 4–9.

50. Report of the Durham School Board, 1928–1929, KPL/SHC/UNC.

51. Mebane, *Mary*, 77, 202–3, was puzzled by her community's ambiguous attitude toward sexuality: "Though the church teaches Biblical chastity and preaches that it is better to marry than to burn, still underlying it is a strong current that says: Better some physical intimacy than none" (202). Mebane resisted the so-

NOTES TO CHAPTER VII

cial pressure, but *Pearl Barbee and *Bernice Jefferson (interviews by Dolores Janiewski, personal holdings) did not, to their eventual regret.

52. *Pearl Barbee, interview.
53. Ozzie Richmond, interview by Lanier Rand, SOHP/SHC/UNC.
54. *Allie Ennis, interview.
55. Rabb and Potter, interviews at Lyons Center.
56. Glenn Hinson, interview.
57. From the papers of Mary O. Cowper. A Durham daycare center was ultimately named after her to honor her efforts in the 1930s and 1940s; MOC/PL/DU.
58. "C. P. Ellis," interview by Studs Terkel, in his *American Dreams: Lost and Found* (New York: Ballantine Books, 1980), 219–33.
59. Annie Mack Barbee, interview.
60. Leonard Rapport, interview.
61. Theotis Williamson, interview by Lanier Rand, SOHP/SHC/UNC.
62. Ozzie Richmond, interview.
63. *Louise Couch Jenkins, interview by Dolores Janiewski, personal holding.
64. Ida L. Moore, "East Durham Mill Village," 12 Sept. 1938, East Durham, NCFWP/SHC/UNC.
65. Mebane, *Mary*, 250–53.
66. Pauli Murray, of course, also escaped by going north to finish her education.
67. U.S. Children's Bureau, "Extracts from Durham Schedules," Child Labor Law series, CB/NA/DC. These were based on interviews by Emma Duke, a Children's Bureau investigator sent to Durham in 1918.
68. Mebane, *Mary*, 203. The entire sentence reads, "And it was my secret guilt that I had longings to do better than that" in reference to a destiny in "field or factory."
69. *Dena Coley, Theotis Williamson, *Allie Ennis, *Louise Couch Jenkins, *Calvin Couch, interviews; *Rose Weeks, interview by Dolores Janiewski, personal holding.
70. Annie Mack Barbee, interview.
71. Esther Jenks, interview by Dolores Janiewski, SOHP/SHC/UNC.
72. *Hetty Love, interview by Linda Wright, personal holding.
73. *Edward T. Williams, interview by Dolores Janiewski, personal holding. One person told Leo Davis that black ministers and businessmen, the church's major financial supporters, feared that unions would compete with them for influence in the black community: Leo Davis, "The History of the Labor Movement among Negro Tobacco Workers in Durham, North Carolina, with Specific References to A.F.L. Locals 194, 204, 208" (Master's thesis, North Carolina Central College, 1949). John Donald Rice, "The Negro Tobacco Worker and His Union in Durham, N.C." (Master's thesis, University of North Carolina, 1941), concurs with this assessment. The chief officer of the Tobacco Workers International Union detected a strictly mercenary motive behind black ministerial opposition to the TWIU campaign in Durham: "They were only looking for the smile you can feel with your hand," he wrote to the TWIU organization about local black ministers. See E. Lewis Evans to Duby S. Upchurch, 28 July 1934, TWIU/ML/UM.
74. The last quotation is from Spencer T. Miller, Jr., and Joseph E. Fletcher, *The*

NOTES TO CHAPTER VII

Church and Industry (New York: Longmans, Green, 1930), 214. Bernard M. Cannon, "Social Deterrents to the Unionization of Southern Cotton Mill Workers" (Ph.D. diss., Harvard University, 1952), found a high correlation between Pentecostalism and anti-union sentiment. Franz Daniel of the Textile Workers Union of America complained about "revivalists paid by the manufacturer who told the workers that we were the agents of the devil and that the mark of the beast was on our forehead" (Textile Workers Union of America, "Building a Union of Textile Workers: Report of Two Years of Progress," Philadelphia, Pa., 15–19 May 1939). Later religious journals such as the *Trumpet* and *Militant Truth* propagandized in the same vein and received contributions from manufacturers. Anti-union lawyer Frank A. Constangy, however, argued that the real reason that the "fundamentalist preacher" opposed unions was "probably and likely competition from Union organizers" for "his position of being the spokesman and leader of his group": Frank A. Constangy to Dr. Frank T. DeVyver, Director of Industrial Relations, Erwin Mills, 24 Oct. 1950, FD/ECMC/PL/DU. John A. Peel, president of the Durham Central Labor Union, and D. C. Parker of the Carpenters pointed to monetary inducements as one of the major reasons for the silence of local churches. According to Peel, "Most of the Churches around here get all their money from the rich mill owners, and would not dare to be open and above board in their support of the unions" (Miller and Fletcher, *Church and Industry*, 212).

75. Rice, "Negro Tobacco Worker"; Weare, *Black Business*; *Horace Mize, interview by Stuart Kaufman, Department of History, University of Maryland, College Park; and Miles Mark Fisher, *Friends: A Pictoral History of Ten Years' Pastorate, 1933–43* (Durham, N.C.: White Rock Baptist Church, 1943) — all concur on the exceptional support given by Fisher to the tobacco workers.

76. *Jessie Ervin, interview; Miller and Fletcher, *Church and Industry*, 212, 210.

77. Bessie Taylor Buchanan and Esther Jenks, interviews.

78. K. P. Lewis to W. D. Carmichael, 1 Mar. 1926; KPL/SHC/UNC. The same incident is also reported in Miller and Fletcher, *Church and Industry*, concerning the film, "Labor's Reward." The mayor gave permission to use the city auditorium but the city council refused, leading to a protest meeting and the film's eventual showing at the Orpheum Theater. Four years later, Lewis advised Will Carr, a member of the city council, to let the "labor people" use the auditorium for an address by the president of the AFL because "we could not afford to add fuel to the flame": K. P. Lewis to W. A. Erwin, 17 Feb. 1930, KPL/SHC/UNC.

79. Miller and Fletcher, *Church and Industry*, 198–99, 193–94.

80. Katherine Norman, interview in MOC/PL/DU; Johnson, "Tobacco Worker," 1: 96.

81. Chester and Roxanne Clarke, interview by Glenn Hinson, SOHP/SHC/UNC.

82. Constangy to DeVyver, FD/ECMC/PL/DU.

83. Johnson, "Tobacco Worker," 1: 105–6, 2: 591–93, 413–14, 417, 427–29.

84. Mebane, *Mary*, 141–44, 151–53, 179–82, 194–97, 237–39, describes incidents of violence and abuse.

85. Constangy to DeVyver, FD/ECMC/PL/DU. The other trade secrets involved

NOTES TO CHAPTER VII

a manager becoming a "part of the community . . . gaining the support of his employees" and "the support of the so-called respectable element of the community" by conforming to the "local mores." Last quotations from David Matza and David Wellman, "The Ordeal of Consciousness," *Theory and Society* 9 (January 1980): 6–7, 26.

86. John Paul Lucas, Duke Power Company, to K. P. Lewis, 5 Jan. 1928; circular by W. Bradford, District Agent, National Merchants and Manufacturers Protective Association, 14 Oct. 1929. These, of course, were letters from manufacturers and industrial espionage agencies attempting to prevent unionization. K. P. Lewis was also in communication with the Railway Audit and Inspection Company, from whom he usually hired operatives for use in Erwin Mills, KPL/SHC/UNC. The use of such professional services apparently began with an agreement among the leading mills of North Carolina, signed on 10 May 1900, during the first concerted campaign to organize the textile industry. The mills agreed to hire an agent, not to work "Union Labor," not to "employ any of the hands" that were involved in a strike or lockout at any mill, and to appoint a "Central Committee of five to watch the labor unions." A copy of the agreement, signed at Charlotte, is located in the North Caroliniana collection, UNC.

87. The culture of the southern mill worker will be most thoroughly discussed in Christopher Daly, Jacquelyn Hall, Lu Ann Jones, Robert Korstad, James Leloudis, and Mary Murphy, *"Like a Family": An Oral History of the Textile South* (Chapel Hill: University of North Carolina Press, forthcoming.)

88. K. P. Lewis to John Paul Lucas, Duke Power, 8 Feb. 1928, KPL/SHC/UNC. The men to whom Lewis referred included several professors at the University of North Carolina, Broadus Mitchell from Johns Hopkins University, and Alfred Hoffman of the Hosiery Workers.

89. Weare, *Black Business*, 193. The quotation is from a speech by C. C. Spaulding written by Rev. M. M. Fisher.

90. Ibid., 225–64.

91. W. H. Gray, Railway Audit and Inspection Co., to "Att. of 700," stamped "received April 16, 1935, Exhibit 169," in U.S. Senate, Subcommittee of the Committee on Education and Labor, 74th Cong., 2d sess., Hearings, Part 1: *Labor Espionage and Strikebreaking: Railway Audit & Inspection Co., Inc., National Corporation Service Inc.*, 21 Aug., 22, 23 Sept. 1936 (Washington, D.C.: G.P.O., 1936), 323; Carl Goerch, publisher of *The State*, to K. P. Lewis, 24 May 1934, KPL/SHC/UNC. Goerch was reporting his conversation with Albert Beck, organizer for the United Textile Workers, and offering his sympathy to Lewis.

92. K. P. Lewis to J. C. Thorne, 23 Feb. 1926; K. P. Lewis to Fred R. Marvin, 24 Feb. 1926; K. P. Lewis to W. D. Carmichael, 26 Feb. 1926; and Margaret C. Robinson to K. P. Lewis, 12 Mar. 1926, KPL/SHC/UNC.

93. *Nellie Carter, interview.

94. MOC/PL/DU.

NOTES TO CHAPTER VIII

CHAPTER VIII

1. Sheila Rowbotham, *Woman's Consciousness, Man's World* (Harmondsworth, Eng.: Penguin, 1974), 33–35.
2. From the title of a book by Sheila Rowbotham, Lynne Segal, and Hilary Wainwright, *Beyond the Fragments: Feminism and the Making of Socialism* (London: Merlin, 1979).
3. For examples of women's activism elsewhere in the textile industry, see Melton A. McLaurin, *Paternalism and Protest: Southern Mill Workers and Organized Labor, 1875–1905* (New York: Negro Universities Press, 1971).
4. *Journal of United Labor*, 6 Aug. 1887.
5. For a discussion of the policy of the Knights of Labor toward working women, see Susan Levine, *Labor's True Woman: Carpet Weavers, Industrialization, and Labor Reform in the Gilded Age* (Philadelphia: Temple University Press, 1984).
6. Raleigh *News and Observer*, 18 Aug. 1900.
7. Raleigh *News and Observer*, 26 Aug. 1900.
8. See Ernest Seeman, *American Gold* (New York: Dial Press, 1978), 173–74, for a fictional account of the strike and its aftermath. See the Durham *Daily Sun*, 30 Aug. 1900, for a report of the actual condition of the strikers and Erwin's charitable decision to open the company store to them (but not to rehire them).
9. Arthur Vance Cole papers, 1917–1920, PL/DU, are the source for this discussion. Cole was the organizer of the TWIU local. For the local's statement of principles, see AVC, 30 Aug. 1919; for the invitation to the ladies, see 26 Aug. 1919.
10. E. Lewis Evans to Arthur V. Cole, 13 Oct. 1919; Henry McAndrews to Arthur Cole, 13 Sept., 26 Dec. 1919. McAndrews, then president of the TWIU, offered Cole a job organizing in Petersburg, Va. Hugh P. Brinton, "The Negro in Durham: A Study in Adjustment to Town Life" (PH.D. diss., University of North Carolina, 1930), covers the same episode.
11. Durham *Herald*, 20 Aug. 1919.
12. Report of Operative No. 230, 23 Jan. 1920, FD/ECMC/PL/DU.
13. Spencer T. Miller, Jr., and Joseph E. Fletcher, *The Church and Industry* (New York: Longmans, Green, 1930), 194–95; Henry Eatough, UTW organizer in Charlotte, report in *Textile Worker*, Aug. 1925, p. 284; Ervin Holt, Local 31, in the *Proceedings, Fifteenth Annual Convention of American Federation of Full-Fashioned Hosiery Workers*, 7 Sept. 1926 (Philadelphia, 1926), 33.
14. Miller and Fletcher, *Church and Industry*, 194; phrase from Report, Builder's Exchange of Durham, Oct. 1926, KPL/SHC/UNC. K. P. Lewis and his allies believed that the employment of a unionized firm to build Duke University's new campus threatened just such an invasion. They also corresponded with John Paul Lucas of Duke Power. See Kemp P. Lewis to J. C. Thorne, 23 Feb. 1926; Kemp P. Lewis to Carmichael, 23 Feb. 1926; John Paul Lucas to Kemp P. Lewis, 5 Jan. 1928; Kemp P. Lewis to John Paul Lucas, 8 Feb. 1928; Kemp P. Lewis to W. D. Carmichael, 19, 22, Feb. 1929, KPL/SHC/UNC.
15. Durham Central Labor Union to President Steele, American Federation of Full-Fashioned Hosiery Workers; Alfred Hoffman, *Proceedings, Sixteenth Annual Convention of the AFFHW*, 6–9 Sept. 1927 (Philadelphia, 1927), 18, 376; Alfred Hoffman, *Seventeenth Annual Convention of AFFHW*, 4–8 Sept. 1928 (Philadel-

NOTES TO CHAPTER VIII

phia, 1928), 376. A brief biography of Alfred Hoffman is contained in his letter to A. J. Muste, 17 July 1928, in which he affirmed his support of Brookwood Labor College and declared that "no attempt was made to empregnate me with Communistic ideas or philosophies, or hair splittings" during "my year's attendance at Brookwood." Brookwood was then under attack in the AFL for leftist tendencies. Hoffman's letter is contained in the Local 189 file, American Federation of Teachers papers, the Archives of Labor History and Urban Affairs, Wayne State University, Detroit, Mich.

16. The surveys are contained in MOC/PL/DU. She collected them for use in an unpublished paper, Mary O. Cowper, "Cotton Cloth: A Type Study of the Community Process," written under the direction of Howard W. Odum, while Cowper was enrolled at the University of North Carolina, 1924–1925, MOC/PL/DU.

17. *Nellie Carter, interview by Dolores Janiewski, personal holding. Cowper's sources include two other women who attended the Bryn Mawr Summer School under the auspices of the Durham YWCA.

18. Mary Frederickson, "The Southern Summer School for Women Workers in Industry: A Female Strategy for Collective Action in the South," paper read at the Berkshire Conference of Women Historians, Mount Holyoke College, Mass., 28 Aug. 1978. Mary Frederickson has a book on the same subject forthcoming from Indiana University Press.

19. *Nellie Carter, interview.

20. Corporation Auxiliary Company report on the convention in 1930 of the N. C. Federation of Labor, KPL/SHC/UNC. Ironically for Lewis, the spy discovered that his sister was one of his opponents.

21. See the Raleigh *Union Herald*, 3, 26 June 1920. The campaign for the constitutional amendment granting women the vote and the new recruitment drive for the revived Ku Klux Klan coincided. North Carolina did not ratify the 19th amendment until 1970.

22. Brinton, "Negro in Durham," 141.

23. Ibid., 146–48. According to Robert L. Allen, *Reluctant Reformers: Racism and Social Reform Movements in the United States* (Garden City, N.Y.: Anchor Books, 1975), racism was prevalent throughout the labor movement, not merely in the South.

24. Durham black leaders are quoted in the Durham *Morning Herald*, 2 Oct. 1919; Charles S. Johnson, "The Tobacco Worker: A Study of Tobacco Workers and Their Families," 2 vols., Division of Review, Industrial Studies Section, NRA/NA/DC, 2: 412. See also "Open Letter to William Green, President of the AFL," in *Opportunity*, Feb. 1930, 56–57, for black criticisms of AFL policies; Horace R. Cayton and George S. Mitchell, *Black Workers and the New Unions* (Chapel Hill: University of North Carolina Press, 1939). For tobacco unions in particular, see Herbert R. Northrup, *The Negro in the Tobacco Industry* (Philadelphia: University of Pennsylvania Press, 1970).

25. *Jessie Ervin, interview by Dolores Janiewski, personal holding. (Here and elsewhere in these notes, an asterisk indicates a pseudomyn.) The arrest of the organizer, Marvin Ritch, was reported in the Durham *Herald*, 19 Sept. 1919. See also the issues of *Southern Textile Bulletin* for 1919–1921.

NOTES TO CHAPTER VIII

26. Hoffman's report on the Henderson strike is contained in *Proceedings, Sixteenth Annual Convention of the AFFHW*, 376. Persuaded by Hoffman's report, the president of the Hosiery Workers pledged to "work more or less in secret gradually educating the Southern workers to a realization of the present day industrial situation." In his remarks Hoffman also noted that many Henderson workers were relatives of Durham workers.

27. For descriptions of the strikes and the Piedmont Organizing Council, see George Sinclair Mitchell, *Textile Unionism in the South* (Chapel Hill: University of North Carolina Press, 1931); see also the Raleigh *Union Herald* and the *Textile Worker* for 1927–1929. Details of the Cone incident are contained in the James Evans interview by Ida L. Moore, NCFWP/SHC/UNC; the R. J. Reynolds incident is reported in Johnson, "Tobacco Worker," 2: 587–89. Simultaneously with the campaign in Winston-Salem, Kemp P. Lewis and W. D. Carmichael were involved in a covert scheme with a man inside the local TWIU to prevent a similar attempt in Durham. Lewis even advised Carmichael to pay the informant several thousand dollars to call off a planned boycott of L and M: Lewis to Carmichael, 19 Feb. 1929, KPL/SHC/UNC. Whether Carmichael followed this advice isn't clear, but the TWIU had ceased activities in Durham by 1930, according to TWIU records, TWIU/ML/UM.

28. *Clara Layton, interview by Ida L. Moore, NCFWP/SHC/UNC.

29. *Henry Laws, interview by Dolores Janiewski, personal holding; David Matza and David Wellman, "The Ordeal of Consciousness," *Theory and Society* 9 (Jan. 1980): 7.

30. James Evans, interview.

31. Southern Summer School for Women Workers in Industry, untitled pamphlet, Summer Session, 1931, Arden, N.C., North Caroliniana Collection, UNC. The last phrase is taken from T. W. Bradford, District Agent, National Merchants and Manufacturers Protective Association, to Kemp P. Lewis, 14 Oct. 1929, KPL/SHC/UNC. Bradford was soliciting Lewis to "allow us to place with you as workers our trained confidential agents . . . We can furnish agents male or female, union or non-union as may best suit the locality or particular situation." Apparently such agencies were aware that employers perceived a widening "gap between employer and employee" that could only be bridged by an agent disguised as a worker, "just 'one of many.'" Although Lewis did not hire this firm, he did use the Railway Audit and Inspection Company's services and amateur industrial spies in 1929 and 1934. He seems to have begun to fear that workers had drawn firmer boundaries between "them and us," had begun to see their interests in opposition to his, and might be organizing against him. These three steps are crucial to the process of forming a class-conscious workers' movement, according to Matza and Wellman, "Ordeal of Consciousness," 7.

32. James Evans, interview.

33. *Maggie Daws, interview by Dolores Janiewski, personal holding.

34. Matza and Wellman, "Ordeal of Consciousness," 9. The authors identify this process of the "transformation of national minorities from isolated periphery to integral core of the working class" as a product of "particular times" involving "a rapid coming together of discrete tendencies which were previously unrelated." If

NOTES TO CHAPTER VIII

southern workers, black and white, can be ascribed "minority status," as I believe, then such a period occurred in the 1930s and 1940s before southern workers were once again pushed to the semi-periphery of the organized working class.

35. This section from the NIRA was quoted in a flyer distributed in Durham; a copy exists in KPL/SHC/UNC.

36. Quotation from E. L. Crouch to E. Lewis Evans, 2 Aug. 1933, E. L. Crouch file, Series 2, TWIU/ML/UM.

37. E. L. Crouch to Evans, 28 July 1933, TWIU/ML/UM.

38. W. B. Culbreth to E. Lewis Evans, 29 July 1933, Local 176 file, Series 3, TWIU/ML/UM.

39. E. Lewis Evans to W. B. Culbreth, 17 Aug. 1933, Local 176 file, TWIU/ML/UM.

40. E. Lewis Evans to Duby S. Upchurch, 22 Jan., 19 Mar. 1934; Duby S. Upchurch to E. Lewis Evans, 19, 24, 31 Mar. 1934, Duby S. Upchurch file, Series 2, TWIU/ML/UM.

41. Duby S. Upchurch to E. Lewis Evans, 5, 11, 23 May 1934, Series 2, TWIU/ML/UM.

42. E. Lewis Evans to Duby S. Upchurch, 28 July 1934, Series 2, TWIU/ML/UM.

43. Reports of Operative No. 3157, Railway Audit and Inspection Service, 25 Mar.–1 Apr. 1934, KPL/SHC/UNC.

44. Carl Goerch to K. P. Lewis, 25 May 1934, KPL/SHC/UNC.

45. John W. Kennedy, "The General Strike in the Textile Industry" (Master's thesis, Duke University, 1947); Durham *Morning Herald*, 24 Aug. 1934.

46. Hoffman, *Sixteenth Annual Convention of AFFHW*.

47. Duby S. Upchurch to E. Lewis Evans, 6 Apr. 1934, Series 2, TWIU/ML/UM.

48. Duby S. Upchurch to E. Lewis Evans, 4 Aug. 1934, Series 2, TWIU/ML/UM; John P. Davis, chairman of the Joint Committee on National Recovery, after a visit to Durham to check on the effects of the NRA code on black tobacco workers, NRA/NA/DC.

49. Duby S. Upchurch to E. Lewis Evans, 2 July 1934, Series 2, TWIU/ML/UM.

50. Charles S. Lakey to E. Lewis Evans, 15 June 1934, Series 1, TWIU/ML/UM.

51. Durham *Morning Herald*, 4 Sept. 1934.

52. A reporter circulated through the crowd to interview participants (including the woman quoted in Chap. 1), Durham *Morning Herald*, 4 Sept. 1934.

53. Kemp P. Lewis, "To the Stockholders and Directors of the Erwin Cotton Mills Company," 26 Jan. 1935, KPL/SHC/UNC.

54. Durham *Morning Herald*, 6 Sept. 1934. Also, see description in Chap. 1.

55. Durham *Morning Herald*, 23 Sept. 1934.

56. James Cavanaugh, Textile Workers Union of America oral history project, to Dolores Janiewski, 21 Nov. 1978, personal holding. Robert Murray, a Durham striker and local leader, was interviewed by John Kennedy for his master's thesis; he reported that pickets in Durham performed their duties without knowledge of the UTW's overall strategy. C. W. Bolick, a UTW organizer, quit the union after the strike. See C. W. Bolick, "Why I Quit the U.T.W.," *Textile Bulletin*, 11 Apr. 1935, pp. 10, 24. The UTW never recovered although it continued to exist.

NOTES TO CHAPTER VIII

57. See also John Wesly Kennedy, "A History of the Textile Workers Union of America, C.I.O." (Ph.D. diss., University of North Carolina, 1950).

58. *Textile Worker*, Dec. 1934; Railway Audit and Inspection Company, Report of Operative No. 3574, 30 Sept. 1934, KPL/SHC/UNC.

59. Durham Hosiery Mills vs. American Federation of Hosiery Workers, 31 Oct. 1934, Federal Mediation and Conciliation Service, NA/DC.

60. Durham Cotton Manufacturing Company vs. Local 2155, Textile Labor Relations Board, 4 Oct. 1934, NRA/NA/DC.

61. Durham Hosiery Mills vs. American Federation of Hosiery Workers' local, Textile Labor Relations Board, 2 Nov. 1934, NRA/NA/DC.

62. Kemp P. Lewis, "Report to the Stockholders," 26 Jan. 1935, KPL/SHC/UNC.

63. Johnson, "Tobacco Worker," 2: 414.

64. Ibid., 2: 413.

65. Ibid., 2: 414.

66. Ibid., 2: 413.

67. "The Tobacco Workers International Union," 16 May 1935, Tobacco Studies Section, NRA/NA/DC.

68. Johnson, "Tobacco Worker," 2: 415.

69. *Ella Faucette, interview by Dolores Janiewski, personal holding.

70. *Rose Weeks, interview by Dolores Janiewski, personal holding.

71. *Maggie Daws, interview.

72. L and M vs. TWIU Local 176, 11 Mar.–30 Oct. 1935, Federal Mediation and Conciliation Service, NA/DC; Local 176 files, 1935, Series 3, TWIU/ML/UM.

73. Local 183 files, 1935–1936, Series 3, TWIU/ML/UM; *Rose Weeks, interview; *Henry Laws, interview by Dolores Janiewski, personal holding.

74. Daisy R. Jones to E. Lewis Evans, 10 Oct. 1938, Local 194 file, Series 3, TWIU/ML/UM. See also Leo Davis, "The History of the Labor Movement among Negro Tobacco Workers in Durham, N.C., with Specific Reference to A.F.L. Locals 194, 204, 208" (Master's thesis, North Carolina Central College, 1949); John Donald Rice, "The Negro Tobacco Worker and His Union in Durham, North Carolina" (Master's thesis, University of North Carolina, 1941).

75. E. Lewis Evans to T. J. Atwater, 23 Oct. 1939, Local 194 file, Series 3, TWIU/ML/UM.

76. Local 204 to E. Lewis Evans, 10 Dec. 1938, Local 204 file, Series 3, TWIU/ML/UM.

77. Durham *Morning Herald*, 25 July 1935.

78. Ibid.; Durham Hosiery Mills vs. A.F.H.W. Local, 23 July, 18 Aug. 1935, Textile Labor Relations Board, NRA/NA/DC.

79. Durham Hosiery Mills report to stockholders, 26 Nov. 1935, KPL/SHC/UNC.

80. Kemp P. Lewis to Mrs. Hargrove Bellamy [Sara Erwin Bellamy], 5 Sept. 1935, KPL/SHC/UNC.

81. Luther Riley, interview by Lanier Rand, SOHP/SHC/UNC.

82. Although Lewis was aware in May 1937 that the "union forces are working at Durham very hard," he received his "first visit from the C.I.O. Committee"

NOTES TO CHAPTER VIII

in mid-November. Kemp P. Lewis to J. C. Thorne, 10 May, 19 Nov. 1937, KPL/SHC/UNC. For information on the TWUA, see Kennedy, "Textile Workers Union."

83. Election results in ECMC/FD/PL/DU.

84. Kemp P. Lewis to W. R. Perkins, 2 Apr., 18 July 1938, KPL/SHC/UNC; N. A. Gregory [Erwin supervisor], "Diary," 19 June 1939, ECMC/FD/PL/DU.

85. Luther Riley, interview.

86. Esther Jenks and *Jessie Ervin, interviews.

87. E. Lewis Evans to P. M. Taylor, 13 Oct. 1937, E. Lewis Evans file, Series 1; Lewis G. Hines to E. Lewis Evans, 20 Oct. 1937, E. Lewis Evans to Lewis G. Hines, 28 Oct. 1937, AFL file, Series 1, TWIU/ML/UM.

88. Stuart B. Kaufman, "The Tobacco Workers International Union," unpublished manuscript, Stuart B. Kaufman holding, Department of History, University of Maryland, College Park, 127–29.

89. H. A. McCrimmon to E. Lewis Evans, 22 May 1937, H. A. McCrimmon file, Series 2, TWIU/ML/UM.

90. E. Lewis Evans to S. E. Blane, 24 June 1937; S. E. Blane to E. Lewis Evans, 26 June 1937; E. Lewis Evans to S. E. Blane, 29 June 1937, T. L. Copley file, TWIU/ML/UM.

91. Much of Evans's correspondence from 1934 to 1940 with H. A. McCrimmon and T. L. Copley, his closest allies in Durham, concerned his efforts to discover the dissidents among local tobacco workers. See the H. A. McCrimmon files and the T. L. Copley files, Series 2, 1934–1940, TWIU/ML/UM.

92. S. E. Blane to E. Lewis Evans, 26 June 1937, T. L. Copley file, TWIU/ML/UM. The investigators for the Johnson survey elicited this comment from an ardent union man in Durham: "I think we're going to get a closed shop . . . The Niggers will have a closed shop, too. They will never get as much as us though. The company couldn't afford that" (Johnson, "Tobacco Worker," 104).

93. Beginning in 1937, the CIO moved into the tobacco industry but its activities were concentrated in centers other than Durham. Most local blacks chose the alliance with white activists, but Oliver Harvey refused to be "Jim Crowed." See Ed McConville, "Oliver Harvey: 'Got to Take Some Risks,' " *Southern Exposure*, 7:2 (1978), p. 24. Harvey refused to join the segregated TWIU local when he arrived in Durham in the 1930s and later went to Duke University where he became involved in forming an independent black local which joined an integrated international union. Robert Korstad, Southern Oral History Program, University of North Carolina, Chapel Hill, is currently completing a dissertation on Local 22 of the United Cannery, Agricultural, and Processing Workers of America, later renamed Food, Tobacco, and Allied Workers, the CIO affliate that organized tobacco workers. See also my article, "Subversive Sisterhood: Black Women and Unions in the Southern Tobacco Industry," in *Southern Women: The Intersection of Race, Class and Gender*, a working paper series published by the Center for Research on Women, Memphis State University, July 1984.

94. Durham *Morning Herald*, 18 Apr. 1939; Ernest Latta, interview by Lanier Rand, SOHP/SHC/UNC. According to Latta, "We emphasized the fact that if they let us have the strike, there'd be no violence . . . It was our intention to have an honorable, peaceful strike."

NOTES TO CHAPTER VIII

95. Contracts for L and M Locals 176, 177, 210, 208, 202, 9 June 1939, ECMC/FD/DU.

96. Lewis, of course, was not pleased to see L and M capitulate, as was revealed by the company's careful monitoring of contracts between the TWIU and L and M. His earlier alliance with W. D. Carmichael in the 1920s had been intended to avert just such a calamity. ECMC/FD/PL/DU.

97. *Horace Mize, interview by Stuart Kaufman, Stuart Kaufman holding, Department of History, University of Maryland, College Park; Chester and Roxanne Clarke, interview by Glenn Hinson, SOHP/SHC/UNC.

98. Annie Mack Barbee, interview by Beverly Jones, SOHP/SHC/UNC; Chester and Roxanne Clarke, interview.

99. Daisy R. Jones to E. Lewis Evans, 17 Mar. 1940, Local 194 file, Series 3, TWIU/ML/UM.

100. Contract between L and M and TWIU Local 194, 3 Oct. 1939, ECMC/PL/DU.

101. As explained by *Oscar Scoggins, interview by Dolores Janiewski, personal holding. See also Jean M. Cary, "The Forced Merger of Local 208 and Local 176 of the T.W.I.U. at L & M in Durham, North Carolina" (Master's thesis, Duke University, 1971), for a continuation of the story.

102. As described by Stuart Kaufman, "Tobacco Workers International Union."

103. As revealed in TWUA Local 246 vs. Erwin Cotton Mills Company before the National Labor Relations Board, ECMC/FD/PL/DU.

104. Erwin Shop Committee reports, ECMC/FD/PL/DU.

105. William H. Ruffin to Kemp P. Lewis, "Memorandum to Mr. K. P. Lewis," 2 Aug. 1939, KPL/SHC/UNC.

106. William H. Ruffin to Kemp P. Lewis, 27 Feb. 1940, KPL/SHC/UNC. Ruffin would later succeed Lewis as president of the company

107. Based on my analysis of the strike records prepared by Erwin Mills for the NLRB in the strike's aftermath, ECMC/FD/PL/DU.

108. Esther Jenks, interview.

109. Kemp P. Lewis to Clairborne Carr, 18 Mar. 1940, KPL/SHC/DU.

110. Kemp P. Lewis to Clyde R. Hooey, 28 Mar. 1940, KPL/SHC/DU. Hooey, a prominent attorney associated with the textile industry before his entry into public office, had prosecuted the Gastonia strikers.

111. Kemp P. Lewis to Magruder Dent, 26 Mar. 1940, KPL/SHC/UNC.

112. Esther Jenks, interview.

113. Luther Riley, interview.

114. *Charlie Riddick, interview by Dolores Janiewski, personal holding.

115. Bessie Taylor Buchanan, interview by Lanier Rand, SOHP/SHC/UNC.

116. Kemp P. Lewis to J. C. Thorne, 17 July 1940, KPL/SHC/UNC.

117. L. P. McLendon to W. R. Perkins, "re: N.L.R.B. vs. Erwin Mills," 19 Apr. 1940, KPL/SHC/UNC.

118. Kemp. P. Lewis to J. C. Thorne, 17 July 1940, KPL/SHC/UNC.

119. Kemp P. Lewis to W. R. Perkins, 10 Sept. 1940, KPL/SHC/UNC.

120. Henry Nathan Mims, "Impact of Union-Management Relations on Management's Industrial Relations Policy: A Study of the Erwin Cotton Mills Company and the T.W.U. of A." (Master's thesis, Cornell University, 1949).

NOTES TO CHAPTER VIII

121. Esther Jenks, interview.

122. Mims, "Union-Management Relations." Frank DeVyver was hired to deal with labor relations after the onset of collective bargaining.

123. *Joe Daniels, *Rachel Medlin, *Ada Scoggins, interviews by Dolores Janiewski, personal holdings.

124. Wilbur Hobby, interview by Bill Finger, SOHP/SNC/UNC; Robert Cannon, "The Organization and Growth of Black Political Participation in Durham, N.C., 1933–1958" (Ph.D. diss., University of North Carolina, 1975); Margaret Elaine Burgess, *Negro Leadership in a Southern City* (Chapel Hill: University of North Carolina Press, 1960); Durham *Labor News*, 1945–1955; and Esther Jenks, *Henry Laws, *Charles Riddick, interviews.

125. Based on the interviews and my own observations of Durham during the years that I spent in that city (1974–1979).

126. *Ella Faucette, interview.

127. *Pearl Barbee and *Oscar Scoggins, interviews.

128. Annie Mack Barbee, interview.

129. Bessie Taylor Buchanan, interview.

130. Wilbur Hobby, interview; Local 208 files, Series 3, TWIU/ML/UM. In the Local 183 files for the 1970s are some newspaper clippings alleging that some members of that local also belonged to the KKK, Local 183 file, Series 3, TWIU/ML/UM.

131. Floyd McKissick in "Tobacco Workers International Union and Local Union No. 208 Hearing," Durham Labor Temple, 26–27 Aug. 1964, Local 208 file, Series 3, TWIU/ML/UM. See Cary, "Forced Merger of Local 208 and 176," for more information on the battle by Local 208 to retain its autonomy and its ultimate defeat.

132. *Charlie Riddick and *Jessie Ervin, interviews.

133. Luther Riley, Ethel and Fannie Jenks, and *Everett Hancock were among the union stalwarts who left the textile industry as a result of the Second World War. West Durham mill village also began to be sold in the same period.

134. *Horace Mize, interview.

135. Sheila Rowbotham warned against this tendency of a "particular oppressed group" to substitute its own narrow definition of oppression rather than to deal with all of the sources of division and exploitation: *Woman's Consciousness*, 27–28.

136. Based on my discussions with Robert Korstad, who is currently completing work on the CIO's tobacco worker unions.

137. Ozzie Richmond, interview by Lanier Rand, SOHP/SHC/UNC.

138. *Rose Weeks, interview.

139. Martha Gena Harris, interview by Dolores Janiewski, SOHP/SHC/UNC.

140. Ernest Latta, interview by Lanier Rand, SOHP/SHC/UNC.

141. As revealed by the files for Roy Trice and George Benjamin, Series 2, TWIU/ML/UM; and *Horace Mize, interview.

142. Bessie Taylor Buchanan, interview.

Index

Addams, Henry I., 158
Agriculture: class conflict in, 49–50; gender relations in, 52–53; labor problems in, 42–53. *See also* Class, relations, in agriculture; Family economy, in agriculture; Gender, relations of, in agriculture; Race, division of labor by, in agriculture; Tobacco cultivation
Allen, G. A., 78
Allen, T. A., 63
American Federation of Full-Fashioned Hosiery Workers, 153–54, 158, 159, 231 n.26. *See also* Hoffman, Alfred
American Federation of Labor, 154–55, 158, 165
American Tobacco Company (1890–1911): dissolution of, 71–72; farmers' attitudes towards, 11–12, 23, 70; labor relations in, 90; number of employees of, 71; origins of, 69–71. *See also* American Tobacco Company (1911–); Blackwell Durham Tobacco Company; Duke, James B.; Tobacco manufacture
American Tobacco Company (1911–): anti-union strategies of, 153; formation of, 69–71; managerial practices of, 107–8, 114, 124, 153, 219 n.44; profits of, 72; sexual division of labor in, 99; workers' attitudes towards, 124. *See also* American Tobacco Company (1890–1911); Blackwell Durham Tobacco Company; Duke, James B.; Tobacco manufacture
Amey, C. C., 79
Austin, Louis, 92–93, 158
Aycock, Charles, 23, 91

Bags, tobacco, making of, 31, 38, 74, 113, 133–34, 146, 197 n.31
Bailey, Mary, 124
Baptists: attitudes towards class conflict, 88, 148; attitudes on gender, 36; attitudes on race, 47. *See also Biblical Recorder*
Barbee, Annie Mack, 119, 144, 147, 167, 173, 175
Barbee, Pearl (pseudonym), 64, 143, 171, 173
Benjamin, George, 168
Biblical Recorder, 47. *See also* Baptists
Blacks: class consciousness among, 18–20, 50–51, 53–54, 84–85, 119–21, 149–51, 161–62, 166–68, 171–74, 210 n.107, 234 nn.92, 93, 235 n.101; color consciousness among, 53–54, 84; disfranchisement of, 22–23, 92–93, 213–14 n.155, 214 n.161; economic condition of, 41–49, 50–54, 57, 66, 78–80, 102, 109–16, 167–68; education of, 39–40, 46, 64, 93, 142–43, 146; as factory workers, 95–105, 108–13, 120–25, 143–44, 167–68, 171, 173–74; housing of, 44, 129–31, 140–41; impact of race upon, 39–40, 41–42, 47–48, 92–94, 129, 139, 140–44, 155, 174–76; and Ku Klux Klan, 39–40, 92, 138, 144, 155, 173–74; reasons of, for migrating, 37, 40, 42, 48, 54–64, 66, 119; during Reconstruction, 39–40; religious activities of, 46, 48, 87–88, 127–28, 139–42, 147–48, 158, 177, 199 n.64, 200 n.75, 201 n.89, 226 n.73; in unions, 161–62, 165–68, 172. *See also* Civil rights, movement for; Dur-

237

INDEX

Blacks (*continued*)
   ham Committee on Negro Affairs; Gender; Ku Klux Klan; lynching; National Association for the Advancement of Colored People; North Carolina Mutual Life Insurance Company; Race; Tobacco workers; Unions, black participation in; Women, racial attitudes of
Blackwell, William T., 68
Blackwell Durham Tobacco Company, 68–70; becomes American Tobacco Company, 71, 90. *See also* American Tobacco Company (1890–1911); American Tobacco Company (1911–); Blackwell, William T.; Carr, Julian S.; Tobacco manufacture
Blane, Sam, 166, 168
Bonsack, James, 69
Bonsack cigarette-making machine, 69, 80–81, 85, 97, 118
Branson, Levi, 65, 86
Brookwood Labor College, 154
Buchanan, Bessie Taylor, 64, 76, 95, 126, 133, 136, 147, 148, 172, 173, 176
Burdette, Mary, 95–96
Butler, Marion, 22. *See also* People's Party, North Carolina

Cameron, Bennehan, 44
Cameron, Duncan, 10
Cameron, Paul Carrington, 10, 52–53
Cannon, Bishop James, 87, 211 n.123. *See also* Methodists; Textile industry, critics of
Carmichael, W. D., 72, 86, 92, 154, 231 n.27. *See also* Liggett and Myers
Carolina Times, 92–93, 158. *See also* Austin, Louis
Carr, A. F., 164
Carr, Elias, 20. *See also* Farmers' Alliance, North Carolina
Carr, Julian S., 57, 65–66, 68–70, 74, 80, 87, 89, 90–92, 145, 205 n.21, 212 n.140, 213 n.147, 213–14 n.155. *See also* Blackwell Durham Tobacco Company; Durham, Duke-Carr rivalry in
Carr, Julian S., Jr., 65, 76, 106. *See also* Durham Hosiery Mills
Carr, Nannie Parrish, 89, 145. *See also* Carr, Julian S.; Parrish family
Carr, W. H., 86, 91. *See also* Durham Hosiery Mills

Carr family, 89, 99, 102, 129, 153–54, 160–61, 163, 169. *See also* Durham Hosiery Mills
Carter, Nellie (pseudonym), 154–55
Cash-crop economy: expansion of, 8, 10, 14–18, 24, 49; consequences of, for women, 17–18, 28–34, 50–51. *See also* Tenancy, causes of; Tobacco cultivation
Child labor: in agriculture, 13–14, 17, 28–29, 31, 52–53; decline of, 114, 119; in industry, 75, 80–81, 91, 95, 98, 104–5, 109–11, 113–16; reasons for, 75, 119, 145–47; in textiles, 75; in tobacco, 72–73, 80–81, 97, 98, 220 n.60. *See also* Family economy
Childbearing: racial differences in, 44, 132; rates of, 34–35, 127–28, 131–32; as system of reproduction, 223 nn.3, 4, 6. *See also* Childrearing
Childrearing, 44–45, 127–28, 131, 136–40, 142–46. *See also* Child labor; Family economy
Christian Advocate, 50. *See also* Methodists
Christian Church, 148
Civil rights, movement for, 92–93, 141, 174–75. *See also* Blacks; Race
Clarke, Chester, 167
Clarke, Roxanne, 149, 167
Class, 5–6, 25–26, 49, 50, 54, 63, 65–67, 75, 80–81, 83–85, 88, 91, 95, 96–99, 117–18, 121–22, 125–28, 129–30, 145–46, 150, 152–53, 156, 162, 177–78, 187 nn.9, 10, 188 n.11, 189 n.14, 190 n.14, 191 n.21, 194 nn.4, 6, 195 n.10, 196 n.21, 205 n.30, 206 n.38, 217 n.32, 223 n.6, 231 nn.26, 81, 231–32 n.34, 236 n.135; consciousness of, among agriculturalists, 10, 18, 20–21, 49–51, 53–54, 75–77, 188 n.11; consciousness of, among capitalists, 67, 69–71, 75–77, 78–81, 82–89, 90–92, 97–99, 107–8, 117–18, 121–23, 148, 160–61, 164–65, 168–70, 206 n.38, 206–7 n.46, 208 n.76, 209 n.81, 210 nn. 103, 107, 211 n.118, 212 n.142, 213 nn. 152, 154, 227 nn. 74, 78, 228 nn.85, 86, 229 n.14, 231 nn.27, 31, 235 nn.96, 110; consciousness of, among industrial workers, 3–4, 63–64, 76–77, 80–81, 82–86, 88–89, 93–94, 97, 104, 108–9, 117–26, 145–78, 215 n.10, 215–16 n.12, 221 n.73, 226 n.73, 227 nn.

INDEX

74, 78, 234 nn.93, 94; interaction of, and gender, 31–34, 51–53, 97, 108–10, 149–51, 175–78, 187 n.10, 195 n.14, 197 n.28, 200 n.77, 215 n.8, 216 nn.14, 18, 219 n.48, 220 n.64, 220–21 n.64, 223 n.6; interaction of, and race, 47, 98, 109–22, 149–50, 155–59, 161–63, 165–68, 171–78, 205 n.30, 206–7 n.46, 230 nn.21, 23, 234 n.93; mobility, 12–18, 25–26, 42–43, 45, 50, 121–22, 222 n.94; relations, in agriculture, 8–23, 25–26, 49–51, 53–54, 194 nn.4, 6, 196 nn.20, 21, 199 n.53, 199–200 n.68; relations, in industry, 63, 69–70, 74–77, 80–86, 91–94, 98, 105–8, 122–26, 148–51, 153–78; religious influences on, 36, 86–88, 97–99, 139–42, 147–49, 177, 200 n.75, 201 n.89, 226 n.73, 227 n.74. *See also* Gender; Race; Textiles manufacture; Textile workers; Textile Workers Union of America; Tobacco manufacture; Tobacco workers; Tobacco Workers International Union; Unions; United Textile Workers; Wages and income; Women, class consciousness of; Women, as . . . workers
Coleman, W. C., 79
Coleman Mill, W. C., 79
Coley, Dena (pseudonym), 82, 136, 147, 171
Committee for Industrial Organization (CIO), 164. *See also* Congress of Industrial Organizations (CIO)
Commonwealth Cotton Mill, 74
Cone family, 156, 231 n.27
Congress of Industrial Organizations (CIO), 166, 175, 233–34 n.82, 234 n.93; includes Industrial Union Council, 172. *See also* American Federation of Full-Fashioned Hosiery Workers; Textile Workers Union of America; Unions, in Durham
Conservative Party. *See* Democratic Party
Copley, T. L., 163
Cotton textile industry. *See* Textiles manufacture
Cotton Textile Institute, 77
Couch, Wilma Mayfield (pseudonym), 59–60, 136, 146, 147
Cowper, Mary O., 83, 86, 151, 154, 210 n.103
Crop lien, 11, 27–28, 33, 189–90 n.5. *See also* Cash-crop economy; Tenancy

Crouch, E. L., 157
Culbreth, W. R., 157–58

Daniels, Joe (pseudonym), 171
Daniels, Jonathan, 29–30, 94
Daniels, Josephus, 22–23
Day, James R., 68
Democratic Party: involvement of Julian S. Carr in, 90–91; as Conservative Party, 40; disfranchisement and, 22–23, 40–41, 213–14 n.155; and Knights of Labor, 19–20; and People's Party, 21–23; use of racism to regain political power, 19–20, 22–23, 39–41, 92; and white supremacy campaign, 22–23, 92. *See also* Blacks; Farmers' Alliance, North Carolina; People's Party, North Carolina; Race; Republican Party
Disfranchisement. *See* Blacks, disfranchisement of; Democratic Party
Domestic labor. *See* Women, as domestic laborers
Du Bois, W. E. B., 78–79, 84
Duke, Benjamin, 68, 70, 79, 81, 83, 86–87, 89, 90, 92. *See also* American Tobacco Company (1890–1911); Duke & Sons Company, W.
Duke, Brodie, 68, 97
Duke, James B., 50, 66, 68–70, 72–74, 81, 83, 145, 170. *See also* American Tobacco Company (1890–1911); Duke & Sons Company, W.; Tobacco manufacture
Duke, Mary (sister of James B.). *See* Leggett, Mary Duke
Duke, Sarah Angier (wife of Benjamin), 89, 145
Duke & Sons Company, W.: becomes Liggett and Myers, 71; capitalization of, 68; development of, 68–71; female employees in, 70–71, 80–81, 99, 105–6, 113, 153; introduction of cigarette production in, 69, 105–6; labor relations in, 69–70, 80–81, 82, 87, 97, 153; mechanization in, 69, 80–81, 85, 97, 105–6. *See also* American Tobacco Company (1890–1911); Duke, James B.; Liggett and Myers; Tobacco manufacture; Tobacco workers
Duke family, 65, 68, 70, 73–74, 80–81, 85, 87, 89, 90–91, 92, 97, 105, 113, 129, 213 nn.146, 147, 215–16 n.11. *See also* American Tobacco Company

Duke family (*continued*)
(1890–1911); Duke & Sons Company, W.; Durham, Duke-Carr rivalry in; Republican Party
Duke Hospital, 143
Duke University, 83, 94, 173, 174
Durham (N.C.): as destination of female migrants, 55–63, 95–96; Duke-Carr rivalry in, 68–71, 74, 90–92; growth of, 68, 80; hosiery industry in, 65, 74–75; housing in, 130–31, 136; industrial development of, 5, 10–11, 57, 63, 65–67, 73–74, 95, 174; race relations in, 48, 78–80, 92–94, 129, 138, 155, 171–76; sex ratios of population, 56–57; spatial organization of, 129–31; textile industry in, 57, 65–66, 74–78, 80; tobacco industry in, 11, 57, 67–73, 97–102, 105–7, 174. *See also* Hosiery manufacture; Race; Textiles manufacture; Tobacco manufacture; Unions, in Durham
Durham Committee on Negro Affairs, 93, 171. *See also* Blacks; Durham (N.C.), race relations in; National Association for the Advancement of Colored People; Race
Durham Cotton Manufacturing Company, 74, 78, 88, 107, 130–31, 140, 160–61. *See also* Textiles manufacture
Durham Hosiery Mills: anti-union strategies of, 85, 106–7, 153–54, 158, 160, 161, 163–64; development of, 65, 74–75, 77, 79, 86, 91, 96, 98, 107, 119, 122, 130, 160–61; industrial democracy in, 76, 106; mill village of, 122, 130, 202 n.13, 216 n.14. *See also* American Federation of Full-Fashioned Hosiery Workers; Carr family; Carr, Julian S., Jr.; Hosiery manufacture; Hosiery workers; Strikes, Durham Hosiery Mills
Durham Industrial Girls Club, 83, 151. *See also* Young Women's Christian Association
Durham Interracial Commission, 92. *See also* Durham (N.C.), race relations in; Race
Durham *Labor News*, 172
Durham *Recorder*, 80, 85, 90

East Durham, 87, 91, 130, 138, 140, 146, 160, 172. *See also* Durham (N.C.), textile industry in; Durham Cotton Manufacturing Company

Edgemont (N.C.), 130, 173
Ellis family, 144
Ennis, Allie (pseudonym), 136, 143, 147
Episcopalians, 87, 148. *See also* Religion
Ervin, Jessie (pseudonym), 120, 156
Erwin, J. Harper, 74, 89, 160–61. *See also* Durham Cotton Manufacturing Company
Erwin, William A., 65, 74–78, 82, 85, 87, 89–91, 95, 105–6, 117, 122–23, 153. *See also* Duke, Benjamin; Durham (N.C.), textile industry in; Erwin, J. Harper; Erwin Cotton Mills Company; Holt family; Lewis, Kemp P.; Textiles manufacture; Textile workers; Unions, in Durham
Erwin Cotton Mills Company: acquired by Burlington Industries, 174; anti-union strategies of, 63, 106, 126, 153, 158, 160–61, 164–65, 168–71; development of, 4, 63–65, 74–78, 88–91, 98, 100, 106–8, 117, 123, 142, 148, 153, 164–65, 170, 171–72, 174; managerial practices in, 75–78, 81, 98, 106–10, 123, 139–40, 153, 164, 168–71, 206 n.38, 206–7 n.46, 218 n.41, 227 n.78, 228 n.86, 231 nn.27, 31; sale of mill village, 172, 202 n.113, 236 n.133; wages in, 122; workers' attitudes towards, 82, 95, 120, 122, 124, 160, 164–65, 168–71. *See also* Duke family; Erwin, William A.; Lewis, Kemp P.; Powe, E. K.; Strikes, at Erwin Cotton Mills Company; Pearl Mill; Textiles manufacture; Textile workers; Textile Workers Union of America; West Durham
Evans, E. Lewis, 157–58, 159, 163, 165–68, 177, 234 n.91. *See also* Tobacco Workers International Union
Evans, James, 156

Fair Labor Standards Act, 134, 168
Family economy: in agriculture, 13–14, 16–18, 28–32, 35–38, 42–46, 51–53, 75, 194 n.5; as a concept, 187–88 n.10, 193 n.1, 194 nn.4, 5, 201 n.82, 215 n.8; as a factor in migration, 57–61; as a family wage-earning economy in Durham, 59–61, 74–75, 109–17, 119, 127, 142–47, 220 n.63. *See also* Gender
Farm laborers: availability of, 14–16, 63–64; condition of, 13–14, 38, 63–64; in Knights of Labor, 18–20; racial characteristics of, 16, 38, 47, 63–64; wages of, 13, 38; women as, 16, 38, 63–64

INDEX

Farmers. *See* Agriculture; Cash-crop economy; Class, consciousness of, among agriculturalists; Class, relations in, in agriculture; Crop-lien; Farmers' Alliance, North Carolina; Tenancy; Tobacco cultivation

Farmers' Alliance, National Colored: arrival in North Carolina, 18, 20; defeat, 21; relations with North Carolina Farmers' Alliance, 20–21. *See also* Farmers' Alliance, North Carolina

Farmers' Alliance, North Carolina: aims of, 19–21; arrival in North Carolina, 18, 20; attitudes towards blacks in, 19, 41, 49, 192 nn.34, 37, 199–200 n.68; cooperatives in, 21; ideology of, 18–22, 31–32, 49–50, 188 n.11, 191 n.21, 199–200 n.68; political activities of, 21; relations with Knights of Labor, 20–21; relations with National Colored Farmers' Alliance, 20–21; rituals of, 18; women in, 19, 31–32, 40, 49–50, 196 n.24. *See also* Farmers' Alliance, National Colored; Knights of Labor; People's Party, North Carolina

Faucette, Ella (pseudonym), 162, 173

Fisher, Reverend Mark Miles, 88, 147, 227 n.75, 228 n.89

Fitzgerald, Richard, 79

Fitzgerald, Robert, 40. *See also* Murray, Pauli (his granddaughter)

Franklin, Julia (pseudonym), 61

Frazier, E. Franklin, 67, 78

Gender, 5–6, 27–36, 51–53, 96–99, 108–10, 117–18, 128–29, 137–40, 150–51, 152, 175–76, 186 n.6, 187–88 n.10, 193 n.1, 194 n.5, 195 nn.10, 11, 14, 196 n.23, 196–97 n.25, 200 nn.77, 79, 200–201 n.81, 201 n.82, 215 n.8, 217–18 n.32, 220 n.64, 223 n.6; consciousness of, 18–19, 29–36, 38–39, 49–54, 61, 83, 86, 96–98, 108–9, 117–18, 125, 128, 135–40, 143–44, 147, 152–53, 157, 162, 175, 177–78, 196 n.24, 196–97 n.25, 221 n.73; interaction of, and class, 49–54, 97, 108–19, 149–51, 175–76, 195 nn.11, 14, 197 n.28, 220 n.62, 220–21 n.65; interaction of, and race, 46–47, 53–62, 97, 99–104, 108–17, 121–22, 138–42, 173, 175, 195 n.11, 196 n.22, 197 n.28, 197–98 n.32, 199 n.64, 200–201 n.81, 216 nn.16, 18, 217–18 n.32; relations of, in agriculture, 25–36, 51–54, 193 n.1, 194 n.5, 195 n.10, 196–97 n.25, 197 n.28; relations of, in industry, 63–64, 72–75, 88–89, 94, 96–105, 108–17, 125, 153, 157–58, 163, 165, 167–68, 173, 175–76, 205–6 n.34, 206 n.35, 207 n.48, 215 n.8, 216 nn.14, 18, 217 n.29, 217–18 n.32, 219 n.48, 225 n.37; religious attitudes towards, 36, 139–40, 197 n.27, 199 n.64, 201 n.89; and sexuality, 19, 30, 34–36, 38–39, 52, 88–89, 97–98, 108, 120, 127–28, 138–40, 197–98 n.32, 200 n.77, 201 n.89, 216 nn.14, 18, 223 nn.3, 4, 6, 224 n.33, 225–26 n.51. *See also* Class, interaction of, and gender; Family economy; Race; Women

Ginter cigarette company, 69. *See also* American Tobacco Company (1890–1911)

Glenn, Bonnie, 164

Golden Belt: development of, 61–62, 74, 78, 90, 96, 111, 133, 149, 158, 160, 164, 172; wages in, 111. *See also* Hosiery manufacture; Textiles manufacture

Goodwin, Mollie (pseudonym), 51

Goodwin cigarette company, 69. *See also* American Tobacco Company (1890–1911)

Graham, Frank Porter, 83, 86, 210 n.103, 211 n.118

Gray, Mamie (pseudonym), 45

Hagood, Margaret Jarman, 31, 50–51, 53, 196 n.22, 196–97 n.25

Hall, H. C., 123

Harris, Carl R., 165–69. *See also* Erwin Cotton Mills Company

Harris, Martha Gena, 95, 175

Harvey, Oliver, 166, 234 n.93

Hayti, 94, 130, 138, 172. *See also* Durham (N.C.), spatial organization of

Hill, John Sprunt, 89, 90. *See also* Watts, George

Hinton, Martha (pseudonym), 140

Hobby, Wilbur, 172, 173

Hoffman, Alfred, 83, 106–7, 154, 156, 159, 213 n.154, 218–19 n.42, 229–30 n.15, 231 n.26. *See also* American Federation of Full-Fashioned Hosiery Workers; Piedmont Organizing Council; Strikes, in textiles; Unions, in Durham

Holt family, 74, 89. *See also* Erwin, William A.

Hosiery manufacture: anti-labor strategies in, 85, 106–7, 153–54, 158–60, 161, 163–64; capitalization in, 74; development of, 74–75, 77, 107, 156–57, 163–64; employment levels in, 74; managerial practices in, 65, 70, 75–76, 85, 98–99, 102–4, 106; racial division of labor in, 75, 99, 102–4; sexual division of labor in, 99–100, 102–4. *See also* Carr family; Durham Hosiery Mills; Golden Belt; Hosiery workers

Hosiery workers: attitudes towards employers, 96, 102–3; characteristics of, 65, 75, 99–100, 102–4, 115; conditions of, 102–4, 119; efforts to organize, 76, 85, 106–7, 149, 153–54, 159–60, 163–65; wages and income of, 111. *See also* American Federation of Full-Fashioned Hosiery Workers; Hoffman, Alfred; Hosiery manufacture; Unions, in Durham; Women, as hosiery workers

Hosiery Workers, American Federation of. *See* American Federation of Full-Fashioned Hosiery Workers; Unions, in Durham; Unions, female participation in

Imperial Tobacco Company, 98
Income. *See* Erwin Cotton Mills Company, wages in; Farm laborers, wages of; Liggett and Myers, wages in; Textile workers, wages of; Tobacco workers, wages of; Wages and income, of industrial workers
Industrialization. *See* American Tobacco Company (1890–1911); Bonsack cigarette-making machine; Child labor, in industry; Class, relations, in industry; Duke, James B.; Duke & Sons Company, W.; Durham Hosiery Mills; Durham (N.C.), industrial development of; Erwin Cotton Mills Company; Hosiery manufacture; Textiles manufacture; Tobacco manufacture
International Association of Machinists, 166

Jenkins, Louise Couch (pseudonym), 146–47
Jenks, Eldred, 64, 169
Jenks, Esther, 95, 147, 148, 165, 169–70, 171, 172
Jenks, Ethel, 169
Jenks, Fannie, 148, 169
Jenks family, 64–65, 169
John Swinton's Paper, 81

Johnson, Charles S., 61–62
Jones, Daisy, 163, 167–68
Journal of United Labor, 13, 19, 81, 153. *See also* Knights of Labor

Kennedy, William, 82. *See also* North Carolina Mutual Life Insurance Company
Kilgo, John C., 87
Kimball cigarette company, 69. *See also* American Tobacco Company (1890–1911)
Kinney cigarette company, 69. *See also* American Tobacco Company (1890–1911)
Knights of Labor: activities of, 13, 18, 21, 85, 153, 211 n.112, 215 n.10; attacks on, 19–21, 85, 192 n.25; goals of, 19–21, 49, 191 n.21, 215–16 n.11; growth of, 18–21, 81, 85–86, 97, 105–6, 118, 153; racial policies of, 18–20, 118, 155; relations with North Carolina Farmers' Alliance, 20–21; rituals in, 18; women in, 18–19, 40, 153, 215–16 n.11. *See also* Class, consciousness of, among agriculturalists; Class, consciousness of, among industrial workers; Farm laborers; Farmers' Alliance, North Carolina; Race, consciousness of, among blacks; Race, consciousness of, among whites; Tobacco workers; Unions, in Durham
Knit-well Hosiery Mill, 74
Ku Klux Klan, 39–40, 92, 138, 144, 155, 173–74, 236 n.130. *See also* Blacks; Democratic Party; Race

Latta, Sam, 157
Lawrence, R. R., 158
League of Women Voters, 83, 86
Leggett, Mary Duke, 68, 145
Lewis, Cornelia Battle, 89
Lewis, John L., 165. *See also* Congress of Industrial Organizations
Lewis, Kemp P., 65, 76–78, 81, 83, 85–86, 89–90, 92, 100, 105–7, 122–23, 142, 145, 150, 154, 158, 160–61, 164, 167, 169, 170, 211 n.118, 231 nn.27, 31, 235 n.96. *See also* Erwin, William A.; Erwin Cotton Mills Company; Textiles manufacture
Lewis, Nell Battle, 83
Lewis, Richard H., 89
Liggett and Myers: anti-union strategies of, 85–86, 106–7, 159, 231 n.27; develop-

ment of, 71–72, 174; employment levels in, 71; labor relations in, 157–59, 161–62, 163, 166–68, 171–78; managerial practices of, 88, 98–100, 122–23, 157, 163, 166–68, 173; mechanization of manufacturing process in, 122–23, 168, 173; origins of managers, 72, 100; origins of workers, 61–62; profits of, 72, 123; race relations in, 121, 125, 173; sexual division of labor in, 99, 168; wages in, 72, 82. *See also* Carmichael, W. D.; Duke & Sons Company, W.; Strikes, at Liggett and Myers; Tobacco manufacture; Tobacco workers; Tobacco Workers International Union; Unions, in Durham; Women, as tobacco factory workers

Lincoln, John (pseudonym), 82
Loman, Bertie (pseudonym), 31
Love, Hetty (pseudonym), 64, 95, 147
Lynching, 45, 47–48. *See also* Blacks, impact of race upon; Ku Klux Klan; Race

McCrimmon, H. A., 163, 166
Mack, Charlie Decoda, 121
Mack family, 64
McKissick, Floyd, 174
Mangum family (pseudonym), 62
Marvin Carr Silk Mill, 85, 106, 153, 159. *See also* Durham Hosiery Mills; Hosiery manufacture; Hosiery workers; Strikes; Unions
Mebane, Mary, 119, 125, 136–37, 141, 146, 147
Mebane, Mary, 119, 125, 136–37, 141, 146, 147
Mebane, Nonnie, 108, 119, 136–37, 146
Mebane, Rufus, 108
Medlin, Rachel (pseudonym), 171
Merrick, John, 57, 66, 78–80. *See also* Blacks, economic condition of; North Carolina Mutual Life Insurance Company; Spaulding, Charles C.
Methodists: and class, 50, 87; and the Dukes, 60, 87, 211 n.120; and gender, 36; and industry, 80; and Julian S. Carr, 87; Orphanage, 60, 121, 136; and race, 7, 50
Migration: causes of, 8, 20, 24, 40–42, 48, 51, 54–67, 72, 74–75, 95–96, 119, 122; class differences in, 36–38, 57, 65–66, 68–70; familial characteristics of, 57–59, 62, 64–65, 95–96, 108–9; gender differences in, 24, 55, 67, 74–75; reverse and temporary, 62, 130, 202 n.13. *See also* Blacks, reasons of, for migrating; Women, reasons of, for migrating

Mize, Horace (pseudonym), 171
Monkey Bottoms, 117, 121, 129, 131, 140, 172, 225 n.38. *See also* Erwin Cotton Mills Company; West Durham
Monkey Top, 117. *See also* Erwin, William A.; Erwin Cotton Mills Company; West Durham
Moore, Aaron, 66, 79. *See also* North Carolina Mutual Life Insurance Company
Murray, Pauli, 129–30, 142

National Association for the Advancement of Colored People (NAACP), 93. *See also* Civil rights, movement for; Durham Committee on Negro Affairs; Race
National Association of Manufacturers, 90
National Defense Mediation Board, 171
National Labor Relations Board, 164, 170, 171
National Negro Business League, 90
National Recovery Administration, 81, 107, 123–24, 157, 159, 172
New South, 4, 5, 6, 186 n.3
Newsome, John, 88, 148
Norman, Katherine, 149
North Carolina Federation of Women's Clubs, 83. *See also* Young Women's Christian Association
North Carolina Mutual Life Insurance Company, 66, 79, 84–85, 89. *See also* Merrick, John; Moore, Aaron; Spaulding, Charles C.
North Carolina Railroad, 10–11, 22. *See also* Southern Railway
Norwood, Clem, 3, 159. *See also* American Federation of Full-Fashioned Hosiery Workers; Hosiery workers; Strikes

O'Daniel, John, 89, 212 n.140. *See also* Carr, Julian S.; Carr family; Durham Hosiery Mills
Oxford Cotton Mills, 89. *See also* Erwin, William A.; Lewis, Richard

Parker, W. S., 63
Parrish, Charles, 159. *See also* Tobacco Workers International Union; Unions, black participation in
Parrish, Edward J., 92. *See also* Parrish family
Parrish, Nannie. *See* Carr, Nannie Parrish

Parrish family, 79, 89, 145
Paul, Hiram Voss, 79–81, 85, 211 n.112, 215–16 n.11. *See also* Knights of Labor
Pearl Mill, 74, 78, 172. *See also* Erwin Cotton Mills Company
Pearson, William G., 66, 79, 92, 213–14 n.155. *See also* Blacks, disfranchisement of; North Carolina Mutual Life Insurance Company; Republican Party
Peavey, Claiborne (pseudonym), 120
Pentacostals, 148, 227 n.74. *See also* Unions, religious deterrents to
People's Party, North Carolina: attempts to fuse with Democrats, 22; establishment of, 21–22; fusion with Republicans, 21–22; ideology of, 10, 21–22, 31–32, 33–34, 41, 49–50, 191–92 n.22, 192 nn.34, 37, 199–200 n.68, 213 n.146; political activities of, 21–22. *See also* Democratic Party; Republican Party
Perkins, W. R., 170. *See also* American Tobacco Company (1890–1911); Erwin Cotton Mills Company
Piedmont Organizing Council, 106–7, 154, 218–19 n.42, 231 n.27. *See also* Hoffman, Alfred
Poe, Clarence, 41. *See also* People's Party, North Carolina; *Progressive Farmer*
Polk, Leonidias L., 20, 22. *See also* Farmers' Alliance, North Carolina; People's Party, North Carolina; *Progressive Farmer*
Populists. *See* People's Party, North Carolina
Powe, E. K., 89. *See also* Erwin, William A.; Erwin Cotton Mills Company
Presbyterians, 87
Progressive Farmer, 20, 22, 31–33, 41, 49–50. *See also* Farmers' Alliance, North Carolina; People's Party, North Carolina; Poe, Clarence; Polk, Leonidias L.

R. J. Reynolds Tobacco Company, 71, 156
Race, 5–6, 38–39, 117–18, 186–87 n.7, 187 n.9, 188–89 n.13, 189 n.14, 193 n.2, 197–98 n.32, 200 n.80, 200–201 n.81, 205 n.30, 215 n.8, 217–18 n.32, 221 nn.71, 73, 231–32 n.34, 236 n.135; consciousness of, among blacks, 5–6, 39–42, 44–46, 48, 50, 52–53, 64, 67, 80, 84, 92–94, 98, 108, 117–18, 119–20, 124–25, 129–30, 136–38, 140–44, 149, 155, 161–63, 165–67, 172–75, 177, 188 n.11, 189 n.15, 210 n.107, 214 n.161, 216 n.18, 217 n.23, 218 n.33, 224 n.28, 231–32 n.34, 234 n.93; consciousness of, among whites, 5–6, 10, 16, 18–20, 22, 31, 33, 38–42, 46–49, 52–53, 63–64, 65–66, 74–75, 84, 92–93, 96–99, 102, 117–18, 121–22, 125, 128, 140–42, 144, 149, 155, 157–59, 163, 166, 168, 171–76, 178, 188 n.11, 192 n.34, 198 n.38, 201 n.85, 206–7 n.46, 208 n.76, 209 n.81, 212 n.140, 213–14 n.155, 216 n.12, 234 n.92; division of labor by, in agriculture, 14–16, 37, 40, 43–44, 49, 52–53, 55, 190 nn.14, 15, 193 n.2, 197 n.28, 201 n.85; division of labor by, in industry, 53, 62, 66, 68, 72–76, 94–105, 107, 109–10, 112–15, 120–25, 127, 131–33, 136, 142–44, 149, 153, 161–63, 166–68, 173–77, 193 n.2, 205 n.30, 205–6 n.34, 206–7 n.46, 207 n.51, 214–15 n.7, 215 n.8, 216 n.12, 217 nn. 26, 29, 217–18 n.32, 234 n.92; relations, in rural society, 10, 13–16, 19–22, 31, 33, 39–42, 45–49, 50, 52–54, 55, 63–66, 188 n.11, 190 nn.14, 15, 192 n.34, 193 n.2, 196 n.22; relations, in urban society, 4–5, 6–7, 64–65, 66–67, 80, 83–84, 91, 92–94, 96–98, 99–100, 108–17, 121, 124–25, 127, 128–31, 135–38, 140–44, 149–50, 155–56, 159, 161–63, 166–68, 171–78, 214 n.161, 225 n.45; and religion, 47–49, 140–42, 199 nn. 64, 66, 200 n.75, 201 n.89, 225–26 n.51; and sexuality, 19, 39, 40, 45, 46–47, 52–53, 88, 97–98, 108, 120, 128, 138–39, 186–87 n.7, 197 n.32, 200–201 n.81, 201 n.89, 216 nn.16, 18, 224 n.33. *See also* Blacks; Civil rights, movement for; Class, interaction of, and race; Gender, interaction of, and race; Ku Klux Klan; Lynching; National Association for the Advancement of Colored People; Segregation; Tobacco workers; Tobacco Workers International Union; Unions, black participation in; Women, racial attitudes of
Raleigh *News and Observer*, 22, 47, 83. *See also* Daniels, Josephus
Raper, Arthur, 42, 47–48
Red Shirts. *See* Democratic Party, and white supremacy campaign
Religion. *See* Baptists; Blacks, religious activi-

ties of; Class, religious influences on; Episcopalians; Gender, religious attitudes towards; Methodists; Pentacostals; Presbyterians; Race, and religion; Unions, religious deterrents to
Republican Party, 14, 19, 21–23, 39–40, 90, 92; Dukes and, 90, 213 n.146. *See also* Democratic Party; People's Party, North Carolina
Richmond, Ozzie, 82, 175
Riddle, Zina (pseudonym), 45
Riley, Lester, 170
Riley, Luther, 64, 164, 170
Rocky Mount Cotton Mills, 89
Roosevelt, Franklin (D.), 160
Ruffin, Callie (pseudonym), 43–45
Russell, Daniel, 22, 213 n.146

Scoggins, Ada (pseudonym), 171, 173
Scoggins, Oscar (pseudonym), 171, 174
Seagrove, Mollie (pseudonym), 104
Seeman, Ernest, 106, 125–27, 129
Segregation, 4, 19, 39, 41, 45, 47, 48, 53–54, 74–75, 84, 94, 99–100, 125, 129–31, 138, 140–42, 166–67, 173, 175–77, 196 n.22, 205 n.30, 210 n.107, 217–18 n.32. *See also* Race
Sexual division of labor. *See* Gender, relations of, in agriculture; Gender, relations of, in industry
Shepard, James E., 66, 79, 88, 93, 210 n.107. *See also* North Carolina Mutual Life Insurance Company; Spaulding, Charles C.
Simmons, Furnifold, 91. *See also* Democratic Party, and white supremacy campaign
Southern Railway, 22, 90
Southern Summer School for Women Workers, 151, 154, 156. *See also* Women, class consciousness of; Young Women's Christian Association
Spaulding, Asa, 85. *See also* Durham Committee on Negro Affairs
Spaulding, Charles C., 57, 66, 79, 84, 87–88, 129, 150, 201 n.107. *See also* Durham Committee on Negro Affairs; Merrick, John; North Carolina Mutual Life Insurance Company
Strickland, Junius, 82, 87. *See also* Knights of Labor
Strikes: at Durham Hosiery Mills, 106, 153–54, 160–61, 164; at Erwin Cotton Mills Company, 3–4, 63, 106, 126, 148, 153, 158–61, 165, 168–70, 213 n.154; at Liggett and Myers, 4, 166–67, 175; in textiles, 76, 106, 156, 232 n.56. *See also* American Federation of Full-Fashioned Hosiery Workers; Congress of Industrial Organizations; Hoffman, Alfred; Piedmont Organizing Council; Textile Workers Union of America; Tobacco Workers International Union; Unions; United Textile Workers
Suitt, Oscar (pseudonym), 52
Swap work, 33, 196 n.21
Swinton, John, 81

Taft-Hartley Act, 174
Tarboro *Farmers' Advocate*, 49
Tenancy, causes of, 8–16, 18, 21, 24–26, 27, 41–42, 49, 50, 54–55, 66; as a concept, 194 n.6, 195 n.10; conditions of tenants, 14–18, 24, 28–33, 36–38, 41–44, 50–53; consequences of, for tenants, 14–18, 24–26, 196 n.20; consequences of, for women, 27–33, 36–38, 42–44, 51–55; decline of, 24; legal framework for, 11, 14, 39. *See also* Cash-crop economy; Class, consciousness of, among agriculturalists; Crop lien; Race, relations, in rural society; Tobacco cultivation
Textile Bulletin (originally *Southern Textile Bulletin*), 86, 210 n.103, 211 n.123
Textile industry, critics of, 83, 86. *See also* Textiles manufacture
Textile workers: attitudes of, towards employers, 76, 82, 88, 95, 98, 107, 109, 117, 119, 122–23, 124, 126, 143, 156, 164–65, 170–71; characteristics of, 65, 74–75, 82, 87–88, 98, 104, 113, 115, 125–26, 135–36, 150, 168–69, 207 n.48; class consciousness of, 117, 120, 122–24, 126, 148, 156, 159–60, 171, 173–74, 231 n.31, 232 n.56; housing of, 130–31, 140–41; wages and income of, 75, 81, 110–12, 219–20 n.54. *See also* Strikes, at Erwin Cotton Mills Company; Strikes, textiles; Textiles manufacture; Textile Workers Union of America; Unions, in Durham; United Textile Workers; Women, as textile workers
Textile Workers Organizing Committee. *See*

Textile Workers Committee (*continued*)
  Congress of Industrial Organizations; Textile Workers Union of America
Textile Workers Union of America, 164, 168, 170, 172, 174, 176–77, 233–34 n.82; Local 246, 168, 170, 171, 174. *See also* United Textile Workers
Textiles manufacture: anti-union strategies in, 76–77, 85–86, 88, 98, 105–7, 153–56, 160–61, 164–65, 168–71, 172, 174, 176, 210 n.103, 211 n.123, 212 n.142, 213 n.154, 218–19 n.42, 224 n.33, 227 nn.74, 78, 228 nn.85, 86, 231 n.31; child labor in, 57, 64, 74–76, 91, 95, 104–5, 109–11, 113–15; development of, 74–81, 106–8, 121–22, 156–57, 160–61, 164–65, 168–71, 172, 174, 206 n.38, 208 nn.68, 69, 214–15 n.7, 215 n.8; managerial practices in, 57, 65, 74–77, 88–89, 99–100, 104–8, 119, 123–24, 164–65, 208 n.63, 216 n.14, 218 n.41, 225 nn.37, 38; manufacturing processes in, 100, 104–5; origins of managers in, 65, 77, 89, 100, 206 n.38; racial policies of, 99–100, 104–5, 206–7 n.46, 207 n.51, 216 n.12; sexual division of labor in, 75, 99–100, 104–5. *See also* Erwin Cotton Mills Company; Golden Belt; Textile industry, critics of; Textile workers; Textile Workers Union of America; United Textile Workers
Thompson, Cyrus, 50
Thompson, Della (pseudonym), 61
Tobacco farmers. *See* American Tobacco Company (1890–1911), farmers' attitudes towards; Cash crop economy, expansion of; Class, relations, in agriculture; Farmers' Alliance, North Carolina; People's Party, North Carolina; Tenancy; Tobacco cultivation
Tobacco cultivation: allotment system in, 24; development of bright-leaf, 10–14, 23–27; labor demands of, 29; labor relations in, 14, 16, 18, 20, 24, 28–31; output per acre, 15; prices paid for product of, 11–12, 16, 21, 23–25; sexual division of labor in, 29–31, 52–53; techniques of, 10–11, 23, 29–30. *See also* Agriculture; Class, relations, in agriculture; Family economy, in agriculture; Farmers' Alliance, North Carolina

Tobacco manufacture: anti-union strategies in, 69, 81, 85, 87, 88, 91, 97, 105–7, 148–49, 153, 156, 158, 162, 166–67, 174, 205 n.28, 215 n.10, 215–16 n.11, 226 nn.73, 78, 229 n.14, 231 n.27; capitalization in, 68–69; child labor in, 72–73, 81; development of, 11, 67–73, 80–81, 85, 97, 99–100, 105, 107, 118, 122–24, 153, 167–68, 174; employment levels in, 68–69, 71, 73, 107, 168, 173, 219 n.43; managerial practices in, 57, 69–70, 72–73, 83, 85, 88, 97, 105–9, 113, 118, 120–21, 122–25, 153, 162–63, 166–68, 174–76; manufacturing processes in, 62, 100–102, 105–6, 107, 122–23; origins of managers in, 68–69, 72, 100; racial division of labor in, 72–73, 94, 96–97, 99–103, 107, 112–13, 114, 121–22, 125, 163, 167–68, 173–74, 175–76; sexual division of labor in, 72–73, 99–102, 106. *See also* American Tobacco Company (1890–1911); American Tobacco Company (1911–); W. Duke & Sons Company; Class, relations, in industry; Gender, relations of, in industry; Liggett and Myers; Race, division of labor by, in industry; Tobacco workers; Tobacco Workers International Union
Tobacco Plant, 80
Tobacco workers: attitudes towards employers, 80–83, 87, 118–20, 122–25, 149, 153, 162–63, 166, 171, 173, 175–76; conditions of, 69–73, 80–83, 85, 97–102, 107–8, 112–13, 118–25, 130–31, 136–37, 166–68, 171–76; housing of, 130–31; wages and income of, 72, 81–82, 110–13, 122–23, 124, 130, 135, 136, 143, 205 n.25, 223 nn.12, 15. *See also* American Tobacco Company (1890–1911); American Tobacco Company (1911–); Blacks, as factory workers; Class, consciousness of, among industrial workers; Class, relations, in industry; Gender, relations of, in industry; Liggett and Myers; Race, division of labor by, in industry; Tobacco manufacture; Tobacco Workers International Union; Unions, in Durham
Tobacco Workers International Union: appeals to black workers, 155, 157–59, 161–63, 165–68, 173–74, 175; appeals

INDEX

to women, 157, 161–63, 166–68; efforts to organize Durham workers, 106, 153, 155–56, 157–58, 161–63, 165–68, 174–78; internal conflicts in, 157–59, 161–63, 165–68, 172–77, 234 nn.91, 92, 93; Local 153, 153; Local 176, 158–59, 162–63, 166, 175–76; Local 183, 158, 162, 163, 172, 173; Local 193, 158, 162; Local 194, 158, 161, 163, 167–68; Local 204, 163, 167; Local 208, 163, 166–67, 173, 174; religious opposition to, 88, 147–48, 158, 212 n.126, 226 n.73. *See also* Blacks, in unions; Class, relations, in industry; Evans, E. Lewis; Strikes, at Liggett and Myers; Tobacco manufacture; Tobacco workers; Unions, black participation in; Unions, female participation in

Toms, Clinton, 72. *See also* Liggett and Myers

Trice, Roy, 168. *See also* Tobacco Workers International Union

Tri-State Tobacco Growers Association, 23–24

Turner, Delia (pseudonym), 61

Turrentine, Lacey (pseudonym), 52

Union Herald (Raleigh), 155. *See also* American Federation of Labor

Unions: black participation in, 4, 18–20, 88, 118, 149–50, 155–59, 161–63, 165–68, 171–78, 234 nn.92, 93; female participation in, 3–4, 18–21, 40, 49, 83, 85, 126, 148–49, 151–56, 158–65, 167–71, 173–78; in Durham, 18, 69, 81, 85–86, 88–89, 91, 93, 106–7, 118, 125–26, 148–49, 150–51, 153–78, 215 n.10, 215–16 n.11, 227 n.28, 229 n.14, 231 n.27, 234 nn.92, 93, 94, 235 n.96; religious deterrents to, 50, 87–88, 147–49, 158, 226 n.73, 227 n.74. *See also* American Federation of Full-Fashioned Hosiery Workers; American Federation of Labor; Blacks, in unions; Class, consciousness of, among industrial workers; Class, relations, in industry; Congress of Industrial Organizations; Piedmont Organizing Council; Strikes; Textile Workers Union of America; Tobacco Workers International Union; United Textile Workers

United States Children's Bureau, child labor investigation, 32. *See also* Child labor

United States Industrial Commission, 70

United Textile Workers, 106–7, 154, 158–61, 174, 176, 232 n.56; Bull City Local 2155, 158–61. *See also* Strikes, at Erwin Cotton Mills Company; Strikes, textile; Textiles manufacture, anti-union strategies in; Textile workers; Textile Workers Union of America; Unions, in Durham

University of North Carolina, 83, 86, 89, 211 n.118. *See also* Graham, Frank Porter

Upchurch, Duby S., 158, 159. *See also* Crouch, E. L.; Evans, E. Lewis; Tobacco Workers International Union

Vickers, Mrs., 134

Wages and income: among agriculturalists, 11–13, 16–17, 20, 23–24, 33, 38, 42, 44, 195 n.10, 196 n.20; among industrial workers, 75, 81–82, 110–13, 123–24, 130, 134, 136, 143, 146, 173, 178, 205 n.25, 219–20 n.54, 223 n.15. *See also* Hosiery workers, wages and income of; Textile workers, wages and income of; Tobacco workers, wages and income of

Walker, A. M., 63

Washington, Booker T., 78–79

Watts, Garrard S., 68

Watts, George, 68, 87, 89–90. *See also* Duke & Sons Company, W.

Weeks, Rose (pseudonym), 64, 147, 162, 176

West Durham, 63–65, 75, 87, 91, 95, 106, 117, 119, 130–31, 138, 140, 148, 158, 160, 168, 169, 172, 173. *See also* Erwin Cotton Mills Company; Monkey Bottoms; Textile workers

Wheeler, John H., 85. *See also* Durham Committee on Negro Affairs; North Carolina Mutual Life Insurance Company

White, Congressman George H., 13, 40–41

White Rock Baptist Church. *See* Fisher, Reverend Mark Miles

White supremacy. *See* Democratic Party, and white supremacy campaign; Race

White Supremacy Club of West Durham, 91. *See also* Democratic Party, and white supremacy campaign

Whitted, Anna Ruffin (pseudonym), 48, 53. *See also* Ruffin, Callie (pseudonym)

Williamson, Theotis, 119, 145, 147, 173

Wilmington (N.C.) race riot, 22, 93. *See also*

INDEX

Wilmington (N.C.) race riot (*continued*) Blacks, disfranchisement of; Democratic Party, and white supremacy campaign; Race

Women: as bag makers, 31, 38, 74, 113, 133–34, 146, 197 n.31; as boardinghouse keepers, 132–33, 140; class consciousness of, 49–54, 93–94, 117–26, 129, 145–49, 151, 152–55, 159–63, 165, 167, 169–71, 173, 175, 177–78; community activities of, 46, 127–28, 141–42, 147; as domestic laborers, 38, 43–44, 53, 59, 114, 127–29, 131–38, 140; education of, 46, 54, 83, 87, 91, 95, 98, 119–20, 127, 140, 142–45, 146–47; familial relationships of, 4, 8, 13–14, 16–18, 26–38, 42–46, 51–54, 57–61, 64, 74–75, 82, 95–96, 108–12, 114–17, 119, 127–29, 131–40, 143–47, 149–50, 152–53, 162, 169–70, 172, 177–78, 186 n.6, 187 n.10, 193 n.1, 194 4n, 5n, 195 14n, 196–197, 25n, 197 28n, 220 62n; as farm laborers, 38, 45–46, 52; as heads of household, 18, 38, 42–44, 57, 59–60, 112, 119, 144, 145, 147; as hosiery workers, 96, 99, 102–4, 119, 144, 149; household labor of, 31–34, 44, 51, 134–38, 143–44; labor force participation of, 37–38, 42–44, 109–17, 131–36; as prostitutes, 128, 138; racial attitudes of, 45–49, 52–54, 120–21, 125, 128–29, 141–44, 175; reasons of, for migrating, 51, 54–57, 59–67, 95–96, 119, 125, 146; religious and moral attitudes of, 36, 47–49, 76, 98, 120–21, 127–28, 142, 147, 216 nn.14, 18, 224 n.33, 225 n.37, 225–26 n.51, 200 n.77, 200–201 n.81, 201 n.89; as textile workers, 81, 95–96, 98–99, 100, 104–5, 108–15, 120, 123–24, 135–37, 148, 150, 207 n.48; as tobacco factory workers, 51, 82, 106–7, 95, 99–102, 110–17, 119–25, 136, 146, 147, 153, 161–63, 166–68, 171, 173–78. *See also* Childbearing; Childrearing; Class, interaction of, and gender; Family economy; Gender; Hosiery workers; Race, consciousness of, among blacks; Race, consciousness of, among whites; Race, and sexuality; Tenancy, consequences of, for women; Textile workers; Tobacco workers; Unions, female participation in

Young Women's Christian Association, 88, 151, 154, 158. *See also* Textile industry, critics of